Twentieth-Century French Poetry: A Critical Anthology

Modern French poetry is unique in the boldness and creativity of its experiments in form and genre, from classical verse to *vers libre*, from *calligrammes* to prose poems and *poésie sonore*. This anthology includes thirty-two poems by French and francophone poets, each followed by an accessibly written, detailed commentary. The different approaches adopted in the close readings by specialists in their field reflect the major trends in current literary criticism and theory. A foreword by one of France's foremost poets, Yves Bonnefoy, a general introduction, and an afterword provide a helpful theoretical framework for the study of modern poetry. An extensive bibliography, concise biographies of the poets, and a glossary of literary terms are included. Students of French and of comparative literature will gain a deeper understanding of the development of French verse and of the artistic movements (especially in the visual arts) that have shaped twentieth-century French poetry.

HUGUES AZÉRAD is Fellow in French at Magdalene College, Cambridge.

PETER COLLIER is Emeritus Fellow in French at Sidney Sussex College, Cambridge.

Twentieth-Century French Poetry

A Critical Anthology

Edited by

HUGUES AZÉRAD AND PETER COLLIER

CAMBRIDGE
UNIVERSITY PRESS

CAMBRIDGE UNIVERSITY PRESS
Cambridge, New York, Melbourne, Madrid, Cape Town, Singapore,
São Paulo, Delhi, Dubai, Tokyo

Cambridge University Press
The Edinburgh Building, Cambridge CB2 8RU, UK

Published in the United States of America by Cambridge University Press, New York

www.cambridge.org
Information on this title: www.cambridge.org/9780521713986

First published 2010

Printed in the United Kingdom at the University Press, Cambridge

A catalogue record for this publication is available from the British Library

ISBN   978-0-521-88642-0 Hardback
ISBN   978-0-521-71398-6 Paperback

In memory of Malcolm Bowie (1943–2007)
and David Kelley (1941–1999)

Contents

Notes on contributors

Elza Adamowicz is Professor of French Literature and Visual Culture at Queen Mary, University of London. She has published widely on Surrealism. Publications include: *Surrealist Collage in Text and Image: Dissecting the Exquisite Corpse* (1998), *Ceci n'est pas un tableau: les écrits surréalistes sur l'art* (2004), and *Surrealism: Crossings/Frontiers* (2006).

Hugues Azérad is Fellow and College Lecturer in French at Magdalene College, Cambridge. He is the author of *L'Univers constellé de Proust, Joyce et Faulkner* (2002), and he has published articles on a range of writers including Proust, Joyce, Faulkner, Reverdy and Nerval.

Victoria Best is Fellow and College Lecturer in French at St John's College, Cambridge, where she works in undergraduate study support. Her research interests focus on modern French literature, with a particular concern for the interplay between identity and narrative. Her books include *An Introduction to Twentieth-Century French Literature* (2002) and, co-written with Martin Crowley, *The New Pornographies: Explicit Sex in Modern French Fiction and Film* (2008).

Michael Bishop is McCulloch Professor of French at Dalhousie University, Canada. Author of numerous books and essays and director of VVV Editions, his latest works include *Jacques Prévert: From Film and Theater to Poetry, Art and Song* (2002), *Altérités d'André du Bouchet* (2003), *L'Art français et francophone depuis 1980* (2005), *The Endless Theory of Days: The Art and Poetry of Gérard Titus-Carmel* (2007), translations of Yves Bonnefoy and Gérard Titus-Carmel, and two volumes of poetry.

Jean-Pierre Bobillot is Professor of French at the University of Grenoble. He specialises in French poetry (1865–1925) and in twentieth-century avant-garde poetry. He has written: *Bernard Heidsieck poésie action* (1996), *Trois essais sur la poésie littérale* (2003) and *Rimbaud: le meurtre d'Orphée* (2004). He has also published several books and CDs of poetry.

Béatrice Bonhomme is a poet and is Professor of French at the University of Nice. In 1994, she co-founded (with Hervé Bosio) the poetry journal *Nu(e)*. She is the president of the Société Pierre Jean Jouve and leads a research team (*Poièma*). She has published widely on poetry and literature.

Yves Bonnefoy is a French poet and essayist. He is Emeritus Professor at the Collège de France where he held the Chair of 'Études comparées de la fonction poétique' in 1981–93.

Roger Cardinal is the author of *Figures of Reality: A Perspective on the Poetic Imagination* (1981) and the editor of *Sensibility and Creation: Studies in Twentieth-Century French Poetry* (1977). He writes on French Surrealism and on the modern visual arts, especially *art brut*.

Mary Ann Caws is Distinguished Professor of English, French and Comparative Literature at the Graduate Center, City University of New York. She has written illustrated biographies of Dora Maar, Virginia Woolf, Marcel Proust, Henry James, Pablo Picasso and Salvador Dalí. Her recent books include *Glorious Eccentrics: Modernist Women Painting and Writing* (2007), *Surprised in Translation* (2006), and two memoirs.

Peter Collier is Emeritus Fellow in French at Sidney Sussex College, Cambridge. He is the co-editor of *Visions and Blueprints* (1988), *Modernism and the European Unconscious* (1990), *Literary Theory Today* (1990), *Artistic Relations* (1994) and *Powerful Bodies* (1999). He is also the author of *Proust and Venice* (1989), and a translator of Bourdieu, Zola and Proust. He is the editor of two series: *Modern French Identities* and *European Connections*.

Tom Conley is Abbot Lawrence Lowell Professor of Romance Languages and Literatures at Harvard University. He specialises in early modern French literature; film and media studies; and the intersection of literature and graphic imagination. His books include *Cartographic Cinema* (2006), *The Self-Made Map: Cartographic Writing in Early Modern France* (1997), and *The Graphic Unconscious in Early Modern French Writing* (1992). He has translated the work of Michel de Certeau, Gilles Deleuze, Marc Augé and Christian Jacob.

Charles Forsdick is James Barrow Professor of French at the University of Liverpool. His publications include *Victor Segalen and the Aesthetics of Diversity* (2000) and *Travel in Twentieth-Century French and Francophone Cultures* (2005). He is co-editor (with David Murphy) of *Francophone Postcolonial Studies: A Critical Introduction* (2003).

Alison Finch is Professor of French at the University of Cambridge. She is a specialist in post-1800 French literature. Her publications include *Proust's Additions: The Making of 'À la recherche du temps perdu'* (1977), *Stendhal: La Chartreuse de*

Parme (1984) and *Women's Writing in Nineteenth-Century France* (2000). She is currently writing *A Cultural History of French Literature*.

Mary Gallagher is Associate Professor of French and Francophone Studies at University College Dublin. Her publications include *La Créolité de Saint-John Perse* (1998), *Soundings in French Caribbean Writing since 1950* (2002), (as editor) *Ici-Là: Place and Displacement in Caribbean Writing in French* (2003), and (as co-editor with Michael Brophy) *Sens et présence du sujet poétique* (2006).

Robert W. Greene is Professor Emeritus of French, State University of New York at Albany. He is the author of *The Poetic Theory of Pierre Reverdy* (1967), *Six French Poets of Our Time* (1979), *Just Words: Moralism and Metalanguage in Twentieth-Century French Fiction* (1993) and *Searching for Presence: Yves Bonnefoy's Writings on Art* (2004). He is also the editor of *Dalhousie French Studies* 21 (Fall–Winter 1991), devoted to 'Art Criticism by French Poets Since World War II'.

Susan Harrow is Professor of French at the University of Bristol. She researches in the field of late nineteenth-century and twentieth-century French poetry and narrative. Her books include *The Material, the Real and the Fractured Self* (2004) and *Zola, the Body Modern: Pressures and Prospects of Representation* (2009). She is President of the Society of Dix-Neuviémistes.

Laure Helms is Associate Research Fellow at the University of Paris X Nanterre. She specialises in nineteenth-century literature and contemporary French poetry. She has published a critical edition of *Pierre et Jean* by Maupassant (2008), and has written articles on Jean-Michel Maulpoix.

Shirley Jordan is Reader in French at Queen Mary, University of London. She has published monographs on the art criticism of Francis Ponge and on new women's writing in France. Other studies explore contemporary writers, film-makers and artists, including Jean-Daniel Pollet, Sophie Calle, Annie Ernaux, Marie NDiaye and Christine Angot.

Jean Khalfa is a Fellow and College Lecturer at Trinity College, Cambridge. He has published widely on philosophy, modern literature (in particular contemporary poetry and writing in French from North Africa and the Caribbean), aesthetics and anthropology. Recently he has edited *Frantz Fanon*, a special issue of *Wasafiri*, 44 (2005); *Pour Frantz Fanon*, special two-part issue of *Les Temps Modernes*, 635–6 (2006); and the first complete edition of Michel Foucault's *History of Madness* (2006).

Roger Little occupied the Chair of French at Trinity College Dublin from 1979 until his retirement in 1998. He has published extensively on modern French poetry and on the representation of Blacks in French literature. He has launched and directed several series including *Critical Guides to French Texts* and *Autrement Mêmes*.

Rosemary Lloyd was Rudy Professor of French at Indiana University until her retirement in 2007. She is the author of studies on Baudelaire, Mallarmé and Flaubert, as well as monographs on jealousy as a literary trope, the representation of childhood in nineteenth-century French literature, and the still life in prose. In addition she has translated writings by Baudelaire, Mallarmé, George Sand, and the contemporary poets Mylène Catel and Philippe Rhamy.

Timothy Mathews is Professor of French at UCL, University of London. He is the author of *Reading Apollinaire: Theories of Poetic Language* (1987) and *Literature, Art and the Pursuit of Decay* (2000), and is the co-editor of *Violence, théorie, surréalisme* (1994).

Jean-Michel Maulpoix is Professor of French Literature at the University of Paris X Nanterre. He has published some thirty titles, poetic texts, critical essays and miscellanies. They have a common aim: the elucidation of what might be called the poetic. His work most frequently evolves on the frontiers of narrative.

Philippe Met teaches literature and film at the University of Pennsylvania. He is editor-in-chief of *French Forum* and the author of articles most notably on poetry and cinema. His books include: *Formules de la poésie* (1999) and *La Lettre tue. Spectre(s) de l'écrit fantastique* (2008). He also edited *Le Savon* for the Francis Ponge Pléiade (2002) and *André du Bouchet et ses Autres* (2003). He is currently completing an essay on the poetics and phenomenology of the notebook (*Fausses Notes*).

Jean-Pascal Pouzet is Maître de conférences at the University of Limoges and Associate Research Fellow at the University of Poitiers. He has published widely on English and French medieval literature.

Margaret Rigaud-Drayton is Fellow and College Lecturer in French at Christ's College, Cambridge, and the author of *Henri Michaux: Poetry, Painting, and the Universal Sign* (2005).

Stephen Romer has lived in France since 1981 where he is Maître de conférences at the University of Tours. A practising poet, he has published four collections, most recently *Yellow Studio* (2008). He has translated widely from modern French poetry. His anthology *Twentieth-Century French Poems* was published in 2002.

Andrew Rothwell is Professor of French at Swansea University, specialising in modern and contemporary poetry with particular reference to the visual arts. He has published books and articles on Reverdy and Bernard Noël. He has also translated a number of Noël's works into English.

Clive Scott is Professor Emeritus of European Literature at the University of East Anglia. Between 1980 and 2002 he published a sequence of books on French verse and versification. More recently, he has turned his critical attention to the subject of translating poetry: *Translating Baudelaire* (2000) and *Translating Rimbaud's 'Illuminations'* (2006).

Michael Sheringham is a Fellow of All Souls College, Oxford, and is Marshal Foch Professor of French Literature at Oxford University. His publications include *French Autobiography: Devices and Desires* (1993) and *Everyday Life: Theories and Practices from Surrealism to the Present* (2006). He co-edited with Johnnie Gratton *The Art of the Project: Projects and Experiments in Modern French Culture* (2005) and edited *Parisian Fields* (1996).

Richard Stamelman is Professor of Romance Languages at Williams College, and is the author of *Lost Beyond Telling: Representations of Death and Absence in Modern French Poetry* (1990), and the editor and principal translator of *The Lure and the Truth of Painting: Selected Essays on Art by Yves Bonnefoy* (1995). His most recent book is *Perfume: Joy, Obsession, Scandal, Sin; A Cultural History of Perfume from 1750 to the Present* (2006).

Thanh-Vân Ton-That is Professor of French at Pau University. Her publications include monographs on Proust (2000), Duras (2005), Léon Cladel (2007) and Mérimée (2008).

Meryl Tyers has taught at Fitzwilliam College, Cambridge, the École Normale Supérieure, St Anne's College, Oxford, and Glasgow University, where she has been an Honorary Research Fellow since 2003. She is the author of *Critical Fictions: Nerval's Les Illuminés* (1998) and has published articles on nineteenth-century bohemians and Bernard Noël.

Emma Wagstaff is Lecturer in French at the University of Birmingham. She is the author of *Provisionality and the Poem* (2006), and of articles about the work of poets André du Bouchet, Philippe Jaccottet and Bernard Noël. She is currently researching French literary responses to the art of Giacometti.

Preface

This book is primarily intended for readers with a good knowledge of French, as the poems are given without translation. However, whenever rare words (from the poems) or particularly difficult quotations or passages in French occur in the commentaries, translations have been given between brackets. Each commentary is followed by a Further reading section, which includes references to existing translations of the volume from which the poem is taken, and of other works by the poet, a short list of critical works not mentioned in the notes, and thus enabling further focused research on the poet. The book includes an Afterword, to be read after the poems, which gives an in-depth survey and reflection on how to read twentieth-century French verse. Even though our contributors have avoided unnecessary jargon, poetry as craft requires an array of critical terms and literary tropes with which we need to familiarise ourselves in order to perceive its internal harmonies and intricate processes. A glossary is therefore provided, regrouping and explaining the most difficult terms used in the commentaries. We also give biographies of the poets (referring to their main works), and finally a select bibliography which is divided into two sections: the first one lists useful reference works and a wide range of French poetry anthologies, in French and in English; the second section, while not claiming to be exhaustive, presents a large number of secondary readings of twentieth-century French poetry and poetics not included in the Further reading. It aims to show that 'poetics' is a fertile field of research in France, where it is often associated with poetry writing and philosophy. This fascinating aspect of French culture tends to be overlooked, and this bibliography should encourage readers to explore some of its richness and engage with it critically.

Acknowledgements

We would like to express our deepest thanks to our editor at Cambridge University Press, Linda Bree, for her trust in this project on French poetry and for her invaluable steering of the book through publication, as well as to Thomas O'Reilly and Maartje Scheltens for their pertinent advice as regards the content and shape of the book. Our gratitude also goes to Yves Bonnefoy for generously allowing us to translate his text on poetry, and to all of our contributors who have unflinchingly shown faith in the project. Their ideas have inflected its overall structure and their writings have brought French poetry to life. Nothing could have been done without the translators and copy-editors, Jane Yeoman, Michèle Lester and Anthony Cummins. We are particularly grateful to the following who so generously offered their support: Marion Schmid, Marie-Josèphe and Julien Azérad, Emma Wilson, Neil Kenny, Michael Tilby, Pierre Brunel, Nicholas Boyle, Robin Kirkpatrick, Julia Dover, Finn Sinclair, Wendy Ayres-Bennett, Andrew Brown, Jean-Pierre Allain, Jean, John and William Gurdon, Aude and James Fitzsimons. Our thanks are also offered to the French Department of the University of Cambridge and to the Master and Fellows of Sidney Sussex College for their generous financial support. Students from the French Department of the University of Cambridge, Sidney Sussex College and Magdalene College have been a ceaseless source of inspiration: they will no doubt recognise their influence and presence in this book.

The book is dedicated to the memory of Professor Malcolm Bowie and Dr David Kelley, who knew how to share their incomparable love and understanding of poetry.

Copyright acknowledgements

Thanks are due to the publishers for permission to reprint the following poems in whole or in part:

Pierre Alferi, 'Une défense de la poésie', from *Sentimentale journée* © P.O.L. (1997).

Guillaume Apollinaire, 'Lettre-Océan', from *Calligrammes* © Éditions Gallimard (1918). Reproduction of 'Lettre-Océan' by kind permission of Victoria and Albert Museum, London (© V&A Images).

Louis Aragon, 'Elsa je t'aime', from *Le Crève-cœur* © Éditions Gallimard (1941).

Marie-Claire Bancquart, 'Essentiel', from *Opportunité des oiseaux* © Belfond (Place des éditeurs) (1986).

Yves Bonnefoy, 'Fin du mandat, besoin d'une alliance' © Yves Bonnefoy and *Semicerchio* (2006); English translation © Peter Collier (2008).

Yves Bonnefoy, 'Rue Traversière', from *Rue Traversière et autres récits en rêve* © Mercure de France (1987).

André du Bouchet, 'Accidents', from *Dans la chaleur vacante* © Mercure de France (1961).

André Breton, 'Vigilance', from *Le Revolver à cheveux blancs*, republished in *Clair de terre* © Éditions Gallimard (1932).

Mary Ann Caws, 'It's Up to Us' © Mary Ann Caws (2008).

Blaise Cendrars, 'Mee Too Buggi', from *Poésies complètes de Blaise Cendrars*, vol. I, 'Tout autour d'aujourd'hui' © Éditions Denoël (1947, 1963, 2001, 2005).

Aimé Césaire, extract 'ô lumière amicale. . .' from *Cahier d'un retour au pays natal* © Présence Africaine (1956).

René Char, 'Gravité. L'emmuré', from 'Seuls demeurent', republished in *Fureur et mystère* © Éditions Gallimard (1948).

Michel Deguy, 'Le Métronome', from *Aux heures d'affluence. Poèmes et Proses* © Éditions du Seuil (1993).

Jacques Dupin, 'Commencer comme on déchire un drap. . .', from 'Moraines', republished in *L'Embrasure* © Éditions Gallimard (1969).

Paul Éluard, 'La courbe de tes yeux fait le tour de mon cœur. . .', from *Capitale de la douleur* © Éditions Gallimard (1926).

Claude Esteban, 'Ils sont riches, mon père. . .', from *Fayoum* (1999), republished in *Morceaux de ciel, presque rien* © Éditions Gallimard (2001).

Édouard Glissant, 'Ô terre, si c'est terre. . .', 'Si la nuit te dépose au plus haut. . .', 'Je t'ai nommée Terre blessée', 'J'écris en toi la musique. . .', 'L'eau du morne est plus grave. . .', 'Je n'écris que pour te surprendre. . .', 'Et n'est que cendre. . .', extracts from 'Pour Mycéa', from *Pays rêvé, pays réel* © Éditions Gallimard (1985).

Bernard Heidsieck, 'Poème-partition B2B3 (Exorcisme)', from *Partition V* © Le Bleu du Ciel (2001).

Philippe Jaccottet, 'L'Ignorant', from *L'Ignorant* © Éditions Gallimard (1958).

Jean-Michel Maulpoix, 'Le bleu ne fait pas de bruit', from *Une histoire de bleu* © Mercure de France (1992).

Henri Michaux, extract from 'Iniji', republished in *Moments* © Éditions Gallimard (1973).

Nguyên Hoàng Bao Viêt, 'Anne Frank' © Nguyên Hoàng Bao Viêt (1959, 1980).

Bernard Noël, 'Les états de l'air', from *Les Yeux dans la couleur* © P.O.L. (2004).

Marie Noël, 'Attente', from *Les Chansons et les heures* © Éditions Gallimard (1920).

Saint-John Perse, 'Écrit sur la porte', from *Éloges* © Éditions Gallimard (1925).

Francis Ponge, 'Le Volet, suivi de sa scholie', from *Pièces* © Éditions Gallimard (1946).

Jacques Réda, 'L'Incorrigible', from *L'Incorrigible* © Éditions Gallimard (1995).

Pierre Reverdy, 'L'Esprit du dehors', from *Le Cadran quadrillé* © Flammarion (1915); 'L'Esprit dehors', from *La Liberté des mers* © Flammarion (1960).

Jacques Roubaud, 'Dès que je me lève', from *Quelque chose noir* © Éditions Gallimard (1986).

Amina Saïd, 'Trois continents dérivent', from *Gisements de lumière* © Éditions de la Différence (1998).

Victor Segalen, 'Aux dix mille années', from *Stèles, Œuvres complètes* © Robert Laffont (1995).

Léopold Sédar Senghor, 'À New York', from *Éthiopiques* (1956), republished in *Œuvre poétique* © Éditions du Seuil (1964, 1973, 1979, 1984 and 1990).

Gérard Titus-Carmel, 'Or battant. . .', from *Seul tenant* © Champ Vallon (2006).

Paul Valéry, 'Le Cantique des colonnes', from *Charmes* © Éditions Gallimard (1922).

Foreword: Ending the mission, inaugurating the pact

YVES BONNEFOY

I

For me the idea of poetry is that it should transgress conceptual thinking, and aim to ensure the proper functioning of what such thinking renders difficult or even impossible: namely to become aware of our essentially finite nature and of the needs and aspirations that it creates in us, to perceive the meaning that poetry can find in life – that is, another way of knowing – and ultimately to renew our relationship with others, which has been spoilt by our inevitably abstract and fragmented approach through analytic thinking. And since this project is never totally attainable, since the poems which it believes that it has set free from the categorisation and intentionality of the conceptual drive are immediately invaded by the daydreams of desire, which are themselves still conceptual, there is – as I persist in thinking – a second degree to poetry, which is to acknowledge this flaw in the poems in their actual form, to deem that they are less poetry than art, and to try to understand their numerous layers of illusion. This is a self-critical undertaking, but one that obviously requires a contribution from the reader, who is often an accomplice but who is in need of guidance in order to attain full awareness. This is therefore an undertaking which creates a field of deconstruction and reconstruction of thinking within the poems, but also within social relationships; and which therefore establishes within society a space for truth.

I also intend to argue that this ongoing exchange, and this linguistic field born under the sign of the poetic, are our sole specifically human reality in an abyss of matter whose phenomena are deprived of meaning: our sole reality, or even our sole being, of which poetry is thus the source. Poetry proposes a pact of alliance which a poet, conscious of the difficulty of his or her enterprise, offers readers, knowing well that – since they too are conditioned by the limits of their language – they experience the same contradictions and the same aspirations as the poet, although often unaware of this. It is a pact whereby readers engage in a struggle to achieve full self-presence, and will face the same perils and vicissitudes that the poets incurred in their initial writing, but will now relive these events in the activity of their own mind, in the hope, even in the harshest times, that one day in the future there will be a grand dialogue of mutual enlightenment: the dialogue which Rimbaud called 'Noël sur terre'.

And poetry? Briefly, it is the most fundamental project of a society, and one that requires the readers of the poem as much as its author to meet on the same level of radical and fundamental questioning. Between the poets, if they live up to their claims, and those who may come to meet them either in the present or the future, this pact is the only relationship which has any significance in the eyes of poetry: a linguistic pact concluded in order to ensure the viability of being on earth.

Which leads me now to consider the idea of the 'mission', first formulated by Walter Benjamin, in 'The Task of the Translator', and more recently by Franco Fortini in *Semicerchio*.

Was the 'mission', which Benjamin mooted in a period now superseded by our own, a means of recognising the value of poetry? Yes, of course, since he refers to the 'symbolic' capacities of the poem. But does this word, 'symbolic', promise to do more than present, through analogy or other figurative means, ways of being and ideas of the world characteristic of any particular social milieu in its historical period? And may we agree to call this the specific characteristic of poetry, true poetry, since I have defined the latter as a transgression of concepts (which themselves inform these analogies) and ideas of the world and existence? Looked at from this point of view – that is, understood as mere literature – poetry is reduced to precisely what poets refuse to accept as the fate of their writing: reduced to just what they want their readers to help them undo. And the 'mission' that we entrust to poetry, which is to exist on its own terms, albeit limiting its repercussions to a search for psychological or aesthetic meaning, is a mission of an order wholly different from the pact which poetic intuition needs in order to live on in the mind.

In truth the notion of a 'mission' is an outright misunderstanding of the poetic. Thinking in terms of a 'mission' of 'letting be', or 'delegating to' the poets without collaborating with them, allowing them into the heart of society, however willingly, but without participating actively in their enterprise, is already a proof that poetry is no longer considered as poetry. The readers who do not understand that authentic poets reject the illusions that constantly flow from their pens, the readers who find meaning in this idea of a 'mission', are the readers who reduce poems to no more than ideas and desires, however forcefully and ingeniously formulated. They do not bother to notice that these networks of meaning remain forms of conceptual thinking, that they signal the failure of a great poetic project, and that this failure consigns the readers in their turn to imprisonment within its walls.

As soon as we conceive of a 'mission' granted to poets, and as soon as we accept this mission, we forget poetry and its vocation, we forget what is specifically poetic in the poem, considered from then on as only one of the forms – albeit more inventive and freer from convention – of self-expression of our everyday consciousness, which thinks in terms of objects to be defined or possessed, rather than of living relationships. And in this case it matters little whether the mission is considered sympathetically, carefully even, or whether it has fallen out of the public eye, as has happened in our own Western society. In both cases the poets, deprived of their truth and their hope, will be in great danger, tempted, for example, as I have said, to find meaning by limiting the range of their art, tempted to render the poem absolute, to privilege its specific language and difference, to indulge in its own private coding – to indulge in what Guido Mazzoni calls 'the self-reference of its own aesthetic canons'.

So rather than bother about the latest developments in the history of the 'mission' accorded to poets, it seems to me that it would be better to try to understand why, at a certain time, the mission replaced the pact which, we believe, did exist in other periods of Western civilisation.

II

Why and how did poetry become reduced to an artistic activity? Insofar as it essentially transgresses the conceptual, we might imagine that its reader-ship collapsed because of the omnipresence of the conceptual at increasingly numerous and profound levels in everyday life, since technology has taken over our lives with its almost totally conceptual products – from the car and other machines through to even our processed food and drink. But this 'total immer-sion' has gone beyond the quantitative, and we need a better understanding of what has been happening if we want a better understanding of the rationale of this 'mission'.

What did happen? Conceptual thought, in its ancient philosophical forms, saturated with metaphysics but also with everyday praxis, had long accepted that it did not control in depth the reality with which it engaged. Faced with the world as a whole, or with objects or persons, it abandoned the entire frame-work of its discourse to another kind of explanation – that is, the divine, and the myths which related it to the world of appearances, as recognised by our senses; thus belief and faith also came to assume the work of ordinary reason.

But reason itself was then used to untangle the network of myths. The day came when Mallarmé could declare them to be 'glorious lies'. What happened then? Taking the hint dropped by God as he departed from this world, that his creation was, like him, supernatural, our conceptual faculty believed itself proudly capable of understanding everything that exists, which implied devot-ing all our thinking to studying phenomena and their laws, with two equally dangerous consequences. On the one hand, the concept focuses on objects in general, without caring for the meaning that one object or another might have in its particular existence – the fruit that I pick, rather than the fruit named in the dictionary – and it follows from this fundamental choice that contact was lost with existence in specific times and places and circumstances, namely with a person's self-awareness, which is nonetheless the centre of his or her real needs and also the site where the real can be comprehended in all its depth and unity, in the most felicitous and intimate way. Having stifled remembrance of the specific and the finite, the networks of the concept have become reduced to a purely schematic representation of the world and being in the world; they provide partial and abstract images, laden with enigma and anxiety.

On the other hand, all of this might prevent us from seeing that the demise of the divine should certainly not imply that we no longer need to admit transcendence as a factor in our relations with the world – quite the contrary. For what is the slightest fragment of empirical reality other than an infinity of irreducible qualities and aspects, whose core remains impenetrable by concepts? This is what we mean by transcendence. And this power of reality to transcend what we can say about it can most naturally be experienced in things that human language has identified – designating them by name, making them familiar, allowing us to love them. And it is this transcendent reality that allows us to glimpse in the site thus constituted a bedrock of reality impenetrable by language – that is, a foundation of unity. Only this will allow individuals, however transitory they perceive themselves to be, to feel that they are a part of the world: 'au monde', to quote Rimbaud once more. It is through transcendence of the basic that we find the proof of our existence.

Having said this, it is the infinity at the heart of everyday reality, the transcendence within immanence, the promise of unity – it is all this, as we know, that is remembered by poetry. And thus I associate with the demise of those 'glorious lies' the demise of our previous belief in the project of poetry: not because what myths said of supernatural worlds was true, but because the demise of their illusory transcendence has led us to forget the fundamental truth of real transcendence – that of all things, whether tree or stone or path, and also that of all people, transcending the appearances offered by conceptual discourse, as well as the ways we use these appearances in our relation to ourselves, in our conception of life. The human mind was confronted with a parting of the ways: in one direction lay religious transcendence, leading beyond the world; in the other, the kind of transcendence I have mentioned, the secular option, the one that gives substance to our stay in the world and enables us to give voice to the One and Indivisible, and link it to our finite existence. Finally, there was also the denial of all transcendence, religious or lay; and a bad choice was made, for between the two other ways the pathway to simple mystery was ignored and untrodden, except by the most lucid poets. A great opportunity was lost, at least at one moment in history.

I think of another crossroads, which occasioned a far better choice, at least for certain great painters: one which occurred at the beginning of the seventeenth century, when Galileo illuminated with his new, sublunary lens the entirely material surface of the moon. Thus crumbled some of the myths that had underpinned traditional religion. The moon, which until then had remained an enclave of symbolism in an environment which had already become a simple natural reality, finally took its place on the horizon of the merely human and terrestrial. But despite this, neither the moon, nor any aspect of its location, was understood as reducible to concepts, as we can see from the great landscapes painted at the time by Annibale Caraccio or Poussin or Gaspard Dughet, where there is such a strong sense of the unity of all things vibrating across the hills, trees, rivers and paths through whose highways and byways they allowed human beings, still breathing freely, to venture forth.

At this initial stage of the demise of the mythological, the transcendence inherent in all things real was in fact revealed to a few great minds, who were, naturally enough, painters, and whose poetic sensitivity was thereby reinforced rather than diminished. And then, three centuries later, in Paris, Georges Bataille published (in *Documents*) that famous photographic enlargement of a big toe: an aspect of something human, yet just as alien as the surface of the moon in Galileo's lens, although interpreted in quite another way. There is nothing in the depth of things other than the dull evidence of their matter, thought Bataille and his friends. Beyond language there is only non-being; we are walled in by language, by relations between words; we are doomed to fear death; we are reduced to self-mockery and its various 'lugubrious games'.

It is the loss of the sense of the infinite in the things – and also the beings – of Nature that has prevented our modern times from hearing poetry, from following poets along their way, which is as much a way of seeing as of writing: to dispose of them otherwise than by allowing them to exist in a sort of Indian reservation of the mind where we may come to watch their dances without bothering to wonder what they mean or rather indicate. Our need therefore is to relearn the positive value of the material world, to sense the 'divinity' of a blade of grass, of the scent of basil, of the laughter of children, of the very shape of a path that we see winding away before us and them, between a line of trees.

And our task, as we meditate on the original moment of the crisis – when the poets were reduced to the mission of doing no more than providing texts for reading, or documents for scholarly analysis – is to return to this fatal crossroads in order to re-establish what in fact is an authentic language: using conceptual thinking, it is true, but providing a fund of key words designating major realities to which the poetic use of language would allow us to regain access, even if only to realise how contradictory and torn we are, and how much more potential tragedy than facile happiness in some *locus amoenus*, some Arcadia, we harbour. In order to enable a new pact to replace the failed mission, we need to acknowledge this poetic supplement, which is actually as evident in our bodies, which we now know to be mortal, as in the world of appearances.

And today there are surely men and women who know this instinctively, which is why some of our friends are absolutely right to draw attention to the ongoing – in fact, the increasing – importance of song. I am glad to say that this does not imply the spoken sing-song which we so often hear in France, which is hardly more than a monologue with a bit of rhythmic support, but rather those songs from all over the world where noises distilled from the natural world and simple, fundamental rhythms predominate over notions. This, in fact, would be a way of describing the more private creative process that leads to similar results in the case of true poetry. Here indeed the auditory qualities of the word transgress the authority of discourse, opening out into a language where our deepest Self becomes aware of its self-presence in all its mortality. And that is really where the heart of the experience of living lies, where the Self can encounter the Other and use this experience to confront its illusions and criticise them, and then offer to society a communal project. Song can help revive the pact between the poet and the common man, which had been interrupted during the period of the mission.

But this does not mean that song can replace poetry, for in its brevity it cannot undertake what the poem can at least attempt: to submit to the authority of the rhythms arising from the body – the rhythms of the finite and the physical – not only a variety of words, but all the bizarre and unpredictable sounds and images that the unconscious, for instance, can suggest through writing, without feeling bound to instantly shape a text, or immediately understand what it says. Poetry, that writing born of intuition, encompasses language in its totality, at the conscious level of action or the unconscious level of desire. It is as much the memory of society's past as the anticipation of its future. It is this desire to embrace everything, which alone can ensure effective action against the illusory, that is the task of poetry. Song is certainly less able than poetry to resist the dream, although its dreams are often truer and closer to our collective needs than the dreams that undermine the self-awareness of writers who are more intricately and specifically involved in the idiom of their era.

III

Who today is really able to give voice to what I have called the divinity of simple things, to transcendence through immanence? Who can recreate this divinity *sans* deity, temporarily scattered throughout the chaos of a world that we perceive as no more than an enigmatic mass of phenomena? Only, I argue, some great poet in the future, and this despite the fact that our present society, in a vicious and potentially fatal circle, is not yet prepared to listen to him or her.

But also today it would perhaps be fitting to think of the other participants in the pact, which once existed and which we wish to revive – that is, readers, whose resources are not as depleted as we are led to believe. Readers? Were the readers not in fact children before yielding to the conceptual thinking that regulates adult life? Children in whose minds this thinking was not yet established, despite the vital language growing inside them, which would mark out the limits of their existence; children who, by the same token, experienced intuitively what poetry would now like to retrieve. Thus it was in their childhood that the great poets – Nerval, Baudelaire and Rimbaud in France, and Leopardi in Italy – first found the nourishment of their vocation, and later the energy to keep it alive. Adolescence is the age of anxiety and myth; it is not the most profound source of poetry, but childhood is the underground water table which, whenever the poetic in society has dried up on the surface, provides those springs which some accident of adult life can suddenly resuscitate. I have often discussed this question of childhood as the source of poetry, and this is not the place to repeat myself. But I can suggest that our chance for the future, if we have one, as I believe we do, depends on our schools: where teachers might consent not to stifle under textual analysis, under meanings so often loaded with ideology, the spontaneous urge of a child to unite with a poem, however naïvely.

Yves Bonnefoy, lecture 'Fin du mandat, besoin d'une alliance' given in Italy, and published in *Semicerchio*, 2006. Translated by Peter Collier.

General introduction

HUGUES AZÉRAD

L'observation et les commentaires d'un poème peuvent être profonds, singuliers, brillants ou vraisemblables, ils ne peuvent éviter de réduire à une signification et à un projet un phénomène qui n'a d'autre raison que d'*être*.

René Char, 'Arthur Rimbaud'[1]

Comme l'arbre, comme l'animal, il [le poète] s'est abandonné à la vie première, il a dit oui, il a consenti à cette vie immense qui le dépassait. Il s'est enraciné dans la terre, il a étendu ses bras, il a joué avec le soleil, il est devenu arbre; il a fleuri, il a chanté.

Aimé Césaire, 'Poésie et connaissance'[2]

Poetry is the plough that turns up time in such a way that the abyssal strata of time, its black earth, appear on the surface. There are epochs, however, when mankind, not satisfied with the present, yearning like the ploughman for the abyssal strata of time, thirsts for the virgin soil of time.

Osip Mandelstam, 'The Word and Culture'[3]

I

In 'Fin du mandat, besoin d'une alliance', Yves Bonnefoy – France's profoundest poet and theorist of poetry of the twentieth century alongside Guillaume Apollinaire, Pierre Reverdy, André Breton, Aimé Césaire and Édouard Glissant – confronts us with what he sees as poetry's urgent task: 'instituer dans la société un espace de vérité'. His conception of poetry and of how we should approach it goes against the grain of what he calls 'conceptual thinking', which would in his eyes be a book of critical readings merely consisting of analyses of poems whose sole role would be to confirm our beliefs of what we want to see in poetry. Good intentions could be the critic's worst enemy when approaching a poem, and Bonnefoy makes explicit what is wrong in our all too tempting need to ascribe a mission or 'mandat' to the poem, our tendency to bring it back to the everyday categories of our thinking lives, but also to the recesses of our desires and fears. For what we perceive as our most human attributes conceal within themselves an unacknowledged inhumanity. Far from being a mystic, as he is sometimes considered by critics, Bonnefoy posits poetry as a transgressive act,

1

a constant struggle against the illusion that we take for our reality, against the concepts which turn us away from the true discovery of ourselves, our sense of immediacy, our presence to the world and to others. Bonnefoy warns us against what is too obvious in poetry, what makes it apparently so necessary to us, and what apparently confers on it its unique status.

Bonnefoy's text makes for difficult reading, not so much because of its density, but because its view of poetry challenges our assumptions of what poetry is, what it should tell us, what poems mean to us. His vast survey of what poetry has meant to mankind and of what it should be could seem either simplistic or plainly wrong. How can a poet indict poetry in such a forceful manner? How can poetry not be about desire, the expression of our innermost anguish, our aspirations, our feelings? Is not poetry the sheer pleasure of wielding words for ludic purposes, for the intrinsic beauty of language?

One thing is certain, Bonnefoy is not speaking as a French poet here, but as a poet who has no time for pseudo-universalisms or sweeping generalisations. His text can be put alongside many similar reflections on poetry written during the course of the last century, from Ezra Pound, T. S. Eliot and Hart Crane to Sylvia Plath, Wallace Stevens, John Ashbery and Louis Zukofsky, from Rilke to Marina Tsvetaeva, Osip Mandelstam and Paul Celan, from Dylan Thomas and W. H. Auden to Eugenio Montale, Federico García Lorca, Derek Walcott and Octavio Paz. It is with true humility and an absolute commitment as a poet that Bonnefoy tells us of the double pitfall which risks wrecking poetry's project: an over-conceptual approach to poetry, in its writing and its reading, even down to its commercialisation, and the more naïve approach, which allows dreams and desire to prevail, however tempting and vertiginous they seem. Conceptual thinking, if allowed to rule unmatched, detaches us from our relation to the world, cuts us off from our acceptance of finitude. In a recent interview, Bonnefoy states that 'la technologie met des concepts en conserve et nous les fait consommer à tous moments de notre vie'.[4] Poetry, in contrast, should allow for the play of chance, the sense of time and the sense of place to be at the centre of our lives, not in order to hem us in or curtail our human aspirations, but in order for us to delight in presence – when we are closer to ourselves; when hope and joy, but also a profound disquiet, take hold of us and urge us to move forward.

This is why poetry is at its best when it takes upon itself to unveil its own defects, when it becomes aware of its lacks, its shortcomings. One is reminded of Pierre Reverdy's aphorism 'La poésie, c'est le bouche-abîme du réel désiré qui manque'.[5] Poetry is also demanding of us, the readers, to be lucid. This is where the alliance proposed by Bonnefoy lies: instead of offering a make-believe, yet another system – conceptual or dreamlike – that would distract us from ourselves, poetry should make the same demands of the readers as it makes of itself; and the poet should seek to forge an alliance through which we, and also poetry, could access the plenitude of presence. Presence is the shared objective of this alliance and it can only exist as a shared experience, when both poet and reader can partake in 'le mode sur lequel l'unité de l'être ou du monde se révèle, en deçà ou au-delà de la saisie conceptuelle que le langage peut en faire, l'évidence de l'Un offerte à une perception qui ne dissocie pas'.[6] This notion of presence was intuited by Bonnefoy after he had studied mathematics, philosophy and logic in the 1940s, and with a learned awareness of psychoanalysis. The only faith Bonnefoy ever had was faith in poetry, and in art's redemptive powers in a world ruled by conceptual thinking: in a recent book on painting, *Remarques sur le regard*, he writes that 'l'art est la guérison du concept'.[7]

The repercussions of presence are multiple, and presence was conjugated by the various theories that were developed in the second half of the twentieth century, in France and in the rest of the world, from structuralism to poststructuralism and deconstruction. Bonnefoy never abnegated the power of reason; his position is not to hanker after a pre-linguistic-turn era. His position complements and balances out the conceptual turn which has been holding sway, often so brilliantly, over the humanities for the last sixty years. Presence does not ignore the developments triggered by Saussure: his assumption that meaning in language is created by opposition and difference, that there is no natural link between language and the world. Indeed, Bonnefoy happily acknowledges the arbitrary nature of the linguistic sign, but he tells us that the story is more complex, that it is only half told if one exclusively follows Saussurean tenets.

Presence – and how could we forget that deconstruction was precisely the debunking of presence – takes linguistic discoveries in its stride as a necessary and even beneficial stage in the course of human thought. But presence is also a constant struggle against the illusional, against misconceived and comfortable notions of identity, against self-congratulatory art and against a world of certainty. If transcendence there is, it will be found in immanence. Bonnefoy was not alone in trying to rectify the balance: Bachelard, but mainly Merleau-Ponty and Ricœur in France, and Gadamer in Germany, also developed ways of breaking through the so-called prison of language. Merleau-Ponty, in his seminal article 'Le Langage indirect et les voix du silence' declared that even though 'le signe ne veut dire quelque chose qu'en tant qu'il se profile sur les autres signes', language is also 'comme un être', and for the writer in particular, 'il devient à son tour comme un univers, capable de loger en lui les choses mêmes – après les avoir changées en sens'.[8] Bonnefoy's view of language is in many respects akin to what Merleau-Ponty calls the 'langage authentique' which he finds in painting and writing in particular: 'Une vision, une action enfin libres décentrent et regroupent les objets du monde chez le peintre, les mots chez le poète.' In a move not dissimilar to the ideas found in 'Fin du mandat', Merleau-Ponty advocates a unique role for art: 'ce qui n'est pas remplaçable dans l'œuvre d'art, ce qui fait d'elle beaucoup plus qu'un moyen de plaisir . . . c'est qu'elle contient, mieux que des idées, des matrices d'idées . . . qu'elle nous apprend à voir et finalement nous donne à penser comme aucun ouvrage analytique ne peut le faire, parce que l'analyse ne trouve dans l'objet que ce que nous y avons mis'.[9]

The crucial awareness that, despite conceptual thinking, language can still offer us access to the world, albeit by 'voies détournées' and also because of them, is why poetry still has a role to play – for each individual, but also for society. Poetry helps us live, it gives us a privileged access to ourselves *in* the world. Bonnefoy puts the cards clearly on the table: 'la poésie n'est rien d'autre, au plus vif de son inquiétude, qu'un acte de connaissance'.[10]

Underlying Bonnefoy's text is the history of philosophy, which was intertwined with the history of poetry throughout the twentieth century, first in Germany, then in France. Even though the style of the text could seem paradoxically conceptual, it is not subservient to concepts, and it does not illustrate or demonstrate. The text is an incarnation of what it propounds, and not what Bonnefoy called an 'excarnation'. His critical essays and his poetry possess the same quality of writing, for both genres of texts seek to establish presence, to bring about 'la parole, laquelle commence à chaque fois que nous secouons dans le discours du langage l'emprise des articulations conceptuelles, de leur regard – ou absence de regard – sur le monde'.[11] This perfect admixture of extreme rigour and poetic style reflects the kind of alliance put forward by Bonnefoy: here, an alliance between philosophy and poetry; there, an alliance between poets and readers.

Bonnefoy shows little patience with 'mandat' – mission or mandate being the other name for conceptual thinking and for a purely conceptual approach to poetry and language. 'Mandat' also refers to any kind of reading that would solely be interested in seeking out psychological or unconscious motifs in the poet's mind or in his or her creation: any kind of interpretation that would seek to substitute its object for the networks of presence or 'présences à vivre' revealed by the poem. His overall prognosis for certain trends in modern poetry and criticism is scathing but not alarmist. His is also an enterprise of debunking certain myths surrounding poetry: either the myth of privileged forms of subjectivity expressed in the poem, or the myth of absolute self-referentiality – two opposite ways of betraying poetry's project.

Poetry's project is to re-establish an alliance that has been lost, against the slow progression of conceptual thinking which has occupied the empty seat left by religion, which itself had replaced mythology. According to Bonnefoy, the world has become a desert in the wake of divinity's withdrawal from the world, which reason alone has been unable to irrigate. The mandate assigned to poetry has failed, despite some apparent successes. Poetry is in urgent need of re-engaging with the world, to break through the veils of self-complacency, of an alluring but ultimately sterile language which privileges the concept, instead of making us feel anew our sense of being in the world, of a simple existence exposed to chance, time and place. But we should also learn how to accept the necessary exile caused by conceptual thinking, by the deceiving world of images, by our illusory beliefs in poetry itself. This erring and forgetting imply that poetry is essentially an act of memory – the memory of forgotten presence, which the simple hearing of the sound of a word can help bring back: 'le son, perçu au-delà des réseaux de significations, c'est de l'immédiat, cet indéfait du monde dont le discours conceptuel dénoue l'unité . . . c'est une présence, là même où la parole tendait de par son jeu de concepts à en empêcher la saisie'.[12] For Bonnefoy, poetry is the memory of what transcends the concept: 'cet infini au sein de la réalité la plus proche, cette transcendance dans l'immanence, cette unité qu'elle offre de vivre, c'est ce dont la poésie a mémoire'.

If poetry is failing, at least in France, it is because its mandate has failed. Most of the poetic enterprises conducted by the Surrealists, Bataille and various other trends of poetry – despite their marvellous discoveries on the plane of language and of the image in particular – became dead ends, even though very few French poets escaped their influence, Bonnefoy included. Painters – and Bonnefoy's passion for painting led him to write brilliantly on art history – fared better, having kept conceptual thinking in abeyance. But for poetry a new alliance is needed, in order for us, for our society, 'de réapprendre la valeur positive de ce qui est, de ressentir la "divinité" du brin d'herbe, de l'odeur du basilic, du rire des enfants, de la forme même de ce chemin que l'on voit tourner devant nous et eux parmi quelques arbres'.

We can of course disagree with what Bonnefoy tells us in his text, but it should not be easily dismissed. His own poetic trajectory throughout the century led him to start writing poetry under the sign of Surrealism, before relinquishing some of its discoveries. But many of the things that Bonnefoy negates have not been abolished: the Surrealist image, for instance, against which Bonnefoy struggled because he saw it as a distraction from presence, as a fascinating but illusory device. This did not prevent him from introducing a new type of image, which Jean Starobinski called 'images précaires', which provide 'un retour à la vérité précaire des apparences . . . si nous évitons de la [l'image] solidifier'.[13] Bonnefoy's prognosis is also not unlike that of Michel Deguy, poet and philosopher, who wrote that 'la poésie n'est plus un royaume enchanté, ni enchanteur . . . La poésie n'est pas seule. Ça veut dire quoi? Qu'elle est avec. Elle accompagne la vie et la vie l'accompagne.'[14]

II

Bonnefoy's text takes stock of what has happened to poetry, in France and probably elsewhere, in the twentieth century, more powerfully than a general history of modern French poetry could do, because it goes to the core of what is at stake, because behind his own prognosis runs an entire poetic tradition which is grinding to a halt.[15] This is not to say that he rejects what the recent and less recent past have created – far from it. French poetry happens to have witnessed a resurgence of creativity in the twentieth century, arguably because of the fact that Paris had become an international hub of artistic effervescence in the late nineteenth century, and in the first half of the twentieth century, when Modernism, exemplified by Baudelaire, Mallarmé, Manet, Cézanne and Picasso, really became a force to be reckoned with. Most poets and artists (from

America, Great Britain, Spain, Italy, Germany, Russia, the francophone countries and from the then colonies of France and Britain in particular) went through Paris before changing tack and moving on artistically. Many an international artist found in France an appropriate ground to develop ideas, get down to work and find an audience. Being at the crossroads between the arts – painting, music, sculpture, dance, photography, sound recording and cinema – but also of scientific discoveries and new theories, French poetry showed a capacity to grow in dialogue with other media, with what René Char called its 'alliés substantiels'. Indeed, the alliance between poetry, the visual arts and music, which was not new as such of course, proved a particularly fecund source of inspiration, as can be seen in Guillaume Apollinaire's 'calligrammes', or word-pictures.

Bonnefoy's call for a new type of alliance – now that, according to him, poetry's mission has expired – is what this volume of close readings would like to start answering, however imperfectly or sketchily. It will afford readers the experience of following an emotional and intellectual journey through thirty-two poems and their accompanying commentaries. The poems were chosen according to a principle of 'elective affinities', the choice being left to the critics, some of whom happen to be poets themselves. Some poems might not be the most celebrated or the most representative, but, given the existence of a number of excellent anthologies of modern French poetry, the critics have felt free to choose works that explore lesser-known aspects of a poet. We trust that the selection will exert sufficient power to make the readers want to explore the many other poems and poets which we regret could not be included here.[16] The variety of approaches adopted reflects the many voices of poetry criticism today, be they predominantly theoretical, historical or stylistic. Thanks to its commentary, each poem becomes a window opening onto the poet and onto poetical and artistic tradition as a whole within a French or international context.

The overall organisation of the volume aims to help the reader rethink the notion of poetic movement, the role of poetics and how we read poetry. Though following a broadly chronological order, the book often groups together poems which were written at different points in time (works by Senghor and Segalen, Michaux and Ponge, for instance), and includes in the same section poets who may seem different at first, but who are working in similar directions and share parallel preoccupations or aesthetic concerns (Glissant and Bonnefoy, for instance). In view of the potential pitfalls of periodisation and classification which 'artificially homogenise literature into linear genealogies',[17] it seemed preferable to think in terms of 'families' or 'constellations' of texts or poets, rather than 'schools' or even 'movements'. To help the reader navigate through this vast corpus of texts, the book is divided into four broad sections which outline the major currents in twentieth-century poetry. The sense of aesthetic and historical development, as well as the play of influences and rebellions, will emerge from the poems and the commentaries themselves, rather than from any rigid categories of literary history.

The opening section 'Traditions and modernisms' brings together Paul Valéry and Victor Segalen (giving voice and vision to Greek columns or Chinese steles), and Apollinaire (celebrating traditional themes in telegraphic style), for instance, not because their works are remotely comparable, but because they adopt a common 'positioning' towards poetic tradition, bent as they were on establishing continuation, albeit sometimes playful, experimental and ironic, rather than a total rupture with France's literary past. There is also a traditional streak in Apollinaire, as there is a Modernist streak in Valéry. The 'Avant-gardes' section regroups not only the Surrealists, including André Breton's moves between urban and oneiric visions, but also poets who embarked on drastically different aesthetic routes, such as Reverdy (master of a spare, elusive and allusive language) and Francis Ponge (creator of encyclo-paedic new linguistic identities for familiar objects). The section devoted to 'Poetics of presence', famously linked to the poets who founded the journal *L'Éphémère*, includes Édouard Glissant, whose now finally acknowledged and celebrated poetics of relation expresses similar concerns about presence, albeit from his own decentring angle. Glissant found poetic experience in the space between image and language, in the spaces opened up between phrases rather than in their synthesis. Finally, and closer to us, the last section 'New voices, new visions' brings together new generations of poets whose concerns vary widely, but who either tend to privilege a more concrete approach to poetry, at the level of voice and of language (Bernard Heidsieck and Michel Deguy), or who embrace a new poetics of vision, not only in the poets' intricate collabora-tion with painters, but also in their trust in the powers of poetry to 'make us see' (Jean-Michel Maulpoix). Straddling both tendencies, but in a similar vein, Pierre Alferi engages with a vocalisation of 'stuttering' and a peripheral vision of everyday ephemera in order to enact the drama of navigating experience through language.

Reading the poems as they are presented should lead to the identification of new resemblances and differences, and thus to the alteration of our still too arti-ficial and 'conceptual categories', and should elicit some new 'lignes de force'. Obvious ones already exist, between the poets who let their art be engulfed by the power of imagination and of the image (although even here a poet such as Valéry calls into question the status of metaphor through his exuberant deploy-ment of the metaphysical conceit, and a poet like Bernard Noël moves beyond metaphor into a world where voice, feeling and vision uncomfortably merge) and those who abnegated the *fulgurance* of the image in order to pursue a more restrained quest – that of the quotidian, for instance, as in the everyday objects that Claude Esteban or Ponge take as the starting point for an exploration of their own dialectical perception. These 'lignes de force' also exist between poetry and prose,[18] and, related to this perplexing dichotomy, between traditional forms of versification and scansion and what Clive Scott calls 'experimental reading'. This new kind of reading would be best qualified to tally with the new

demands of modern poetry, as its 'move from the linear to the tabular transforms a perspectival vocality (a single voice moving towards an horizon) to a
planar vocality (a voice shifting between the vocal, the devocalised, different
kinds of oral enunciation)'. Scott adds: 'We need to recover the qualitative and
the heterogeneous in our experience of accent and syllable; we need to make
the ear more responsive to latent performance features in verse'.[19] Here Henri
Michaux's oral glossolalia disturbs and excites with its ludic deconstruction of
representational linguistic signs.

Older poetic topoi are revisited too: landscapes (geology and geography
being an intrinsic part of what nature already represented for Romanticism) or
'paysages' will appear in many poems (by Segalen, Char, Jacques Dupin, André
du Bouchet, Glissant, Michaux, Aimé Césaire, Amina Saïd), becoming what
Jean-Pierre Richard called 'pages-paysages', some calling monuments of former
civilisations into question (Valéry, Segalen, Saint-John Perse), and therefore
acting as a kind of obverse side of Modernity, while others plunge into urban
landscapes (Léopold Sédar Senghor, Jacques Réda, Reverdy, Breton). These
landscapes are not objects of representation but complex 'modes of feelings',[20]
sometimes addressing societal developments (Senghor, Césaire, Glissant), sometimes seeking to escape the individual/society dichotomy, and searching for an
in-between threshold (Philippe Jaccottet, Alferi). In that sense, they are possibly
the only outlets left to modern lyricism, which Adorno defined in his seminal
essay 'On Lyric Poetry and Society':

> It is precisely what is not social in the lyric poem that is now to
> become its social aspect . . . the lyric reveals itself to be most deeply
> grounded in society when it does not chime in with society, when it
> communicates nothing, when, instead, the subject whose expression
> is successful reaches an accord with language itself, with the inherent
> tendency of language . . . When the 'I' becomes oblivious to itself in
> language it is fully present nevertheless.[21]

One thinks of the hauntingly disjuncted images of Nguyên Hoàng Bao Viêt's
poem, where random missed buses and the occasional bomb-blasted doll recalling Anne Frank interrupt any smooth flow of postcolonial interpretation. As the
self becomes more alienated from its historical coordinates, it draws us more
insidiously into a questioning of our own cultural identity.

Many poems will stake out a claim for 'diversity', thus displacing poetry
from its arrogantly assumed French centre. Glissant will engage with French
(and Western) poetic tradition complicit in colonisation, first theorised by
Segalen, in order to relocate it within the larger context of the 'Tout-monde',
but he will also deliberately blur the traditional dualism relating self to nature
in nineteenth-century poetry. In fact, Apollinaire revising pastoral tradition in
Paris, Blaise Cendrars confronting a capitalist Easter in New York, and Senghor
in the same city coming to terms with a new feeling of 'négritude' rather than

assimilation, have already used shock juxtapositions in order to force the reader to question how they constructed their cultural identity.

Other poems will remind us that poetry and philosophy have been in tense but fruitful dialogue throughout the last century: poets have engaged with philosophers ranging from Bergson, Dilthey, Bachelard and Heidegger, to Merleau-Ponty, Ricœur, de Certeau, Nancy and Deleuze. Philosophers and theorists (particularly Blanchot, Derrida, Cixous and Kristeva) wrote texts which explicitly blurred the boundaries between poetry and philosophy, more to the advantage than to the detriment of both. Thought is not the apanage of conceptual thinking. Marie-Claire Bancquart explores identity through the notion of time, as did Proust and Bergson. Jaccottet's sonnet on ignorance, and the immanence of death within knowledge, or Ponge's elaborate consultation of caressed and constructed 'objeux', also bear witness to this philosophical search for identity through a phenomenology of perception and an enquiry into the boundaries of time and space.

It is not a coincidence that a philosopher such as Jean-Luc Nancy recently found the need to talk on behalf of poetry in his splendidly and cogently named *Résistance de la poésie*, not so much to defend poetry on the basis of what it is, but on what is external to it, yet motivates it: 'Si nous comprenons, si nous accédons d'une manière ou d'une autre à une orée de sens, c'est poétiquement. Cela ne veut pas dire qu'aucune sorte de poésie constitue un moyen ou un milieu d'accès. Cela veut dire – et c'est presque le contraire – que seul cet accès définit la poésie, et qu'elle n'a lieu que lorsqu'il a lieu.'[22] In effect, theory and philosophy often took their own inspiration in poetry – poetry as a 'matrice d'idées' which unravel themselves in recent and future theoretical debates, whether they be on gender, race or ethics – and this is perhaps where poetry's true avant-garde nature has always lain.

Twentieth-century poetry was a poetry of desire – from Marie Noël's ambiguous appeals to Valéry's celebration of sculpted female figures, and a celebratory exploration of love (Paul Éluard, Aragon). It was also notoriously a 'poetry of voice' and self-enquiry, as nearly every poem in this volume tends to turn into a covert re-enactment of the process of creation, from Alferi's interstitial spaces to Glissant's fusion with the earth, from the sparse questioning of Bernard Noël and Pierre Reverdy to the media-conscious linguistic disturbances of Michaux and Heidsieck. If the twentieth century saw the apotheosis of the image (Pound, Eliot, Reverdy, Breton), it also saw the demise of the metaphor and the rise of a new poetic voice, searching for its own imaginary space, creating rather than reflecting its own identity, listening to rather than dictating its own language.

This *was* the twentieth century, but, since the poems presented here have resisted the test of time, we rather hope and believe that they have already started to herald our own new times, and that they will give birth to further fertile critical study and further creative writing.

III

Yves Bonnefoy's text which we have chosen as a Foreword serves as a blueprint and as an antidote (in the Derridean sense of *Pharmakos*) to what this volume of close readings hopes to offer. It should be used as a blueprint when reading this volume in light of what it tells us about the new alliance that needs to be found between poets and readers, which requires schools and universities to put younger generations into contact with as wide a range of poems as possible. This book should be seen as an invitation to a series of encounters with poems first, then with the readings which accompany them. But in the same way as Bonnefoy gives us his interpretation of what poetry is or should be, close readings, if done in a manner that does not impose too rigid an ideology or a conceptual grid, offer a window onto the world of the poem and of the poet; and yes, perhaps onto the craft of poetry as well. The danger incurred by any interpretation is also what redeems it in our eyes.

If, as Césaire told us in an article-manifesto published in 1945, poetry is knowledge,[23] but a kind of knowledge that countervails the balance which has so far tipped too much in favour of conceptual thinking, reading a poem, listening to it being read, voicing it ourselves, indeed becomes an adventure. Even though we often remain perplexed when faced with a poem for the first time, and because of this first reaction of incomprehension, dismay even, we all know that, slowly, something happens and the encounter turns out to be a mutual discovery. Poetry requires courage, for true poetry faces you with the unknown, and this unknown is all the more frightening (hence also fascinating) that it is soon revealed to be within ourselves: 'Pour voir le monde, il faut rompre notre familiarité (acquise) avec lui', Merleau-Ponty tells us.[24] This is why poetry makes not so much an aesthetic demand on us as an ethical one. In the act of reading a poem, ethics and aesthetics find themselves, at last and if only momentarily, conjoined.

But what are we going to make of Bonnefoy's stern warning against interpretation? For the reason just mentioned, interpretation can become poetry's ally, and this is what the critics and poets in this book, some of them belonging to the long tradition of 'critical poetry' or 'poésie critique' which started in the era of German Romanticism,[25] set their hearts and minds to do. Commentaries can be either 'musique d'accompagnement' (Deguy) or could be compared to the best of art criticism, when a painting comes truly alive before our eyes thanks to the words of a John Ruskin, Walter Pater, Erwin Panofsky or, more recently, Daniel Arasse or Georges Didi-Huberman. Our eyes switch their attention back and forth from painting or poem to the text. It can create the vertiginous pleasure of partaking in a creative act: what some philosophers called an act of interpretation. In that sense, reading a poem critically should ideally be the symmetrical image of writing a poem, thus giving us an insight into poetry *en acte*. And if courage is required when faced with a poem, humility is also necessary, which is not synonymous with servile passivity or tantamount to paying lip service to complacent idolatry or to our own narcissism. Heidegger reminded us of such humility in his preface to his study of Hölderlin: 'Pour l'amour de ce qui vient en poème, l'éclaircissement doit viser à se rendre lui-même superflu. Le dernier pas, mais le plus difficile, de toute interprétation consiste à disparaître devant la pure présence du poème. Le poème se tenant alors sous son propre statut apporte de lui-même immédiatement une lumière aux autres poèmes.'[26] As long as we bear in mind this caveat, alongside René Char's remark in our first epigraph, written whilst engaged in a critical reading of Rimbaud, this series of close readings will help readers discover freely the rich veins of poetic creation written in French throughout the century, and encourage them to reassess what seemed definite about the modern French poetic tradition through new juxtapositions of poets and poems.

Asking the question of why poetry is important, and answering by way of a stern warning, Yves Bonnefoy utters his anti-Platonic faith in defence of poetry. His prognosis of the world is no different from that of Shelley when the English poet lucidly wrote two centuries ago that 'the cultivation of poetry is never more to be desired than at periods when, from an excess of the selfish and calculating principle, the accumulation of the materials of external life exceed the quantity of the power of assimilating them to the internal laws of human nature'.[27] Shelley was eerily aware of the true dangers facing humanity caught in the thrilling wave of nascent Modernity.[28] It did not prevent him, however, from telling us that 'hope creates from its own wreck'.[29] If we were to replace 'hope' with 'poetry' in this phrase, Bonnefoy's text might yield a little more light. For one element remains certain throughout the century, and through all the poems presented here, even those which speak of the unspeakable – poetry is nothing if it is not a figure of hope. Its future, about which poetry does not care, exists only if poetry tirelessly posits the possibility of a better future for others:

> un avenir qui est bien celui de la poésie. Celle-ci, c'est toujours dans un enfant, encore en deçà de l'emprise du conceptuel sur les mots, puis dans un adolescent, une jeune fille, eux encore à leur espérance, qu'elle commencera, recommencera. Rien ne peut remplacer ni même égaler l'élan de ces enthousiasmes, la lucidité de ces inquiétudes, la vérité de ces impatiences.[30]

Notes

1 René Char, 'Arthur Rimbaud', in *Œuvres complètes* (Paris: Gallimard, 1983), p. 729.
2 Aimé Césaire, 'Poésie et connaissance', *Tropismes*, 12 (1945), p. 163.
3 Osip Mandelstam, 'The Word and Culture', in *The Complete Critical Prose and Letters*, trans. Jane Gary Harris and Constance Link (Ann Arbor, MI: Ardis, 1979), p. 113.
4 Yves Bonnefoy, *Le Magazine littéraire*, April 2008, p. 94.
5 'Poetry stops the gaping mouth of the desired real which is lacking', in *En vrac: notes* (Monaco: Éditions du Rocher, 1956), p. 139.

6 John E. Jackson, Postface to Yves Bonnefoy, *Rue Traversière* (Paris: Gallimard, 1992), p. 208.

7 Yves Bonnefoy, *Remarques sur le regard* (Paris: Calmann-Lévy, 2002), p. 14.

8 Maurice Merleau-Ponty, *Signes* (Paris: Gallimard, 1960), pp. 68, 69.

9 *Ibid.*, pp. 91, 125.

10 Yves Bonnefoy, 'La Présence et l'image', in *Entretiens sur la poésie (1972–1990)* (Paris: Mercure de France, 1990), p. 199.

11 *Yves Bonnefoy et l'Europe du XXe siècle*, ed. Daniel Lançon, Michèle Fink and Maryse Staiber (Strasbourg: Presses Universitaires de Strasbourg, 2003), p. 483.

12 Yves Bonnefoy, 'L'Enjeu occcidental de la poésie', in *Identité littéraire de l'Europe*, ed. Marc Fumaroli, Yves Bonnefoy, Harald Weinrich and Michel Zink (Paris: Presses Universitaires de France, 1996), p. 210.

13 Preface to Yves Bonnefoy, *Poèmes* (Paris: Gallimard, 1982), p. 28.

14 Michel Deguy, *Des poètes français contemporains*, ed. Michel Deguy, Robert Davrey and Hédi Kaddour (Paris: ADPF Publications, 2001), p. 22.

15 For excellent introductions, see Michael Bishop's chapter 'Poetry', in *The Cambridge Companion to Modern French Culture*, ed. Nicholas Hewitt (Cambridge: Cambridge University Press, 2003), pp. 224–47, and Jean Khalfa and Emma Wagstaff's entry 'Poetry', in the *Encyclopedia of Modern French Thought*, ed. Christopher John Murray (London: Fitzroy Dearborn, 2004), pp. 518–24.

16 Good poetry anthologies (see Select bibliography) will reveal many more wonderful poets: Paul Claudel, Robert Desnos, Tristan Tzara, Antonin Artaud, Jules Supervielle, Benjamin Péret, Lorand Gaspar, Joë Bousquet, Pierre-Jean Jouve, André Tardieu, Jacques Prévert, Eugène Guillevic, André Frénaud, Louis-René des Forêts, Gisèle Prassinos, Lionel Ray, Salah Stétié, Edmond Jabès, Georges Schehadé, Kateb Yacine, Tchicaya U'Tamsi, Emmanuel Hocquard, James Sacré, etc.

17 See the editors' introduction in *A New History of French Literature*, ed. Denis Hollier (Cambridge, MA: Harvard University Press, 1989), p. xix. Ideally, as Julien Gracq tells us, a history of literature should be able to substitute the titles of poems, plays and novels for the names of their authors, therefore implying that, unlike History, it records only its victories, and not its defeats, which benefit no one. See Julien Gracq, *En lisant en écrivant* (Paris: José Corti, 1980), p. 169.

18 Giorgio Agamben has proposed insightful remarks about the impossible poetry/prose dichotomy, in his *Idée de la prose* and *The End of the Poem* (see Select bibliography). Jean-Luc Nancy also dismisses easy categorisations, as well as current trends towards 'prosaïsation' in modern French poetry: 'autant il est clair . . . qu'on n'en peut plus, du poétique et de la poétisation, de l'exaltation grandiloquente, des suavités évocatoires . . . pour ne rien dire des académismes romantiques, symbolistes, mallarméens, surréalistes ou "post-modernistes", autant, donc, n'est pas clair ce qu'on demande avec la prose', Jean-Luc Nancy, *Résistance de la poésie* (Bordeaux: William Blake and Co, 2004), p. 23.

19 See Clive Scott's Afterword, p. 292–3.

20 Raymond Williams, *The Raymond Williams Reader*, ed. John Higgins (Oxford: Blackwell, 2001), p. 32.

21 Theodor Adorno, *Notes to Literature*, vol. I, ed. Rolf Tiedemann, trans. Shierry Weber Nicholsen (New York: Columbia University Press, 1991), pp. 37–46.

22 Nancy, *Résistance de la poésie*, p. 9.

23 Césaire, 'Poésie et connaissance'.

24 Maurice Merleau-Ponty, *Phénoménologie de la perception* (Paris: Gallimard, 1945), p. viii.

25 See Walter Benjamin's article 'The Concept of Criticism in German Romanticism', in

Walter Benjamin, Selected Writings (1913–1926), vol. I, ed. Marcus Bullock and Michael Jennings (Cambridge, MA: Harvard University Press, 1996), pp. 116–200.

26 Martin Heidegger, *Approche de Hölderlin*, trans. Henry Corbin, Michel Deguy, François Fédier and Jean Launay (Paris: Gallimard, 1979), p. 8. See Françoise Dastur's coruscating analysis of this text in *À la naissance des choses* (Paris: Encre marine, 2005). Against 'éclaircissement' and against any notion of tranparency, Glissant develops his own ethics of reading, dwelling on the necessary 'opacity' or resistance of the text itself: 'La pratique d'un texte littéraire figure ainsi une opposition entre deux opacités, celle irréductible de ce texte, quand bien même il s'agirait du plus bénin sonnet, et celle toujours en mouvement de l'auteur ou d'un lecteur'. Édouard Glissant, *Poétique de la relation* (Paris: Gallimard, 1990), p. 129.

27 Percy Bysshe Shelley, *A Defence of Poetry*, in *The Norton Anthology of English Literature* (New York: Norton, 1975), p. 1816.

28 Sharing a similar faith in poetry, but reflecting on the withdrawal of divinity from the world of modernity, Hölderlin also advocated a new alliance between poetry and mankind:

> [ce] qui rend [la puissance poïétique de la poésie] supérieure à la théorie comme à la pratique, à la philosophie comme à la politique, c'est ce pouvoir d'*instauration* auquel Hölderlin fait allusion lorsqu'il écrit dans son poème *Andenken*: 'Was bleibet aber, stiften die Dichter' ['Mais ce qui demeure, les poètes l'instaurent']. Cette force poïétique est fondatrice de l'être-ensemble des hommes parce que la parole poétique est nomination des figures des dieux, c'est-à-dire de ces libres créations poétiques dans lesquelles les hommes se donnent à voir à eux-mêmes leur vie supérieure.

See Françoise Dastur, 'La Signification ontologique de l'image', in *Puissances de l'image*, ed. Jean-Claude Gens and Pierre Rodrigo (Dijon: Éditions Universitaires de Dijon, 2007), pp. 37–48, at p. 41.

29 Shelley, *Prometheus Unbound*, p. 1774.

30 *Yves Bonnefoy et l'Europe du XXe siècle*, p. 8. I would like to thank Peter Collier and Marion Schmid, who greatly contributed to the writing of this introduction.

Part I

Traditions and modernisms

1 Paul Valéry, 'Le Cantique des colonnes'

PETER COLLIER

Le Cantique des colonnes

à Léon-Paul Fargue[1]

1	Douces colonnes, aux Chapeaux garnis de jour Ornés de vrais oiseaux Qui marchent sur le tour,	4
2	Douces colonnes, ô L'orchestre de fuseaux ! Chacun immole son Silence à l'unisson.	8
3	– Que portez-vous si haut, Égales radieuses ? – Au désir sans défaut Nos grâces studieuses !	12
4	Nous chantons à la fois Que nous portons les cieux ! Ô seule et sage voix Qui chantes pour les yeux !	16
5	Vois quels hymnes candides ! Quelle sonorité Nos éléments limpides Tirent de la clarté !	20
6	Si froides et dorées Nous fûmes de nos lits Par le ciseau tirées Pour devenir ces lys !	24
7	De nos lits de cristal Nous fûmes éveillées Des griffes de métal Nous ont appareillées.	28

8   Pour affronter la lune,
      La lune et le soleil,
      On nous polit chacune
      Comme ongle de l'orteil !   32

9   Servantes sans genoux,
      Sourires sans figures,
      La belle devant nous
      Se sent les jambes pures.   36

10   Pieusement pareilles,
      Le nez sous le bandeau
      Et nos riches oreilles
      Sourdes au blanc fardeau,   40

11   Un temple sur les yeux
      Noirs pour l'éternité,
      Nous allons sans les dieux
      À la divinité !   44

12   Nos antiques jeunesses,
      Chair mate et belles ombres,
      Sont fières des finesses
      Qui naissent par les nombres !   48

13   Filles des nombres d'or
      Fortes des lois du ciel,
      Sur nous tombe et s'endort
      Un dieu couleur de miel.   52

14   Il dort content, le Jour,
      Que chaque jour offrons
      Sur la table d'amour
      Étale sur nos fronts.   56

15   Incorruptibles sœurs,
      Mi-brûlantes, mi-fraîches,
      Nous prîmes pour danseurs
      Brises et feuilles sèches,   60

16   Et les siècles par dix,
      Et les peuples passés,
      C'est un profond jadis,
      Jadis jamais assez !   64

18

17   Sous nos mêmes amours
         Plus lourdes que le monde
         Nous traversons les jours
         Comme une pierre l'onde !   68

18   Nous marchons dans le temps,
         Et nos corps éclatants
         Ont des pas ineffables
         Qui marquent dans les fables. . .   72

From *Charmes*

Poetry has traditionally been a kind of spoken song. Its rhymes and rhythms, whether chanted aloud or echoed silently, were for centuries the most eminently vocal kind of literature. A change occurred about a century and a half ago, when the regularity of the voicing of verse was challenged by the proponents of prose poetry (Baudelaire, Rimbaud) and *vers libre* (Laforgue, Eliot).

One effect of this dislocation of the regularity of prosody was to move away from the traditional forms and rhythms of poetry, and draw attention to the emotional as well as the physical aspects of breathing and phrasing as in, say, Walt Whitman's *Leaves of Grass* (1855). But another effect was to highlight the raw linguistic matter of poetry: that is, its sound and even shape. The visually decorative and sonorously awkward aspects of poetry were foregrounded in such works as the *Poèmes barbares* (1862) of Leconte de Lisle and Mallarmé's *Un coup de dés* (1897), where expectations of grammatical fluency and clarity of meaning were deliberately undermined. Thus, towards the end of the nineteenth century we find that Romantic and Symbolist poetry gave way to a poetry in which classical form is present, but where form is knowingly played with. We might call this 'baroque', by analogy with the music, art and architecture of the seventeenth century, with their formal elaboration of a simple theme into an elaborate pattern. One thinks also of the *trompe l'œil*, the stucco marble and the false perspectives of Italian churches.

In the 1890s Paul Valéry was a Symbolist poet and a disciple of Mallarmé, but as he rewrote his early verse, published in 1920 as his *Album de vers anciens* and his new volume, *Charmes* in 1922,[2] he moved towards a paradoxical, neo-baroque kind of Modernism.

Charmes is famous above all for the elegy 'Le Cimetière marin', but I propose here to analyse a poem which is apparently less philosophical and meditative, a more playful and ornamental poem: 'Le Cantique des colonnes'. Looking at this poem, even before we decipher a line or a verse, we cannot help but see – well, a column of verse. The poem appears to present itself in vertical rather than horizontal form. The lines are short. They are in fact 'hemistiches', that is, half-alexandrines. The twelve-syllable alexandrine, used in French verse over the centuries from the plays of Racine and Molière to the verse of Baudelaire, corresponds roughly to a spoken sentence, as does the five-foot iambic pentameter of Shakespearean blank verse. Superficially, short verses seem somehow simpler. Yet, on reflection, we have to admit that they are in fact more difficult for the writer to handle and the reader to follow, requiring the rhyme scheme to repeat twice as often and shortening the length given to expressing a thought.

Valéry's playful rhyme scheme is very rich – rhyming the previous consonant as well as the final vowel – and complex, shifting from ABAB in the first stanza (colonnes, aux / de jour // oiseaux / le tour) to AACC in the second (colonnes, ô / fuseaux // immole son / l'unisson) and ADAD in the third (si haut / radieuses // sans défaut / studieuses).

The rich over-determination of these interwoven sonorities is underlined visually by the spelling, so that even as we move into stanza 4 with its EFEF rhyme, the reader's eye is still visually rhyming 'cieux', 'voix' and 'yeux' (stanza 4) with the preceding 'aux', 'oiseaux' and 'fuseaux' (stanzas 1 and 2) , as well as hearing the assonance of the echoes of 'cieux' and 'yeux' (stanza 4) repeated from 'radieuses' and 'studieuses' (stanza 3). Valéry mostly observes the classical alternation between masculine rhymes (ending in an accented vowel sound) and feminine rhymes (ending in a mute e), as for instance in stanza 9 (genoux/figures/nous/pures), but he is no longer systematic. There are stanzas which have only masculine rhymes (stanza 2, ô/fuseaux/son/unisson) and others with only feminine rhymes (stanza 12, jeunesse/ombres/finesse/nombres). He also modulates this pattern by sometimes contrasting a simple vowel with a diphthong (stanza 13, d'or/ ciel/s'endort/miel).

Valéry's poem is not merely sonorous and visual; it is dramatic. Above all, it stages a dialogue. For the first two and a half stanzas, the poet's voice apostrophises the columns, repeating his address 'Douces colonnes' twice, before asking the question 'Que portez-vous si haut / Égales radieuses'. From then on, starting with the reply in the third stanza 'Au désir sans défaut / Nos grâces studieuses' right through to the eighteenth and last stanza, the voice of the poem is taken over by that of the columns themselves, which, given the gendered nature of the French language, automatically become female voices. This personification leads the reader to begin to attribute human, feminine characteristics to the carved stone columns. At the same time the metaphors, from the start of the poem, feminise the architecture, treating the capitals as if they were ladies' hats. As the poem proceeds we find references to nail varnish (line 32), maid servants (line 33), girls (line 49), and sisters (line 57).

The voices are given an accent which is at once artistic and coquettish. The female figures insist almost narcissistically on the beauty and richness of their decoration and presentation and on their mathematical and quasi-divine precision. These attributes of human beauty and desire are married to an ongoing undercurrent of references to art, architecture, sculpture and music. I shall discuss these complex metaphors and visual conceits in a moment. But first we should note the presence of what has been called the 'linguistic conceit': that is, the term which playfully draws attention to its own creative ambiguity.

Valéry's language is often either 'precious' like that of John Donne or the Pléiade, but also often awkward as in Mallarmé, in both cases drawing attention to its own artificial crafting. This self-conscious linguistic performance contrasts with the superficially limpid quality of the extremely short sentences, whose very brevity and lack of specific reference, however, make them enigmatic, as in:

> Il dort content, le Jour,
> Que chaque jour offrons
> Sur la table d'amour
> Étale sur nos fronts,

where the reader hesitates whether to construe 'étale' as a verb ('spreads') or as an adjective ('smooth'). This type of grammatical ambiguity is symptomatic of a more fundamental search throughout the poem for shifts in meaning and an interplay between the abstract and the concrete. The columns evoke girls, organ pipes and lilies but, on the other hand, call our attention to abstract or formal entities such as music, sculpture and religion, all the time emphasising one of the main themes of the poem, which is creativity. As the cold, sleeping, feminine figures were chiselled by the sculptor from their rock, so they are polished like verse or calculated by architects.

Valéry spoke memorably of poetry as 'une longue hésitation entre le son et le sens'.[3] The first two stanzas are a musical incantation whose beautiful sonorities appear to override logical meaning with their columns wearing hats and their organ pipes sacrificing silence. The poet systematically mingles abstract and concrete notation in order to confound any simple match between signifier and signified. In stanza 13 the columns as girls are embodiments of the Greek golden section but are also embraced by the sun god who is the colour of honey. The theoretical 'Lois du ciel' and 'nombres d'or' conflict with the sensual 'couleur de miel' and 'tombe et s'endort'.

The poem, then, is a dramatic and a visual meditation. Its simple vertical linearity is modulated by its sinuous interchange of rhymes and sonorities. It looks like a column but its internal echoes spiral around its fall, as acanthus leaves or caryatids on a Greek column delay and deflect the descending eye.

The poem is a festival of shifting metaphor. In stanza 2 the columns are a set of organ pipes. The musical analogies are developed as it were in the form of a fugue rather than literally, with verbs such as 'chantons / chantes' (stanza 4) and nouns such as 'voix' (stanza 4), 'hymnes' and 'sonorité' (stanza 5).

It is typical of Valéry that just as he develops a crystallising metaphor, so he modifies it. Metaphor for Valéry is not intended as an illustrative image of reality but as a sign of its transformation in the mind, where the interplay between image and reality continually sparks off new images and new ideas which modify our view of reality. As the thematics of song and music develop, so does that of architecture. The function of the columns, which might be merely radiant and graceful, is given in stanza 4 as bearing the weight of the heavens, and in stanzas 6, 7 and 8 they also reveal how they were hewn, chiselled and polished as artefacts.

But in this imaginary journey from music to sculpture, images of the feminine are rarely absent. Already in stanza 1 the columns were feminised as 'douces' and wearing hats; their 'grâces' occur in stanza 3; in stanza 4 we interpret them as caryatids, in stanzas 6 and 7 they are drawn from their beds, in stanza 8 they are polished like toenails. Stanza 9 is all smiles and legs, stanza 10 all earrings and headscarves.

Valéry's art is often the art of the oblique. The 'jeunesse' of the feminised colums is 'antique' (stanza 12), they are girls, but only as daughters of the mathematical golden mean; they are honey-coloured, but only as lit by the setting sun (stanza 13). They make love, albeit only to the daylight (stanza 14); they dance, but are neither wholly ardent nor wholly innocent, and in an intermingling of nature and art these hybrid creatures have intercourse not only with the wind and the trees, but also with people and history (stanzas 15 and 16). One thinks of Keats's 'Ode on a Grecian Urn', where it is hard to make a distinction between the voice of the viewer and that of the figures.

When reading a Valéry poem it is so difficult to hold a single image in the mind, and relate the interwoven thematics to it consistently. But perhaps it is precisely the interferences that matter. Legs waking from beds are also flesh crafted from stone. Birds' nests on tree tops are also carved capitals. Organ pipes are the metallic equivalent of the fluted voice. Stone sings.

The poem does not so much describe as enact. It is not a landscape, although it evokes paintings by Poussin or Claude of classical ruins in a landscape viewed in a certain artistic light. It is not a moment of perception but rather a process of visualisation. It is a voice reflecting on its imagery and on its own linguistic creativity.

The columns are also columns of poetry. The visual effects invoked by the imagery are sometimes underscored, sometimes undermined by the linear, columnar nature of the verse. In a Modernist turn, Valéry, like his recent contemporary Apollinaire (*Calligrammes*, 1916) plays with two different sources of our visual imagination: the shape of the words on the page and the visions triggered by language. As we try to visualise the austere proportions of classical marble, helped by the simplicity of Valéry's layout, we are distracted by the flamboyant flourishes (hats, headscarves, earrings, lilies).

The reader's mind wants both to colour and decorate the rigorous verse form and yet to pattern the wild and disparate metaphorical connotations. Such poetry could easily become rococo rather than baroque, but the burgeoning images are given a harmonious overall tonality as their tones remain within the almost colourless contrasts of light ('candide', 'jour', 'cristal', 'clarté', 'lys', 'miel', 'onde') and dark ('matte', 'ombre', 'noir').

Valéry's poetry has been called by Christine Crow and Kirsteen Anderson a 'poetry of voice'.[4] The poem sings of the senses, of sound ('orchestre', 'chantons', 'hymnes') of touch ('froides, 'griffes', 'polis') of movement ('danseurs'), of desire (stanzas 13 and 14), as well as of visual delight. In addition to giving a voice to music, sculpture, architecture and erotic desire, each expressed in terms of the others, the poem is a dramatic dialogue and narrative, leading from bed to myth, from the chisel to the polished work. It takes us from the mathematical calculation of the building (similar to the prosodic structure of the poem) and its spiritual and artistic aspirations (the 'message' of the writer), through its formal perfection (as with the polished verse), up to its moment of decay and recuperation by history and nature (perhaps echoing the absorption of poetry by the minds and bodies of its once and future readers). The effort of retrieving Valéry's meaning from his intricate, lyrical but enigmatic verse moves the reader through the stages of the birth, life and death of a work of art and uses its linguistic play and experiments as a model for reading and writing, a model based on a kind of Proustian fantastic wandering, where the downward drift of the reading eye interacts with the almost erotic upsurge of the pleasure principle in the enjoyment of tactile imagery, implying the idea of artistic creation as a projection of the desired and desiring body and an introjection of natural beauty, as in some paintings by Valéry's contemporary, Matisse, where creative energy is expressed in terms of dance, desire in terms of design, vision in terms of ornament.

Notes

1 Léon-Paul Fargue (1876–1947) was the author of *Pour la musique* (1912), which draws on Symbolism and music.
2 Paul Valéry, *Charmes* (Paris: Larousse, 1968).
3 Paul Valéry, 'Rhumbs', in *Œuvres complètes*, vol. II (Paris: Gallimard, 1960).
4 Kirsteen Anderson, *Paul Valéry and the Voice of Desire* (Oxford: Legenda, 2000); Christine M. Crow, *Paul Valéry: Consciousness and Nature* (Cambridge: Cambridge University Press, 1972).

Further reading

Austin, Lloyd James, *Poetic Principles and Practice: Occasional Papers on Baudelaire, Mallarmé and Valéry* (Cambridge: Cambridge University Press, 1987).
Bloom, Harold (ed.), *Paul Valéry* (New York: Chelsea House, 1989).
Crow, Christine, *Paul Valéry and the Poetry of Voice* (Cambridge: Cambridge University Press, 1982).
Gifford, Paul (ed.), *Reading Paul Valéry: Universe in Mind* (Cambridge: Cambridge University Press, 1998).
Ince, Walter Newcombe, *The Poetic Theory of Paul Valéry: Inspiration and Technique* (Leicester: Leicester University Press, 1970).
Jarrety, Michel, *Valéry devant la littérature* (Paris: Presses Universitaires de France, 1991).

Mairesse, Anne, *Figures de Valéry* (Paris: L'Harmattan, 2000).

Marx, William, *Naissance de la critique moderne* (Arras: Presses Universitaires d'Artois, 2002).

Putman, Walter, *Paul Valéry Revisited* (New York: Twayne Publishers, 1995).

Valéry, Paul, *The Collected Works of Paul Valéry*, vol. II, *Poems in the Rough*, ed. Jackson Mathews, trans. Hilary Corke (London: Routledge, 1969).

The Art of Poetry, trans. Denise Folliot (Princeton, NJ: Princeton University Press, 1989).

Notebooks, ed. Brian Stimpson, trans. Paul Gifford (Frankfurt am Main: Peter Lang, 2000).

Charms and other Pieces, trans. Peter Dale (London: Anvil Press Poetry, 2007).

2 Victor Segalen, 'Aux dix mille années'

CHARLES FORSDICK

Aux dix mille années

Ces barbares, écartant le bois, et la brique et la terre, bâtissent dans le roc afin de bâtir éternel !

Ils vénèrent des tombeaux dont la gloire est d'exister encore ; des ponts renommés d'être vieux et des temples de pierre trop dure dont pas une assise ne joue.

Ils vantent que leur ciment durcit avec les soleils ; les lunes meurent en polissant leurs dalles ; rien ne disjoint la durée dont ils s'affublent ces ignorants, ces barbares !

o

Vous ! fils de Han, dont la sagesse atteint dix mille années et dix mille milliers d'années, gardez-vous de cette méprise.

Rien d'immobile n'échappe aux dents affamées des âges. La durée n'est point le sort du solide. L'immuable n'habite pas vos murs, mais en vous, hommes lents, hommes continuels.

Si le temps ne s'attaque à l'œuvre, c'est l'ouvrier qu'il mord. Qu'on le rassasie: ces troncs pleins de sève, ces couleurs vivantes, ces ors que la pluie lave et que le soleil éteint.

> Fondez sur le sable. Mouillez copieusement votre argile. Montez
> les bois pour le sacrifice : bientôt le sable cédera, l'argile
> gonflera, le double toit criblera le sol de ses écailles :
>
> Toute l'offrande est agréée !
>
> o
>
> Or, si vous devez subir la pierre insolente et le bronze orgueilleux,
> que la pierre et que le bronze subissent les contours du bois
> périssable et simulent son effort caduc :
>
> Point de révolte : honorons les âges dans leurs chutes successives
> et le temps dans sa voracité.
>
> From *Stèles*

A month after their arrival in Beijing, Victor Segalen and his travelling companion Gilbert de Voisins took a train to Xiling to visit the thirteen tombs of the Qing dynasty. In a letter to his wife Yvonne (25 July 1909), Segalen recorded the immediate impact the site had both on him and on his understanding of Chinese monumental architecture:

> Mais ici, quel mépris à rebours du Temps lui-même! Il dévore? Qu'on
> lui donne à dévorer. Il ruine? Il décatit, il abrège, il tronçonne, il
> éventre et pourrit? Qu'on lui donne à détruire. Qu'on nourrisse sa
> faim: et non pas avec des aliments durs et indigestes. . . voici des mets
> plus apprêtés: des bois odorants. . . des tuiles que délitera la pluie, et
> que la charpente effondrée versera comme des gravats sur le sol. . . . . .
> Le temps est repu. – Ici le monument est indurable et léger. . . Mais il se
> réclame d'une autre puissance: le Monument chinois est *mobile*, et ses
> hordes de pavillons, ses cavaleries de toits fougueux, ses poteaux, ses
> flammes, tout est prêt au départ, toujours, tout est nomade: Rendons-
> lui donc son en-allée, sa fuite, son exode, et sa procession éternelle.[1]

In embryo, the passage outlines what Segalen would dub the 'Orchestique' of Chinese statuary, i.e. its dependence not on duration, stability and immobility, but rather on progressive erosion, impermanence and other forms of constant mobility.

The response to the tombs at Xiling becomes a central strand of *Briques et tuiles*, the series of poetic fragments produced by Segalen during his first major Chinese journey (1909–10). The passage sent to Yvonne Segalen appears to have been reproduced almost verbatim from notes in this text, part of a longer reflection on the 'dynamisme lent' of this site and on the inherent ephemerality of the monuments of which it consists.[2] In early September, while in Shanxi province, Segalen began to elaborate further on this theme. He drafted two versions of a prose text ('Aux années. Au temps dévorateur' and 'Aux dix mille années') in which the Emperor, addressing a merchant ('Toi qui reviens des étranges contrées occidentales') who has observed architectural practice in Europe, ridicules Western faith in the permanence of stone monuments and praises the use of perishable materials, most notably wood. This was followed by a further text ('Notes sur les restaurations architecturales chinoises'), which casts contemporary Chinese attempts to conserve stelae as a form of vandalism, contrary to the poetics of ruins inherent in the steady deterioriation of these edifices and in 'la nudité de leurs arêtes sèches dans l'air incessamment léger, voltigeant autour de leur stabilité'. Finally, a short draft, from December 1909, presents the beginning of an 'essai d'orchestique sur l'architecture chinoise', a revisionist account of the history of monumental art, substituting 'tout un cortège de. . .' for 'définitions pesantes et géométriques tout un cortège de rythmes, d'ondulations, de dynamique et d'impérennité'.[3]

In terms not only of theme but also of vocabulary and phrasing, these extracts from *Briques et tuiles* – written directly in the field of travel, and consequently reflecting with spontaneity and immediacy specific 'moments chinois' (the original title of *Stèles*) – represent the first drafts of 'Aux dix mille années'. At the same time, they reveal the centrality of that particular poem to the genesis of the collection. Segalen was a 'polygraphic' author, selecting significant events in his life or key ideas, and exploring them, often in a variety of genres, through multiple rewritings. In such a process, *Briques et tuiles* plays a matrical role, for the text contains what Segalen classes the 'germes' of a number of subsequent projects, most notably *Stèles* itself. He began work on this poetry collection in September 1910, writing over the next two years the forty-eight poems that would constitute the first edition published in August 1912, the year following the Chinese Revolution. (The second edition, published in 1914 in the bibliophile 'collection Coréenne' that Segalen founded and directed for Georges Crès, contained an additional sixteen texts.) 'Aux dix mille années' was one of the first *stèles* to be written, and was itself subject to substantial redrafting and rewriting, with the three versions of the poem extant in manuscript form revealing a progressive tightening and shortening of its prose.[4]

Segalen's encounter with China constituted a radical new departure in his thinking on intercultural contact, and permitted the renewal – in texts such as *Stèles* – of what he dubbed his 'esthétique du Divers'. A naval doctor by training, he had spent an initial posting in Polynesia (1903–4), where he had been struck by the damaging, even fatal implications of Western expansion, especially in its most aggressive form: colonialism. His ethnographic novel *Les Immémoriaux* (1907) is an attempt to recount the beginnings of such processes of contact from an indigenous viewpoint. The text, written in a *français tahitien* that proved unpalatable for most contemporary readers, exoticises the Methodist missionaries on whose arrival and impact it focuses. Dissatisfied with this early work and by the tepid critical reaction to it, Segalen sought in China not only new manifestations of diversity, but also new literary models through which to explore this concept. *Stèles* is evidence of such a shift, and Segalen enthusiastically acknowledged Henry Manceron's discovery in his collection of an 'éclatement de la formule', a major departure from the exoticism that had characterised Segalen's previous work.[5]

This radically new departure was a matter not only of theme, but also of literary form, and depended on an aesthetic conception of exoticism in which the two elements of theme and form were interdependent. When Segalen died, prematurely and mysteriously, in 1919, he left a vast unpublished oeuvre, of which significant parts still remain in manuscript form. Whilst alive, he published only three books, *Les Immémoriaux* (mentioned above), *Stèles* itself, and *Peintures* (1916), a second collection of prose poems inspired by Chinese painting. The Tahitian novel, produced *à compte d'auteur*, had attracted little attention, and *Peintures*, released at the height of the First World War, also appeared without significant contemporary comment. *Stèles*, however, enjoyed a very different publishing history, the bibliophilic dimensions of which reflect the conception of poetry for which the book serves as a vehicle.[6] Produced in several editions during its author's own lifetime,[7] the first version of the work is a beautiful material artefact in its own right: printed *à la chinoise* on the presses of the Lazarists in Beijing, its pages are folded concertina-like, held between covers made of camphor wood (traditionally selected to prevent damage by insects), and bound with yellow silk. Each poem follows the distinctive tripartite layout of the Segalenian *stèle*: a rectangular black outline – reminiscent of the blocks of stone that inspired the form – encloses two bodies of text; the epigraph, in Chinese characters, appears in the right-hand corner of this frame; and the main body of the poem, in French, dominates the page, with its sections divided by small circles in imitation of the simple punctuation of classical Chinese texts. Those privileged enough to receive copies of the first edition, of which only eighty-one copies appear to have been produced, would have been faced with a genuinely exotic object, designed to engage the reader multi-sensorially, through sight, hearing, touch and smell.

Modern paperback editions of *Stèles* cannot, of course, reproduce this effect, but it is essential to remember that for Segalen his work was more than the words on the page. Not only was layout important, not least for the effects of juxtaposition it triggered, but also the book, as a material support for the poetry it contained, also reflected the ritualistic understanding of poetry, almost Mallarméan in conception, echoed in the work's language. The genesis of this poetic form can be tracked through Segalen's correspondence. To Claude Debussy, he describes the emerging work as 'un recueil de proses courtes et dures' (6 January 1911),[8] but it is in a letter to his *maître à penser* Jules de Gaultier (26 January 1913) that the wider project of *Stèles* is outlined:

> Ce n'est pas l'esprit ni la lettre, mais simplement la forme *Stèle* que j'ai empruntée. Je cherche délibérément en Chine non pas des idées, non pas des sujets, mais des formes, qui sont peu connues, variées et hautaines. La 'forme Stèle' m'a paru susceptible de devenir un genre

littéraire nouveau, dont j'ai tenté de fixer quelques exemples. Je veux dire une pièce courte, cernée d'une sorte de cadre rectangulaire dans la pensée, et se présentant de front au lecteur.[9]

The confrontational nature of the form – 'se présentant de front au lecteur' – is part of the collection's perceived difficulty or resistance, encapsulated in what Victor Bol described as its 'hermétisme de surface'.[10] Nevertheless, of all Segalen's works, it is *Stèles* that has attracted the most sustained critical attention, with an early analysis of the work, by readers such as Henry Bouillier, as post-Symbolist literature, progressively eclipsed by an emphasis on the poems' intercultural status and their often ambiguous grounding in Chinese culture.[11]

Stèles is structured by a meticulously conceived internal architecture, dividing the poems into thematic clusters based on the four cardinal points and two supplementary locations. 'Aux dix mille années' figures in the first of these six sections, devoted to 'Stèles face au midi' (the south is traditionally the most important cardinal point in China, often associated with the Emperor) and containing fifteen poems. Together these constitute a critical reflection on religious and philosophical themes. At the same time, subtle connections are created within each section between individual texts. 'Aux dix mille années', for instance, is closely related, diptych-like, to 'Ordre de marche', the epigraph of which – '10,000 li, 10,000 times 10,000 li', derived from the Chinese expression '10,000 years, 10,000 times 10,000 years' – clearly echoes the earlier poem's title. This *stèle*, like the fragment in *Briques et tuiles* that shares its title, presents itself as an imperial declamation, adopting the imperative tone common throughout the whole collection. The Emperor ridicules the vanity of the Western architectural tradition, which seeks to build enduring, permanent edifices, and contrasts this with its Chinese equivalent, in which the construction materials are deliberately perishable (or, in cases where durable materials are used, given an appearance of perishability). Concealed in the opening section of the poem, behind the references to tombs, bridges and temples, are allusions to the now 'dead' civilisations – Egyptian, Roman and Greek – that the Chinese Empire had long outlived.

The poem's structure reveals a progressive shift from architectural observation, grounded in Segalen's own archaeological work, to metaphorical reflection. The group of 'Stèles face au midi' constitutes a general engagement with 'reason', the subject of 'Hommage à la raison', one of the later poems in this section. Noël Cordonier accurately describes an assault on 'le rationalisme à prétention universalisante de l'Occident',[12] and 'Aux dix mille années' constitutes a reflection on the architectural manifestation of such epistemological assumptions, here related to questions of memory and vanity, and associated with a certain hubris located in links between the durability of stone and the desire for immortality. There is undoubtedly (and, for Segalen, characteristically) a sideways glance at the Gospels and the parable of the two builders (Matthew 7: 21–7). Moreover, faith in constructing 'dans le roc' is countered by a conception of a fragmented sense of matter (reminiscent of Heraclitus), as well as by an understanding of history related to the Nietzschean eternal return, suggesting that the upheaval of dynastic change is underpinned by a residual continuity. Simon Leys has demonstrated convincingly the ways in which this poem-*stèle* is primarily a reflection on Chinese attitudes towards the past.[13] Despite the concluding admonition 'Point de révolte', this is not, however, a quietist call for resignation to the all-eroding effects of time, but a reflection on the nature of eternity, and on its relationship to interior and exterior worlds. In claiming that '[l]'immuable n'habite pas vos murs, mais en vous', the poet criticises a Western faith in the endurance of material yet ultimately perishable objects; he foregrounds instead an alternative vision of the world, in which reality exists elsewhere, beyond material phenomena, and in which the interpersonal transmission of tradition is privileged. There remains nevertheless a residual ambiguity, not least because this poem, rejecting the durability of construction materials such as stone, is itself a *stèle*, but it is possible – as Bouillier suggests – to read the text as a comment on poetry itself, existing beyond the fluid material world described and constituting in itself the 'immuable' at the text's core.[14]

The counter-cultural, even counter-intuitive manoeuvre that the poem performs is inherent within its subject matter, for 'Aux dix mille années' is dependent on an exoticising reversal of the gaze, with the Western reader equated with the 'barbares' evoked in its opening line (and repeated chiasmically at the end of the opening section). This effect is equally apparent in the language of the poem, which thematically – with its references to water and architectural form – is linked to a number of others in the collection. More striking than symbolism and vocabulary, however, is the issue of voice. In the preface to *Stèles*, Segalen describes the linguistic effect sought: 'Le style en doit être ceci qu'on ne peut pas dire un langage, car ceci n'a point d'échos parmi les autres langages et ne saurait servir au langage quotidien: *le Wên*.'[15] The poetic voice of 'Aux dix mille années', with its dense syntax (e.g. 'hommes lents, hommes continuels') and concise, elliptical style (e.g. the two 'que' omitted in the third paragraph), is undoubtedly that of the Emperor himself, addressing his people, the 'fils de Han' of the opening line of the second section. The result, for the francophone reader at least, is one of defamiliarisation, as the French language is in part 'sinified' and endowed with unfamiliar ritual tones.

Reminiscent of Mallarmé's comments on Poe (presented as giving 'un sens plus pur au mots de la tribu'), the shock of formal, linguistic and thematic exoticisation of the everyday is central to Segalen's conception of poetry. Such a process is crystallised in the presence of the *stèles*' Chinese epigraphs (quotations from classical literature, proverbs, lines of poetry, idiomatic phrases or inventions by the poet himself), whose visual impact on readers is one of the distinguishing features of the collection. Those faced with the *stèle* are struck, even before they begin decoding the text, by the unaccustomed interplay on the page of Chinese characters and Roman script. For the majority of readers, with a limited or non-existent knowledge of Chinese, the effect of the epigraph remains therefore unsettling, even disruptive, at least until a translation is provided. In the case of 'Aux dix mille années', Segalen offered his own: 'Exclamation rituelle: "Dix mille ans! Dix mille dix milliers d'années"', revealing the characters to be a truncated version of the Chinese equivalent of 'Long live the King!', without in this case any reference to the Emperor (i.e. 'Long live!').[16]

Close analysis of a poem requires the reader to undertake an unaccustomed deceleration of sense-making processes. In this case, there is a need to unpick the stages of interpretation: the initial, primarily iconic, apprehension of the structure, letters and characters laid out on the page, which is related to the rare, epiphanic moments of shock – or 'regard par-dessus le col' – recounted in Segalen's *Equipée*; the interpretation of the main body, i.e. the text in a 'sinified' French; the processing of the epigraph, either resistant to translation for those without Chinese, or decoded through critical apparatus; and finally the return to a holistic reaction, in which the three previous stages are reconfigured into a general response. The role of the epigraph in this process is essential, for it plays a metonymic role in relation to the general exoticising effect that Segalen endeavours to create in the poem as a whole. To translate the epigraph is in a way to domesticate it, to defuse the charge of its alterity, although such a reading assumes an ignorance of Chinese and fails to acknowledge the fascinating ways in which *Stèles*, now translated into Chinese, has itself travelled, adding new, unexpected stages to its reception history.

Scholars of Segalen have long been preoccupied by what Christian Doumet has classed the 'question sinologique', exploring – on the one hand – the creative, exoticising exclusions inherent in those readings of *Stèles* based on a relative ignorance of Chinese culture and language, and – on the other – the very different reactions that knowledge of China may trigger. Segalen himself, in the letter to Gaultier cited above (26 January 1913), states: 'j'ai fait mon possible pour éviter tout malentendu chinois, toute méprise, toute fausse note. Mais dans ce moule chinois, j'ai placé simplement ce que j'avais à exprimer.'[17] This is a claim that he develops in a slightly later letter to Henry Manceron (3 February 1913), in which the transcultural potential of the form is made clear:

> Un pas de plus et la 'Stèle' se dépouillerait entièrement pour moi de son origine chinoise pour représenter strictement, précisément: un genre littéraire nouveau. . . Il est possible que plus tard, dans très longtemps, je donne un nouveau recueil de *Stèles*, et qu'elles n'aient de la Chine même pas le papier.[18]

The challenge for the reader of *Stèles* is to negotiate the various levels on which these poems operate, grounded as they are in a privileged contact with Chinese culture, but freighting at the same time their author's elevated, even aristocratic conception of the purposes of poetry. Permitting this meeting of the textual and metatextual, of the culturally specific and the poetically abstract, the *stèle*-poem is defined by Haun Saussy as 'a parallax or interlanguage produced by the encounter of two semiotic systems': we may even identify here the first stirrings of a poetry that operates – in the terms of one of Segalen's most subtle post-colonial readers – 'en présence de toutes les langues du monde'.[19]

Notes

1 See Victor Segalen, *Corrrespondance*, ed. Henry Bouillier, 2 vols. (Paris: Fayard, 2004), vol. I, p. 933.
2 Victor Segalen, *Briques et tuiles*, in *Œuvres complètes*, ed. Henry Bouillier, 2 vols. (Paris: Laffont, 1995), vol. I, pp. 845–959 (p. 859).
3 See Segalen, *Briques et tuiles*, pp. 871–2, 873–4, 900–1.
4 The manuscript versions are reproduced in Mauricette Berne, 'Segalen: "Aux dix-mille années"', *Genesis*, 9 (1996), pp. 139–48.
5 See Segalen, *Correspondance*, vol. II, p. 73.
6 See, for a discussion of the bibliophilic materiality of the volume, Victor Segalen, 'Aux lettrés d'Extrême-Orient', in *Œuvres complètes*, vol. II, pp. 137–43. The complete text of the poems from the original 1914 Beijing edition of *Stèles* is available at: www.steles.org/StelesComplete.html.
7 The main critical editions of *Stèles* were produced by Henry Bouillier (Paris: Mercure de France, 1982 [1963]) and Christian Doumet (Paris: Librairie Générale Française, 1999). There are also several translations of the collection into English, including those by Nathaniel Tarn (Santa Barbara, CA: Unicorn Press, 1969) and Andrew Harvey and Iain Watson (London: Jonathan Cape, 1990). A parallel-text edition has recently been published (reproducing the 1914 edition in facsimile), translated, edited and annotated by Timothy Billings and Christopher Bush (Middletown, CT: Wesleyan University Press, 2007). This contains substantial critical apparatus, and is supported by a second volume, *Chinese Sources and Contexts*, available exclusively on-line (www.steles.org).
8 See Segalen, *Correspondance*, vol. I, pp. 1147–8.
9 See Segalen, *Correspondance*, vol. II, pp. 69–70.
10 Victor P. Bol, *Lecture de* Stèles *de Victor Segalen* (Paris: Minard Lettres modernes, 1972), p. 14.
11 Among the principal studies of *Stèles*, in addition to Bol, are Noël Cordonier, *Segalen et la place du lecteur: étude de* Stèles *et d'*Equipée (Paris: Champion, 1999), Christian Doumet, *Le Rituel du livre: sur* Stèles *de Victor Segalen* (Paris: Hachette supérieur, 1992), Marc Gontard, *La Chine de Victor Segalen:* Stèles, Equipée (Paris: Presses Universitaires de France, 2000), and Yvonne Hsieh, *Segalen,* Stèles (Glasgow: University of Glasgow French and German Publications, 2007).
12 See Cordonier, *Segalen et la place du lecteur*, p. 121.
13 See Simon Leys, 'L'Attitude des Chinois à l'égard du passé', in *Essais sur la Chine* (Paris: Laffont, 1998), pp. 739–56.
14 See Henry Bouillier, *Victor Segalen* (Paris: Mercure de France, 1986 [1961]), p. 299.
15 See Segalen, *Stèles*, in *Œuvres complètes*, vol. II, p. 36.
16 For a discussion of the epigraph, see Shushi Kao, 'Écriture et imaginaire idéogrammatique chez Segalen', in Yves-Alain Favre (ed.), *Victor Segalen: Actes du colloque international de Pau, 13–16 mai 1985*, 2 vols. (Pau: Université de Pau et des pays de l'Adour, 1987), vol. I, pp. 72–4.
17 Segalen, *Correspondance*, vol. II, p. 70.
18 *Ibid.*, p. 73.

19 See Haun Saussy, 'Foreword: *Impressions de Chine*, Or How to Translate from a Non-existent Original', in Segalen, *Stèles*, trans. and ed. Billings and Bush, pp. xi–xxxiv (p. xi); Édouard Glissant, *Introduction à une poétique du divers* (Paris: Gallimard, 1996), p. 40.

Further reading

Cordonier, Noël, *Victor Segalen, l'expérience de l'œuvre* (Paris: Champion, 1996).

Dollé, Marie and Doumet, Christian, *Victor Segalen* (Paris: Éditions de l'Herne, 1998).

Forsdick, Charles, *Victor Segalen and the Aesthetics of Diversity: Journeys between Cultures* (Oxford: Oxford University Press, 2000).

Forsdick, Charles and Marson, Susan (eds.), *Reading Diversity/Lectures du divers* (Glasgow: University of Glasgow French and German Publications, 2000).

Fourgeaud-Laville, Caroline, *Segalen ou l'expérience des limites* (Paris: L'Harmattan, 2002).

Ha, Marie-Paule, *Figuring the East: Segalen, Malraux, Duras and Barthes* (Albany, NY: State University of New York Press, 2000).

Hamdan, Dima, *Victor Segalen et Henri Michaux: deux figures de l'exotisme dans la poésie française du vingtième siècle* (Paris: Presses de l'Université de Paris-Sorbonne, 2002).

Hsieh, Yvonne, *Victor Segalen's Literary Encounter with China: Chinese Moulds, Western Thoughts* (Toronto: University of Toronto Press, 1988).

Laügt, Elodie, *L'Orient du signe. Rêves et dérives chez Victor Segalen, Henri Michaux et Émile Cioran* (Oxford: Peter Lang, 2008).

Winspur, Steven, *La Poésie du lieu: Segalen, Thoreau, Guillevic, Ponge* (Amsterdam: Rodopi, 2006).

3 Guillaume Apollinaire, 'Lettre-Océan'

TIMOTHY MATHEWS

From *Calligrammes*[1]

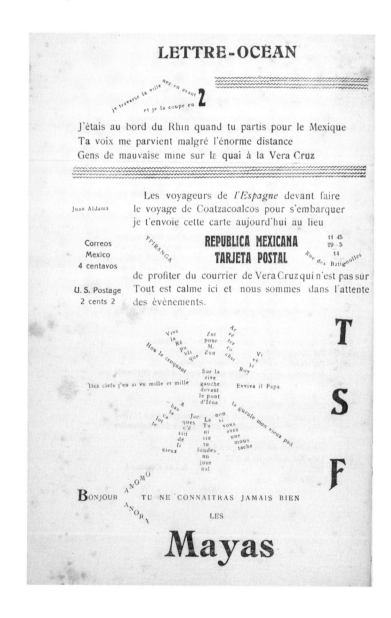

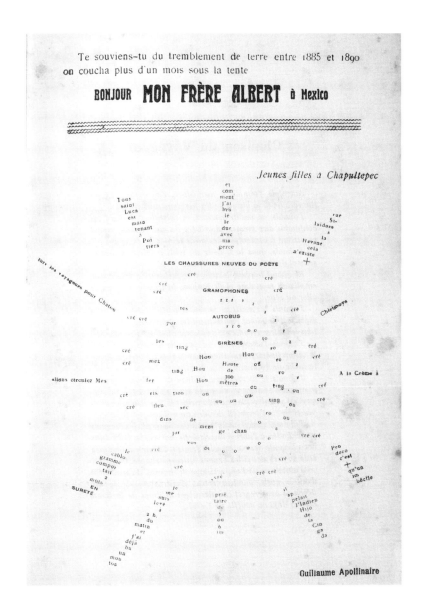

I

Two wheels, or two circles, both with a centre and lines going out, both with concentric circles moving away from the centre – or towards it. But what are these forms? What do they represent? Two points of view in any case, and two ways of representing a circle: one looking into a central reference point, one looking at a flattened surface. But both involve representations on a flat page, and as the distinction between the two collapses we are left wondering what we are looking at. What do Apollinaire's shapes actually mean? After all, they are made of words; surely that will tell us what these shapes show or symbolise? But what are we to make of an offering which confuses the messages of word and image? Can we read and look at once?

Apollinaire's picture poem suggests we cannot. Looking, we see circles. Reading, we peer more and more closely at the words, and as we try to make them out in their unusual places we lose a sense of the visual whole. But, equally, the idea that we cannot use all our senses at once is counter-intuitive: we use them together to move and think. We might think of reading as sequential and seeing as synthetic. But that opposition soon disintegrates as both reading and seeing engage with memory to produce meaning. One intuitive certainty is then confirmed: for the senses to work in tandem there has to be movement and time. But the circles in the poem are flat, they do not move, and even though they are made of words and are not pure shapes, each remains in its own space, each facing the other across the spine of the book.

But, somehow, the two circles need to work together, like the wheels on a bicycle, if we are to make sense of them. Perhaps as readers, we are the ones who need to move for the visual and verbal impacts to articulate each other spontaneously. Perhaps we need to remember walking as we sit and read; and we can read that the poet himself is walking, his new shoes make a noise as he goes around; perhaps they are uncomfortable, perhaps they trigger further memories. Apollinaire's poet is walking in circles, and that makes one at least of the concentric circles we see on the right-hand page. Close by lie other bits of meaning to do with sound: bells on buses and the engines revving, a gramophone needle crackling away at the end of a 78 rpm record, all the indoor and outdoor urban cacophony that makes the song of ancient sirens into mere noise – or is that simply the sound of ambulance sirens we read and see, adding its own circuit to the others? Another such circuit is made by imitating the sound of interference on radio transmission. TSF – 'Télégraphie sans Fil', the acronym of that day's development in communications technology – stands in the position of a hinge between the two sets of circles, the two frames of vision, the two ways in. And looking at all the concentric circles together, as readers we might now see one further iconic convention: the use of circles to represent airwaves, the 'ondes' which give the title to this chapter in *Calligrammes*, Apollinaire's second book of verse, published in 1916.

So the circles do work together, creating movement and the circulation of meanings. But how? And what kind of meaning? The title itself is an expression of solidarity between poetry and the variety of types of communication on offer, feeding modern life and feeding into it. 'Une lettre-océan' was a type of letter sent at sea from one liner via another. Autobiography is in play: Apollinaire's brother was called Albert and he had travelled to Mexico in 1913, the year the poem was published. Allusions to Mexico are spread over the first surface in the poem, and the conflation of narrator into author continues. But as readers we are free to take at face value the phrase in bold at the top of the second page – 'bonjour MON FRÈRE ALBERT'. Guillaume is writing to Albert and not the other way around; sending a message to Mexico and receiving one have become confused. The greeting loses its biographical reference, takes its mobile and indeterminate place amongst other bits of conversation overheard out of context, and which we can read in any order even though their position in the poem is fixed. There is a cornucopia of methods of communication alluded to in the poem and scattered all over its surfaces for the reader to peruse. The Spanish words for a postcard appear in bold on the first page, and postmarks are also replicated – a Parisian and a US one, moreover, rather than just a Mexican one. Sender and recipient are joined almost immediately, separated only by the spaces on the page, which the eye can so easily cross. Telephone cables might be suggested in the wavy lines at the top of each page, which are also a further iconic diagram of the wireless radio messages. The visual form of these textual sketches combines with the verbal one to put modern communication into practice – a communication of *impressions*: impressions of some worldwide community; of rejuvenated intimacy; of messages translated immediately from any person to any other in any place.

Moreover, at this level of perusal it is not simply the present moment that is embraced in the dimensions of the poem, but also the past, both immediate and anthropological. We might read some of the words around the bold-type 'Tarjeta Postal' as the message on the back of this Mexican postcard – one a traveller would jot down to give someone the feel of what is happening: 'tout est calme ici et nous sommes dans l'attente des événements'. The Mexican civil war of 1911–14 is still going on in 1913, and everyday utterances like this one conflate the political and the affective. This flattening of distinction is not only categorical but temporal. Not only contemporary but pre-Columbian culture is present in the visible surface of the poem: '**Mayas**' shouts in bold from the bottom of the first circle. The clash of the reforming presidency and the radical peasantry, in this civil war, echoes the colonial wars which finally brought the Mayan civilisation to an end in 1697. And, more than echoes, what this surface recreates and rediscovers is the power of surface itself. Perspective, whether we look straight on at the two pages, or imagine ourselves above looking down, has been escorted from the stage. Depth has been brought to the surface, into the surface and onto it: temporal as well as spatial depth. Memory and what is lost to it have both been made apparent. What is about to pass from view is held there. And if we think again of the circles, side by side, as wheels, that allows us to introduce movement into thinking about what we see and how it affects us. Along with things passing and things there, reading and seeing are also reintegrated. The poem's surfaces recreate the power of the senses to work together; and rediscover the power of thought to synthesise its perceptions, its memories, and be free to start again.

What if now we saw the two circles not only as two wheels but as two eyes as well? Each has a centre, or hub, or pupil. But now it becomes clear that the relation between the two 'eyes' is not producing the unified vision we are used to. Reading interrupts that seamlessness. We read first in one circle then the other, look at one eye and then the other, trying to read their messages. But within each messages are piled on to others; messages show through others only to be stamped out by them as well. Transmission between them is interrupted, though taken up in a different form elsewhere. Once any of the messages is engaged with in its verbal form, its relation visually to others is not now one of synthesis, but simple contiguity; not one of metaphor, but of metonymy. Far from limiting the signifying scope of each utterance, the contiguity of each in relation to the other stresses just that: closeness, rather than distances needing to be crossed and the signifying systems required. At the visual level, again perspective ceases to apply. Things are not made visible by means of sidelining others. The integration of the two focal points, one from each 'eye', is suspended, the line to the horizon interrupted; and the reader can move in reading and viewing from one focal point to the other, combining them spontaneously and in different ways continually. Mexico figures in one of the eye-forms, and then again in the other. So does the idea of a postcard: 'Tarjeta Postal' in one, and 'Jeunes filles à Chapultepec' in the other, which evokes in French rather than Spanish the title of the picture on the card. The language of the sender, the receiver, the writer and reader, of the European and Mayan civilisations present and past, all occupy the same space and also overtake each other continually. Words disappear under images, images under words. Which is the front and which is the back of the postcard? The point of departure and the point of reception of any message stand in the closest possible contiguity with each other, yet still are not absorbed or lost in one another's seeing or words. If sense impressions are shown to work together, this spontaneity of perception we know so well is now coming not from their integration, nor even its break-up; but from a sense of the ever-so-close.

The indeterminacy of integration and contiguity – the question opens itself out rather than being foreclosed. Here is another: when did we start to look at the poem as readers, and to read the words of the forms? Looking at the centre of each of these circles or wheels, since when might a reader have known that they each describe the Eiffel Tower, separately and in conjunction? 'Sur la rive gauche devant le pont d'Iéna'; and 'Haute de 300 mètres': one gives some horizontal coordinates for it, the other describes its vertical dimension. But only the poem as a whole can hope to communicate the power of this Modernist icon – the poem and its forms. Messages of all kinds emanate in spokes and concentric waves from its two epicentres, but it is their forms which show the optimism carried there as a whole. The horizontal approaches the vertical, approaches still further, and then closer still, but they do not meet, for the conventions of their meeting have once again been suspended. The trajectories of sending and receiving have lost their organisation, and been replaced with other networks made in immediacy and democracy. The movement which the circles both show and interrupt is neither circular nor conclusive, but improvised, responsive and open. Walking begins life in the poem as a metaphor of writing it, then of reading it, then gloriously loses its own metaphoric power to cross distances, and opens the eye to crossing itself – or wandering, or perusing. The reading eye responds to the shifts and starts of perception, at once drenched in the intimate mnemonics of self, and cleansed of them. We read as we *might* walk about and look, self-made *flâneurs* all, within the formal circuits of this imaginary city, and the imagined communications it fosters. In its formal concentrations and contiguities, its tantalisingly never-completed squeezing of time into space, the poem opens itself out to the light of this urban magic; and to the light of living. Just as 'Les Fenêtres' does, which Apollinaire had written a few months earlier, 'Lettre-Océan' opens out its frames to everything they might let in:

> La fenêtre s'ouvre comme une orange
> Le beau fruit de la lumière

II

Is 'Lettre-Océan' a manifesto of the modern art of Apollinaire's time? Or of Futurist art? In *Manifeste du futurisme*, published on the front page of *Le Figaro* in 1909, Marinetti affirms the power of the once-and-for-all, the shock of the new. Symbolically, his target is *The Victory of Samothrace*, displayed in the Louvre; and affectively, it is classical art itself. Marinetti wants to remove the classical form from our adoration and replace it with the car. He appeals to speed and its power to take the temporality out of vision and transform time into space. The simultaneity of points of view championed by Cubist painters is cast as hopelessly removed from the immediacy it claims to espouse. 'Paroles en liberté', words in freedom, words without strings, wireless messages – such are the methods and messages of this Futurist energy. Apollinaire understood its confidence in the power of art to reform the world. 'Lettre-Océan' looks like a translation of Futurist practice from the verbal, and the visual, to the verbal–visual: words are made to move from one place to another, from one time, even one civilisation to another. They leap out of their contexts and are no longer constrained there.

But is pasting hybrid things together a sign of disregard for context, or a further immersion in the labyrinth of provenance and becoming? The visual and verbal–visual collage developed at the same time by Cubist practitioners is driven as much as Futurist artefacts by the desire to reconceive the subject matter of art, to draw it from the here and now of seeing, from whatever comes into view now. But it does not suggest an aspiration to suppress time. The Cubist aspiration is not simply to refashion perception; the issue is not what we think or see, but how. As well as 'Lettre-Océan', Apollinaire published *Les Peintres cubistes* in 1913, although the volume contained pieces written from 1905. There he describes Picasso 'imitant les plans pour représenter les volumes'.[2] Perspective had always exploited surfaces – 'les plans' – to try and give the illusion of depth – 'pour représenter les volumes'. But in Picasso, Apollinaire sees the capacity to do more than simply subvert that rationalist practice. Cubist art shows what is lost to view because of where we stand, and because of the surfaces we see; but it also shows that what is lost to view is still receptive to the power of form, to the imagination, and a different kind of reason.

The *impressionism* of Futurist painters such as Boccioni and Severini ultimately disappoints Apollinaire. Apollinaire shares with many the awareness that to disrupt the frame of viewing is not enough to nullify its effects. There are other wheels evoked by the two wheels of 'Lettre-Océan', and alluding to them gives Apollinaire the space to explore that awareness. 'Les Fenêtres' has the same title as Robert Delaunay's sequence of paintings which he produced in 1912. This time implicitly, in 'Lettre-Océan' Apollinaire makes further intertextual dialogues with some of Delaunay's other paintings, and the wheels and circles on display there. The Ferris wheel, symbolising the new globalism, figures in *L'Équipe de Cardiff FC* of 1912–13. In *Soleil* (1913) the wheel has lost its material referent in contemporary modernity, but gained a structural one. That wheel or disc is made in the primary colours of the rainbow, the colours which make light; they are invisible in ordinary seeing and yet integral to seeing. The intervention of a prism makes the colours of light apparent, and science allows us to know they are there, but in seeing they are invisible. This is the dynamic of Delaunay's wheel. It parts company with the Futurist adoration of modern appearance, with the pursuit of progress and its supervised utopias. A power is rediscovered to see what is presented to us without being dominated by it; or at least to imagine such a power. This art suggests that emancipation comes not from what can be made accessible and visible alone, but from examining seeing itself, and consuming, and what our own seeing hides from view.

'Lettre-Océan' takes part in that ambition for art. The joy it expresses at Modernist communication comes with the sense of a need to *invent* communication rather than be subjected to it. The wheels in the poem as well as the picture do not seek to describe movement, or espouse or exploit it, or silence their own immobility; but instead show with brilliance that we may understand what we cannot see. The messages in the poem are not delivered in the sentences of a telegram, or a 'Lettre-Océan', or any hybrid; their form makes them obscure. Words make a form in which they resonate and in which their varied mobility is revealed. Words do not simply substitute themselves for pictures we might imagine on postcards of the Eiffel Tower or Mayan monuments. Pictures are covered in words which bring these icons to life, undermine their solidity – but also confirm their power. And yet in *not* reading and seeing together, perhaps we learn a form of interpreting able to reinterpret and un-interpret. For still we walk away from the page with an integral word-image in mind: one we can understand and work with, work on, walk on with, confidently.

With Delaunay, then, in 'Lettre-Océan' Apollinaire shows the optimistic critical power of an art he calls Orphism. But what if a different dialogue emerges, with a different wheel, the one in Marcel Duchamp's *The Bicycle Wheel*? This *Readymade* was also made in 1913, and it is a kind of Dadaist manifesto. It consists of a bicycle wheel in its bracket, upended and screwed into the seat of a kitchen stool. Both the wheel and the stool are prevented from functioning. The wheel is detached from the machine which depends on it, and no-one can sit on the stool. Cubist collage has come into its own; the bits of disrupted context cannot be put together again; viewers do not know where they stand or what they are looking at, even though elements can be recognised in isolation. Recognition itself is being scrutinised, and as consumers we are left to wonder what it is we are looking for and how we are to find it. The world is made up of so many recognisable things, things made desirable *because* we recognise them, and still we do not know what we see. At the same time, the irredeemable lack of cohesion shouting at us from the piece forms the basis of a mode of viewing that criticises viewing itself. 'Lettre-Océan' and *The Bicycle Wheel* together testify to that art 'in the age of mechanical reproduction' identified by Walter Benjamin.[3] The subject-matter of art itself is made responsive to the industrial age; reproduction, representation and the knowing they convey have been taken out of the hands of patronage like cars swept away in a tornado. Or has knowing itself been swept aside, displaced by an ineffective catalogue of clichés, a stream of replicas which we fail to interrupt as it builds empires out of supervising our desires? Poised indeterminately between authority and its subversion, frame and its dissolution, distance and invasion, the texts of Apollinaire, Duchamp and Benjamin leave us only to wonder.

Still, there are two wheels in 'Lettre-Océan', and perhaps two is always better than one, for they offer the prospect of dialogue rather than the imposition of the one true and permitted word. Max Ernst recognises but also challenges that hope in his own *La Roue de la lumière* – recognises it in Apollinaire, challenges it in his work. Produced in 1925, after the First World War, well into the Surrealist effort to make art expose censorship and violence, the picture is a testament to the continuing impact of Apollinaire on the following generation of avant-garde radicals. The wheels continue their appearances in Apollinaire's aesthetic journeys of construction and collapse. Here is another, along with his critical, poetic account of painting and light:

> J'aime l'art d'aujourd'hui parce que j'aime avant tout la lumière et tous les hommes aiment avant tout la lumière, ils ont inventé le feu.

Quand l'homme a voulu imiter la marche, il a créé la roue qui ne ressemble pas à une jambe.[4]

Put together, these two fragments of critical prose poetry tell of the intellectual oxygen coming in through the holes in our understanding. It seems that, for Apollinaire, the ability to tell the stories of art and life is always gloriously discovered somewhere other than where we expected, and in another form. And still it comes naturally, along with confidence in the power to engage with life and to create. I think Max Ernst reads Apollinaire's wheels, and tests their confidence against his own experience and practice; and in a Surrealist condensation of his own produces the picture, and the title, *La Roue de la lumière*. I think his title is a self-conscious though silent allusion to Apollinaire's wit and vision.

Visually, *La Roue de la lumière* is a mixed-media picture, inherently composite and plural in the way it is made. There are allusions to optical physics as well as engineering. Material reality, natural, biological and applied science are all in play in Ernst's complex form, built up through overlay and draughtsmanship. But this artist's breaking loose from the techniques and frames of art also signals an embrace by other, further, larger, still more all-encompassing frames of knowing, and surveillance. Looking out at us from the picture is a single eye, and however much we look into it with both of ours, its implacable singularity is never diminished. This is the invasion of the voyeur, the unbreakable surveillance of orthodoxy, as well as the self-regard of paranoia allowing us to accept surveillance and even enjoy it, whatever the cost. By working Apollinaire's remark over in his title, I think Ernst makes his single-eyed picture into a commentary on the two-eyed kaleidoscope of 'Lettre-Océan'; on Apollinaire's own elaborate embrace of the art of his time in the circles and wheels of the poem. In his own immediate history, Ernst now sees only ever increasing constriction, a continual forcing of the freedom to create down the funnels of censorship, of fear and permitted knowing. Still, living in his own time after the mass nationalist slaughter of the First World War, he seems to address a wave of nostalgia and respect to the confidence of Apollinaire, who composed his piece beforehand and alongside his own visions of assassinated poets. And composition 'Lettre-Océan' certainly is: suspended as Apollinaire always wanted between order and adventure, it reaches out to the twin possibilities of beautiful and alienated knowing, composes them together, inviting us to keep each of those impostors close by as we make our own ways through the icons of our lives.

Notes

1 Guillaume Apollinaire, *Œuvres poétiques*, ed. Marcel Adéma and Michel Décaudin (Paris: Gallimard, 1965), pp. 183–5.
2 Guillaume Apollinaire, *Méditations esthétiques, Les Peintres cubistes*, in *Œuvres complètes*, ed. Michel Décaudin, with portraits and facsimiles compiled by Marcel Adéma, 4 vols. (Paris: A. Balland et J. Lecat, 1965), vol. IV, p. 30.

3 Walter Benjamin, 'The Work of Art in the Age of Mechanical Reproduction', in *Illuminations*, ed. and intro. Hannah Arendt, trans. Harry Zohn (London: Fontana, 1973).
4 Apollinaire, *Méditations esthétiques, Les Peintres cubistes*, p. 26; and *Les Mamelles de Tirésias*, in *Œuvres poétiques*, ed. Marcel Adéma and Michel Décaudin (Paris: Gallimard, 1965), pp. 885–6.

Further reading

Adamson, Walter L., *Embattled Avant-gardes. Modernism's Resistance to Commodity Culture in Europe* (Berkeley, CA: University of California Press, 2007).
Apollinaire, Guillaume, *Alcools*, trans. Donald Revell (Hanover: Wesleyan University Press, 1995).
   The Cubist Painters, illustrated translation and critical edition by Peter Read (Berkeley, CA: University of California Press, 2002).
   Calligrammes: Poems of Peace and War (1913–1916), trans. Anne Hyde Greet, intro. S. I. Lockerbie and commentary by Anne Hyde Greet and S. I. Lockerbie (Berkeley, CA: University of California Press, 2004).
Breunig, Leroy C. (ed.), *Apollinaire on Art: Essays and Reviews 1902–1918*, trans. Susan Suleiman (New York: Viking, 1972).
Décaudin, Michel, *Apollinaire* (Paris: Librairie Générale Française, 2002).
Green, Christopher, *The European Avant-Gardes: Art in France and Western Europe 1904–c.1945* (London: Zwemmer, 1995).
Hubert, Étienne-Alain, *Circonstances de la poésie: Reverdy, Apollinaire, surréalisme* (Paris: Klincksieck, 2000).
Jean, Raymond, *La Poétique du désir: Nerval, Lautréamont, Apollinaire, Éluard* (Paris: Seuil, 1974).
Mathews, Timothy, *Reading Apollinaire: Theories of Poetic Language* (Manchester: Manchester University Press, 1987).
   Literature, Art and the Pursuit of Decay in Modern France (Cambridge: Cambridge University Press, 2000).
Read, Peter, *Picasso et Apollinaire, les métamorphoses de la mémoire* (Paris: Jean-Michel Place, 1995).
Renaud, Philippe, *Lecture d'Apollinaire* (Lausanne: L'Âge d'homme, 1969).
Terdiman, Richard, *Present Past: Modernity and the Memory Crisis* (Ithaca, NY: Cornell University Press, 1993).

4 Marie Noël, 'Attente'

ALISON FINCH

Attente

J'ai vécu sans le savoir
    Comme l'herbe pousse. . .
Le matin, le jour, le soir
    Tournaient sur la mousse.

Les ans ont fui sous mes yeux   5
    Comme à tire-d'ailes
D'un bout à l'autre des cieux
    Fuient les hirondelles. . .

Mais voici que j'ai soudain
    Une fleur éclose.   10
J'ai peur des doigts qui demain
    Cueilleront ma rose,

Demain, demain, quand l'Amour
    Au brusque visage
S'abattra comme un vautour   15
    Sur mon cœur sauvage.

Dans l'Amour, si grand, si grand,
    Je me perdrai toute
Comme un agnelet errant
    Dans un bois sans route.   20

Dans l'Amour, comme un cheveu
    Dans la flamme active,
Comme une noix dans le feu,
    Je brûlerai vive.

Dans l'Amour, courant amer,   25
    Las ! comme une goutte,
Une larme dans la mer,
    Je me noierai toute.

Mon cœur libre, ô mon seul bien,
    Au fond de ce gouffre,   30
Que serai-je ? Un petit rien
    Qui souffre, qui souffre !

Quand deux êtres, mal ou bien,
    S'y fondront ensemble,
Que serai-je ? Un petit rien   35
    Qui tremble, qui tremble !

J'ai peur de demain, j'ai peur
    Du vent qui me ploie,
Mais j'ai plus peur du bonheur,
    Plus peur de la joie   40

Qui surprend à pas de loup,
    Si douce, si forte
Qu'à la sentir tout d'un coup
    Je tomberai morte.

Demain, demain, quand l'Amour   45
    Au brusque visage
S'abattra comme un vautour
    Sur mon cœur sauvage. . .

. . . .

Quand mes veines l'entendront
    Sur la route gaie,   50
Je me cacherai le front
    Derrière une haie.

Quand mes cheveux sentiront
    Accourir sa fièvre,
Je fuirai d'un saut plus prompt   55
    Que le bond d'un lièvre.

Quand ses prunelles, ô dieux,
    Fixeront mon âme,
Je fuirai, fermant les yeux,
    Sans voir feu ni flamme.   60

Quand me suivront ses aveux
    Comme des abeilles,
Je fuirai, de mes cheveux
    Cachant mes oreilles.

Quand m'atteindra son baiser,   65
   Plus qu'à demi-morte,
J'irai sans me reposer
   N'importe où, n'importe

Où s'ouvriront des chemins
   Béants au passage,   70
Éperdue et de mes mains
   Couvrant mon visage ;

Et, quand d'un geste vainqueur,
   Toute il m'aura prise,
Me débattant sur son cœur,   75
   Farouche, insoumise,

Je ferai, dans mon effroi
   D'une heure nouvelle,
D'un obscur je ne sais quoi,
   Je ferai, rebelle,   80

Quand il croira me tenir
   À lui tout entière,
Pour retarder l'avenir,
   Vingt pas en arrière !. . .

S'il allait ne pas venir !. . .   85

From *Les Chansons et les heures*

Until the advent of identical schooling for both sexes, which came to France relatively late in the twentieth century, French women poets started with a signal disadvantage: unless they were lucky enough to have enlightened fathers who not only hired tutors for them but also allowed them to be taught like boys, their education did not include the versifying in French, Latin and Greek that men's schooling did. And of course many had no formal education at all. Thus the great nineteenth-century poet Marceline Desbordes-Valmore learned the rules of French verse only via an acting career that introduced her to such dramatists as Racine, while others simply 'picked up' the rules from an extensive reading of, and love for, poetry. Despite this, many did master and practise the technicalities with remarkable skill; and by the time Marie Noël published her first major collection *Les Chansons et les heures* in 1920, it had also become acceptable for women to publish verse in their own names. During the previous century, some female poets had been recognised by the literary establishment: they had been given prizes, even small pensions; they wrote to, and received direct encouragement from, such illustrious men as Hugo; and Desbordes-Valmore herself had obtained two ultimate accolades: approval from the Baudelaire who viscerally, and seemingly on principle, detested women's writing; and acceptance into the fraternity of 'poètes maudits' by Verlaine.[1] Delphine de Girardin, wife of the press baron Émile de Girardin, had been one of the few nineteenth-century female playwrights to bring out verse drama under their own signatures. Furthermore, women poets had been moving into hitherto uncharted territory: Marie Krysinska has some claim to be the first practitioner of *vers libre*, while Louise Ackermann had, in the late nineteenth century, written outspokenly atheistic poetry which would be drawn on by Valéry – startlingly recognisable fragments of her lines appear in his verse. And the far from shy Anna de Noailles (1876–1933) was a star on the French literary scene during Noël's youth. When, therefore, we ask where Marie Noël came from – what shaped this poet, with her technical brilliance and her avowals of erotic feeling – we should remember that she had bold predecessors and that her culture was – by stages – allowing women to partake in the prestige of verse.

None the less, we do see elements of conformity to gender stereotype in Noël. Like many nineteenth-century female predecessors, she will disavow her own verse with self-deprecatory remarks (in, for example, 'Les chansons que je fais': 'J'hésite, à plusieurs fois tâtant le son qu'il faut, / Accrochant çà et là ma voix gauche et peu sûre').[2] And to an extent she shelters behind the protection of religious subjects. Since the Middle Ages, it had been permissible for women to express devotion to God in writing, and many of the subtle-minded ones, such as Marguerite de Navarre, had carefully blended the twin principles of 'pleasure and instruction' to develop ostensibly pious thoughts while at the same time joking about the body, writing without embarrassment about female sensuality, sophisticatedly teasing the reader, and being perfectly irreverent, if not downright hostile, towards clerics themselves. So too Noël as it were 'sanctifies' much of her verse by bringing it within an overtly or implicitly religious context. But at her slyest and boldest – and like a latter-day, more self-aware Saint Theresa – she mingles the erotic and the devotional to a point where they become indistinguishable, and in doing so raises questions about both the quasi-religious passion that may enter into sexuality and conversely the extent to which religious belief has a sexual component. 'Attente' is such a poem. For whom is the narrator waiting? The lover, or the bridegroom Christ who will consume her with fervour?

'Attente' is one of two poems by Noël included by the poet and publisher Pierre Seghers in his mid-twentieth-century *Le Livre d'or de la poésie française*, an anthology that covers the whole range of French verse from its origins to 1940; furthermore, she is one of only nine female poets in the whole collection. The poem rewards close reading, all the more if we set it in context. First, its mainstream literary one: 'Attente' is part of that turn-of-the-century 'syndrome' that Edmund Wilson would famously and rather crudely diagnose in his *Axel's Castle* of 1931: the dream is better than its realisation, the waiting is better than the awaited event, as in Huysmans's *À rebours* (1884), Proust's *À la recherche du temps perdu* (1913–27), Valéry's 'Les Pas' in *Charmes* (1922).

'Attente' also has its Third Republic political setting. Conflicts between state and church had become ever more fraught during the preceding thirty years. While tensions between secular and religious interpretations of literature can be found in any era of French culture, they might be especially self-conscious during this period. A child brought up under the Third Republic could not be unaware of conflicts between laity and clergy, between faith and the positivism that was the educational banner of the Republic. Thus, the love invoked in 'Attente' is sometimes reminiscent of a Christian context in which the self is both rescued and painfully purified by the fire of God's Love (capitalised in ll. 17 and 21). But the recurrent hunting imagery also suggests pagan religion: Racine's Venus 'tout entière à sa proie attachée' – and Noël does invoke 'dieux', not 'Dieu', in line 57, and echoes Racine's 'tout entière' in the last full stanza. Hers is not the full-blooded syncretism of a Nerval, but rather a tentative apologia for Christianity that borrows where it needs to.

Finally, Noël's 'nature imagery' could be seen, blandly, as a throwback to Romantic verse: as apparently ignoring Baudelaire's attacks on tenderness for the vegetable world and those lilies of Rimbaud's that are embedded in the word 'enema' ('c*ly*stères d'ecstase', in 'Ce qu'on dit au poète à propos des fleurs'). But, more interestingly, it might be interpreted as a promotion of rural France: like Nerval and George Sand before her, Noël had a quasi-anthropological interest in the customs and songs of the countryside. Thus, in the prefatory note to her *Chants sauvages*, she remarks that some were 'nés comme des chansons populaires avec des airs que j'ai notés et des accompagnements maladroits, qui pourtant ont part à leur poésie'.[3] The stress on dissonance and inelegance is significant. A dissenting regionalism had, since the nineteenth century, had its cultural charge, representing a reaction against the drive to create thoroughly 'French citizens' by rooting out local differences. Such poems as 'Attente', in other words, are not entirely politically innocent on this score.

Turning now to a more detailed consideration, we see that 'Attente' represents both different kinds of time and different types of religious or erotic desire – from a delicate, expectant arousal to the ferocity of a savage possession. Indeed, it can be difficult to know whether we are looking at temporal or erotic experience: the fact that the two sometimes fuse is part of the power of the poem.

Many different experiences of time are suggested. First, a straightforward chronological progression: the narrator has lived her life unheedingly, as grass grows (ll. 1, 2). 'Comme l'herbe pousse. . .' (l. 2) will remind the reader of Hugo's 'l'herbe pousse et . . . les enfants meurent', also suggesting an onward – if unfair and cruel – march of time. But already in the second stanza the picture becomes more complex: now the years fly like swallows fleeing 'from one end of the skies to the other' (ll. 5–8): this suggests a circular movement round a horizon – at any rate, it is not certain in which direction the swallows flee. Then, in rapid

succession, we move from suddenness (l. 9) to tomorrow (l. 11) to the introduction, early in the fourth stanza, of the suspenseful 'quand' clauses that will
henceforth dominate the poem. But these (as we shall see) are not usual 'quand's:
they lead not to resolution but to a heightened uncertainty as to what, exactly,
will happen when (for example, in ll. 33–5, 'Quand' raises only a further question about identity: when two beings melt together, 'Que serai-je?'). We do not
have here the sense of 'whenever' of Baudelaire's famous 'Spleen' poem, 'Quand
le ciel bas et lourd', which also repeats 'quand's, but through them creates a continuous present: in 'Attente' all the 'quand's point to an indeterminate future,
and indeed in the twelfth stanza, just before the crucial mid-point break in the
poem, they do not even make a complete grammatical structure – the 'when'
clause is simply left hanging (ll. 45–8).

The loss of self is compared, in the fifth stanza, to a lamb wandering in a
pathless wood; so here the temporal has, as with the swallows but now more
clearly, become spatial – a directionless space. And this sense of immersion in a
vast, undefined 'something' continues with the image of the tear in the sea (l.
27), or the 'petit rien' (l. 35) that the narrator will become tomorrow, when –
emerging from this vast vagueness – suddenness strikes again: joy so 'surprises'
that, from having felt it 'tout d'un coup', she will fall dead: 'Je tomberai morte'
(ll. 41–4).

By now, about half-way through the poem – a point Noël marks with spaces
and a line-long ellipsis – we have a sense of the narrator wandering, tossing,
sinking, seized by a 'time' that may be tomorrow, that may be much longer.
In the second part of the poem, these images become more corporeal. The
narrator's veins will hear the beloved come, she will hide her face behind a
hedge, her hair will feel his fever rush towards her (ll. 49–54). Veins, hedges and
hair suggest entangled networks, symbolic of experience that proceeds not in
straight lines and obvious divisions but whose components and pathways are
inextricably interwoven. (Once more, too, we remember Racine's Phèdre, whose
famous declaration of love turns the labyrinth into female sexuality, almost
female anatomy.) And now the narrator, like the swallows of the second stanza,
flies as it were anywhere; on the beloved's approach, she will jump away like a
hare, she will flee as if from a bee-sting (ll. 62–3), she will ceaselessly seek refuge
wherever she can among 'gaping' paths (ll. 67–70). Yet this image is also bound
to suggest the 'opening' of the female to receive the male. Even when this male
has possessed her – and now we approach the end of the poem – she will, in
order to slow down the future, take twenty paces back: 'Je ferai, rebelle, / . . .
Pour retarder l'avenir, / Vingt pas en arrière !. . .' (ll. 80, 83–4). But then, in a final
line that stands alone, we have deliberate bathos in the conversational, almost
prosaic, 'S'il allait ne pas venir !. . .'. The fantasy is punctured: the longing for,
yet fear of, fiery passion, as well as the whirling of time and space – all subside
in a return to 'reality' that is reminiscent of much nineteenth-century literature.
The imagination soars; then there is the bump back to earth (as in, for example,

the poignant bareness of Rimbaud's 'Mais, vrai, j'ai trop pleuré !' that initiates the coda of 'Le Bateau ivre').

All this sense of an irregular time, of a hesitant eroticism, of a multifarious interweaving, is created too by the poem's structures and its linguistic play. 'Attente' is written in the asymmetrical *vers impair*, the odd-syllabled line, here 7 + 5. The *vers impair* was favoured by Desbordes-Valmore and Verlaine, among others. It often suggests something pleasurably off-balance: a tripping dance, a lilting song. And there are song-like 'refrains' in 'Attente'. But these, and the twisting *vers impair* itself, can also be grim (Love plunging down on its prey like a vulture: ll. 15, 47), or at least convey unease: is it really comforting to read 'Dans l'Amour, si grand, si grand' (l. 17), where the second 'grand' suddenly discomfitingly removes the idea of love as 'great' and makes it appear unfathomable instead? (Verlaine had used *vers impair* for dissonance as much as harmony.) Furthermore, the 7 + 5 syllable pattern in itself suggests ephemerality and rapid changeability (we have only to compare it to a hypothetical 7 + 7, let alone the more stately, fluid alexandrine or the relatively dignified decasyllable). In 'Attente', the five-syllable lines in particular dramatically present single impressions, only for these to be whisked away: 'Une fleur éclose' (l. 10), 'Je brûlerai vive' (l. 24). And the very brevity of the lines, combined with the use of the syllabic 'e atone', means that Noël can render time elastic in the metre itself, as in for example the second line, where the final pronounced 'e's of 'Comme' and 'l'herbe' represent the long-term growing of the grass – these four syllables taking up almost the whole line; and if the following 'pousse' has only its one syllable, the ellipsis Noël places after it can extend that too.

Noël uses the five-syllable line not only to make experience elastic but also to theatricalise it, as in 'Que serai-je ? Un petit rien / Qui souffre, qui souffre !' and 'Que serai-je ? Un petit rien / Qui tremble, qui tremble !' (ll. 31–2, ll. 35–6). The last lines of each pair arguably have 'coupes lyriques' after the first 'souffre' and 'tremble'. That is, to take the second example, the line has to be read thus: 'Qui tremble' is a three-syllable phrase where, extraordinarily, the stress falls on the last 'e' of 'tremble', whereas the repetition 'qui tremble !' has a quite different accentuation: only two syllables, with a diminution, a fading-out, of the second trembling despite the exclamation mark.

Noël deploys verbatim repetition to still more dramatic effect in lines 68–70, which bridge the gap between two stanzas. We read:

> N'importe où, n'importe
>
> Où s'ouvriront des chemins
> Béants au passage

Here the enjambement, not just between lines but between stanzas, combined with the terrific new emphasis on the second 'Où', opens up the poem to an indeterminate space (both 'anywhere' and 'where?') that is reinforced both by the image of gaping paths and the attention inevitably drawn to the 'gaping path' of the space between the stanzas. (And, of course, by the immediately juxtaposed 'ou' assonance of '**Où**' and 's'**ou**vriront', l. 69.)

As readers of Mallarmé's octosyllables know, the short-syllabled line also makes wordplay stand out, sometimes almost dominate the line. 'Attente' has a similar liking for wordplay. Noël uses the same double meaning of 'pas' as would Valéry in his more famous 'Les Pas': it functions as a final climax here, in those last two lines (ll. 84, 85): the narrator will make 'Vingt **pas** en arrière! . . .' but then: 'S'il allait ne **pas** venir !. . .'. (The wordplay had been adumbrated in the earlier statement that the narrator fears joy 'Qui surprend à *pas* de loup' (l. 41): a line that itself 'surprises' the reader 'à pas de loup', since, like the one we were just looking at, it too is the second line of a between-stanza enjambement.) 'Bien' rhymes with 'rien' in two successive stanzas (ll. 29–36) but in each the 'bien' has separate grammatical functions. In one case it is a noun, part of an apostrophe in which the narrator states with passion that her free heart is her only 'good', but in the next case it functions as an adverb to indicate that the melting together of two beings may be 'bad' or 'good': thus the noun is swallowed by the adverb just as the narrator's freedom is swallowed up by her uncertainty about the nature of the union. The wordplay means that the feared yet longed-for consummation becomes an object of moral confusion as well as of temporal and spatial anxiety.

Other double meanings stud the poem, for instance those of 'mousse' (l. 4), which makes the narrator's experience of passing time both frothy and solidly rooted in the slow time of flora, 'mousse' meaning both foam and moss. Phonetic networks criss-cross stanzas and lines: a '**Las** !' of one line will lead into the '**la**rme' of the following line (ll. 25–6); the lover's '**aveux**' will follow the narrator like '**abeilles**', again in the very next line (ll. 61–2). Not that all such echoes serve to reinforce meanings: some are jolting. Thus the 'v', 's' and '[k]' alliterations in lines 14 to 16 bring together, with unexpected force after the conventional 'rose' image of the third stanza, the ferocity of Love with the wildness of the waiting heart:

> Demain, demain, **qu**and l'Amour
> Au brus**qu**e **v**isage
> **S**'abattra **c**omme un **v**autour
> **S**ur mon **c**œur sau**v**age.

And the end-rhyme of the antepenultimate stanza surprisingly suggests that the lover's quasi-military conquest is not a conquest at all: the rhyme of 'prise' and 'insoumise' indicates that the possession has scarcely succeeded, and (as we have seen) the following two stanzas 'rewind' the experience as the narrator moves backwards from consummation and from him.

The poem's rhymes are mostly 'suffisantes', with only two phonetic elements coinciding, but the 'riches', where three elements coincide, are often provocative in their semantic unions (thus 'forte' / 'morte', ll. 42, 44). Even more disturbing are the rhymes that are either 'léonines' or nearly so, with two syllables rhyming (or virtually). Here the rhymes can take the poem off on pathways that (as Leiris would famously suggest à propos of the words and music of songs) do not necessarily support anticipated meanings but can apparently go their own way. Readers may respond differently to the degree of 'coincidence' and 'tension' in the examples with which I shall end this discussion. Among the *rimes riches* are, for instance: 'tire-d'ailes / hirondelles' (ll. 6, 8); 'gouffre / souffre' (ll. 30, 32), but also, less easy to associate, 'fièvre / lièvre' (ll. 54, 56); 'demi-morte / n'importe' (ll. 66, 68). Among the 'léonines' or near-'léonines' are: 'cheveu / le feu' (ll. 21, 23); 'amer / la mer' (ll. 25, 27); 'aveux' / 'cheveux' (ll. 61, 63); 'vainqueur / son cœur' (ll. 73, 75), and, most conclusively and now unequivocally 'léonines', the three at the end: 'tenir, avenir, venir' (ll. 81, 83, 85).

'Attente' deserves its place in Seghers's anthology: it is troubling, exquisite and conceptually sophisticated, and if it is less well known than it should be, that is because French women's poetry has taken time to achieve due consideration in its native culture.

Notes

1 For these and the following facts see my *Women's Writing in Nineteenth-Century France* (Cambridge: Cambridge University Press, 2000).
2 Marie Noël, *Les Chansons et les heures* (Paris: Crès, 1928), pp. 11–13 (p. 13).
3 See Marie Noël, *Chants et psaumes d'automne* (Paris: Stock, 1999), p. 13, n. 1.

Further reading

Blanchet, André, *Marie Noël* (Paris: Seghers, 1962).

Blaise Cendrars, 'Mee Too Buggi'

CLIVE SCOTT

Mee Too Buggi

Comme chez les Grecs on croit que tout homme bien élevé
                                    doit savoir pincer la lyre
Donne-moi le fango-fango
Que je l'applique à mon nez
Un son doux et grave
De la narine droite   5
Il y a la description des paysages
Le récit des événements passés
Une relation des contrées lointaines
Bolotoo
Papalangi   10
Le poète entre autres choses fait la description des animaux
Les maisons sont renversées par d'énormes oiseaux
Les femmes sont trop habillées
Rimes et mesures dépourvues
Si l'on fait grâce à un peu d'exagération   15
L'homme qui se coupa lui-même la jambe réussissait dans le
                                    genre simple et gai
Mee low folla
Mariwagi bat le tambour à l'entrée de sa maison

From *Dix-neuf poèmes élastiques*

'Mee Too Buggi' is the seventeenth of Cendrars's *Dix-neuf poèmes élastiques* (1919), most of which were written between 1913 and 1914, and published individually at that time or shortly afterwards. 'Mee Too Buggi' itself first appeared in *Les Soirées de Paris* (July–August, nos. 26–7) in 1914.[1] Cendrars's notion of the elastic is usually related to contemporary Futurist celebrations of elasticity, whether in Boccioni's painting of the dynamism of a horse and rider, entitled simply *Elasticity* (1912), in which forms are translated into energies, so that subject and context interpenetrate, and divisions between matter and space, inside and outside, outline and movement, melt; or in Marinetti's use of the word in relation to consciousness, or intuition, or to the adaptations of linguistic elements to each other. The new poet creates an equally new free verse able to cope with the dynamic of these elasticities and the shifting contours of ever-changing experience.

Thanks to the investigations of Jean-Pierre Goldenstein,[2] whose critical edition (1986) of the *Dix-neuf poèmes élastiques* is an indispensable companion,[3] we know that most of this text, apart from the first line, is a highly edited version of passages taken directly from a French translation (November 1817) of John Martin's account of the Tonga islands (1817).[4] Was this poem written on the assumption that the reader would discover the source? In a poetic world like the one posited by Lautréamont (Cendrars edited *Les Chants de Maldoror* in 1920), 'le plagiat est nécessaire. Le progrès l'implique. Il serre de près la phrase d'un auteur, se sert des ses expressions, efface une idée fausse, la remplace par l'idée juste' (*Poésie II*).[5]

Plagiarism is one of the means whereby another of Lautréamont's axioms – 'La poésie doit être faite par tous'[6] – can be achieved. In his adoption of plagiarism as a creative principle, Cendrars anticipates Oulipian writers[7]: literary texts are works that have realised themselves before properly envisaging their manifold potentialities. Plagiarism (with permutation) is a text's path to a liberation from itself, to a release of expressive energies that would otherwise remain unrevealed. Our way of responding to plagiarism is overly prejudiced by nineteenth-century notions of literary ownership and of the sacrosanctity of the original text. In an Oulipian conception, plagiarism is a form of literary prosthetics, of tweakings and retouchings, which gives no privilege to chronological priority. In fact, John Martin's text is, in relation to Cendrars's poem, 'plagiat par anticipation'. The source is superseded, or rather diverted, by the needs of Modernity. To insist on an original text, and on authorship as a guarantee of its authenticity, is an act of wilful fossilisation, an act that condemns the work to growing irrelevance or erroneousness. In any literary text, the field of meaning will always exceed authorial intention.

All works are in transition, between themselves and another form of themselves. Different layouts produce different rhythmic configurations of the same material, different rhythmic interactions. Cendrars tells us that he cares little for syllable-counting.[8] Rhythm becomes an inexact or approximate or changeable percept: we neither know how many syllables a line has nor the degree to which it is accentuated. Does the first line, for example, have 20 syllables or 22 (do I count the e's of 'Comme' and 'homme' or not?). Do I read it prosaically with as few as three accents, or more 'intensively' with as many as seven? As we see, these uncertainties are not just a symptom of layout, but an integral part of the reading process. Is this poem rhymeless or rhymed? If rhymeless, is it unrhymed (because it does not intend to rhyme) or anti-rhymed (because it intends not to rhyme, as a polemical gesture)? If rhymed, is it as much half-rhymed ('grave/droite/paysages/folla'; 'lyre/Papalangi') as full-rhymed ('fango-

fango/animaux/oiseaux'; 'nez/passés/habillées/gai'; 'exagération/maison')? But then what rhymes with what? Are these rhymes paired, or, in the larger groups, tripled, or quadrupled? And do we perceive some rhymes more vividly, or more consciously than others? Variation of the interval between rhymes allows the poet to set rhymes at different levels of consciousness. Would we in fact hear the rhyme between 'lyre' and 'Papalangi', for instance, or between 'nez' and 'gai'? Or do these occur at some aurally subliminal level? 'Elastic' means that the reader passes through a range of discourses with different dynamics, different degrees of connotative or perceptual intensity, different rhythmic coherences.

If one is to judge from notes taken in shorthand by a listener at a lecture given by Cendrars in São Paulo, 12 February 1924,[9] Cendrars is fascinated by phenomena of 'slippage', particularly as these bear witness to the psychic underpinning of poetic expression. This fascination relates to the replacement, at the time, of generical criticism, the criticism of literary categories, by the burgeoning science of linguistics. The slippages that Cendrars makes mention of are those between the vocal and the non-vocalisable (when psycho-rhythmic peaks become too frequent, the voice has difficulty in negotiating them), between conscious and unconscious pronunciation, and a variety of other slippages between what the mind envisages and what the body (vocally) produces (acoustic and syntactic configurations, verbal images). Cendrars makes special mention of the early-century experimental phonetics pursued by the abbé Rousselot at the Collège de France: 'ses travaux touchent tous au domaine si mystérieux de la formation de la parole et la mise en branle des organes vocaux, c'est-à-dire aux sources mêmes du lyrisme'.[10] Why is linguistics so significant for the new poets? Because linguistics establishes links between linguistic production and mental processes, and thus begins to understand those slippages which occur between 'les formes les plus aiguës de la civilisation' and 'les terreurs les plus anciennes de la vie'.[11]

But does the *bricolage* of textual fragments from a traveller's tale, to make a poem for the armchair traveller, smack of late colonial exotic, of touristic pick-and-mix, and what Victor Segalen would call 'impressionism', à la Pierre Loti?[12] To a certain extent, yes. 'Mee Too Buggi' uses a motley collection of exotic materials as a kind of publicity, but where publicity is the necessary accompaniment of a polyglot, cosmopolitan existence, suffusing practical activity with the magic of the imaginary, with a spirit of restless aspiration and curiosity. Cendrars picks up the lead given by Apollinaire when he writes: 'Ce qui caractérise l'ensemble de la publicité mondiale est son lyrisme.'[13] And here lyricism is an existential condition, an aptitude for being and responding, a way of consuming the world. 'Bolotoo' is perhaps a tutelary site of this lyricism: John Martin's definition of this word runs: 'An imaginary island to the north-westward of Tonga, the residence of the immortal gods, and of the souls of deceased chiefs and matabooles [nobles, next below a chief]'.[14]

And yet Cendrars is also an *exote* in the purer Segalenian sense, a traveller who savours difference, distance, the incomprehensibility of the other, who, above all, has the ability to inhabit the object as a subject, to enjoy the *reciprocity* of difference. In adopting the fango-fango (nose-flute) as his instrument of expression, the poet not only calls into question the pre-eminence of our Graeco-Roman cultural heritage, but also adopts a Tongan way of interpreting the world: lines 6–8 are about the content of Tongan songs, and lines 11–13 are Tongan glimpses of the oddities of Europe ('Papalangi'). But perhaps, too, Cendrars is mischievously shuffling the cards, so that we do not know through whose spectacles we are looking.

In similarly 'exotic' fashion, plagiarism is not only an act of appropriation but also of textual alienation; borrowed words become a vehicle of self-expression, yes; but, at the same time, the poet quotes them, as something other, untranslatable. If we take 'Mee too buggi' ('a dance standing up with paddles: a day dance'), 'fango-fango', 'Bolotoo', 'Papalangi', 'Mee low folla' ('a dance with the arms outspread: a night dance') and 'Mariwagi' (a particular individual), we must ask: can the poet say these, can he assimilate them into his own speech? And our question is motivated by two considerations. First, the variants: in the Bibliothèque nationale dossier of manuscripts, 'fango fango' has no hyphen (does Tongan have a linguistic concept like the hyphen?); in the original publication (*Les Soirées de Paris*), 'Bolotoo' is spelt 'Bo lo too' and 'Mariwagi' appears as 'Marigavi'. Second, we do not know how to pronounce them. Are they French transcriptions of Tongan words? Or English transcriptions borrowed from the source text? Or French translations of English transcriptions? Do we, for example, say /fãgofãgo/ or /fæŋgəufæŋgəu/? If we go back to the English source text, we find not 'Mee too buggi' but 'Mëë too buggi', and instructions that would amount to a pronunciation something like /meetubʌgi:/. And how are these words accentuated? This picture is further complicated by other factors. English readers of this text (and French, too, perhaps) may fall into colonial misapprehensions: for example, that the names of the two dances are versions of pidgin, with anachronistic importation from the Afro-American world – Walter Albert translates 'Mee Too Buggi' as 'Me Too Boogie',[15] and 'Mee low folla' as 'Me low fellah'.[16] And it is not just English translations of Cendrars's text which generate creative misreadings: the French translation of Martin by A.-J.-B. Defauconpret, used by Cendrars, translates the English 'and at the *mooa* [the capital town of an island] there are houses that are pulled along by enormous birds'[17] as 'Les maisons sont renversées par d'énormes oiseaux',[18] which, in turn, is translated back into English by 'Houses are toppled over by enormous birds',[19] or 'Houses are bowled over by enormous birds',[20] or 'The houses are turned over by enormous birds'.[21] And, for his part, Cendrars's 'translation' of the French translation lets indefinite articles drift into the definite: 'Beaucoup de leurs chansons contiennent des descriptions de paysages' becomes, in 'Mee Too Buggi', 'Il y a la description des paysages'; 'le récit de quelque événement passé' becomes 'Le récit des événements passés'; 'une relation de contrées qu'ils ne peuvent que connaître d'imagination' becomes 'Une relation des contrées lointaines'. In this way, the picture shifts from the unidentified, the random, the speculative, to items that are generical and/or referentially specific, known rather than unknown. By all these devices, Cendrars seems to court, even celebrate, creative misreadings, mispronunciations, misapprehensions, drifts of consciousness, as constant negotiations between self and other. This is another form of elasticity: our involvement in a pliable world whose temporal and spatial dimensions are, as in a Cubist painting, in a state of continual reconfiguration, so that points of view are multiplied and multipliable.

Parataxis, a syntax of main clauses, without subordination, might, as we find it in 'Mee Too Buggi', be read as a colonial gesture, as an imputation of infantilism, whether one rejects the Graeco-Roman heritage or not. But it is more likely that parataxis is cultivated by Cendrars as a dimension of the cinematic, as a device to facilitate the interchangeability of verse-lines. And even more, perhaps, parataxis makes a provocative enigma of the way things relate to each other and problematises the notion of a presiding subjectivity. Is the cinematic eye an embodied or a disembodied point of view and, correspondingly, what kind of voice does it have?

It is common to associate the construction of modern verse with cinematic techniques of cutting and montaging, to create sequences in which there will be more coherence than cohesion, even if of a precarious kind. It is noticeable that, on several occasions, Cendrars has, in his poem, changed the order of the materials as they appear in (the French translation of) Martin. For example, in Martin, the elements of line 5 precede those of line 4, just as those of line 15 precede those of line 14; and 'Mee low folla' is the first element to occur in the original. The world has no fixed shape. Any element is likely to displace itself, to set up new relationships with its context, depending on one's perceptual position. In his 'L'ABC du cinéma', Cendrars speaks of cinematic vision in these terms: 'Cent mondes, mille mouvements, un million de drames entrent simultanément dans le champ de cet œil dont le cinéma a doté l'homme. Et cet œil est plus merveilleux, bien qu'arbitraire, que l'œil à facettes de la mouche. Le cerveau en est bouleversé. Remue-ménage d'images.'[22]

Cendrars's world, like that of the Cubists, the Futurists and the Orphists, is dedicated to the transformation of the consecutive into the simultaneous. The poet sensorily gathers the world at a stroke, if rather untidily, haphazardly. And, as a result, the task of making meaning gives way to the intoxicated absorption of unprocessed experience: 'Le réel n'a plus aucun sens. Aucune signification. Tout est rythme, parole, vie.'[23] The absence of punctuation helps reinforce this sense of the unprocessed, which, in turn, brings us back to elasticity.

For our purposes, the significance of the omission of punctuation is threefold:

first, it reinforces the collage/*bricolage* technique by implying the mobility, the shufflability, of textual items (structural elasticity). Second, it helps to devocalise the text. In punctuated texts, patterns of voice (intonation, pausing, tone) are partly captured in the punctuation. Without punctuation, the voice loses these vocal reference points and as it were floats free of the text, becomes a set of multi-vocal potentialities, unanchored in the text (vocal elasticity). Third, inasmuch as punctuation generates temporality, measuring phrase-lengths, respiration, rests, a text without punctuation will tend either to erase our sense of unfolding time or to internalise it, to make it more fluid and heterogeneous (temporal elasticity). Just as plagiarism interferes with the temporal order of literary history and de-chronologises it, so the removal of punctuation makes Cook's voyages peculiarly available to all kinds of re-embarkation.

Notes

1 Blaise Cendrars, *Du monde entier. Poésies complètes 1912–1924* (Paris: Gallimard, 1967), p. 102. See also *Œuvres complètes*, 8 vols. (Paris: Denoël, 1960–65).

2 Jean-Pierre Goldenstein, 'Blaise Cendrars sur les traces du capitaine Cook', *Revue d'Histoire Littéraire de la France*, 73 (1973), pp. 112–17.

3 Jean-Pierre Goldenstein (ed.), *Dix-neuf poèmes élastiques de Blaise Cendrars* (Paris: Klincksieck, 1986).

4 The edition of Martin's work referred to in this analysis is John Martin, *An Account of the Natives of the Tonga Islands in the South Pacific Ocean. With an Original Grammar and Vocabulary of Their Language. Compiled and Arranged from the Extensive Communications of Mr. William Mariner, Several Years Resident in those Islands*, second edition with additions, 2 vols. (London: John Murray, 1818).

5 In Isidore Ducasse, comte de Lautréamont, *Lautréamont/Germain Nouveau. Œuvres complètes*, ed. Pierre-Olivier Walzer (Paris: Gallimard, 1970), p. 281.

6 *Ibid.*, p. 285.

7 OULIPO (Ouvroir de Littérature Potentielle) was founded in 1960 by Raymond Queneau and François Le Lionnais, and dedicated itself to the renewal of literature through the application of 'creative constraints', or systems of linguistic transformation, permutation and combination, often with a basis in mathematics. These applications might be devoted to works already in existence or act as structural blueprints for new work. OULIPO has counted among its fellowship Albert-Marie Schmidt, Jacques Roubaud, Georges Perec and Italo Calvino.

8 'Il ne s'agit pas de compter la menue monnaie des syllabes sur ses doigts'. *Aujourd'hui 1917–1929 suivi de Essais et réflexions 1910–1916*, ed. Miriam Cendrars (Paris: Denoël, 1987), p. 193.

9 *Ibid.*, pp. 99–114.

10 *Ibid.*, p. 114.

11 *Ibid.*

12 Victor Segalen, *Essai sur l'exotisme: une esthétique du divers et Textes sur Gauguin et l'Océanie*, ed. Gilles Manceron (Paris: LGF, 1986), p. 51. Segalen was working on his essay on exoticism from 1904 until his premature death in 1919. His notes, jottings and related letters give a good idea of the shape it would have taken. Pierre Loti (1850–1923), a naval officer for forty-two years and much travelled, was both a novelist of faraway places (e.g. Africa, *Le Roman d'un spahi* (1881); Oceania, *Le Mariage*

de Loti (1882); Far East, *Madame Chrysanthème* (1887)) and a travel writer (e.g. *Au Maroc* (1890); *Vers Ispahan* (1904)).

13 Cendrars, *Aujourd'hui 1917–1929*, p. 118.
14 Martin, *An Account of the Natives*, vol. II, n.p.
15 'Boogie', the dictionary tells us, a twentieth-century borrowing, derives probably from Kongo *mbugi* ('devilishly good'). The Tongan 'buggi-buggi' is 'a certain kind of club' (Martin, *An Account of the Natives*, vol. II, n.p.).
16 Walter Albert (ed. and trans.), *Selected Writings of Blaise Cendrars*, intro. Henry Miller (New York: New Directions, 1966), pp. 178–81.
17 Martin, *An Account of the Natives*, vol. II, p. 319.
18 Goldenstein, *Dix-neuf poèmes élastiques*, p. 99.
19 Albert, *Selected Writings*, p. 181.
20 Peter Hoida (trans.), *Blaise Cendrars: Selected Poems*, intro. Mary Ann Caws (Harmondsworth: Penguin Books, 1979), p. 36.
21 Ron Padgett (trans.), *Blaise Cendrars: Complete Poems*, intro. Jay Bochner (Berkeley, CA: University of California Press, 1993), p. 78. If one were to translate this text, transferring back into it the relevant phraseology from the English original, from which the French is only indirectly derived, one would arrive at:

> Like the Greeks we believe that every well-educated man should know
> how to pluck the lyre
>
> Give me the fango-fango
> That I may put it to my nose
> A sound soft and grave
> From the right nostril
> There is the description of scenery
> The description of past events
> An account of places which are out of [their] reach
> Bolotoo
> Papalangi
> The poet describes among other things the animals [belonging to the
> country]
> The houses are pulled along by enormous birds
> The women are too covered with dress
> Neither regular measure nor rhyme
> Excepting a little exaggeration
> The man who cut off his own leg was very expert in the composition of
> humorous pieces
> Mëë low folla
> Mareewagee beats the drum at the entrance of his hut

> (Martin, *An Account of the Natives*, vol. II, pp. 317–22, 308).

22 Cendrars, *Aujourd'hui 1917–1929*, p. 35.
23 *Ibid.*, p. 36.

Further reading

Boder, Francis, *La Phrase poétique de Blaise Cendrars: structures syntaxiques, figures du discours, agencements rythmiques* (Paris: Champion, 2000).
Bozon-Scalzitti, Yvette, *Blaise Cendrars: ou la passion de l'écriture* (Lausanne: L'Âge d'homme, 1977).

Brunel, Pierre (ed.), *Le Roman du poète: Rilke, Joyce, Cendrars* (Paris: Euredit, 2004).

Colvile, Georgiana M. M., *Blaise Cendrars, écrivain protéiforme* (Amsterdam: Rodopi, 1994).

Flückiger, Jean-Carlo (ed.), *L'Encrier de Cendrars* (Neuchâtel: La Baconnière, 1989).

Leroy, Claude, *La Main de Cendrars* (Villeneuve d'Ascq: Presses Universitaires du Septentrion, 1996).

6 | Saint-John Perse, 'Écrit sur la porte'

MARY GALLAGHER

J'ai une peau couleur de tabac rouge ou de
mulet,
    j'ai un chapeau en moelle de sureau couvert
de toile blanche.
    Mon orgueil est que ma fille soit très-belle   5
quand elle commande aux femmes noires,
    ma joie, qu'elle découvre un bras très-blanc
parmi ses poules noires ;
    et qu'elle n'ait point honte de ma joue rude
sous le poil, quand je rentre boueux.   10

*

    Et d'abord je lui donne mon fouet, ma
gourde et mon chapeau.
    En souriant elle m'acquitte de ma face
ruisselante ; et porte à son visage mes mains
grasses d'avoir   15
    éprouvé l'amande de kako, la graine de
café.
    Et puis elle m'apporte un mouchoir de tête
bruissant ; et ma robe de laine ; de l'eau pure
pour rincer mes dents de silencieux :   20
    et l'eau de ma cuvette est là ; et j'entends
l'eau du bassin dans la case-à-eau.

*

    Un homme est dur, sa fille est douce. Qu'elle
se tienne toujours
    à son retour sur la plus haute marche de la   25
maison blanche,
    et faisant grâce à son cheval de l'étreinte
des genoux,

il oubliera la fièvre qui tire toute la peau du
visage en dedans.   30

*

J'aime encore mes chiens, l'appel de mon
plus fin cheval,
    et voir au bout de l'allée droite mon chat
sortir de la maison en compagnie de la guenon. . .
        toutes choses suffisantes pour n'envier pas   35
les voiles des voiliers
        que j'aperçois à la hauteur du toit de tôle
sur la mer comme un ciel.

From *Éloges*

'Écrit sur la porte' is the threshold poem of Saint-John Perse's magnum opus, the Pléiade edition of his *Œuvres complètes*, which the poet himself composed for publication in 1975 in Gallimard's 'Bibliothèque de la Pléiade' series. This fine leather-bound collection, printed on Bible-thin paper, symbolically consigns the work of French writers to the literary pantheon. The four-stanza poem, signed Saint-Léger Léger, was first published in 1910 in the literary review, *La Nouvelle Revue Française,* some fourteen years before Alexis Léger had chosen his definitive pseudonym, and was dated 1908 (the poet would have been just twenty-one at the time of composition). The poem subsequently appeared as the opening text of the 1925 edition of the volume of poems entitled *Éloges*, which was first published without this opening poem in 1911. This collection includes three poem sequences, entitled 'Images à Crusoé' (dated 1904), 'Pour fêter une enfance' (dated 1907) and the eponymous sequence 'Éloges' (dated, like 'Écrit sur la porte', 1908). *Éloges* is, without any doubt, the work most deeply marked by nostalgia for the poet's Caribbean childhood; it celebrates not just the atmosphere of a tropical, colonial childhood, but also the world of the Creole plantation and town. In opening his (revised) first volume, and eventually his collected poetic work and indeed his 'Complete Works' as such, with 'Écrit sur la porte', Saint-John Perse lends the text successively different resonances. The poem's title presents it first and foremost as a piece of writing located in relation to threshold space. The title can be read as referring to the outcome of an act of writing accomplished 'upon a door', or as a piece of writing placed upon a door, or indeed as a piece of writing about a door or doorway. This liminal text thus opens into the work, functioning as a frontispiece from which the reader will be tempted to draw conclusions about the poetics of the entire work which it inaugurates or prefaces.[1]

The fundamental prosodic unit of all of Saint-John Perse's published poetry is the *verset*, a hybrid form between verse and prose, deeply marked by the biblical origins that give it both the solemnly oratorical lyricism which also imbues Claudel's *verset* and the oracular tone that can be heard in the ample periods and in the evocation of ritual of 'Écrit sur la porte'. What are particularly striking about Saint-John Perse's *verset* throughout his poetic work are the traces of the conventional octosyllabic line or of the alexandrine that often underlie it. However, this underlying conventional scansion is loosened by the flexibility of the *verset*, the musicality of which is often further enriched by stress patterns more typical of English prosody and by intensive use of the harmonic patterning already noted in 'Écrit sur la porte' (even if the poet only develops his extensive use of paronomasia in his later works). The solemnity of tone associated with the biblical origins of the *verset* and the shadow presence of regular versification are both evident in 'Écrit sur la porte' in the declaration 'Un homme est dur, sa fille est douce', which scans as an octosyllabic line. However, as has often been noted, although the *verset*, partly because of its extensible length, lends itself to a certain epic stamina, the compactness of 'Écrit sur la porte' and its tidy division into just four regular stanzas mean that, on a formal level, it contrasts with the epic breadth (and breath) of Saint-John Perse's poetics as it evolves through *Anabase*, *Exil*, *Vents*, and *Amers*, just as the poet(h)ics of spatial, temporal and cultural openness and expansion of the poet's later work stand out against the more constrained canvas of 'Écrit sur la porte'.

The first two stanzas of the poem are arranged in five *versets*; the second two in four *versets*. The first stanza defines the speaker by his property; the second recounts the sequence of actions and observations triggered by the speaker's return home after a working day in the plantation fields. The third stanza, in the optative mode, enunciates the wish that the current domestic order might prevail forever, while the final stanza provides a supplementary proclamation of the speaker's fulfilment in his present situation.

The poem opens with a deictic reference to the colour of the speaking (or writing) subject's skin: 'j'ai une peau couleur de mulet ou de tabac rouge'. Although it is unclear whether the colour of the speaker's skin is a function of pigmentation or of contact, of race or of staining, the word 'mulet', which refers to cross-breeding, has strong racialist undertones. The second line repeats the reference to possession ('j'ai un chapeau en moelle de sureau'). Just as the hues of the speaker's skin colour imply the earth and the sun, the reference to the hat points towards the sun from which it protects the skin. This particular sunhat is recognisably a colonial-style pith helmet, woven from the pith of the 'sureau' (elder) tree and covered with white voile cloth.

One of the most striking structural and semantic features of the entire poem is the hyperbolic enumeration of possessives, suggesting that the speaker's identity is defined less by what he is than by what he owns. It is tempting to relate this preoccupation to the ethics of two prominent twentieth-century Jewish thinkers. Emmanuel Levinas for his part stigmatises the 'jeu du même' by which the human being is imprisoned in an identity defined by aesthetic, affective and material capital. Similarly, Martin Buber deplores the restriction of human meaning to the 'avoir rapport': 'celui qui dit Tu n'a aucune chose, il n'a rien. Mais il s'offre à une relation.'[2] In 'Écrit sur la porte', there is no room for the 'tu' or for face-to-face relationality, as the 'moi' stakes out its claim to an identity founded on property. In this poem there is, then, no foregrounding of speech as allocution or relation: first-person markers are the only deictic references in the text and the emphasis is on the exposition of Levinas's cardinal points of proprietorial identification: 'le corps, la possession, la maison, l'économie'.[3]

In the first stanza, the two *versets* beginning with the possessive 'j'ai' are followed by two *versets* opening on possessive adjectives in the first person: 'mon orgueil', 'ma joie'. The three final *versets* of the stanza relate the speaker's pride and joy to his daughter ('ma fille'), filiation being thus represented as a variant of possession. The speaker takes vicarious pride in the girl's beauty (when she gives orders to black women); and his joy relates both to her revealing a very white arm that stands out against her black hens, and to the fact that she is not ashamed of his rough and unshaven cheek when he returns home 'boueux', soiled by labour.

The sequence of ritual gestures in the second stanza again relates the speaker to his daughter. In a choreography of give and take, the speaker first hands her his whip, gourd and hat; then, with a smile, she soothes him of his streaming face. Having brought his work-stained hands to her face, she proffers a starched cloth, a woollen robe and pure water to rinse his teeth. The theme of ritual purification is continued in the further emphasis on water (the water in the speaker's basin and the water flowing in the tank of the 'case-à-eau' or water-hut). The ritual actions take place in the static present of a sacred order, and the fact that the speaker/writer is described as 'silencieux' is not just consonant with the poem's title (for his words are written, not spoken), but also underlines the visual fixity of the scene.

The third stanza situates the pair in the third person: 'Un homme est dur, sa fille est douce'. Articulating the wish that she might always stand on the highest step of the white house to await his return, the enunciator inscribes this scene in the timelessness of an eternal present. If that condition is met, then he will continue, upon his return, to release his horse from the embrace of his knees, and will forget the fever that pulls the skin of his face inwards. Thus, although the enunciative perspective has shifted in this stanza from first person to third person, instead of opening up the perspective, this shift simply produces an effect of consecration by universalisation. Moreover, the continuity of the prevailing self-centredness is confirmed by the centripetal force of the sensation evoked at the end of the stanza: 'il oubliera la fièvre qui tire toute la peau du visage en dedans'.

The final stanza, returning to the first-person perspective, evokes the speaker's love of his dogs, of the call of his finest horse, and of the sight of his cat emerging from the house accompanied by the monkey. This menagerie, added to the other domestic sights and the domestic ritual heretofore evoked are deemed to be 'sufficient' to prevent the enunciating subject from envying the sails of the yachts that he can discern against the line of the sea at the level of the tin roof. Thus, at the very end, the poem widens its reach from the domestic realm to the vast open stretches of the sea and sky beyond, the one being compared with the other in the poem's sole simile. The poem has thus moved from the realm of ownership to the horizon of desire, and from a statement of possession to a reference to lack – albeit to a lack that is denied. The enunciator of this text thus positions himself in relation to desire twice: in the third stanza he explicitly expresses his desire for unchanging return: 'Qu'elle se tienne toujours' (the alliteration of 'toujours' and of 'tienne' underlining the static tenor of 'tienne'); and in the final stanza he expresses his lack of desire (for mobility and adventure). Both declarations imply a consistent rejection of the vast scale of sky and ocean, but also of change and movement, metonymically connoted here by the sailing vessel. The enumeration of various domestic elements, all linked by their common ownership by, or attachment to, the speaker, is held to outweigh the pull of the non-appropriated, indeed non-appropriatable space of sky and sea. The plantation order, a circumscribed universe of possession and production, is thus affirmed in this poem in opposition to a rejected expanse of openness and movement. Thus, a poetics of contraction within the familiar and predictable is opposed to the Baudelairean poetics of imagination and to the Mallarméan dream of the 'brise marine'. And yet, the word 'envie' itself breathes a certain antiphrastic vitality into the poem, just as the very statement of the absence of desire (envie) paradoxically asserts its presence.

A poetics of the plantation/habitation

The socio-geographical space evoked by the poem is that of a tropical plantation, unequivocally located by references to the colonial helmet, the cocoa bean crop, the elevated, white plantation house with the avenue leading up to it, the 'case-à-eau', the shack with its 'toit de tôle', heat, sun, thirst, and the racial dynamic between whites and blacks. To the extent that the domestic space of the plantation is so closely linked in the text to the agricultural space of the crop fields, the universe represented here recalls the small-scale plantation of the tiny French-speaking Caribbean islands, where plantations are locally referred to as 'habitations'. This euphemism (by which a space of production – or 'exploitation' – is referred to as a dwelling space) is based on scale, in that the scale of the Caribbean plantation meant that the dwelling space was much more prominent and visible, much more up-close and determining, than in the vast continental latifundium. The localised tropical or Caribbean poetics of this poem is not typical, however, of the much more deterritorialised epic poetic vision of the rest of Saint-John Perse's oeuvre.

An aesthetic of contrasts

'Écrit sur la porte' presents above all an aesthetic of contrasts. In other words, it is antithetical in structure (opposing blackness and whiteness, pride and shame, grime and purification, hardness and tenderness, silence and water, sea and sky, earth and sky, earth and sea, singularity (the single, elevated, white house) versus plurality (the many low-lying – grey or black – tin roofs). These dichotomies are coloured by affect, as, for example, when the speaker characterises his pride, his joy, his daughter's lack of shame, etc. in relation to them. They are also situated in relation to a certain hierarchy, in that they are linked to the giving of orders, and to superlatives ('très-belle', 'très-blanc', 'mon plus fin cheval', 'la plus haute marche de la maison blanche'). The singular whiteness of the house is the backdrop to the black women and chickens who serve as a foil to the whiteness of the speaker's 'very-beautiful' daughter. Not only is this aestheticised contrast racialised, but the black women are pejoratively compared, by an unspoken parallelism, to the black chickens. This equation of beauty with the contrast between epidermic whiteness and blackness resonates with the 'Song of Songs' ('I am black, but I am beautiful'), just as the references to a hierarchy of values (via the use of superlatives, for example) suggests an immutable aesthetic order, a suggestion reinforced by the age-old mythical echoes of the white-armed Greek goddess Hera. The hieratic poses of the two figures (the pale-skinned girl on the top step of the threshold of the white house and the silent man astride his horse) reinforce the hypnotic harmony of these dichotomies. The static balance of opposites is lent further stability by the expression of a lack of longing for anything else or for anything more. The strictly ordered stanza form of this poem enacts that same controlled regularity of an ordered mind.

The poem's rich textual dynamic can be seen in the recuperation of the image of the ships' sails which are linked by assonance with the image of the veiled sunhat protecting the speaker's complexion from the sun ('toile', 'voile', 'moelle'). Internal rhyme also links the idea of shame with the image of the sombre, unshaven face ('point/poil' and 'joue/boueux'). Perhaps the most striking use of verbal texture, however, lies in the dissemination of the word 'eau' throughout a text that ends by turning its back so ostentatiously on the sea. The reference to water is thus covertly present in the word 'peau' ('j'ai une peau' and 'la peau du visage') and 'sureau' (elder). But it is implicit above all in the water contained in receptacles or basins: 'case-à-eau', 'l'eau de ma cuvette', 'l'eau du bassin', 'de l'eau pure pour rincer', in the 'gourde' and in the speaker's 'face ruisselante'.

There is a preponderance of visual reference, relating principally to epidermic realities, such as skin colour, although the references to the unshaven skin ('joue rude sous le poil'), to the muddied appearance of the speaker ('boueux'), to his greasy hands, to the starched handkerchief, and to the speaker's grip on his horse, introduce tactile or kinetic imagery, just as the final reference to the speaker hearing the 'eau du bassin dans la case-à-eau' and to the 'appel' of his best horse suggests certain sound effects. The poem also features the play of centripetal and centrifugal forces across thresholds: the cat emerging from the house; the daughter standing on the highest step of the house; the man returning to the house ('quand je rentre', 'à son retour'). Similarly the sound of water emanates from the interior of the 'case-à-eau', and at the end of the poem, the thresholds between land and sea and land and sky are evoked. Moreover purification rituals imply the crossing of a threshold between one state and another, just as the skin functions, in corporeal terms, as a boundary or threshold space between 'inside' and 'outside'.

An ante-poetics or an anti-poetics?

To the extent that a Creole poetics runs through Saint-John Perse's entire oeuvre, this poem can be read as a foretaste: an ante-poetics. Yet, in another sense, to the extent that his poetics is one of desire and of movement, a poetics that disparages domestication, to the extent that it is a poetics of epic historical reach, cosmic span, climactic or nomadic desire (in *Anabase, Vents, Exil, Amers, Chronique*, etc.), 'Écrit sur la porte' could be read as an anti-poetics. The epic scale of movement and reference is nowhere in evidence in this poem, except perhaps at the very end of the text, where it is renounced. Instead, the poem extols location as opposed to dislocation or impulsion. In that sense it is a poem of continence and even satisfaction. And yet an undercurrent of desire flutters beneath this containment, this closure and fixity, as longing intrudes into the poem in its very negation. There are other sources of ambiguity in the text: for example, the question concerning the speaker's identity and the matter of racial difference. Insofar as the notion of a certain social hierarchy is superimposed on racial difference (a superimposition latent in the image of the beauty of the speaker's girl/daughter being somehow related to her giving orders to black women), much of the affect of the first part of the poem is related to skin colour. The speaker indeed seems to feel some discomfort or even shame about his own skin colour, even though it is surely not (simply) a matter of pigmentation, but one linked to his work in the plantation fields. Yet, if he is white, the question is whether or not a white 'propriétaire' or 'colon' would himself be working in the fields. On the other hand, a (usually mixed-race) 'commandeur' or foreman, might be unlikely to have a white daughter, though the latter's arms might well appear 'very-white' (the hyphenated expressions in the text are typical of Creole linguistic structures) when set against those blacker than herself. It is noteworthy in this connection that the 'white house' is not claimed as the speaker's own home.

The other 'Écrit sur la porte'

In the 1925 edition of *Éloges*, the poet symmetrically closes the volume with a poem bearing the same title as the opening text: 'Écrit sur la porte'. This closing text had been published initially in the third issue of the review *Commerce* in autumn 1924 under the title 'Chanson'. It was subsequently integrated into editions of the collection *La Gloire des rois* (where it remained in the *Œuvres complètes*) as 'Chanson du présomptif'. The original and ultimate titles of this second bookend text of the 1925 edition of *Éloges* identifies it as a song, rather than as a written text. And although the song is that of (or is about) an individual (the 'présomptif' or presumed heir), the first-person deictic references in this text are sometimes in the plural. This gregarious subject, 'nous les vivants', contrasts with the rigid singularity of the 'je' of the 'Écrit'. Moreover, there is no mention of subalterns in the 'Chanson', where all 'vivants' seem to be on an equal footing. A further point of contrast concerns the favouring of appearances, and even of purely epidermic values, in the 'Écrit' as opposed to the favouring of the interior world of the singer in the 'Chanson'. For the 'Chanson' replies to the emphasis on material realities in 'Écrit sur la porte', to the emphasis on skin, particularly the skin of the face ('face ruisselante', 'joue rude sous le poil'), by the very relational, allocutional statement 'j'ai face parmi vous'. The figures of the 'Chanson' are all steeped in mobility or interiority: one boards boats, another 'parle dans le bruit de son âme', and yet another 'marche dans les songes et s'achemine vers la mer'. The speaker himself is in motion and in relation: 'j'ai hâte parmi vous'. This text presents the same competing sets of values as does 'Écrit sur la porte', although, when both are weighed up, the singer finds that 'la maison chargée d'honneurs et l'année jaune entre les feuilles' in no way outweighs the call of the road; indeed he declares that they are 'peu de chose au cœur de l'homme s'il y songe'. Thus, in the final line of this poem, the speaker declares that 'tous les chemins du monde nous mangent dans la main !' The poetics of the 'Chanson', in its openness to the addressed other, to interiority, and to the vastness of the world, and in its favouring of movement and rupture, is much more typical of Saint-John Perse's poetic vision than 'Écrit sur la porte', thereby revealed as a tongue-in-cheek aberration designed to highlight by contrast the ethics and poetics of the rest of the poet's work.

Saint-John Perse's place in the French poetic tradition is not easy to sum up on the basis of a reading of this poem alone. If his articulation of a planetary perspective locates him in the family of French traveller-poets as diverse as Segalen and Claudel, his art and his voice have imprinted themselves, far beyond this family, on the poetics of francophone poets with startlingly different planetary perspectives to his: most notably, Senghor, Césaire and Glissant.

Notes

1 Interesting critical perspectives on this poem include Jacques Robichez's judgement that it provides a poor introduction to Saint-John Perse's poetics; May Chehab's comments on the Nietzschean intertext; and Claude Thiébaut's article on the insights provided by the Creole translation of the text. See Jacques Robichez, *Sur Saint-John Perse:* Éloges, La Gloire des Rois, Anabase (Paris: SEDES/CDU, 1982); May Chehab, *Saint-John Perse, neveu de Nietzsche* (Paris: Champion, 2009); Claude Thiébaut, ' "Écrit sur la porte" de Saint-John Perse à l'épreuve de la traduction en créole', in *Pour Saint-John Perse*, ed. Pierre Pinalie (Paris: L'Harmattan, 1988).

2 Quoted in Jacques Derrida, *L'Écriture et la différence* (Paris: Seuil, 1967), p. 139.
3 Quoted in Martin Buber, *Je et tu*, trans. G. Bianquis (Paris: Aubier Montaigne, 1967), p. 21.

Further reading

Caduc, Eveline, *Saint-John Perse, Connaissance et création* (Paris: José Corti, 1977).
Camelin, Colette and Tamine, Joëlle Gardes, *La Rhétorique profonde de Saint-John Perse* (Paris: Champion, 2002).
Gallagher, Mary, *La Créolité de Saint-John Perse* (Paris: Gallimard, 1998).
Knodel, Arthur, *Saint-John Perse: A Study of his Poetry* (Edinburgh: Edinburgh University Press, 1966).
Little, Roger, *Saint-John Perse* (London: Athlone Press, 1973).
    Études sur Saint-John Perse (Paris: Klincksieck, 1984).
Perse, Saint-John, *Anabasis*, trans. T. S. Eliot (London: Faber and Faber, 1959).
    Selected Poems, ed. Mary Ann Caws (New York: New Directions, 1982).
Rigolot, Carol, *Forged Genealogies: Saint-John Perse's Conversations with Culture* (Chapel Hill, NC: University of North Carolina Press, 2001).
    Saint-John Perse, la culture en dialogues (Paris: L'Harmattan, 2007).
Sacotte, Mireille, *Saint-John Perse* (Paris: Belfond, 1991).
    Éloges et *La Gloire des rois* (Paris: Gallimard, 1999).
Ventresque, Renée, *Les Antilles de Saint-John Perse* (Paris: L'Harmattan, 1993).
Winspur, Steven, *Saint-John Perse and the Imaginary Reader* (Geneva: Droz, 1988).

7 Léopold Sédar Senghor, 'À New York'

ROGER LITTLE

À New York
(pour un orchestre de jazz : solo de trompette)

I

New York ! D'abord j'ai été confondu par ta beauté, ces
   grandes filles d'or aux jambes longues.
Si timide d'abord devant tes yeux de métal bleu, ton sourire
   de givre.
Si timide. Et l'angoisse au fond des rues à gratte-ciel   5
Levant des yeux de chouette parmi l'éclipse du soleil.
Sulfureuse ta lumière et les fûts livides, dont les têtes fou-
   droient le ciel
Les gratte-ciel qui défient les cyclones sur leurs muscles
   d'acier et leur peau patinée de pierres.   10
Mais quinze jours sur les trottoirs chauves de Manhattan
  – C'est au bout de la troisième semaine que vous saisit la
   fièvre en un bond de jaguar
Quinze jours sans un puits ni pâturage, tous les oiseaux de
   l'air   15
Tombant soudain et morts sous les hautes cendres des
   terrasses.
Pas un rire d'enfant en fleur, sa main dans ma main fraîche
Pas un sein maternel, des jambes de nylon. Des jambes et
   des seins sans sueur ni odeur.   20
Pas un mot tendre en l'absence de lèvres, rien que des
   cœurs artificiels payés en monnaie forte
Et pas un livre où lire la sagesse. La palette du peintre
   fleurit des cristaux de corail.
Nuits d'insomnie ô nuits de Manhattan ! si agitées de feux   25
   follets, tandis que les klaxons hurlent des heures vides
Et que les eaux obscures charrient des amours hygiéniques,
   tels des fleuves en crue des cadavres d'enfants.

II

Voici le temps des signes et des comptes
New York ! or voici le temps de la manne et de   30
  l'hysope.
Il n'est que d'écouter les trombones de Dieu, ton cœur
  battre au rythme du sang ton sang.
J'ai vu Harlem bourdonnant de bruits de couleurs
  solennelles et d'odeurs flamboyantes   35
– C'est l'heure du thé chez le livreur-en-produits-pharma-
ceutiques
J'ai vu se préparer la fête de la Nuit à la fuite du jour. Je
  proclame la Nuit plus véridique que le jour.
C'est l'heure pure où dans les rues, Dieu fait germer la vie   40
  d'avant mémoire
Tous les éléments amphibies rayonnants comme des soleils.
Harlem Harlem ! voici ce que j'ai vu Harlem Harlem !
  Une brise verte de blés sourdre des pavés labourés par
  les pieds nus des danseurs Dans   45
Croupes ondes de soie et seins de fers de lance, ballets de
  nénuphars et de masques fabuleux
Aux pieds des chevaux de police, les mangues de l'amour
  rouler des maisons basses.
Et j'ai vu le long des trottoirs, des ruisseaux de rhum blanc   50
  des ruisseaux de lait noir dans le brouillard bleu des cigares.
J'ai vu le ciel neiger au soir des fleurs de coton et des ailes
  de séraphins et des panaches de sorciers.
Écoute New York ! ô écoute ta voix mâle de cuivre ta
  voix vibrante de hautbois, l'angoisse bouchée de tes   55
  larmes tomber en gros caillots de sang
Écoute au loin battre ton cœur nocturne, rythme et sang
  du tam-tam, tam-tam sang et tam-tam.

III

New York ! je dis New York, laisse affluer le sang noir
  dans ton sang   60
Qu'il dérouille tes articulations d'acier, comme une huile de vie
Qu'il donne à tes ponts la courbe des croupes et la souplesse
  des lianes.

Voici revenir les temps très anciens, l'unité retrouvée la
  réconciliation du Lion du Taureau et de l'Arbre   65
L'idée liée à l'acte l'oreille au cœur le signe au sens.
Voilà tes fleuves bruissants de caïmans musqués et de laman-
  tins aux yeux de mirages. Et nul besoin d'inventer les
  Sirènes.
Mais il suffit d'ouvrir les yeux à l'arc-en-ciel d'Avril   70
Et les oreilles, surtout les oreilles à Dieu qui d'un rire de
  saxophone créa le ciel et la terre en six jours.
Et le septième jour, il dormit du grand sommeil nègre.

From *Éthiopiques*

'À New York' could scarcely be more central to Senghor's output. Occupying a crucial position in Senghor's third collection of poems (out of six), from the middle of his life, *Éthiopiques*, first published in 1956, has proved attractive to readers, commentators and anthologists alike.[1] Its tripartite structure lends itself to carefully balanced dialectical treatment – thesis, antithesis and synthesis – and these are based, in the circumstances, on geographical and racial considerations with reconciliation as the ultimate watchword and hope.

It is important to know that Senghor was a man who devoted his life to building bridges between his native culture and that of the colonial power, France, in which he was no less steeped. As to the title 'À New York', it is both location, evocation, invocation and provocation, depending on how the preposition is understood, and the musical indication which follows it gestures both towards a particular manner in which the poem is to be read or accompanied and towards the cultural association of jazz with the history of African Americans in the United States. The geography is thus transatlantic, recalling the so-called 'middle passage' of the slave trade, misnamed for the slaves themselves for whom it was final. It is as if Senghor were pursuing that journey towards Europe on behalf of his people, by writing – masterfully – in French. But the geography is also local to New York, from which two areas are selected symbolically for special attention: Manhattan and Harlem. The first, the centre where skyscrapers, high finance and round-the-clock high living are concentrated, represents the values of 'white' civilisation. The second, where Blacks congregate north of Central Park in what became a ghetto of material deprivation but human vitality, smacks sufficiently of Africa for Senghor to use Harlem as a point of contrast. A recent commentator of Cameroonian origin neatly captures the contrast: 'Le Noir américain qui vit à Harlem-la-Noire se mire dans l'opulence arrogante de Manhattan-la-Blanche et finit par réclamer sa part du gâteau.'[2]

The values embodied by Manhattan are characterised by mineral rigidity, technical progress and prowess, and a lack of human warmth. It is like Baudelaire's nightmarish vision in his 'Rêve parisien' from which 'le végétal irrégulier' is banished and whose 'murailles de métal' echo a 'Babel d'escaliers et d'arcades'.[3] In declaring that 'tout, même la couleur noire, / Semblait fourbi, clair, irisé', Baudelaire's purely chromatic notation even seems to anticipate Senghor's racial theme. The association of mineral inflexibility with Whites contrasting with the lithe animality of Blacks became a useful assumption of the Negritude movement founded in the 1920s by Senghor and his fellow students Aimé Césaire from Martinique and Léon Gontran Damas from Guyana. An episode in the Senegalese Cheikh Hamidou Kane's celebrated novel *L'Aventure ambiguë*, written in 1952 but only published nine years later, recounts a West African's first visit to France in terms similar to Senghor's discovery of New York: 'Mon regard parcourait toute l'étendue et ne vit pas de limite à la pierre. Là-bas, la glace du feldspath, ici, le gris clair de la pierre, ce noir mat de l'asphalte. Nulle part la tendre mollesse d'une terre nue. Sur l'asphalte dur, mon oreille exacerbée, mes yeux avides guettèrent, vainement, le tendre surgissement d'un pied nu.'[4]

However, at first sight, Manhattan offers attractions, if intimidating ones: the apposition 'ta beauté, ces grandes filles d'or aux jambes longues' functions both to evoke richly dressed young women and to present lanky metaphorical skyscrapers.[5] The sun is blocked out, as is animal warmth: the city's muscles are made of steel and its skin is covered with stone. A fortnight is enough for the poet to be revolted by the baldness of the sidewalks, the absence of living springs and pastures; fever pounces on you like a jaguar, the epitome of supple natural strength so lacking in the Manhattan of Senghor's vision. The anaphoric series 'Pas un. . .' underlines the missing human warmth, and the first section ends significantly on murky flood-water flushing downstream its jetsam of condoms and aborted foetuses.

A switch to biblical references (Senghor was brought up as a Roman Catholic and here he links the Old Testament exile, through references to hyssop and manna, to the exile of Africans in the New World) emphasises, by contrast, Harlem, with its houses on a human scale, buzzing with vitality and natural warmth. Trombones introduce a jazz note, the backing group being the life-pulse of the poet's own bloodstream which provides its strong beat: 'Il n'est que d'écouter les trombones de Dieu, ton cœur battre au rythme du sang ton sang.' In his 1950 essay, 'La Poésie négro-américaine', Senghor refers to James Weldon Johnson's 1927 collection of poems, *God's Trombones*, where the traditional black preacher is a source of inspiration with 'his wonderful voice, a voice – what shall I say? – not of an organ or a trumpet, but rather of a trombone, the instrument possessing above all others the power to express the wide and varied range of emotions encompassed by the human voice – and with greater ampli-tude.'[6] Johnson's volume has further resonances in Senghor's poem, as when we read (p. 5) that 'oratory . . . is a progression of rhythmic words more than it is anything else. Indeed, I have witnessed congregations moved to ecstasy by the rhythmic intoning of sheer incoherencies.'

Unlike the bald pavements of Manhattan, those in Harlem are alive with the throb of barefoot Dan dancers[7] who seem to plough the stone and make wheat grow from it just as God is said to summon protozoan life from the streets. Contrasts are clearly established between the two zones: love, hygienic and cold in Manhattan, is linked to succulent mangos in Harlem; women, silken sylphs, undulate sensuously, their breasts like darting snakes,[8] their swaying dances like those of water-lilies. Senghor calls on New York, and specifically Manhattan, to listen attentively to these life-giving, life-enhancing forces encapsulated by jazz, to allow itself to be revitalised by its soul music, to pay heed to its despised Black citizens, even to accept what may be perceived as excess.[9] Brass and oboe are backed by African drums in a further historical allusion to the origins of this community; and 'l'angoisse bouchée' presents a telling transferred epithet for *suppressed* anguish from a *muted* brass instrument, the semantic area of the adjective 'bouchée' covering both the words italicised here. To end the section, the persistent rhythm of the music to which New York should pay heed is foregrounded through repetition in which the pulse of coursing blood is associated with insistent percussion: 'Écoute au loin battre ton cœur nocturne, rythme et sang du tam-tam, tam-tam sang et tam-tam.'

Writing of the poets of the Harlem Renaissance, Senghor declares that:

> la qualité essentielle du style poétique nègre est le *rythme* . . . Le rythme . . . est l'élément le plus vital du langage: il en est la condition première et le signe . . . Ce rythme explique que la plupart des poèmes soient faits pour être déclamés ou chantés . . . les voix nègres ont toujours eu des aptitudes pour la diction et le chant. À tel point que plusieurs poètes accompagnent leurs œuvres d'annotations pour les musiciens . . . Vous le sentez, rien de codifié dans ce rythme, rien de rigide: il est libre comme le vers. Sa seule loi est d'être un accompagnement à l'émotion – comme la batterie d'un jazz. (*L 1*, pp. 111–12)

Black American poets of that generation thought, as Senghor clearly did himself, that belief in their race 'apporte, avec des valeurs neuves, une sève de printemps, qui fera refleurir la Civilisation américaine . . . L'Afrique est, ainsi, un refuge de paix contre la dureté du monde américain, un bain de vie primitive contre la sophistication de la culture blanche' (*L 1*, pp. 117, 120).

The third section opens with yet another direct address to New York (how insistent the repeated vocatives are!), here as so often restricted to Manhattan in people's minds, and invites the city not just to listen to the beat of Harlem but to learn from the lessons of its freedom and inventiveness. Senghor calls for the fusion of 'Black' and 'White' blood, not so much for physical as for cultural miscegenation, the 'métissage culturel' which became a slogan for the poet–president in his tireless quest for some substance to be injected into the French Revolutionary motto: 'Liberté, Égalité, Fraternité'. In his 1950 essay 'De la liberté de l'âme ou Éloge du métissage', he writes:

> Notre vocation de colonisés est de surmonter les contradictions de la conjoncture, l'antinomie artificiellement dressée entre l'Afrique et

l'Europe, notre hérédité et notre éducation. C'est de la greffe de celle-ci sur celle-là que doit naître notre liberté . . . Supériorité, parce que liberté, du Métis, qui choisit où il veut, ce qu'il veut pour faire, des éléments réconciliés, une œuvre exquise et forte . . . Trop assimilés ou pas assez assimilés? Tel est exactement notre destin de métis culturels. (*L 1*, p. 103)

The next and final stage in Senghor's thinking, the slogan for which was a plea for a 'Civilisation de l'Universel', was a natural outgrowth from this cultural criss-crossing.[10]

The unbending features of mineralised Manhattan need the lubrication of Harlem's vital oil. 'Il ne s'agit plus d'infériorité non plus que de supériorité ni d'antagonisme, mais de différence féconde' (*L 1*, p. 107). Reconciliation is sought in everyone's interest,[11] and the poet assumes the role of the prophet, evoking both *illud tempus*, a primeval time before things were separated into distinct categories, and a mythical future which will rediscover such perfect unity. There is wishful thinking manifestly at play here, and a willing suspension of intellectual refinement: were it really true that at any time ideas and actions were in complete accord, the ear totally attuned to the heart or the sign to its meaning, we would be in some cloud cuckoo land which in some respects at least – that of signifier and signified being identical for example, long since satirised by Swift in *Gulliver's Travels* – would be as nightmarish as Manhattan. Senghor is on firmer ground in envisaging the invasion of American rivers by creatures he associates with Africa such as the 'lamantin', the manatee or 'Mami-Wata' whose form and habit purportedly gave rise to the legend of the mermaid and which, like members of the crocodile family, is indeed found in both African and American waters, though not in the Hudson or East Rivers which hold Manhattan in their embrace, and which, with the Harlem River, make Manhattan an island. The closing lines turn heavenwards, towards the biblical symbol of reconciliation, the rainbow, and a decidedly jazz-loving black Creator. Senghor affirms at the close of 'Ce que l'homme noir apporte': 'Le service nègre aura été de contribuer, avec d'autres peuples, à refaire l'unité de l'Homme et du Monde; à lier la chair à l'esprit, l'homme à son semblable, le caillou à Dieu' (*L 1*, p. 38). And if a black God ripples with laughter, it is because '[l]'humour nègre . . . exprime la perception d'un déséquilibre entre deux faits et deux situations – d'un déséquilibre inhumain. Mais le Nègre, au lieu de protester [as Whites do] au nom de la raison, d'affirmer, dans un sourire, le primat de l'intelligence, le Nègre affirme, dans un éclat de rire, le primat de la vie' (*L 1*, p. 115).

There is, however, something disquieting about the essentialism of Senghor's characterisation of Whites and Blacks, since it implies an acceptance of the white man's traditionally supercilious view of Blacks. It is encapsulated in his notorious declaration, emphasised in the original: '*L'émotion est nègre, comme la raison hellène*' (*L 1*, p. 24). Yet such essentialism, implicit throughout the poem

and inherent in the very philosophy of Negritude, is fundamental to its dialectical structure. Redemption comes not only through reconciliation and laughter,
but also through the cultural synthesis of the poetry itself. Senghor brings to his
discovery of New York his experience of black West African and white French
languages and cultures, even though he highlights only the former in his text.

In the important postscript to *Éthiopiques*, 'Comme les lamantins vont boire
à la source', Senghor first alludes to the African world 'où la parole se fait spontanément rythme dès que l'homme est ému',[12] adding unambiguously: 'Cette
poésie n'est pas tout à fait d'Europe' (p. 106) while acknowledging French influences on him. 'À New York' is suffused with the stylistic influence of biblical
verses (known as *versets* in French), particularly as mediated in French through
the mature poetry of Paul Claudel and Saint-John Perse. Senghor claims as his
principal merit that of having been among the first to write 'des vers nègres en
français' (*PA*, p. 185), however suspect we may find this formulation. Certainly
his comments on and translations from traditional African poetry[13] suggest significant affinities with the *versets* of Bible and Claudelian practice. Repetitions
in general and anaphora in particular are familiar features, and Senghor stresses
in his writings that repetition does not imply monotony:

> Le mot est repris avec une variante, à une autre place, dans un autre
> groupe. Il rend un autre accent, une autre intonation, un autre timbre.
> L'effet d'ensemble en est intensifié – non sans nuance. Cela rappelle
> les chants africains, où une oreille musicale découvre, bientôt, sous
> l'apparente simplicité et monotonie, une richesse et une subtilité peu
> communes. (*L 1*, p. 112)

So multiple sources and resources familiar to the poet reinforce his confidence
in the general accessibility of his style and in the universality of his message.
Senghor returns to rhythm as the key to the reader or hearer being both
engrossed and moved: 'Seul le rythme provoque le court-circuit poétique et
transmue le cuivre en or, la parole en verbe', quoting the Surrealist André Breton
to give further weight to his view: 'Les grands poètes ont été des "auditifs", non
des visionnaires' (*OP*, pp. 160–1). And he attributes to French, with a degree
of exaggeration which English speakers are well placed to measure, a range of
sound-production which includes an African dimension: 'Le français, ce sont les
grandes orgues qui se prêtent à tous les timbres, à tous les effets, des douceurs
les plus suaves aux fulgurances de l'orage. Il est, tour à tour ou en même temps,
flûte, hautbois, trompette, tam-tam et même canon' (*OP*, p. 167).

Drawing on this range of cultural experience, the style of the poem offers
a synthesis which reflects that of the narrative content. For the best reading,
Senghor recommends treating it as 'une partition de jazz . . . et lorsqu'en tête
d'un poème, je donne une indication instrumentale, ce n'est pas une simple
formule. Le même poème peut donc être récité – je ne dis pas: déclamé –
psalmodié ou chanté' (*OP*, p. 167). In bringing a new and exciting synthesis to

poetry in French, Senghor is building on the kind of disjunctions and syncopations which have their origins in the inception of the prose poem around 1840, in the prosodic developments of free verse and the *verset* later in the nineteenth century, and culminating around the First World War and its aftermath with the experimentations of Futurism, Dada and Surrealism. The neat formal garden of traditional French versification, whatever its subtleties, was seen by Senghor as too restrictive for his purposes, and in terms of his theme in 'À New York', the poet gives us a fine example of 'l'art du compromis dynamique' (*PA*, p. 338), in the still valid hope of better understanding between peoples.

Notes

1 In the first edition (Paris: Seuil, 1956), 'À New York' follows rather than precedes the long poem 'Chaka', so making its position even more central to the collection. In *La Poésie de l'action* (henceforth abbreviated in the text as *PA*), Senghor declares (pp. 136–7): 'Les *Éthiopiques*, du [grec] *aithiops*, "noir", ce sont, en somme, des poèmes qui s'inspirent de la Négritude.' Léopold Sédar Senghor, *Œuvre poétique* (Paris: Seuil, 1990); *Poésie complète*, critical edition coordinated and ed. Pierre Brunel (Paris: CNRS Éditions, 2007); *Anthologie de la poésie nègre et malgache de langue française*, précédée de 'Orphée noir' par Jean-Paul Sartre (Paris: Presses Universitaires de France, 1948); *La Poésie de l'action: conversations avec Mohamed Aziza* (Paris: Stock, 1980); *Ce que je crois: négritude, francité et civilisation de l'universel* (Paris: Grasset, 1988).
2 Gaston Kelman, *Au-delà du Noir et du Blanc* (Paris: Christian Bourgois, 2007), p. 27, n. 1.
3 Charles Baudelaire, 'Rêve parisien', poem CII in *Les Fleurs du mal* [1861], in *Œuvres complètes*, ed. Claude Pichois (Paris: Gallimard, 1975), vol. I. Dedicated to the painter Constantin Guys, the poem, an important point of reference for Senghor which seems to have gone unnoticed so far, depicts the poet's flashy mineral vision just as in 'À New York': 'La palette du peintre fleurit des cristaux de corail.'
4 Cheikh Hamidou Kane, *L'Aventure ambiguë* [written 1952, first pub. 1961] (Paris: Christian Bourgois, 1979), p. 103. From the dates of original composition and publication, it is clear that neither author could have been directly influenced by the other's observations.
5 The later 'jambes de nylon' have the man-made fibre, patented in 1935 as Pierre Brunel observes in his notes to the poem (*Poésie complète*, pp. 294–7), mask human flesh. In 1946, Saint-John Perse, of whom Senghor was an avid reader, uses the word *nylon* in *Vents*, vol. II, 1. Saint-John Perse, *Œuvres complètes* (Paris: Gallimard, 1972), p. 201.
6 See Senghor, *Liberté 1: négritude et humanisme* (Paris: Seuil, 1964), pp. 108–9, where he refers to this collection, however, as *Les Trompettes* [as opposed to *Les Trombones*] *de Dieu*, a significant slippage in the context of his paratextual musical notation in 'À New York' of 'solo de trompette', an instrument which does not figure further in the poem. James Weldon Johnson, *God's Trombones: Seven Negro Sermons in Verse* (New York: Viking Press, 1927), pp. 6–7. From the very first essay in *Liberté 1*, dating from 1937, Senghor shows his familiarity with and admiration of poets of the Harlem Renaissance. References to the volume *Liberté 1* are abbreviated as *L 1*, followed by the page number.
7 The 'danseurs Dans' have been widely misinterpreted. Several English translations give the nonsensical 'dancers In'. The Senegalese critic Papa Guèye N'Diaye,

Éthiopiques, poèmes de Léopold Sédar Senghor: édition critique et commentée (Dakar and Abidjan: Nouvelles Éditions africaines, 1974), p. 82, over-sensitive to biblical references in this section, restricts his commentary to: 'mot biblique, tribu d'Israël'. Far more relevant is the Dan tribe of West Africa (Liberia and Ivory Coast), famous for its smoothly elegant oval masks. Fernando Lambert, *'Lire. . .' Éthiopiques de Senghor* (Paris: Présence Africaine, 1997), p. 59, n. 14, further refers to the etymology of the West African country Dahomey (now Benin): *Dan Homè*, the source of many slaves taken to the New World.

8 In the context, 'fers de lance' refer far more probably to the trigonocephalus than to spearheads.

9 Gutters beside Harlem pavements flow with 'rhum blanc' and 'lait noir', the latter astutely interpreted as whisky by Brunel (in his *Poésie complète* notes) with reference to Claudel's play *L'Échange*, where the term clearly has that meaning.

10 See also Senghor, *Liberté 3* (Paris: Seuil, 1977). Just as in the French West Indies, where Césaire championed *Négritude*, subsequent generations of writers have developed the concepts of *Antillanité*, *Créolisation* and *Tout-Monde* (Glissant) and *Créolité* (Chamoiseau and Confiant).

11 A similar plea for reconciliation between Black and White, but also between North and South, is found in the 'Épîtres à la Princesse', also in *Éthiopiques*.

12 Senghor, *Œuvre poétique*, p. 156. Abbreviated below as *OP* in the text.

13 The first of these appended to *OP*, 'Chant du feu (chant bantou)' (p. 409), is a good example, but the degree to which Senghor's creative practice impinged on the manner of his translation, inevitably considerable, is impossible to assess accurately without knowing the original.

Further reading

Brunel, Pierre, Bourrel, Jean René, and Giguet, Frédéric (eds.), *Léopold Sédar Senghor* (Paris: ADPF, 2006).

Djian, Jean-Michel, *Léopold Sédar Senghor: genèse d'un imaginaire francophone* (Paris: Gallimard, 2005).

Kluback, William, *Léopold Sédar Senghor: From Politics to Poetry* (New York: Peter Lang, 1997).

Lebaud-Kane, Geneviève, *Imaginaire et création dans l'œuvre poétique de Léopold Sédar Senghor* (Paris: L'Harmattan, 1995).

Senghor, Léopold Sédar, *Prose and Poetry*, trans. John Reed and Clive Wake (London: Heinemann, 1976).

   The Collected Poetry, trans. Melvin Dixon (Charlottesville, VA: University Press of Virginia, 1991).

Spleth, Janice, *Critical Perspectives on Léopold Sédar Senghor* (Washington, DC: Three Continents Press, 1993).

Vaillant, Janet G., *Black, French and African: A Life of Léopold Sédar Senghor* (Cambridge, MA: Harvard University Press, 1990).

Part II
Avant-gardes

8 Pierre Reverdy, 'L'Esprit du dehors'

STEPHEN ROMER

L'Esprit du dehors

Les mains tremblent sous la lampe où
le papier blanchit
        Et l'abat-jour coupe toutes les têtes
Dans le seul coin de la salle où la clarté remue
        On entend quelquefois la pendule et le chat
Personne n'oserait entrer dans ce silence
On craint pourtant le bruit du doigt
cherchant la porte
        Quelle nuit
Quelqu'un passe en criant sur le
trottoir d'en face
        La plume grince
Et là-haut
        Le vent rugueux frôle le toit

From Le Cadran quadrillé

L'Esprit dehors

Les mains s'étirent sous la lampe où le papier blanc se déploie, où le tranchant de l'abat-jour coupe les têtes. Dans le seul coin de cette salle où la clarté remue on entend quelquefois la pendule qui bat. Personne n'oserait entrer dans ce silence.

On craint pourtant le bruit du doigt cherchant, dans le secret, les lignes de la porte. Au débouché funèbre de la nuit, quelqu'un passe en criant dans la rue qui s'efface.

Murmures sans écho, chagrins de trop grand poids, la plume grince tard sur la feuille du livre, comme le vent rugueux sur la pente du toit.

From La Liberté des mers

81

A genius of unease

Pierre Reverdy is a genius of unease. He is the paradoxical poet of the intimate space and the cosmic cold. We enter a Reverdy poem as we might a domestic interior, one of those comfortable scenes, represented in a painting such as *Sous la lampe* by Vuillard. But once we have settled into a reassuring womb-like space, a black wind rips through the room, its solid framework dissolves, and we are on the outside, dispossessed of stable identity, in an obscure cold place, peering into another cold place. The original room has been devastated and turned inside out. As readers we seem to be attached to an organ of extraordinary and anguished acuity, an eye and an ear, that registers phenomena such as falling shadow, trembling light, a noise at the door, intangible things that co-exist with solid, everyday objects, in an atmosphere from which the oxygen has been sucked out. Common objects of everyday familiarity take on the precise appearance of being preserved under glass, and the whole experience is obscurely linked to a powerful emotional charge.

'L'Esprit du dehors'[1] is a poem that manages to be at once a dispassionate inventory of a disposition of phenomena in and outside a room, and a deeply subjective description of an emotional state that swings between reassurance and dismay, and over which presides an undefined menace. The objects are therefore an objective correlative of this state, felt by the unnamed and possibly discontinuous speaker, disguised behind the grammatically neutral pronoun 'on'. Something of considerable import seems to be at stake here, though the procedure is always one of showing, not telling. This is a phenomenology of perception in which the stakes are appreciably higher, and the emotional disturbance greater, than would normally be the case in a serene philosophical enquiry. The central dichotomy, as the title suggests – the spirit without, or the spirit (seen from) without – is between the inside and the outside, and is a kind of inner sanctum within the interior space, that seems to inspire fear or respect – 'Personne n'oserait entrer dans ce silence'. This space is threatened, however, apparently from all sides, by a finger at the door, a cry from the pavement, and that ubiquitous wind testing the roof overhead.

The blessed space, under the lamplight, where it eventually becomes clear, but only in the pre-penultimate line – 'La plume grince' – that someone is in the act of writing, is a space inherited from the poets of the late nineteenth century. Mallarmé sat up, night after night, 'dans la clarté déserte' of his lamp, poring over 'le vide papier que la blancheur défend', and the stakes of Mallarmé's poetics were high indeed. But in his 'Brise marine', the domestic interior – the poet at his table under the lamplight, the young woman nursing her child nearby – is framed for the viewer in just the way a Vuillard interior might be framed – unproblematically. Something very different has happened in Reverdy's 'L'Esprit du dehors', and it has to do with viewpoint and with perspective. We are no longer looking in at a scene with a fixed frame. The frame rather seems elastic; in pictorial terms we might say that there is no vanishing point which would otherwise govern or even dictate a single viewpoint. The focalisation constantly shifts about; the perceiving subject observes 'le seul coin de la salle où la clarté remue'; then seems inside it: 'personne n'oserait entrer dans ce silence'; and then looks up and through to where 'le vent rugueux frôle le toit'.

In other terms, a struggle has been enjoined between the reassuring elements of a cosy interior – the lamplight, the clock, the cat – and the various elements from without – a hand at the door, a cry on the street, the wind tugging at the roof – that might be inimical to it. And at the centre of the scene are those hands, trembling over the paper, blanched in the lamplight. For the moment, all seems nevertheless to be well, the implication being that things are under control as long as 'la plume grince', as long as the writing continues. The difficult equilibrium between these components must be maintained if the pen is to keep scratching away. The hands holding the pen are the spider at the centre of this web, and the acute concentration of the perceiver, receiving and processing the ambient visual and aural phenomena, holds the elements of this scene in place. In a moving, late letter to his old friend Georges Braque, Reverdy reiterates what Braque the painter does when he arranges objects on a canvas, and here at least the analogy with his own poetic practice is clear: 'Vous savez que si on entre dans une maison ou une pièce désertées, inhabitées, les choses y sont dans un isolement glacial qui peut serrer le cœur et l'esprit. Ce qui lie les choses dans la vie, c'est l'atmosphère que la vie des êtres animés y apporte . . . En art, ce qui les lie c'est la poésie'.[2] In Reverdy's poetics, as we shall see, it is the poet's 'esprit' – mind, spirit, soul – that orders, filters, elevates, disposes and above all *brings together into an image* object and emotion. On one level, then, our poem seems to enact, in a self-reflexive and disjunctive way that is exemplary in its modernity, the struggle of the mind to create. The risk is that the charmed circle of the room, with the hands under the lamplight at its centre, fly apart into a state of desolation and dispossession, a threatening nightmare that comes increasingly to haunt the poetry of Pierre Reverdy.

Every reader responds to the uncanny in these poems, created by constantly shifting viewpoint, emotionally laden verbs, and ambiguous ellipses of all kinds. There is at times something of the metaphysical *whodunnit* about his work, with traces of blood, and mysterious phenomena occurring in the curtains of the library. And Reverdy the poet might be well pleased with this reader response, because it is precisely the *unheimlich*, the *intime étrangeté* in Michel Collot's phrase,[3] the defamiliarisation of the everyday, that he aims for in his early poems, which are also those most closely associated with his Cubist years. The poem is not, and should not be, too readily accessible. The pioneers of Cubism in painting declared war on conventional perspective with its framing devices, inviting the viewer instead to 'piece together' the evidence in an act of co-production, and to rediscover (often with mysterious pleasure) everyday objects. Reverdy notes of Picasso[4] how he chooses objects that are most intimate and near at hand – the guitar, the pipe, the favourite tobacco packet – and suggests by analogy that the Cubist experiment required the painter to put to one side all the painterly knowledge previously acquired, and to start from scratch, with the nearest objects that came to hand. The artistic effort is always against the too readily conceptualized; both poetry and painting must slow down the process of mental categorisation, or 'pigeon-holing'. In Britain, the founder of the Imagist movement, T. E. Hulme, was saying similar things, 'Verse is a pedestrian taking you over the ground, prose – a train which delivers you at a destination.'[5] Addressing the same matter, the supposed obscurity of his poems, Reverdy says this: 'Chacun d'eux est une chambre close où le premier venu ne peut entrer. Il faudra prendre la peine et le soin d'allumer sa lampe avant de pénétrer. Ici, c'est l'esprit du lecteur qui sert de lampe. Et cette lampe, l'intelligence et le sens poétique seuls sont propres à l'alimenter.'[6]

To return to our poem, it appears that we can extend its reflexive nature – by which I mean the way in which the poem describes, and comments upon, its own creation – and say that the 'chambre' becomes a metaphor for the text itself, and the *chambre noire* the darkened room or the darkroom in which it is elaborated. Andrew Rothwell puts it thus: 'As an enclosed, isolated domain, the textual *chambre* is a space where the new semantic and figural relations which will constitute the poem's non-realist "atmosphère" are created.'[7] In terms applied to Braque's still-lifes, but which present clear analogies with his own poetics, Reverdy writes on Cubism's basic aims:

> Il s'agit seulement d'une figuration dans l'espace sans l'aide de la perspective; de l'utilisation de la matière sans l'atmosphère qui l'enveloppe, et au total d'une création à l'aide d'objets reformés et conçus par l'esprit, d'une œuvre qui est le résultat d'une émotion au lieu d'en être la répétition; c'est par là que les œuvres qu'apporte cette esthétique nouvelle constituent des réalités en elles-mêmes. Il s'agit de réalité artistique, bien entendu, par opposition à l'œuvre d'art imitative de la réalité.[8]

I quote at length, both because of the richness of the thought, but also to give an example of the kind of deeply pondered aesthetics that Reverdy was elaborating during the years he ran his famous avant-garde journal *Nord-Sud* (1917–18). Reverdy stands, with Apollinaire, as the fountainhead of that aspect of Modernism in France which allied poets and painters so closely, and which has no exact equivalent elsewhere. It is, of course, an alliance that goes back to Baudelaire's championing of Courbet, Delacroix and Constantin Guys, through Mallarmé's friendships with the likes of Manet, Monet and Whistler, and it comes down, via the frenetic activity of the Surrealists, to more recent times – for instance the constellation of poets that gathered around Giacometti

– René Char, Yves Bonnefoy, André du Bouchet and Jacques Dupin. Guillaume Apollinaire was the original poet-champion of *la peinture nouvelle* (and Blaise Cendrars's connection with the Delaunays should not be passed over), but it was Reverdy who went into the matter most deeply, and most sustainedly. Part of the result was a series of magnificent collaborative *livres d'artistes*, in which texts by Reverdy were juxtaposed with works by, pre-eminently, Juan Gris, Picasso and Braque.

Such a collaboration made sense, because the Cubists were emphatically anti-mimetic and anti-anecdotal, and, for Reverdy, the poets that mattered were striving for the same effects. Even though Reverdy, in the essay quoted above, stated flatly 'La poésie cubiste n'existe pas', in order to dispel a straightforward *confusion des genres*, there is no doubt he was attempting something *analogous* to the painters, especially in his strictly selective use of materials – the windows, doors, tables, lamps etc. that make a Reverdy poem instantly recognisable. The problem was how to free up language in a way resembling the media of the visual arts. But language is by nature a profoundly conceptual medium, made up as it is of a fixed lexicon, a syntax and a grammar – which is why we are always returned, forcibly, to Mallarmé's ideal flower, his 'notion pure, l'absente de tous bouquets'. Whereas in painting the creation and disposition of plastic form and shape can lead towards pure abstraction, language is locked into meaning which, if syntax is respected, words produce, as they unfold along Saussure's *chaîne signifiante*. For despite the poet's best efforts, language does have this vexatious conceptual tendency, making abstraction in the sense we use it when speaking of painting, and indeed of music, unachievable.

Reverdy's solution was primarily through what he calls *L'Image*, a notion he elaborates in the famous eponymous essay in *Nord-Sud*: 'L'Image est une création pure de l'esprit. Elle ne peut naître d'une comparaison mais du rapprochement de deux réalités plus ou moins éloignées.' It was this statement that André Breton took over for his own purposes, by adding that the more *arbitrary* the two elements brought together the stronger the image. But Reverdy does not say that; he seems indeed to counter the Surrealist thrust when he writes 'une image n'est pas forte parce qu'elle est *brutale* ou *fantastique* – mais parce que l'association des idées est lointaine et juste.'[9] In these terms, the notorious meeting of an umbrella and a sewing machine on a dissecting table is not the kind of image Reverdy desired. His silent, brooding decors are not littered with sofas metamorphosed into horse-carcasses pulled about on ropes by Catholic priests, as in the unbridled fancifulness of Dalí and Buñuel. The image, for Reverdy, and the poem itself, is always the coincidence of the inner reality of the poet, and the internal pressure that seeks an outlet, with the outer reality of the world, the poem being the *réalité imaginée*, the crystalline deposit (a frequent trope) left by their collision. The most striking 'image' of this occurs in perhaps his most celebrated single poem, 'Les Ardoises du toit':

Sur chaque ardoise
    qui glissait du toit
        on
    avait écrit
      un poème

La gouttière est bordée de diamants
    les oiseaux les boivent

So the 'image' in question, in 'L'Esprit du dehors', is really its existence as metaphor: the process whereby we as readers effect the transfer from the concrete exterior décor of the room, and *understand it* as representing the internal world of the poet in the workshop of creation. It is an ideal image for Reverdy because it manages to enclose both inner and outer worlds within the space of the poem – the huge ambition of poetry since Mallarmé enclosed the stars of the *septuor* within the frame of the mirror, or transcribed a celestial constellation in *Un coup de dés*.[10] It is the primordial act of the Imagination, profoundly metaphorical in nature, of the kind Coleridge theorised, and enacted in a poem such as 'Frost at Midnight' where, similar to, though on a larger scale than, 'L'Esprit du dehors' or than 'Les Ardoises du toit', the 'secret ministry' of the frost becomes fused with the secret ministrations of the poet in the act of creation. Like the frost, he hangs his poems up in icicles, or according to Reverdy, in rows of diamonds, along the edge of the gutter.

Icicles, water-drops – these are phenomena that would count among Reverdy's *éléments purs*, that would include the simple, constant, unchanging things. In the 1924 essay 'Poésie',[11] he instances the cloud, the table, sun, rain and shadow as among the *réalités* for a poet, whereas the specific type of clothing worn by someone, or – even more controversially perhaps – all 'réminiscence livresque', by which I suppose he means all literary echo or allusion, are *irréalités*. One senses here the beginnings of futile aesthetic debate of the kind between free and dependent beauty, which for many vitiates Kant's *Critique of Judgment*. When it comes to the idea of purity, a whole aesthetics could be devoted to it, insofar as it haunts French poets, and it would still not exhaust this perplexing question. Once again, the filtering of the world into *éléments purs* and the rest recalls Mallarmé's division of language into the *brut* and the *essentiel*, and Valéry's description of poetry as a language within a language. In the end, such taxonomies, so beloved of the French mind, invariably come to grief, or else they are ignored by their exponents in practice. The exclusion of all 'réminiscence livresque' in the case of Reverdy is a particularly tall order, though it follows on logically enough from his determination to be, following Rimbaud's war cry, absolutely modern. Reverdy probably meant by the phrase unconscious literary echo, and falling into cliché, but it is curious to note also that it is diametrically opposed to the practice of two great Modernists across the Channel, Pound and Eliot, whose poetry consists, on the contrary, of a dense network of self-conscious literary allusion as a procedure for forging, by parataxis, fresh meaning. That the hordes of commuters crossing London Bridge should remind Eliot of the damned in Dante is an immensely rich allusion that would, presumably, be disallowed by Reverdy as an example of 'réminiscence livresque'. The rigorous exclusiveness of the French poet's elements begins in his work as a strength, but ends – as he himself came to see – as a damaging limitation.

The 'éléments purs' were to be stripped of their 'enveloppe sentimentale' and deployed in a novel arrangement that would, again like a Cubist still-life (which was effectively the only Cubist genre acceptable to Reverdy), constitute a new reality, not merely a representation or copy of an old one. The suggestive phrase 'enveloppe sentimentale' is in reality a revised version of the 'film of familiarity' which the Romantics were to strip away from the 'things of everyday'.[12] What is new is the magnetic current the poet is to set up between his chosen elements, in the closed circle of the room. And so we find, through their reiteration, objects recurring in the early poems (one critic commented of *Les Ardoises du toit* merely that there seemed to be an awful lot of windows). Some of these objects do indeed come to constitute, through their repetition, almost as leitmotif, a symbolic status that is nevertheless not wholly interpreted. In 'L'Esprit du dehors' the lamp is clearly crucial to the process, both as a concentrating agent in whose light the pen traces its script, and as an excluder: the lampshade cuts across all the other heads (although whose heads these might be, given the overwhelming solitariness of the perceiver in the poem, it is not clear). In the poem immediately following this one, which comes from the collection *Le Cadran quadrillé*, the lamp stops the shadow that has crept down from the roof, while in *Au soleil du plafond*, in the poem called 'La Lampe', which is really a sister piece to our poem, it is a beacon and a lighthouse for the mind against an obscure assailant: 'Le vent noir qui tordait les rideaux ne pouvait soulever le papier ni éteindre la lampe'.[13]

What I hope is clear from the foregoing is the very high degree of self-consciousness that is involved in the composition of a poem like 'L'Esprit du dehors'. As much would be true of the vast majority of the poems Reverdy wrote, though there are certain significant changes of emphasis in the later work: for example, a more liberal use of the personal pronoun 'je', a more explicitly moral tenor combined with a more openly emotional, less impersonal manner. This self-consciousness, which is the opposite of 'doing what comes naturally', extends of course into the formal arrangement of the poem. Discussion of the form of the poem is complicated somewhat by the fact that Reverdy revised 'L'Esprit du dehors', as he revised a great deal of his earlier verse, and the revisions, as we shall see, are not without serious consequences. The original version of 'L'Esprit du dehors' is clearly written according to Reverdy's own prescription of the kind of syntax and typography adequate to the Modern movement:

> Pour un art nouveau une syntaxe nouvelle était à prévoir; elle devait
> fatalement venir mettre dans le nouvel ordre les mots dont nous

devions nous servir . . . La syntaxe est un moyen de création littéraire. C'est une disposition de mots – et une disposition typographique adéquate est légitime.[14]

'L'Esprit du dehors' is composed in the kind of free verse that Ezra Pound favoured, when he called on poets to 'compose in the sequence of the musical phrase, not in sequence of a metronome'.[15] Reverdy's elegant *vers libre* is beautifully chiselled in precisely this spirit; the syntax is in fact orthodox for the most part, though the lack of punctuation allows for a free-flowing ambiguity. To which phrase, for example, is the line 'Quelle nuit' attached grammatically? It is, in fact, a free-floating exclamative, surrounded by blank space, which adds to the controlled ambiguity of the text. The spatially composed, paratactic arrangement of phrases enhances the sense that we are receiving a second-by-second printout from a finely-tuned seismograph.

How curious, then, that Reverdy should have chosen to rewrite this poem, and so many others, and transform them into un-indented blocks of prose. A comparison of the two versions is instructive. The later prose version (published in *La Liberté des mers*, a sumptuous *livre d'artiste* illustrated by Braque) makes explicit much that was left ambiguous. 'Le tranchant de l'abat-jour', for instance, or 'les lignes de la porte', and the much more explicit 'au débouché funèbre de la nuit' replaces that enigmatic 'Quelle nuit'. As for the newly imported phrase 'chagrins de trop grand poids', it changes the mood of this poem radically. The grammatical ambiguity of the title is also flattened into 'L'Esprit dehors'. More information is supplied; readers are 'told' what to think, they are not simply presented with the facts as in the earlier version. Critics have put this wholesale revision on the part of Reverdy down to a growing loss of faith in his early Cubist poetics, even to an assimilation of the lacunary nature of the texts to his own growing conviction and terror of the lacunary nature of his own personal experience: the failure of his version of the avant-garde, followed some years later by the loss of the religious faith that sent him into voluntary exile in 1926, to live in the shadow of the monastery at Solesmes. It appears he felt the need, for his own metaphysical health, literally to 'fill in the gaps' of his own poems.[16] Be that as it may, the body of Reverdy's poetry is impressive testimony to a high ideal. The discipline required amounts to a veritable ascesis, and the work exhausts his particular line of approach. The unspoken suffering of his later years is hard even to contemplate. But the best of his poems are still as fresh, nearly a century on, as when he wrote them.

Notes

1 I have taken the original version of Reverdy's poem 'L'Esprit du dehors' as the basis for my discussion. This is an early poem, dating from 1915, that was to be included in the projected (though never published) collection *Le Cadran quadrillé*. The editor of Reverdy's *Collected Works*, Étienne-Alain Hubert, established the collection after the

poet's death as accurately as existing records allow. The revised version, 'L'Esprit dehors', printed here alongside, was published by Aimé Maeght in the collection *La Liberté des mers* (Paris: Maeght, 1960), a *livre d'artiste* with original lithographs by Georges Braque.

2 Pierre Reverdy, *Ancres* (Paris: Éditions Maeght, 1977), p. 72.

3 See Michel Collot's 'Le Lyrisme de la réalité', in *Pierre Reverdy*, special issue of *Europe*, 777–8 (Paris, 1994), p. 41.

4 Pierre Reverdy, *Nord–Sud, Self defence et autres écrits sur la poésie 1917–1926* (Paris: Flammarion, 1975), pp. 185–204. See also Pierre Reverdy, *Le Livre de mon bord, notes 1930–1936* (Paris: Mercure de France, 1948); *Cette émotion appelée poésie 1932–1960* (Paris: Flammarion, 1974); *En vrac: notes* (Monaco: Édition du Rocher, 1956); *Le Gant de crin: notes* (Paris: Flammarion, 1968); *Note éternelle du présent: écrits sur l'art 1923–1960* (Paris: Flammarion, 1973).

5 T. E. Hulme, *Selected Writings*, ed. Patrick McGuinness (Manchester: Carcanet, 1998), p. 80.

6 Reverdy, *Nord–Sud, Self defence*, pp. 206–7.

7 For a lucid and extended study of these and other matters in Reverdy, see Andrew Rothwell, *Textual Spaces: The Poetry of Pierre Reverdy* (Amsterdam: Rodopi, 1989), esp. pp. 91–106.

8 Reverdy, *Nord–Sud, Self defence*, pp. 145–6.

9 *Ibid.*, pp. 73–5.

10 Such at least was Paul Valéry's first impression of his mentor's poem. See his moving account in Paul Valéry, *Œuvres complètes*, vol. I, (Paris: Gallimard, 1965), pp. 622–30.

11 Reverdy, *Nord–Sud, Self defence*, pp. 204–7.

12 See S. T. Coleridge, *Biographia Literaria*, ch. XIV, in *Coleridge: Selected Poetry and Prose*, ed. Stephen Potter (London: Nonesuch Press, 1933), p. 248.

13 Reverdy, *Au soleil du plafond* (Paris: Gallimard, 1980), p. 17.

14 Reverdy, *Nord–Sud, Self defence*, pp. 81–2.

15 Ezra Pound, *Literary Essays*, ed. T. S. Eliot (London: Faber, 1974), p. 3.

16 On the dramatic effect of Reverdy's revisions see Rothwell, *Textual Spaces*, pp. 173–202.

Further reading

Bishop, Michael, 'Pierre Reverdy's Conception of the Image', *Forum for Modern Language Studies*, 12 (1976), pp. 25–36.

Brée, Germaine, Caws, Mary Ann and Bent, Timothy (eds.), *Reverdy: Selected Poems* (Newcastle: Bloodaxe, 1991).

Caws, Mary Ann, *La Main de Reverdy* (Geneva: Droz, 1979).

Chol, Isabelle, *Pierre Reverdy, poésie plastique* (Geneva: Droz, 2006).

Collot, Michel and Mathieu, Jean-Claude (eds.), *Reverdy aujourd'hui* (Paris: PENS, 1992).

Du Bouchet, André, *Matière de l'interlocuteur* (Montpellier: Fata Morgana, 1992).

Greene, Robert W., *The Poetic Theory of Pierre Reverdy* (Berkeley, CA: University of California Press, 1967).

Hubert, Étienne-Alain, *Circonstances de la poésie: Reverdy, Apollinaire, surréalisme* (Paris: Klincksieck, 2000).

LeHardy Sweet, David, *Savage Sight/Constructed Noise* (Chapel Hill, NC: North Carolina University Press, 2003).

Para, Jean-Baptiste, *Pierre Reverdy* (Paris: La documentation française, 2006).

9 | Paul Éluard, 'La courbe de tes yeux. . .'

RICHARD STAMELMAN

La courbe de tes yeux fait le tour de mon cœur,
Un rond de danse et de douceur,
Auréole du temps, berceau nocturne et sûr,
Et si je ne sais plus tout ce que j'ai vécu
C'est que tes yeux ne m'ont pas toujours vu.   5

Feuilles de jour et mousse de rosée,
Roseaux du vent, sourires parfumés,
Ailes couvrant le monde de lumière,
Bateaux chargés du ciel et de la mer,
Chasseurs des bruits et sources des couleurs,   10

Parfums éclos d'une couvée d'aurores
Qui gît toujours sur la paille des astres,
Comme le jour dépend de l'innocence
Le monde entier dépend de tes yeux purs
Et tout mon sang coule dans leurs regards.   15

From *Capitale de la douleur*

In the autumn of 1996 Lancôme, the French perfume and cosmetics company, launched a new scent called 'Poême' for which it chose as the fragrance's slogan a line from a poem written by Paul Éluard in 1950. Entitled 'Je t'aime', Éluard's lyric describes the poet's love for a woman whose power over him is celebrated in cosmic and heliotropic terms; it ends with a verse Lancôme could not resist borrowing: 'Tu es le grand soleil qui me monte à la tête.'[1] Aside from the revised spelling of the word *poème* – a circumflex replaces the *accent grave* – and the paradoxical announcement that 'Poême' says more than words (i.e. a poem) could ever say, print advertisements for the scent were striking in the way they set a golden-yellow perfume bottle against a background of celestial blue.[2]

Blue and yellow, signs of infinite sky and expansive light, give colour to a landscape that, for Éluard, is almost invariably feminine. 'Je suis', he writes in the poem 'L'Extase', 'devant ce paysage féminin / Comme un enfant devant le feu /. . . / Je suis devant ce paysage féminin / Comme une branche dans le feu' (II, p. 107). While the child, from a safe distance (according to Éluard's vision of the scene), stares at the fire with eyes of wonder, imagining all sorts of marvellous forms pulsating within the flames, the branch joyfully welcomes union with the pyre. Similarly, the poet, standing before a landscape he imagines as a woman and a woman he imagines as a landscape, perceives wondrous, ever-changing forms in the limitless geography before his eyes, until he, like the branch consumed by the fire, becomes one with its (or her) body.

The union between poet and world, poet and landscape, poet and woman is reflected as well in Lancôme's borrowed verse: 'Tu es le grand soleil qui me monte à la tête.' For here the poetic *I* is enveloped by the encroaching sun of the beloved woman, whose light, climbing his body, ultimately plants the flag of erotic possession in his skull and in his imagination. Invaded by the other, the poet becomes literally drugged by the opiate of the woman's presence within himself. Henceforth, he lives only by her command, by the *fiat lux* she has announced. Like the phoenix he is reborn from the fire and heat of her love. Like the sunflower (a prophetic Surrealist symbol for André Breton), Éluard is instinctively pulled towards the light of this pure, life-giving solar woman: 'Tout existe tout est visible / Il n'y a pas une goutte de nuit dans tes yeux / Je vis dans une lumière exclusive la tienne' (I, p. 441).[3]

Not only does the poet's being revolve, like some planet, around the sun of his love; the entire physical, concrete world with its stones, flowers, trees, rivers, birds, stars, dawns, and colours in which he and his beloved dwell, owes its existence to the woman's sustaining illumination, as the penultimate line of 'La courbe de tes yeux' proclaims: 'Le monde entier dépend de tes yeux purs' (I, p. 196). The dependence of the natural world on the woman's eyes – mirrors of light whose surface reflects not only an image of the poet looking at her but also the image of the woman gazing back into his own eyes, and the image of a fantastic world that this choreography of intersecting and self-reflecting gazes has brought into being through love – goes beyond what the mere verb 'dépend' signifies. The universe literally 'hangs on' the woman's gaze. When she looks, she gives new configurations and identities to the objects in the world upon which her fervent glance, inspired by love, alights; her dreams 'en pleine lumière / Font s'évaporer les soleils' (I, p. 140), illuminating the universe with a dynamic and magical force that reinvents it. Indeed, the cosmos *depends* on these eroticising eyes, because they give birth to a non-transcendental, immanent paradise, an Eden of timeless presence that knows no past or future and that lives within the eternity of an instant. 'Let there be light' (*fiat lux*), the woman's eyes command, and from the dream world of her unconscious – and, of course, from Éluard's poetic and sensual imagination – emerges a plenitude of brilliant light that reconfigures and regenerates a reality transformed into a sur-reality. For as Éluard argues, 'tout ce que l'esprit de l'homme peut concevoir et créer provient de la même veine, est de la même *matière* que sa chair, que son sang et que le monde qui l'entoure' (I, p. 516). Since thought, dream and poetry are as material as blood, flesh and the senses, a poem is – and Éluard believes this intensely – as tangible and concrete as a kiss: 'que parler / Soit aussi généreux / Qu'embrasser' (I, p. 822).

Indeed, when Éluard calls poetry 'the art of light' (I, p. 527), he does not wish to be understood metaphorically. Rather, the poem *gives* light; it commands that there be light; it creates through light; it has the physical luminescence of light; it is, finally, an act of light – as well as enlightenment. Thus, the importance of seeing and visuality in Éluard's work must not be underestimated. The beloved woman is pure visuality: 'Je t'appellerai Visuelle / Et multiplierai ton image' (I, p. 293). Through her loving gaze ('tes yeux purs') she gives visibility to the infinite elements of the world, a gift of revelation that love and poetry also offer, for sight is also the *giving* of sight: a 'donner à voir' (I, p. 917); it initiates a new Genesis:

> Je n'invente pas les mots. Mais j'invente des objets, des êtres, des événements et mes sens sont capables de les percevoir . . . Le poème désensibilise l'univers au seul profit des facultés humaines, permet à l'homme de voir autrement, d'autres choses . . . Il découvre un nouveau monde, il devient un nouvel homme. (I, pp. 979–80)

The opening line of 'La courbe de tes yeux fait le tour de mon cœur', the next-to-last poem in Éluard's *Capitale de la douleur* published in 1926, begins with an easily visualised metaphor of bodily invasion that, despite its concreteness and ingenuity, goes well beyond what, according to the physiology of cardiac and optical function, is conceivable or logical. Like many of Éluard's surreal images, which seek to contradict the infallible principles of physics, logic, thought, psychology and perception – the most striking of which is 'La terre est bleue comme une orange' in his *L'Amour la poésie* from 1929 (I, p. 232) – the penetrating curve of the woman's eyes are to be read not as metaphor but as reality: a new vision of the physical interaction of eyes, heart and body that the poem, in its celebration of the joyful fusion of love, imagines and thus makes real.[4] This is why, after declaring in 'La terre est bleue. . .' that the earth is both 'blue' and 'orange' – a contradiction that juxtaposes opposites such as insubstantiality (blue) and pulpiness (orange), abstractness and concreteness, formlessness and roundness, expansiveness and compression, the blueness of oranges and the 'orangeness' of the earth – Éluard announces in the next line that 'Jamais une erreur les mots ne mentent pas' (I, p. 232). In a Surrealist world, where imagination and its creations are real, there can never be error or contradiction, because every reality can be joined with or compared to every other reality; there are no limits to the possible associations that can be imagined:

> Voici que l'objet virtuel naît de l'objet réel, qu'il devient réel à son tour, voici qu'ils font image, du réel au réel, comme un mot avec tous les autres . . . Deux objets ne se séparent que pour mieux se retrouver dans leur éloignement, en passant par l'échelle de toutes les choses, de tous les êtres. (I, pp. 938–9)

Moreover, hierarchies of distinctions based on good and bad, high and low, possible and impossible, real and unreal, lived and dreamt, rational and irrational, no longer exist. 'Tout est comparable à tout', Éluard writes, 'tout trouve son écho, sa raison, sa ressemblance, son opposition, son devenir partout. Et ce devenir est infini' (I, p. 527).

If truth exists for the Surrealist, it is to be found in what issues forth from the unconscious or the imagination or dream life through unconstrained linguistic, artistic and automatist expression and through the unforeseen workings of chance. Such creations have their own 'devenir', their own process of ceaseless metamorphosis, by means of which they perpetually replace and renew each other. In Éluard's world every instant effaces the moment preceding it and is, in turn, erased by the moment that follows. Time is defined by the immediacy of the *now*, by a constantly self-renewing present, unique in its newness, innocence and purity. Great artists and poets recognise this eternal recurrence of the *new*, Éluard observes; for them, 'tout est encore à faire, et non à refaire . . . Nous partons sans cesse d'aujourd'hui, aujourd'hui je commence, demain je ne recommencerai pas, je commencerai et ainsi tous les jours je naîtrai à moi-même et au monde. Le temps ne passe pas, le temps commence' (II, pp. 520–1).

Thus, existence is a state of unending and transformative becoming, which the poem creates: 'Plus rien ne nous fera douter de ce poème / Que j'écris aujourd'hui pour effacer hier' (II, p. 366). Love suppresses the past, wipes it clean, transforms it into a tabula rasa, a new beginning: 'l'amour est au monde pour l'oubli du monde' (I, p. 216). Such forgetting gives the poet the freedom of creative amnesia and the licence to destroy and then create things by naming them: 'nous vivons dans l'oubli de nos métamorphoses' (II, p. 83), one poem declares, while another announces that 'C'est ici que l'on voit le créateur de mots / Celui qui se détruit dans les fils qu'il engendre / Et qui nomme l'oubli de tous les noms du monde' (I, p. 181). To name what is forgotten is to substitute a new word or reality or life for the absence or void left behind; effacement thus becomes creation, destruction birth.

In the first of the three five-line stanzas that structure 'La courbe de tes yeux', the *I* who speaks establishes his cardiological identity in contrast to the optical nature of the *you*; the beloved is all eyes, the poet all heart. In fact, the entire fifteen-line poem refers to the poet rarely in the first person: twice as the subject pronoun, 'je' (l. 4), twice as the possessive adjective, 'mon' (ll. 1, 15), and once as the direct object pronoun, 'me' (l. 5). The beloved, however, is unvaryingly designated by the possessive adjective 'tes' (ll. 1, 5, 14), as if her being were more stable and certain than the poet's. Interestingly, more than half of the poem's lines (ll. 2–3, 6–12) offer no direct personal identification, although they are dense with epithets and associations referring to the dynamism and world-generating force of the woman's eyes, lovingly glorified by the poet's voice (and declared in the first line). Not only do her eyes move literally to the heart of the poet's being, where they tenderly encircle, embrace, caress and cradle the organic center of his life; they initiate a circularity, a closed system of rhythmical contraction and dilation, of recurring centrifugal and centripetal movements, evoked by images of roundness – the curve of an eye encircling the heart, a dance that comes full circle, a halo of self-sufficient light and of time made luminescent, a cradle rocking back and forth. As blood circulates through the body, giving life and feeling to legs, arms and head, only to return to the heart, so light moves out from the woman's eyes to the poet and the world, only to return to its source where it will begin again its life-giving journey. Flowing through the world, light makes whatever it touches visible, awakens it into being, gives it birth. No wonder that one of Éluard's collections is entitled *Les Yeux fertiles* (I, p. 491) and that images of birth and dawn, of openings and beginnings – 'berceau', 'jour', 'rosée', 'ailes', 'sources', 'éclos', 'couvée', 'aurores', 'innocence' – fill the lines of 'La courbe de tes yeux'.

In addition to the symbiotic circulation of blood and light, the poem presents images of expansion, emanation, fluidity, and birth: images that, because they fuse two different realities into a compressed, highly visual metaphor, can be read in several contradictory yet imaginative ways, which to the non-Surrealist mind would seem blatantly impossible. Leaves ('feuilles de jour', l. 6) unfold like the day or, conversely, the day becomes green through the freshness of leaves or, yet again, it comes alive through the verdant coolness of a mossy dew or a dewy moss ('mousse de rosée', l. 6). Reeds ('roseaux du vent', l. 7) dance in the wind or the wind, blowing through them, makes them chatter. Smiles ('sour-ires parfumés', l. 7), transformed into vapour, saturate the air like perfumes; or perfumes, because of the delight they give, make the air softly smile. Light from birds' wings (l. 8) spreads tenderly over the world in a maternal gesture of protection. Cargoes of sky and sea (l. 9), despite their expansive immensity, fill the holds of ships en route to new shores. Fountains of colours ('sources des couleurs', l. 10) bubble up from the earth, simultaneously watery and prismatic. Fragrant dawns hatch from eggs (l. 11), while cosmic scents emanate from astral nests of straw (ll. 11–12). Innocence and purity (ll. 13–14) are born from the day, from the world, and from the confluence of blood and light, heart and eyes, self and other. The poem's second and third stanzas teem with an effervescent, foaming reality, with a profusion of exuberantly dynamic things, an ecstatic *omnium gatherum* of newly generated natural and human phenomena.

Even though this chain of descriptive epithets celebrates the movement of the beloved's eyes as they curve around the poet's heart and circulate in the world, and even though these compressed metaphors express the gift of light and illumination – the gift of creation – that her eyes offer the poet, it is the very words and images of the poem itself, as they move from object to object, from reality to reality – from the day's leaves to the dew's moss (l. 6), for example – and as they join image to image and noun to noun in a crescendo of joyful Surrealism, creating an imaginary world that becomes physically and sensually real. A landscape of love, at once concrete and cosmic, particular and universal, corporeal and planetary, is born out of the infinitely reciprocal and unending relations existing among all the objects, realities, phenomena, associations, juxtapositions and links that the poem brings together for the first time. Poetry, like love, is revelation, because before the poem even existed and before the poet even encountered the life-giving eyes of the beloved, the world was an empty, colourless, uneventful place where nothing existed: no love, no light, no knowledge, no life; 'si je ne sais plus tout ce que j'ai vécu / C'est que tes yeux ne m'ont pas toujours vu', lines 4 and 5 declare. Without sight – that vision that accompanies and is informed by love – there is no being. Light, which makes the world visible, flows through the universe like blood coursing through the veins and arteries; light is to the world what blood is to the body. And imagination circulating through and among the words of the poem is the *blood* of language, giving it warmth, colour, flesh and life.

It could be said, then, that the curve ('la courbe') of the poem – the trajectory of its recurrence, of its embracing vision of a joyous surreal life – encircles not just the heart of the poet but that of its readers, to whom it offers a new way of simultaneously seeing and participating in the world. Turning round and round each other, like a 'rond de danse et de douceur' (l. 2), the poem's words and sounds – the abundant 'ou' and 'r' sounds and the syllabic repetition of 'rosée' in 'roseaux', 'parfums' in 'parfumés', 'chargés' in 'chasseurs', 'jour' in 'toujours' – perform a repetitive 'dance' that mirrors the 'pas de deux' of poet and beloved ceaselessly circling around and circulating within each other, all in rhythm with the beating of their hearts and the blinking of their eyes.

'La courbe de tes yeux' seems, thus, to end where it began: namely, with the image of eyes and heart; however, a significant chiastic reversal (yet another 'turning round') has taken place. Whereas the poem's first line described the encounter of the *organ* of sight with the *organ* of circulation (i.e. eyes and heart), the final line invokes the *emanations* (blood and gaze) these organs produce. And while the eyes in the opening line move to encircle the heart ('fait le tour') – one imagines that they merely touch or envelop the heart muscle – it is only in the final line that, all barriers having been removed, blood and light finally flow ('coule') freely into each other: a confluence of bodies and selves made real through unimpeded and unmediated love.

So the poem comes full circle and is itself a circle because the movement of the woman's eyes toward the poet's heart in line 1 is reversed in line 15; the poet's blood now advances towards and is united with the woman's sight. Like the heart, the poem becomes a closed system of circulation. What had moved from the *you* to the *I* in the first line ('*tes* yeux [font] le tour de *mon* cœur') reverses course at the poem's end, pumped back as it were, from the *I* to the *you*: '*mon* sang coule dans leurs regards' (i.e. 'les regards de *tes* yeux'). From the selfless exchange of identities, from the generous sharing of a man's and a woman's being, and from the blending of blood and light, self and world, subject and object, a couple comes into being. From the union of an *I* and a *you* is born the *we*: a word so irreducible, so indivisible, so tautological that its few letters express all that can be said about Surrealist life and love: 'nous étions vraiment ensemble, nous étions vraiment, nous étions, nous' ('Nuits partagées', I, p. 373). One unremarkable syllable, 'we' / 'nous', articulates everything about Surrealist experience that needs to be said. Only one other single-syllable word can be read as equally essential for Éluard: 'La femme que j'aime, je veux lui dire qu'il n'y a qu'un mot concret: *aime*, et pour qu'il lui tombe encore sous les sens, je le compléterai ainsi: *aime* à jamais' (I, p. 930, italics mine).

Notes

1 Paul Éluard, *Œuvres complètes*, 2 vols. (Paris: Gallimard, 1968), vol. II, p. 439; hereafter cited in the text.
2 For a detailed analysis of Éluard's poem and Lancôme's perfume, see Richard Stamelman, *Perfume: Joy, Scandal, Obsession, Sin; A Cultural History of Fragrance from 1750 to the Present* (New York: Rizzoli, 2006), pp. 204–12.
3 See André Breton's automatic poem 'Tournesol' and his commentary on the 'nuit du tournesol' in *Clair de terre* and *L'Amour fou* respectively. *Œuvres complètes*, 3 vols. (Paris: Gallimard, 1988–9), vol. I, pp. 187–8; vol. II, pp. 712–35.
4 When Éluard wrote, 'Que le langage se concrétise !' (I, p. 937), he meant it literally. Let words, he suggests, coalesce, and in their coming together within a poem let them create the realities they designate. Éluard's line, for example, 'L'amour est un caillou riant dans le soleil', upon which Lacan comments in his 'L'instance de la lettre dans l'inconscient' (*Écrits* (Paris: Seuil, 1966), p. 508), can be read, the psychoanalyst François Gantheret argues, as the demand that 'soudain un mot vient, le temps d'un éclair, non pas combler, non pas représenter, mais *présenter* . . . Ce caillou riant dans le soleil, ce ne sont pas mots qui parlent de l'amour, c'est l'amour naissant à ce moment-là dans les mots eux-mêmes, dans la chair des mots', *Moi, monde, mots* (Paris: Gallimard, 1996), p. 172.

Further reading

Bergez, Daniel, *Éluard, ou le rayonnement de l'être* (Seyssel: Champ Vallon, 1982).
Bowie, Malcolm, 'Paul Éluard', in *Sensibility and Creation: Studies in Twentieth-Century French Poetry*, ed. Roger Cardinal (New York: Barnes and Noble, 1977), pp. 149–67.
Decaunes, Luc, *Paul Éluard: l'amour, la révolte, le rêve* (Paris: Balland, 1982).
Éluard, Paul, *Last Love Poems*, trans. Marylin Kallet (Boston, MA: Black Widow Press, 2006).
  Capital of Pain, trans. Mary Ann Caws, Nancy Kline and Patricia Terry (Boston, MA: Black Widow Press, 2007).
  Love, Poetry, trans. Stuart Kendall (Boston, MA: Black Widow Press, 2007).
Gateau, Jean-Charles, *Paul Éluard, ou le frère voyant, 1895–1952* (Paris: Robert Laffont, 1988).
Guedj, Colette (ed.), *Éluard à cent ans: Actes du colloque de Nice (janvier 1996)* (Paris: L'Harmattan, 1998).
Jean, Raymond, *Éluard* (Paris: Seuil, 1997).

McNab, Robert, *Ghost Ships: A Surrealist Love Triangle* (New Haven, CT: Yale University Press, 2004).

Mingelgrün, Albert, *Essai sur l'évolution esthétique de Paul Éluard* (Lausanne: L'Âge d'homme, 1977).

Nugent, Robert, *Paul Éluard* (New York: Twayne Publishers, 1974).

Parrot, Louis, and Marcenac, Jean, *Paul Éluard* (Paris: Seghers, 2006).

Richard, Jean-Pierre, *Onze études sur la poésie moderne* (Paris: Seuil, 1964).

André Breton, 'Vigilance'

ELZA ADAMOWICZ

Vigilance

À Paris la tour Saint-Jacques chancelante
Pareille à un tournesol
Du front vient quelquefois heurter la Seine et son
    ombre glisse imperceptiblement parmi les remor-
    queurs   5
À ce moment sur la pointe des pieds dans mon sommeil
Je me dirige vers la chambre où je suis étendu
Et j'y mets le feu
Pour que rien ne subsiste de ce consentement qu'on
    m'a arraché   10
Les meubles font alors place à des animaux de même
    taille qui me regardent fraternellement
Lions dans les crinières desquels achèvent de se con-
    sumer les chaises
Squales dont le ventre blanc s'incorpore le dernier   15
    frisson des draps
À l'heure de l'amour et des paupières bleues
Je me vois brûler à mon tour je vois cette cachette
    solennelle de riens
Qui fut mon corps   20
Fouillée par les becs patients des ibis du feu
Lorsque tout est fini j'entre invisible dans l'arche
Sans prendre garde aux passants de la vie qui font
    sonner très loin leurs pas traînants
Je vois les arêtes du soleil   25
À travers l'aubépine de la pluie
J'entends se déchirer le linge humain comme une
    grande feuille
Sous l'ongle de l'absence et de la présence qui sont de
    connivence   30

Tous les métiers se fanent il ne reste d'eux qu'une
    dentelle parfumée
Une coquille de dentelle qui a la forme parfaite d'un
    sein
Je ne touche plus que le cœur des choses je tiens le fil   35

From *Le Revolver à cheveux blancs*

'Je me livre à ceux qui me lisent, les yeux bien ouverts'. (André Breton)

'Le sujet de ce livre est un être mobile', reads the publicity for André Breton's collection of poems *Le Revolver à cheveux blancs* (1932), where 'Vigilance' was first published.[1] Written in 1930–2, it is one of a sequence of longer poems in which Breton moves away from the partly automatic texts of *Clair de terre* (1923) to more consciously composed poems, often with a narrative development.

Critical interest in André Breton has focused primarily on his theoretical writings, his prose works and, more recently, his automatic texts. His poetry has largely been bypassed, disparaged as illustrations of his poetic theory, or dismissed as mantissa. In Julien Gracq's classic 'comprehensive' study of Breton's life and work, for example, the poems are conjured away in a phrase – 'les poèmes, – pour une bonne part manqués', and are never once quoted.[2] Such harsh judgements seem to be corroborated by Breton himself in a conversation with Charles Duits: 'Mes poèmes? Mais ils ne valent rien, cher ami! Je n'ai jamais écrit un seul vers qui me satisfît.'[3] Critical references to poems such as 'Vigilance' have thus tended to focus on isolated fragments, chosen to exemplify Breton's central theory of the poetic image as the encounter between disparate images ('Je vois les arêtes du soleil / à travers l'aubépine de la pluie'), developed in his 1924 *Manifeste du surréalisme*; or the concept of 'le point suprême' or resolution of opposites ('Je ne touche plus que le cœur des choses je tiens le fil'), elaborated in his second *Manifeste* of 1929.[4] This approach is inadequate, however, because Breton's poetic theory, focusing on the isolated hallucinatory image rather than sustained development, does not fully account for this poem.

The very mobility of a poem like 'Vigilance', its dense semantic interweaving of themes, its palimpsestic appearance, its enigmatic narrative development linking oneiric, alchemical, erotic and metapoetic elements, can make the reading of Breton's poetry difficult. Yet it presents a challenge for the reader and critic to consider the poem less as an enigma than as a mystery to be experienced, since, as J.-B. Pontalis writes, whereas the enigma can be deciphered, 'le mystère, lui, n'est pas déchiffrable, il échappe au langage, il va de pair avec la révélation, avec le dévoilement'.[5] If the poem unveils its meanings or reveals its mysteries, it is less in the sudden illumination resulting from the juxtaposition of disparate elements than in the gradual *dépaysement* experienced by the narrator in the initiatory process, and by the reader in the reading process. Above all, the poem is an open text: its poetic and narrative density – its shifting geographical spaces (from the Tour Saint-Jacques and the Seine, to the bedroom and the dream, and finally the ark), its mobile identities (the subject of enunciation as double, as Tour), its tensions between an account of an initiation and an affirmation of unity, its hallucinatory images – lends it a mysterious quality which simultaneously suggests several threads of interpretation and resists any single reading.

The poem can be read in relation to other texts by Breton. Indeed, he himself linked it to his early poem 'Tournesol' (1923),[6] which he later read as prophesying events of 'la nuit du Tournesol' (1934): the account of a walk through Paris at night with Jacqueline Lamba, who was to become his second wife, an experience which he considered as the realisation of the events recounted in the early poem, the imagined experience giving impetus and direction to the lived experience.[7] The poem is thus part of a constellation of texts and events, its significance inextricably linked for Breton with lived experience. 'L'imaginaire est ce qui tend à devenir réel', he writes in 'Il y aura une fois', the preface to *Le Revolver à cheveux blancs*.[8]

If we consider the poem itself, it appears to present a relatively coherent narrative framework, the topos of initiation, the account of a passage towards a state of illumination identified by Breton as the surreal. In fact, the poem can be considered as a paradigmatic development of the opening words of the preface: 'Imagination n'est pas don mais par excellence objet de conquête'.[9]

The poem's opening (ll. 1–5) evokes an image of Paris transformed, with its echoes of the poets Cendrars and Apollinaire, the painters Chagall or Delaunay. The Tour Saint-Jacques, both 'tour' and 'tournesol', tottering and falling into the Seine, transforms Paris into an imaginary space. The image of the tower, analogous to the mobile identity of the narrator of the poem, can be read as an indirect representation of the poet, through a process of identification common in dreams. Like the Tower, the subject moves from a vertical ('Je me dirige vers la chambre') to a horizontal position ('je suis étendu'); he shifts from an urban to an oneiric space; and he is doubled as narrator and participant of his dream, both actor ('j'y mets le feu') and spectator of his own transformation ('je me vois brûler').

In the second section (ll. 6–21), the bedroom becomes a site of metamorphosis, and is equated with the space of the dream. The subject-dreamer sets fire to the objects of his room, transforming its furniture into tamed animals: chairs into lions, sheets into sharks, and his own body, now food for the 'ibis du feu', into invisibility. In this gradual transformation, the subject as dreamer is disembodied ('brûler'), as lover he is feminised ('cette cachette solennelle de riens / . . . Fouillée'), and as poet depersonalised ('invisible'). Breton is staging a form of ritualistic loss of self, a burning where the poet purifies through fire the everyday reality around him, then his own body, in order to efface the 'consentement' which social reality has wrested from him. In this perspective, the 'vigilance' of the title can be read as a state of heightened awareness, a form of resistance to enforced consent to the everyday. This erasure of the poet as a restricted subjectivity, and the opening onto the experience of otherness, is central to the Surrealist experience.

The stage of ritualistic purification through fire gives access, in the last section of the poem (ll. 22–35), to a privileged, mythical space ('l'arche') distinct from reality (identifed with the distant 'passants de la vie'), where the metamorphosis of reality and self has been accomplished. 'Connivence' has replaced 'consentement': here, opposites come together ('sous l'ongle de l'absence et de la présence') and fire and water merge ('Je vois les arêtes du soleil / À travers l'aubépine de la pluie'). The essence of the experience is expressed, not on a cosmic scale, but in the erotic intimacy of metonymy ('paupières bleues', 'une coquille de dentelle qui a la forme parfaite d'un sein') evoking a sensual, feminised world with echoes of Mallarmé. Yet that world, even as it is glimpsed, is already lost. The weaving looms fade like flowers ('Tous les métiers se fanent'); all that survives is 'une dentelle parfumée', which becomes a simple 'fil', in a process of gradual dematerialisation (from 'drap' to 'linge', 'dentelle', and ultimately 'fil'). The final illumination can only be expressed in negative terms ('il ne reste d'eux qu'une dentelle. . . / Je ne touche plus que. . .'), the repetition of negative signifiers, as in Rimbaud, serving to point to rather than (re)create the 'inconnu'. Similarly the last line stresses discursively the presence and unity brought about by the poetic experience: 'Je ne touche plus que le cœur des choses je tiens le fil'. A tension is created between the revelatory sensuous apprehension of the dream ('Je. . . touche') and the mental activity of the dream process ('je tiens'), represented metaphorically by 'le fil', in an image which comments on the Surrealist practice of establishing poetic associations between disparate elements, unveiling a *'tissu capillaire'*[10] which unites inner and outer reality in a dynamic interchange. As Georges Durozoi writes: 'Tenir le fil, c'est tenir l'unité, ce qui relie les choses les unes aux autres'.[11] Our poet-Theseus may have tamed the monster, but he is still in the labyrinth, his Ariadne an insubstantial 'coquille de dentelle', the sensual memory of a female breast, the trace of a perfume.

Breton's poetry stages the desire to transcend opposites and abolish polarities, yet that desire is rarely fully realised, whence the importance of narrativisation, as in this poem, which focuses on the passage towards the surreal, the evocation of a partial surrealisation of space rather than a confident *être-là* of surreal space. Thus in Breton's poems the 'arche' – and its avatars the crystal, the castle or the prism – are only fleetingly alluded to, rarely fully inhabited. The poem reveals moreover an analogy between the concepts of *l'ailleurs* and *l'autre*: both are based on the parallel processes of *dépaysement* and depersonalisation, which we have seen at work in this poem. Access to the surreal must pass for Breton through the familiar *pays* – from Paris seen to Paris imagined, from bedroom to dream space – just as access to alterity can only be accomplished through the death of the subject.

'Quoi de plus cohérent qu'un poème pourtant d'inspiration onirique comme "Vigilance"', claims Philippe Jaccottet.[12] Yet the relative coherence presented by the development of the initiatory narrative discussed above is disrupted by the presence in the poem of disjunctive discourses: on the one hand the duality of the narrating and dreaming 'I'; and on the other hand the tensions between the affirmation of unity and the play of contradictions. Firstly, the 'je' alternately or simultaneously experiences and reflects on his dream, a duality characteristic of Surrealism which was as interested in the conscious interpretation of dream material as it was in recording the mind's unconscious workings: 'il a tout intérêt à les capter, à les capter d'abord, pour les soumettre ensuite, s'il y a lieu, au contrôle de notre raison'.[13] Thus the poet, far from simply coinciding with the flux of the unconscious, appears also as the lucid observer of his own visions: both *voyant* and agent of his own metamorphoses and *voyeur* of the operations of his imagination. In this context, the title 'Vigilance' suggests attentiveness to both the content and the processes of the dream. The poem is thus self-generating and self-reflexive. Breton kept safely away from the abyss of madness: the *garde-fou* which protected the poet was a form of lucidity of the irrational, recalling Dalí's paranoia-criticism, in which the poet achieves a schizoid form of consciousness in a self-reflexive movement where he is at once self and other, through a process described by Maurice Blanchot as 'cet effort suprême par lequel l'homme veut se retourner sur soi et se saisir d'un regard qui n'est plus le sien'.[14]

Disruption also operates on the global level of the poem, which stages a dialectical tension between contradiction and synthesis. The search for the resolution of opposites or 'point suprême' lies at the heart of Breton's theoretical writings and on the horizon of his poetic works. In his *Manifeste du surréalisme* he defines the surreal as 'la résolution future de ces deux états, en apparence si contradictoires, que sont le rêve et la réalité'.[15] Note that the resolution is projected into the future, and often displaced, as in this poem, by a focus on the dialectic as process, passage and transformation, suggesting the gradual dispossession of the material, a journeying towards the surreal rather than a fulfilment or the confident inhabiting of the 'point suprême'. The poet creates a space of complicity, of dynamic interrelations between opposites ('Sous l'ongle de l'absence et de la présence qui sont de connivence'). Indeed it is rare to find in Breton's texts a final 'illumination' or synthesis. As he writes in *L'Amour fou*: 'J'ai parlé d'un certain "point sublime" dans la montagne. Il ne fut jamais question de m'établir à demeure en ce point.'[16] While Breton advocates a philosophy of unity, he practises a poetics of the fragment or of passage – 'une poétique de l'étincelle longue', in the words of Jacqueline Chénieux-Gendron[17] – and the narrative structure charts the stages of this process.

The reference to the Hegelian dialectic, which underpins the narrative structure of the poem, is interwoven with allusions to the alchemists' search for the philosopher's stone or 'point suprême'. Indeed, in his writings Breton constantly underlines the parallel between Hegelian, alchemic and poetic processes. The alchemic reference is over-determined in this poem by the implicit metonymical link between alchemy and the Tour Saint-Jacques. Quoting the first two lines of the poem in *L'Amour fou*, Breton comments explicitly on the convergence of the motifs of the Tower, the sunflower, and alchemy:

> Le rapprochement ainsi opéré rend un compte satisfaisant de l'idée complexe que je me fais de la tour, tant de sa sombre magnificence assez comparable à celle de la fleur . . . que des circonstances assez troubles qui ont présidé a son édification et auxquelles on sait que le rêve millénaire de la transmutation des métaux était étroitement lié.[18]

The poetic or oneiric transformations of everyday reality are linked, through the metaphor of fire, to the alchemic process, where fire has the power to transmute base reality. The transformation of the Tour Saint-Jacques is effected through the alchemic paradigm: 'tournesol' (in its double meaning as flower and litmus paper) contains, prolongs, and transubstantiates 'tour'. Alchemic imagery thus functions metaphorically both on the narrative and metapoetic planes. The burning of the furniture and of the self acts as a *mise en abyme*: the dream process itself transforms reality, thus providing an analogy for the poetic process. Moreover, the erotic metaphor has often been used as a paradigmatic narrative of alchemic transmutation. In this perspective the opening lines can be read as an allegory of the sexual act, where the tower is the alter ego of the subject. The erotic paradigm continues in the image of fire, of the sexual act consummated ('le dernier frisson des draps' / 'J'entends se déchirer le linge humain'), and in the allusion to the female body as fetishistic fragment ('Une coquille de dentelle. . . sein'). The poem can thus be seen to materialise Breton's concept of 'beauté convulsive': 'érotique-voilée' (allegory of erotic encounter), 'explosante-fixe' (burning of banal reality, metamorphosis by fire into animals), 'magique circonstancielle' (transformation of the Tour Saint-Jacques).[19]

Although alchemic interpretation proposes a key to decipher the enigmas of the world, offering a totalising account of natural and mental processes, encompassing all signs within a grand narrative, one should not conclude too quickly that alchemy can provide a comprehensive interpretive model for the poem. References to alchemy in fact provide less a hermeneutic key than a poetic analogy between artistic creation and the process of transformation of base matter. Alchemic imagery points to the hermeticism of images rather than proposing a hermeneutics, and the poem, as suggested above, remains a mystery, not an enigma.

The interweaving of themes, the intertextual allusions, and the disruptions of the narrative resist any single interpretative strategy, presenting a challenge to the reader to experience such poems as an open-ended mental adventure, 'un être mobile'. As the Surrealist poet Paul Éluard wrote – well aware of both the complexity and revelatory aspect of Breton's poems – when offering Breton a signed copy of *Ralentir Travaux*: 'Mon cher André, nous parlons la même langue. Mais je ne suis pas encore habitué à ta pensée. J'en vois toujours s'ouvrir de nouvelles portes, toutes les aubes en sont nouvelles.'

Notes

1 André Breton, *Le Revolver à cheveux blancs* (Paris: Éditions des Cahiers Libres, 1932), p. 156. This edition contains poems from Breton's earlier collections of poems, *Mont de piété* (1919), *Les Champs magnétiques* (1920) and *Clair de terre* (1923), and a section of more recent poems (1924–32). 'Vigilance' was subsequently published in *Poèmes* (Paris: Gallimard, 1948), *Clair de terre* (Paris: Gallimard, 1966) and *Œuvres complètes*, vol. II (*OCII*) (Paris: Gallimard, 1992), p. 94.

2 Julien Gracq, *André Breton* (Paris: José Corti, 1948), p. 98.

3 Charles Duits, *André Breton a-t-il dit passe* (Paris: Denoël, 1969), p. 166.

4 The only substantial published analysis of the poem to my knowledge is by Rainer Stiller, 'André Breton: *Vigilance*', in Helmut Köhler (ed.), *Interpretationen. Französische Gedichte des 19. und 20. Jahrhunderts* (Stuttgart: Philipp Reclam, 2001), pp. 252–64.

5 J.-B. Pontalis, *Frère du précédent* (Paris: Gallimard, 2006), p. 133.

6 *Œuvres complètes*, vol. I (*OCI*) (Paris: Gallimard, 1988), p. 187.

7 *L'Amour fou* (1937), in *OCII*, p. 717.

8 'Il y aura une fois', in *OCII*, p. 50.

9 *Ibid.*, p. 49.

10 *Ibid.*, p. 202.

11 Gérard Durozoi and Bernard Lecherbonnier, *André Breton. L'Écriture surréaliste* (Paris: Larousse, 1974), p. 184.

12 Philippe Jaccottet, 'Un discours à crête de flamme', *La Nouvelle Revue Française*, 172 (1 April 1967), p. 803.

13 Breton, *Manifeste du surréalisme*, in *OCI*, p. 316.

14 Maurice Blanchot, *La Part du feu* (Paris: Gallimard, 1949), p. 100.

15 *OCI*, p. 319.

16 *OCII*, pp. 782–3.

17 Jacqueline Chénieux-Gendron, 'Plaisir(s) de l'image', in *Du surréalisme et du plaisir* (Paris: José Corti, 1986), p. 89.

18 *L'Amour fou*, p. 717.

19 *OCII*, p. 687.

Further reading

Adamowicz, Elza, *Ceci n'est pas un tableau: les écrits surréalistes sur l'art* (Lausanne: L'Âge d'homme, 2004).

Bonnefoy, Yves, *Breton à l'avant de soi* (Tours: Farrago, 2001).

Balakian, Anna, *André Breton: Magus of Surrealism* (Oxford: Oxford University Press, 1971).

Bonnet, Marguerite, *André Breton: naissance de l'aventure surréaliste* (Paris: José Corti, 1975).

Breton, André, *Poems of André Breton*, trans. Jean-Pierre Cauvin and Mary Ann Caws (Boston, MA: Black Widow Press, 2005).

Breuil, Eddie, Pair de terre *d'André Breton* (Paris: Gallimard, 2009).

Caws, Mary Ann, *André Breton, Revisited* (New York: Twayne Publishers, 1996).

Gracq, Julien, *André Breton: quelques aspects de l'écrivain* (Paris: José Corti, 1989).

Rabaté, Jean-Michel, *La Pénultième est morte: spectographies de la modernité* (Seyssel: Champ Vallon, 1993).

11 Louis Aragon, 'Elsa je t'aime'

TOM CONLEY

Elsa je t'aime

Au biseau des baisers
Les ans passent trop vite
Évite évite évite
Les souvenirs brisés

Oh toute une saison qu'il avait fait bon vivre   5
Cet été fut trop beau comme un été des livres
Insensé j'avais cru pouvoir te rendre heureuse
Quand c'était la forêt de la Grande Chartreuse
Ou le charme d'un soir dans le port de Toulon
Bref comme est le bonheur qui survit mal à l'ombre   10

Au biseau des baisers
Les ans passent trop vite
Évite évite évite
Les souvenirs brisés

Je chantais l'an passé quand les feuilles jaunirent   15
Celui qui dit adieu croit pourtant revenir
Il semble à ce qui meurt qu'un monde recommence
Il ne reste plus rien des mots de la romance
Regarde dans mes yeux qui te voient si jolie
N'entends-tu plus mon cœur ni moi ni ma folie   20

Au biseau des baisers
Les ans passent trop vite
Évite évite évite
Les souvenirs brisés

Le soleil est pareil au pianiste blême   25
Qui chantait quelques mots les seuls toujours les mêmes
Chérie Il t'en souvient de ces jours sans menace
Quand nous habitions tous deux à Montparnasse

La vie aura coulé sans qu'on y prenne garde
Le froid revient Déjà le soir Le cœur retarde   30

    Au biseau des baisers
    Les ans passent trop vite
    Évite évite évite
    Les souvenirs brisés

Ce quatrain qui t'a plu pour sa musique triste   35
Quand je te l'ai donné comme un trèfle flétri
Stérilement dormait au fond de ma mémoire
Je le tire aujourd'hui de l'oublieuse armoire
Parce que lui du moins tu l'aimais comme on chante
Elsa je t'aime ô ma touchante ô ma méchante   40

    Les ans passent trop vite
    Au biseau des baisers
    Évite évite évite
    Les souvenirs brisés

Rengaine de cristal murmure monotone   45
Ce n'est jamais pour rien que l'air que l'on fredonne
Dit machinalement des mots comme des charmes
Un jour vient où les mots se modèlent aux larmes
Ah fermons ce volet qui bat sans qu'on l'écoute
Ce refrain d'eau tombe entre nous comme une goutte   50

    Évite évite évite
    Les souvenirs brisés
    Au biseau des baisers
    Les ans passent trop vite

From *Le Crève-cœur*

'Doing with' Aragon: 'Elsa je t'aime'

Contradictory as their other views may be, specialists in communication and psychoanalysts agree that life begins with separation. In communication theory an original statement, a first act of communication, is 'originary' because it is made *in response* to another act that prompts its expression. Whatever begins is preceded by something that causes it to gain cognisance of its own beginning. The words or signs that initiate a dialogue imply that whoever or whatever emits them is separated in some way in time and space from what elicits the expression, as it were, in the first place. The grounding conundrum is that communication begins 'in the second place' and that as a consequence for the communicator, communication inaugurates a sense of displacement at the very site of its expression. Almost invariably every statement contains an element of deixis indicating that the speaker is 'here' and the receiver is 'there'. Yet, at the same time the speaker or writer at once locates and loses the place he or she occupies in the process of speaking and writing.[1]

For the psychoanalyst, whether of Freudian or Kleinian bias, the 'originary' moment of life to which a person always returns in most instances of communication is that of separation 'into' the world at large. The speaker frequently feels isolation, which prompts an often traumatising sense of existence as soon as words are spoken: when they are sent into space without the assurance that they will find receivers or, if they do, that they will bear meaning. In the secure surrounding of the hourly session the analysand rehearses, sometimes consciously and sometimes not, the anxiety that comes with the eternal return to separation that inspires symbolic activity. The patient having money and leisure enough to undergo analysis gains the unsettling reward of recalling how communication is built upon an affirmation of absence, indeed what Montaigne asserted – and what we imagine him saying – in the isolation of his tower: 'nous n'avons aucune communication à l'estre'. We have no communication with being or presence; as a result we persist in speaking and writing in order to cope with what their expression brings forward.

French poets writing in the heyday of psychoanalytical discoveries often build their verse on the fact that separation is a vital component of communication. The verse that we recall from the great writers belonging to the age of Freud and his followers brings us 'back' to a searing but paradoxically enthusing anxiety of separation. It carries greater pathos insofar as it is written in the midst of limit-situations – of imminent or current war, carnage and death – in which the presence of a sender and a receiver is in doubt. Wherever it intones of love and of sublimities of wonder and aura, the poetry is exceptionally fragile and, no less paradoxically, borne by creative force. Such are the poems Louis Aragon assembled and published under the title of *Le Crève-cœur* (1941)[2], that tell of the effects of being shattered both into love and into the Second World War. The poems tell of the stakes of writing poetry when circumstance would otherwise be cause for silence: when words fall short of actions and deeds that in themselves are in deficit in view of the exodus and Occupation of 1940. The poems attest to the fact that affection and empathy are crucial for the very survival of poetry as such. Many of Aragon's most unforgettable poems – unforgettable because they cause their reader to return to trauma through masterful lyrical control and sparkle of wit – are gathered in this collection.

With 'Richard II Quarante', 'Elsa je t'aime' counts among the most remembered (and, as it will be shown below, *recited*) among all of Aragon's verse. Standing as the last poem in the collection, 'Elsa je t'aime' is set in place to recall the epigraph of the book in which it first appears. At the headpiece, 'À Elsa, chaque battement de mon cœur', suggests that each poem might be a heartbeat. At the same time the name of the dedicatee aims the eyes of the reader towards the poem that would seem to be the keystone of the collection.[3] A correspondence is established within the collection, and so also is a suggestive sense of destiny, a *destinataire* or receiver, and a destination. The title can be construed to be a whisper, a sigh or a cry that may or may not be heard, and what follows to be words that could bear a fate similar to a poem in a corked bottle tossed into the sea. The poem anticipates 'Les Yeux d'Elsa', published in the following year (1942) while suggesting that the words that follow are immediate, unabashed, and drawn *literally*, as both the epigraph and title indicate, from a poet's heart.

'Elsa je t'aime' is said to have been written after the fall of France, while the author, who had been in the French armed forces as an auxiliary aide, was stationed in Carcassonne in October 1940.[4] It is set in the context of 'vers de circonstance', all carefully dated to mark the vagaries of the instant in which the creation takes place. Each poem in the collection thus becomes an *event* because of a sense of fragility, of plight and of isolation of the sender from the reader. War is so invasive that a companion piece, *Le Poème interrompu* reflects the very moment when the author is forced to post the verse in the mail early in the morning on 10 May 1940, just as he is sent on assignment from his billet in Audencourt.

The simplicity of the title that seems born of breath or *souffle* is bespoken by the formal control of the refrain (reiterated six times) that introduces, punctuates and completes the verse. On cursory glance five stanzas of six alexandrines each, in *rimes plates* (aabbcc) are set in alternation with the refrain of four lines, in hexameter, in *rimes embrassées* (abba). Closer inspection reveals that on two occasions – perhaps because the poem marks the haste of its composition, hence the fragility of the occasion – faulty rhymes (stanza 1, ll. 5–6 and stanza 4, ll. 1–2) break the otherwise self-containing effects of symmetry. The inaugural refrain responds to the title as if it were an inner reflection of fear and longing. It could be apprehension mixed with regret and warning associated with a *carpe diem* or *carpe noctem* issuing from a place, *on ne sait où*, outside, elsewhere, like Baudelaire's *anywhere out of this world*. The stanzas are composed of paratactic lines that in themselves are units, as it were, of inner monologue. Each stanza thus accumulates six 'events' or thought-flashes, first coming out of the past, that bear on the present moment of the writing of the poem. Yet at the very point of its conclusion the refrain turns the poem back on itself and causes it to 'loop' in indefinite repetition.

The visual shape can be seen both as circular in form (much like that of the eternal return implied by the refrain of Apollinaire's 'Le Pont Mirabeau', a poem that seems present in 'Elsa je t'aime') and serial or ordered in spatial units, whereby the refrain stands in emblematic relation with what is printed above or below. In the first instance, in accord with the formal design of an emblem, 'Au biseau des baisers. . .' (ll. 1–4) would be a visual shape, an *inscriptio* or an image

set below the *superscriptio* or 'motto' of the title. It would beg for oblique explication by the verse in *subscriptio* below. Each block of verse that follows would
then change its role in being now a superscription, then an inscription, then
again a subscription, and so on, in order to call attention at once to the visual
and lexical form of a poem designed to be seen as it is read (and vice versa). From
this standpoint the poem also resembles a ballad reminiscent of the thirteen
ballads intercalated in François Villon's *Grant Testament* (c. 1463, first printed
in 1489), that play on the repetition and difference emerging from the various
inflexions of the refrain at the end of each of their three stanzas and their final
flourish or *envoi* that recoups and redirects the play of meaning.

The refrain inaugurates the poem much like an *incipit* of a late medieval
rondeau that 'strikes back' (from *fraindre*) in the final lines of each stanza, with
the difference that here the quatrain is detached or separated from the groups
of alexandrines that tell of the past moments two lovers had shared before the
voice turns to the present moment of the poem in its unfinished creation. 'Au
biseau des baisers': what is it to be on the *biseau*, the bevel of kisses? Implied
is that the lovers' lips are chamfered and that they are an embrasure, and that
from the aural and visual resemblance of *bisou* to *biseau* a labial fantasy is born:
both in the figure of two pairs of lips that might meet from indirect angles and
in recall of a highly charged feminine image, belonging to feminine poetry, in
which breath and speech are figured flowing over soft labial ridges.[5] The breath
of the soul seems to carry the line in an effectively simple alliteration in which
the arcs of the letter *B* that meet at a mouth in the middle of the vertical bar are
said to evoke the very shape of lips that close before the slightly plosive consonant is voiced.[6] The implied grammar of the first two lines suggests that 'years
are passing too quickly on the bias of *baisers*'. The second line would be what
is literally whispered or spoken on the bevel of the lips, and the third either a
response to the second or piece of confused inner monologue – confused in
meaning but limpid in form – in which the call to avoid or to veer (obliquely)
away is homonymous with acceleration: *et vite et vite et vite*. The person to whom
the poem is addressed is asked to steer away from the 'broken memories' of the
last line: yet in the simple syntax, breakage is one with the aural and visual
form of the 'biseau des baisers'. In the last line the shattered memories carry a
sense of anticipation, of something 'underneath' (*sous*, the preposition that slips
obliquely into *biseau* by way of association with *bisou*) or unknown that may
come (*venir*). The refrain thus becomes a perfect tourniquet whose inflection
changes with each repetition in what follows.

Beyond its recall of Louise Labé, the apostrophe inaugurating the first stanza
underlines further the mix of parataxis and formal control. Each of the alexandrines seems built about a brief syncopation or break at the hemistich. The effect
is one where otherwise ephemeral flickers of memory are suddenly eternalised
in classical form. 'Oh toute une saison. . .': like the Rimbaldian flash of the
sun going off with the sea in 'L'Éternité' ('C'est la mer allée / Avec le soleil'),[7]

the *incipit* underscores how much the interlocutors are separated at once from one another and how much, too, they are at a remove from the emotive landscape they had shared. The first line of the second stanza further indicates that the poem is entrenched in the tradition of *seasons*. Like the troubadours, the rhétoriqueurs, Ronsard (of the *Hymnes*), and even Baudelaire and Mallarmé, Aragon stages the poem in the turmoil of autumn, the moment when, in the midst of war, the promise of a return of spring or of growth (say, Hugo's 'palpitation sauvage du printemps' when Pan inspires the awakening of nature in 'Le Satyre') is faint and even remote. In the last two lines the voice that speaks to itself in its chronicle of bygone bliss suddenly turns to address the reader who is Elsa. In asking her to *see* his eyes in hers (much as does Éluard in his verse), he wonders if she might *hear* his heart and his madness. As in the literature of early modern print culture, the existence of a receiver or a reader is cast in doubt. For that reason the third instance of the refrain, unlike the second that seeks recall of the days before the invasion and exodus (in June), draws attention to a voice that seems to echo from *anywhere out of the past*, the toponyms and events mentioned in the first stanza notwithstanding.

The third stanza nonetheless returns, like a refrain, to moments and places shared in the recent past. As in the two that precede, the keynote rhymes – that juxtapose words that would hardly be contiguous – are set in the centre, at the end of the third and fourth lines. '*Chérie*' (in italics at the beginning of the third line), an unlikely apostrophe recalling the beginning of the poem, would be the pallid but vital 'sunshine' of memory taken from popular songs. The poet affirms that the most intensely lived experience belongs not in higher realms of sublimity but in everyday circumstance. For the first time the fluid sense of passage in the refrain is echoed in the body of the poem. The fifth line displaces the sensation of passage the reader gathers from recalling Apollinaire's 'Pont Mirabeau' by the Seine, below the Eiffel Tower, to Montparnasse (a site, as it will be shown, that contains a secret that will become variously shared among different generations of readers). When fluid passage of time is cast into the future anterior the topos of the *carpe noctem* is enhanced when set in the implied season of winter ('Le froid revient'). Seasonal alternation is stopped where the upper-case D of *Déjà* signals that whatever is 'already' is always both done and yet to come. The uncanny spacing of 'Le froid revient Déjà le soir Le cœur retarde' removes signs of 'punctuation' that would otherwise mark the shifts in time being described.

By virtue of its spatial design and mix of formal control and free play (notably with only faint alternation of masculine and feminine rhyme) the poem correlates the last words of the third stanza, 'Le cœur retarde', to the now accelerated tempo of the refrain just below. Although the quatrain emphasises the sheer velocity of affective time the fourth stanza that follows takes pause by turning the reflection towards the very writing and shape of the words and letters on the page. The poem folds upon itself while holding to its own measure. It draws upon its own resources and gains distance from itself in telling of its own genesis and of Elsa, who, in the words of Jean Ristat and his team of exegetes, becomes 'not only the object of the love poetry, but the interlocutrix of the poet . . . The love for Elsa immediately turns reflexively upon itself, recounting too the beloved's reception of the poem being addressed and dedicated to her.'[8] Reiteration of the title in the poem, at the beginning of the last line (that offers visual contrast to '*Chérie*' thirteen lines above) engages the almost contractual condition in which the poem is enjoined to speak for, or, as one reader would have it, in the name of its name.[9] The quatrain that has carried the poem is now described as a matter of fact. If it is an infertile object that the author draws from a 'forgetful closet', it is taken, too, from a rich and vast memory-bank of poetry and poems.[10] In this context the fifth instance of the refrain lays stress on the verse as a piece of machinery or a highly efficient system engineered to hold and retrieve a variety of affective matter.

The autonomy that the words gain in respect to its author or speaker becomes the object of reflection in the last stanza. A mechanism likened to a TSF (*télégraphie sans fil*) or a gramophone emitting a 'murmure monotone', 'Elsa je t'aime' appears to evacuate itself of its own pathos. What it describes in the final alexandrine as its 'refrain d'eau' that 'falls between us' – in the space (of) its own form, in the gap between the narrative gist and the refrain itself – at once emphasises the fluid and funereal character of memory (*eau tombe* can be read as a spoonerism that echoes *tomb-eau* which would be the very 'armoire' or vault of the lyric) and its continuous looping. When *Eau* is heard as the homophone of *Oh*, the apostrophe that begins the poem proper, it points to the sixth instance of the refrain as that which both begins and ends the tale told in verse. Already the stanza recoups two different 'speeds' of poetry by saying the air the poet hums ('fredonne') utters words 'mechanically'. But then again, the form reminds us of the presence of classical notes, 'charmes', of words which (from *carmen*) sing and seduce. From this standpoint the refrain at once entrances and repeats itself like a broken record. The one tone or mood calls the other into question.

The legacy of 'Elsa je t'aime' indicates how it has been read and what, given the passage of almost seventy years and various technological revolutions, can be done with it.[11] Jean-Luc Godard cites the refrain at a crucial turn in *À bout de souffle* (1960), ostensibly in order to recall the brilliance of Aragon's verse and to have it figure in the loose tessellations of a love story told at a time, at the height of the Cold War, when the destiny of the world is in doubt. In *À bout de souffle* Patricia (Jean Seberg), an American college student, has encountered Michel (Jean-Paul Belmondo), a French hooligan and car thief, who identifies with the persona of Humphrey Bogart. He is madly in love with her, but she is unsure if her attraction is to him or to the language and culture she believes he embodies. Having unwittingly murdered a motorcycle cop after being apprehended for violating the speed limits in the stolen car he was delivering from Marseille to Paris, Michel finds her and, awaiting the money he will obtain for delivering a car (not the Oldsmobile he had been driving, but another that he steals during his adventures in Paris), he invites her to find bliss and solace with him in Italy. The police cast a dragnet over Paris. In evading the law the couple take sanctuary in a cinema (the Napoléon) by the Champs-Elysées where they embrace while a Western is being shown.[12]

In its economy, in strong contrast to the others, the sequence in the cinema lasts no more than thirty seconds. Patricia and Michel, in close-up and in profile in the darkness of the theatre, embrace each other. Two voices over, one masculine and the other feminine, reply to each other through two poems that each recites. Godard's voice intones the refrain of 'Elsa je t'aime' before a woman quotes a piece from Apollinaire's 'Cors de chasse' (from *Alcools*). Aragon's verse begins with an apocryphal line, 'Méfie-toi Jessica' just as Apollinaire's begins with 'Et Thomas de Quincey buvant' (as if to cue the alcoholic origin of what will follow), which leads into 'L'opium poison doux et chaste / À sa pauvre Anne allait rêvant / Passons passons puisque tout passe / Je me retournerai souvent / Les souvenirs sont cors de chasse / Dont meurt le bruit parmi le vent.' Aragon (male) and Apollinaire (female) are whispered or *soufflés* into the film in such a way that it is impossible to discern to whom the voices belong, who is thinking what, and whence comes the verse itself. The poems are enigmas that distinguish a knowing viewer – bred on modern French poetry – from his or her counterpart – a neophyte – who stands to learn not only from the charm of the allusion and mix of voices but also the words as they figure in a gamut of citations that turn the film into a moving hieroglyph. The graft of 'Les ans passent trop vite / Évite évite évite' onto 'Passons passons puisque tout passe' establishes a 'rupture of contact' doubled by the lips of the two protagonists who kiss in the cinema. The poems attest to a history and an affiliation with the 'modern' that both Apollinaire and Aragon had espoused in their re-enactment of the *Querelle des anciens et des modernes*, the former in 'Zone', his poem-paean to the Eiffel Tower, and the latter in *Le Paysan de Paris*, a manual for the spatial practice of everyday life in the City of Light.

Surely in the formula 'au biseau des baisers', the 'bevel' or 'bias' refers to how Aragon's poem is incised (or again, whispered, *soufflé*) into the film and shown, seen in its absent presence. When the poem is spoken (remarkably in Godard's grainy voice) or slipped anamorphically into the image of the lovers, its *graphic* traits become keynote. Marie-Claire Ropars notes that when the refrain is quoted,

> the vocalisation of the poem – O biso de bésé – allows the alphabet that it nonetheless takes up to be deviated: in order to read A b s d b s in this line the text would need to be seen and not heard. The phonetisation thwarts the repetitive alphabetisation; in the concatenation [*engrenage* or even montage] of letters the[re is a] fracture of an aberrant sonority: the voice is what allows the inaugural *a* to be suppressed and replaced by an *o* in echo, an *é* that is prolonged over three measures [bésé . . . évite].[13]

She argues that through Aragon and Apollinaire, two authors who are instances of the letter A, we witness a 'conspiracy of writing' in which neither poet is mentioned nor any attribution made. Each begins by apocryphal deviation ('Méfie-toi' and 'Et Thomas. . .') where invention meets citation. She argues that by eradicating the signature the origins of the poems are endowed with the originary force of pure poetry. 'The quotation [*citation*] becomes recitation [*récitation*], and the text that is written, that informs the montage of the film, is both at once doubled [one would say quoted, even ventriloquised] and erased.'[14]

By way of this reading it can be said that the film brings forward virtues that already inhere in the poem. In Aragon's melody, especially in the refrain of 'Elsa je t'aime', which is both a machine and a piece of lyrical memory, we read and see verse based on the 'interpenetration of the sign and the figure' or of voice and the montage of writing. Elsewhere in the film Aragon is indirectly recalled proverbially. The casual remark 'il n'y a pas d'amour heureux' bears on the two protagonists' puppy-love and the finale that replays the Orphic ending of a variety of Hollywood films (from *High Sierra* to *Gun Crazy*).[15] Here and elsewhere Aragon is ubiquitous in *À bout de souffle*. Close inspection reveals that the memories of his love poetry seep into a context in which, in the later post-war years, the verse might otherwise be forgotten. The circumstance of separation that inflects, indeed that 'bevels' the writing of Aragon's poem, is projected upon two lovers. Wherever they are they are shown far from each other in the midst of their proximity. Contrary to the voice and writing of 'Elsa je t'aime', they are far from the political and historical context in which they circulate. In the long sequence (of nine minutes and fifteen seconds) immediately preceding the recitation of the refrain, Patricia and Michel scurry, one after the other, through a crowd (filmed from the second floor of an apartment) pressed along the two sides of the Champs Elysées. Earlier a radio report was heard, like the poem itself – whispered into the field of the image – announcing that De Gaulle and Eisenhower were to meet at the tomb of the Unknown Soldier and be part of a great parade from the Arc de Triomphe to the eastern end of the boulevard. Before the couple take refuge in the cinema and remain oblivious to the recitation of the poems, the camera records wedges of motorcycles moving down the Avenue, in the midst of a fanfare, just before the film cuts short of displaying the two leaders in their motorised cavalcade. The editing of the sequence implies that the two powers, France and America, are, like the two lovers, far from one another; and further, it suggests that the precarious state of the world almost goes without notice until, in the next sequence, Aragon intervenes. The invasion and exodus of France in 1940, the backdrop to 'Elsa je t'aime', reminds us of the failed 'accords' (especially the Hitler–Stalin pact) that led to worldwide disaster.

The pathos of the circumstance in which both leaders and lovers fail to reach agreement in 1959 is made clear through the persisting memory of the poem in the final sequences of the film. Patricia and Michel spend their last hours in a photographer's studio located in Montparnasse on the rue Campagne-Première. Before Patricia informs the police about where they are, she and her companion share a brief moment – another rupture of contact or contact of separation – at a site indicated by the lines of the third stanza: 'Quand nous habitions tous deux à Montparnasse / La vie aura coulé sans qu'on y prenne garde / Le froid revient Déjà le soir Le cœur retarde. . .'. Aragon's exegetes note that reference is made to an apartment at 5 rue Campagne-Première, where the author and Elsa Triolet resided from April 1929 until they moved to rue de la Courdière in February 1935, which is indeed the street in which Godard films the Orphic conclusion to *À bout de souffle*.[16] It is said that Godard had an apartment on the same street and that he was folding an autobiographical secret into the film. If a secret it was, it was recited (or whispered) through the memory of Aragon, with whom identification is not only serendipitously typographical and topographical but also sentimental and, in its critical force, entirely existential. Godard lives *through* Aragon. He does 'with' Aragon what the poet did so masterfully with his own poem.

Notes

1 It suffices to superimpose Jacques Derrida's conclusions to 'signature événement contexte' in *Marges de la philosophie* (Paris: Éditions de Minuit, 1975) over those of Michel de Certeau in his chapter of *L'Invention du quotidien*, vol. I: *Arts de faire*, ed. Luce Giard (Paris: Gallimard, 1990) on speech and spatiality. For Certeau discourse and dialogue – or communication *tout court* – are forces that turn the inertia of 'place' into the agency of 'space'. Derrida reminds his readers that whatever goes by the name of 'communication' is not what many believe it to be: it does not bear the fullness or warmth of 'presence' (in the philosophical and theological notions of the word) because all communication presupposes a distance or absence that it must necessarily fail to overcome.

2 Louis Aragon, *Le Crève-cœur, Le Nouveau Crève-cœur* (Paris: Gallimard, 1980), pp. 58–60.

3 A slight exception might be made for 'Les Lilas et les roses', Aragon's most famous poem recounting the chaos, confusion and ultimately the tragedy of the fall of France, insofar as *Elsa* is the name, written across the title, that ties the lilacs to the roses.

4 Jean Ristat, 'Hors d'œuvre', note appended to Aragon, *L'Œuvre poétique*, vol. IX (1939–42) (Paris: Livre Club Diderot, 1979) n. 19 (p. 398) and n. 33 (p. 400).

5 The well-named Louise Labé, the poet par excellence of kisses, draws attention to the erotic beauty of labia at the end of her thirteenth sonnet, 'O si j'estois en ce beau sein ravie' (l. 1), when she sighs, hoping that in tenderness her lover 'me baiseroit, / Et mon esprit sur les lèvres fuiroit, / Bien je mourrois, plus que vivante, heureuse.' Here, as in Aragon's poem, the soul of the beloved is exhaled on the lips of her lover in 'an eternal kiss'. See François Rigolot, a propos the *mors oculi* in his edition of *Louise Labé: Œuvres complètes* (Paris: Garnier/Flammarion, 1986), p. 128.

6 See [Robert] Massin, *Lettre et image*, with a preface by Raymond Queneau (Paris: Gallimard, 1973), p. 100, fig. 272 – from *ABC Trim. Alphabet enchanté* (Paris: Hachette, 1861). Massin cites the epigraph: 'Plus d'enfant récitant ses lettres de travers ! En une heure on apprend l'alphabet et cent vers !' (p. 286).

7 In Daniel Leuwers (ed.), *Rimbaud: Poésies complètes* (Paris: Librairie Générale Française, 1984), pp. 109–10.

8 In Jean Ristat (ed.), *Aragon: Œuvres poétiques complètes*, vol. I (Paris: Gallimard/Pléiade, 2007), pp. 1453–4.

9 Jacques Derrida, 'Le Titrier: Titre à préciser', in *Parages* (Paris: Galilée, 1986), pp. 219–47. The essay was written after a public reading of Francis Ponge's *Pour un Malherbe* (Paris: Gallimard, 1976), where Derrida met Aragon and Jean Ristat. Shortly afterwards he collaborated with the latter on the journal *Digraphe*.

10 Most immediate would be Rimbaud's 'Le Buffet', a sonnet in which the furnishing is described as a *fouillis de vieilles vieilleries*. See Leuwers, *Rimbaud*, p. 55.

11 Reference is made to Michel de Certeau's concept of *faire avec* by which what is done with or made from an object is a creative collaboration or extension of and variation upon an inherited form. The concept is mobilised in Certeau, *L'Invention du quotidien*, vol. I: *Arts de faire* (n. 1), a book closely affiliated with Louis Aragon's *Le Paysan de Paris* (Paris: Gallimard, 1972 [1926]), and it is elegantly theorised through Freud in the last two chapters of Certeau, *L'Écriture de l'histoire* (Paris: Gallimard, 1975).

12 In her reconstruction of the film, Marie-Claire Ropars-Wuilleumiers emphasises that the feature is *classical* in design, composed of twelve segments (chapters, or even stations) separated by seven fadeouts in black, two iris-fades, and two lap-dissolves. She calls the twelve units 'entities demarcated by the film itself, whose punctuating inserts rhyme with the development of the narrative as a function of its own laws', in 'L'Instance graphique dans l'écriture du film', *Littérature*, 46 (May 1982), p. 76. The late and deeply regretted author of this analysis was the first to call attention to the importance of the poetic patterning of film and writing in this founding feature of the French New Wave.

13 *Ibid.*, p. 69.

14 *Ibid.*

15 'Il n'y a pas d'amour heureux', published in the autumn of 1943, is said to have been written when Elsa Triolet wanted to leave Aragon in order to work for the Resistance, 'the rules of security requiring that couples be separated'. See Ristat, *Aragon*, p. 1563. It can be read along the same lines as 'Elsa je t'aime', and its oblique presence in Godard's film attests to the effect of separation, which the variation on the final refrain shows: *Il n'y a pas d'amour heureux / Mais c'est notre amour à tous deux*. See Ristat, 'Hors d'œuvre', p. 317; and Ristat, *Aragon*, p. 1004.

16 Ristat, *Aragon*, p. 1453, n. 4.

Further reading

Aragon, Louis, *Paris Peasant*, trans. Simon Watson Taylor (Boston, MA: Exact Change, 1994).

Louis Aragon Anthologie (Audio CD, Epm musique, 2005).

Barbarant, Olivier, *Aragon: la mémoire et l'excès* (Seyssel: Champ Vallon, 1997).

Hilsum, Mireille, Trévisan, Carine and Vassevière, Maryse (eds.), *Lire Aragon* (Paris: Champion, 2000).

Nicolas, Alain and Zoughebi, Henriette, *Aragon, le mouvement perpétuel* (Paris: Stock, 1997).

Piégay-Gros, Nathalie, *Esthétique d'Aragon* (Paris: SEDES, 1997).

Aragon et la chanson (Paris: Textuel, 2007).

Ray, Lionel, *Aragon* (Paris: Seghers, 2002).

12 Henri Michaux, 'Iniji'

MARGARET RIGAUD-DRAYTON

Iniji

Ne peut plus, Iniji

Sphinx, sphères, faux signes,
obstacles sur la route d'Iniji

Rives reculent
Socles s'enfoncent   5

Monde. Plus de monde
seulement l'amalgame

Les pierres ne savent plus être pierres

Parmi tous les lits sur terre
où est le lit d'Iniji ?   10

Petite fille
petite pelle
Iniji ne sait plus faire bras

Un corps a trop le souvenir d'un autre corps
un corps n'a plus d'imagination   15
n'a plus de patience avec aucun corps

Fluides, fluides
tout ce qui passe
passe sans s'arrêter
passe   20

Ariane plus mince que son fil
ne peut plus se retrouver

Vent
vent souffle sur Araho
vent   25

Anania Iniji
Annan Animha Iniji
Ornanian Iniji
et Iniji n'est plus animée

Mi-corps sort   30
mi-corps mort

Annaneja Iniji
Annajeta Iniji
Annamajeta Iniji
. . .

Extract from 'Iniji', *Moments, traversée du temps*

Enigmatic, gap-ridden, and seemingly locked into unequal combat with silence, 'Iniji' has much to say about the twentieth century's loss of faith in the capacity of language to give us access to what we might call the 'Real', or even to allow for a truthful account of human experience. Yet, if the elliptic and paratactic poetics of 'Iniji' conjure a pessimistic meditation on the absurdity of human life, its elegiac lyricism nevertheless does not suggest radical nihilism. Indeed the interrelated webs of echoes which resonate throughout 'Iniji' like tenuous yet curiously persistent musical movements, suggest that the flirtation with nonsense which led Michaux to strip the French language of its rigid lexical and syntactical carapace did not reflect an unambiguous disenchantment with words. Instead, even as it calls the French language into question by testing the limits of its capacity to signify, Michaux's text introduces a powerful reflection on the enduring power of poetry to conjure life from the sonorous but vacuous forms that are words.

Unfolding in irregular, river-like undulations on the white page, 'Iniji'[1] describes a world in flux, where nothing is ever stable. Although 'souvenir' (l. 14) is perhaps the only word in the text that explicitly evokes the precariousness of the present, 'Iniji' is nevertheless haunted by a sense of the ephemeral. All the conjugated verbs in the text are in the present indicative, but the presence to the world which this tense usually correlates is punctured by a heightened awareness of transience. The repeated framing of the tense with the backward-looking construction 'ne. . . plus' evokes a present hollowed out by the past (see ll. 1, 8, 13, 15, 16, 22, 29). Verbs such as 'passe', 'reculent' and 's'enfoncent' (ll. 18–20, 4, 5) intensify this effect by also connoting the passage of time. Evoking transitoriness, the threefold repetition of 'passe' simultaneously conjures up the continuous *passage* of the present, as it transforms into what is *passé*. In turn, 'reculent' and 's'enfoncent' (ll. 4–5) recall familiar spatial images of the present receding into the past. The motif of the passage of time is emphasised further by the Heraclitean metaphor of the river of time which runs through the text.

117

Evoking a river the banks of which are receding, '*Rives* reculent' (my emphasis, l. 4), in particular, suggests that 'la route d'Iniji', 'le lit d'Iniji' and Iniji's 'bras' (ll. 3, 10, 13) describe a riverpath, among other things. While the verbs in the third stanza inflect the image of a river journey with temporal connotations, it is in the text's ninth stanza that the image's Heraclitean undertones are most explicit: 'Fluides, fluides / tout ce qui passe / passe sans s'arrêter / passe'. As in that river where one only bathes once, elemental, possibly watery 'fluides' come to anticipate and exemplify the continuous crumbling away of the present. The stanza performs this wreckage in the slippage into sibilance of an initial alliteration in 'f', while these semantic and phonetic images of dissolution retrospectively illuminate the process of disintegration at work in lines 4–8. As riverbanks shift, geological platforms slip, and stones lose their rock-like qualities, boundaries between words begin to blur through alliterations, paronomasia, and those partial anagrams which Saussure called *les mots sous les mots*. The echoing *ondes* which '*monde*' (my emphasis) conjures in 'Monde. Plus de monde' (l. 6) foreshadow the disintegration of the world into 'l'amalgame' in the following line. In much the same way, the *hier* which resonates in '*Pierres*' (l. 8, my emphasis) confines the solidity of stones to a lost era. Conversely, in 'Socles s'enfoncent' (l. 4), sibilance and the interplay of oral and nasal vowels ('o'/'on' and 'e'/'en') between a noun which grammatically and semantically evokes stasis, and a verb which grammatically and semantically denotes movement, perform the shifting of foundations described in the line by blurring these two linguistic categories. Indeed, the line also anticipates the ninth stanza's phonetic performance of dissolution in the interplay which it stages between the fricative consonants 'f' and 's'. Similarly, in 'Rives reculent' (l. 5) an alliteration in 'r' emphasises the line's transposition of the grammatical and semantic motion inherent in the verb *reculer* to a static noun which evokes solid ground (as opposed to water) as well as anything that is *rivé*, by paronomasia. In turn, and as in line 4, the unsteadiness which the alliteration brings to mind also anticipates the ninth stanza, through the line's paronomastic evocation of the river (***rivière***) of time. Breaking down the boundaries between usually dichotomous linguistic and conceptual categories, these echoing phonetic patterns anticipate the dissolution of the conventional French lexis into assonantic and alliterative chains of words at the end of the extract.

Although a destructive movement sweeps 'Iniji' onward towards the unravelled language at the end of the extract, the text does not flow along a straightforwardly linear path from life to death, or from sense to nonsense. Instead, the repetitions and interruptions which pervade the extract emphasise its circularity and opacity long before its glossolalic ending. From the opening line onwards, ellipsis and parataxis undermine the coherence and continuity of 'Iniji'. In turn, phonetic and semantic echoes both reinforce this pattern by delimiting the short-circuited fragments which compose the text, and undermine it by interweaving them with the rest of the text through insistent, if usually more subtle, webs of echoing sounds, words, and images. The text's curiously disrupted yet continuous flow is particularly evident in the powerful rhetorical devices of repetition and interruption which structure the stanzas. Introducing breaks into the text through their capitalised opening lines, the stanzas are themselves pervaded by jarring gaps. Yet, even though their onward movement from line to line is regularly interrupted by parataxis, they are compellingly bound together by anaphora, epiphora and anadiplosis (cf. stanzas 7, 8, 9, 11, 12, 13, 14) when they are not framed by the repetition of the same word (cf. stanzas 5, 8, 11). Giving the stanzas a certain formal coherence in spite of the discontinuity introduced by their paratactic structure, these devices simultaneously undermine their forward movement. For even as such reiterations may sometimes allow for antanaclasis (the repetition of the same word but with different meanings) such interpretations nevertheless remain too precariously uncertain to be persuasive. Instead, confined to the wavering obscurity of non-determination, the stanzas remain ambiguously poised between movement and repetition. The same paradoxical dynamic pervades the lines which compose them, through ellipses and phonetic echoes which reinforce further the text's repeatedly stalling, or permanently stalled, progress. The combination of ellipsis and epanadiplosis (the reiteration of a word at the start and end of a line) (ll. 6, 8, 14, and 17) dramatises the text's open-ended circularity particularly powerfully by producing lines which hover uncertainly between introducing change and intimating stasis. This contradictory movement animates even the most apparently non-circular lines of the text. The opening line, 'Ne peut plus, Iniji', is a case in point. Composed of an elliptic French phrase and an invented word/name, 'Ne peut plus, Iniji' is both phonetically and morphologically heterogeneous. A comma, however, underlines the division of the line into two equally enigmatic, tri-syllabic and elliptic utterances. Although it anticipates the text's movement from elliptic but lexically conventional French fragments to glossolalia, the line's well-balanced rhythm simultaneously pre-empts the notion of textual progresssion (or regression) toward formal and semantic disintegration. With the ellipsis and negation on which its first section ('*Ne* peut *plus*') opens and closes reduplicated within its second section ('I*niji*') the word/name 'Iniji' repeats, as much as it emphasises, the linguistic powerlessness which 'Ne peut plus' invokes and performs, through ellipsis. Even as the text begins, then, the power of language, and, correlatively, of the Iniji-like poet, to account meaningfully for human experience is already in doubt. Rehearsing 'Ne peut plus, Iniji' in literal repetitions of 'ne peut plus' (l. 22), 'ne. . . plus' (ll. 8, 13, 15, 16, 29), 'plus' (l. 6), and 'Iniji' (ll. 3, 10, 13, 26–9, 31–3), as well as in more or less scrambled assonantic and alliterative variations on its inaugural line, the text as a whole seems condemned to ever more deformed and/or fragmentary reiterations of the failure of words to provide the text's disempowered narrator with a solid hold on the sand-, water- and wind-like experiences which slip through his/her fingers before they can even be named.

The mystery of death is of course at the centre of the text's elegiac poetics. Indeed, by the time Iniji's demise is made explicit in 'Et Iniji n'est plus animée' (l. 29), her death has been in the air for some time. Even as the text opens, Iniji, whose name repeats the text's founding motif of disempowerment, already emblematises that ultimate mark of human powerlessness: mortality. Hovering on the verge of nothingness, she anticipates her alter-ego, the lost Ariane, who, 'plus mince que son fil' (l. 21) not only evokes the tenuousness of the thread of life through a transferred epithet, but hints at the Fates who cut that thread through a *minceur* which conjures the old French verb *mincier* (to cut) even as it describes her near insubstantiality. Paronomastically pointing to the funerary inscription *ci gît* and the fragility of the ego (*-ni je*) while resonating with the shrill echo of a cry (i-i-i), Iniji's very name anticipates the eponymous text's elegiac poetics of dissolution. Indeed, the text as a whole invites a reading as a poignant attempt to find a language for the nonsensical vacuum which death imprints onto life. However, just as the enigma of the 'Sphinx', invoked in line 2, gives a simultaneously linear and almost circular account of human life (which, having begun on four legs, develops into a two-legged affair before regressing to a three-legged experience) the relationship of life and death is ambiguous in 'Iniji'. Indeed, much as the moth that the 'Sphinx' also emblematises evokes both the fragility of life and the survival of the soul, so life and death interreact in the text. Not only is there life in death, and death in life, in 'Iniji', but life and death can be difficult to tell apart. Even as 'Et Iniji n'est plus animée' is reiterated, making explicit Iniji's long-hinted demise, still the resonances with contradictory images in the lines which precede and follow combine to raise questions about what differentiates life from death. Anticipating 'Et Iniji n'est plus animée', the word/name 'Animha' (l. 27) in particular introduces a tension between the mortal body and the immortal soul, which undermines the certainty of Iniji's disappearance, in line 29 as elsewhere in the text. The doubt which 'Animha' introduces on the meaning of death in the text is emphasised further in 'Mi-corps sort / mi-corps mort' (ll. 30–1). Whereas in line 31 the internal rhyme between 'corps' and 'mort' encourages a reading of 'corps' as 'corpse', the death that the line and stanza evoke is nevertheless neither absolute nor final. Not only does the prefix 'mi-' suggest that annihilation in death is merely partial, but the end-line rhyme between 'mort' and 'sort' presents death as a *sortie*, indeed as *ce qui fait sortir*, while also bringing to mind our mortal fate. In turn, the double movement in the stanza between death-as-ending and death-as-escape, forces a rereading of the imagery of dissolution which pervades the text. Rather than evoking the straightforward destruction of the self in death, this imagery introduces a more complex and open-ended process of transformation. If 'tout ce qui passe / passe *sans s'arrêter* / passe' (my emphasis) conjures up a simultaneously cosmic and human journey toward dissolution, for example, it nevertheless makes clear that death itself cannot stop this self-propulsing movement toward 'l'amalgame'.

If the nonsensical vacuum introduced in the text by ellipses and parataxes can evoke a radical nihilism, the ambiguously open-ended and non-determined process that is the cycle of life and death in 'Iniji' rather challenges such ideological certainties. As all things transform into fluids, the inanimate world and text are revealed to be alive with elusive and unfamiliar traces of human passage. Even though it invokes mortal wreckage, the coldly ephemeral world conjured by 'tout ce qui passe' (l. 18) calls forth the lingering shadows of *tous ceux qui passent* by homophony. A nameless *lui* is inscribed and disseminated into the impersonal 'fl*ui*des' (l. 17) which the world and text move towards. Even the vanished world of certainties in which stones knew how to be stones described in line 8 still resonates with the name of its long-discredited founding father, Pierre. Indeed, even an inanimate, manufactured 'petite p*elle*' locates the *elle* of the 'petite fille' which preceded it, and which it also evokes anaphorically (ll. 11–12). More generally, the wind of dissolution which blows over the text is alive with the breath of life, as suggested by the immediate juxtaposition of 'vent' and 'souffle' (l. 24), which etymologically refers to the movement of respiration. In much the same way, the more or less scrambled echoes, in the glossolalic catalogue with which the extract ends, of the Sanskrit for 'breath' and 'life', *anana*, locate traces of life within what could at first have conjured no more than lexical destruction. If the text's 'amalgame', 'fluides' and 'vent' (ll. 7, 17, 23–5) evoke the finitude of life, then, they simultaneously point to its improbable endurance in increasingly fragmented, inanimate, particles of matter, words and sound. Indeed, the text evokes the tenuous survival of past lives in the precarious and ever more dispersed echoes which run through its lexis. This is clearest in the glossolalic onomasticon at the end of this extract. If the reduction of conventional French words to alliterative and assonantic nonsense confirms both the dissolution of all things and the failure of language to make sense of annihilation, the capitalisation of words simultaneously underlines the power of their music to conjure life from devastation and meaninglessness. In 'Anania', a number of barely remembered and more or less faceless ancient figures overlap, from the biblical Hanania, a descendant of King David evoked in 1 Chronicles 8, and Hananiah (spelt Hanania in French), the false prophet in the prophecies of Jeremiah, to an entire nation, the Hananians, of whom all that is left today are funerary monuments, not to mention the anonymous lives which *anana* points to. Similarly, in 'Ornanian' (l. 28) echoes of the name 'Hanania' and its correlates resonate with other names, including 'Ornan', who conjures up the figure (sometimes spelled Araunah) in 1 Chronicles 21 and 2 Samuel 24 and the kingdom of Araunah, where the oldest of Indo-European languages, Hittite, has its roots. Highlighting the density of even the most apparently random words, these limited insights into the lingering resonances carried by just two of the names in the extract's final onomasticon suggest that it probably resonates with allusions to many other long-vanished peoples, languages and cultures. Naming, or echoing the names of, long-forgotten figures and their lost worlds, the text points to the fragility of human experience only to highlight its ghostly endurance in the hollow shells of words.

As shadowy figures are conjured up from oblivion in what initially may have seemed like gratuitous glossolalic incantations, the text as a whole begins to challenge the boundary between proper and common names. Just as the name 'Pierre' resonates in the mineral 'pierres' of line 8, so 'Iniji' as a whole invites a reading as an onomasticon celebrating the Protean capacity of the empty and inadequate forms that are words to retain the disseminated traces of the past, even as it exposes the inability of language to make sense of loss. Bringing the ghosts of the past back to the consciouness of the living in the insistent but tenuous and perhaps haphazard music of alliterative and assonant words, 'Iniji' returns modern twentieth-century French poetry to the primitive, mantra-like invocations in which it has its roots. As its discontinuous and circular narrative of powerlessness acquires the rhythms of incantation, the performative force of naming is revealed alongside the text's very modern meditation on the limitations of language. As lost worlds, languages, and peoples are summoned from its apparently vacuous web of echoes, 'Iniji' asks us, along with many other twentieth-century French poetic texts, to reconsider the power of poetry.

Note

1 Henri Michaux, *Moments, traversée du temps* (Paris: Gallimard, 1973), pp. 189–90.

Further reading

Ball, David, *Darkness Moves: An Henri Michaux Anthology 1927–1984* (Berkeley, CA: University of California Press, 1997).

Bowie, Malcolm, *Henri Michaux: A Study of his Literary Works* (Oxford: Clarendon Press, 1973).

Broome, Peter, *Henri Michaux* (London: Athlone Press, 1977).

Edson, Laurie, *Henri Michaux and the Poetics of Movement* (Saratoga, CA: Anma Libri, 1985).

La Charité, Virginia, *Henri Michaux* (Boston, MA: Twayne Publishers, 1977).

Michaux, Henri, *Selected Writings*, trans. Richard Ellmann (New York: New Directions, 1968).

Ideograms in China, trans. Gustav Sobin (New York: New Directions, 2002).

Parish, Nina, *Henri Michaux: Experimentation with Signs* (Amsterdam: Rodopi, 2007).

Rigaud-Drayton, Margaret, *Henri Michaux: Poetry, Painting, and the Universal Sign* (Oxford: Oxford University Press, 2005).

13 Aimé Césaire, *Cahier d'un retour au pays natal*

JEAN KHALFA

ô lumière amicale[1]
ô fraîche source de la lumière
ceux qui n'ont inventé ni la poudre ni la boussole
ceux qui n'ont jamais su dompter la vapeur ni l'électricité
ceux qui n'ont exploré ni les mers ni le ciel   5
mais ceux sans qui la terre ne serait pas la terre
Gibbosité d'autant plus bienfaisante que la terre déserte
davantage la terre
silo où se préserve et mûrit ce que la terre a de plus terre
ma négritude n'est pas une pierre, sa surdité ruée contre la clameur
     du jour   10
ma négritude n'est pas une taie d'eau morte sur l'œil mort de la terre
ma négritude n'est ni une tour ni une cathédrale

elle plonge dans la chair rouge du sol
elle plonge dans la chair ardente du ciel
elle troue l'accablement opaque de sa droite patience.   15

Eia pour le Kaïlcédrat royal !
Eia pour ceux qui n'ont jamais rien inventé
pour ceux qui n'ont jamais rien exploré
pour ceux qui n'ont jamais rien dompté

mais ils s'abandonnent, saisis, à l'essence de toute chose   20
ignorants des surfaces mais saisis par le mouvement de toute chose
insoucieux de dompter, mais jouant le jeu du monde

véritablement les fils aînés du monde
poreux à tous les souffles du monde
aire fraternelle de tous les souffles du monde   25
lit sans drain de toutes les eaux du monde
étincelle du feu sacré du monde
chair de la chair du monde palpitant du mouvement même du monde !
Tiède petit matin de vertus ancestrales

Sang ! Sang ! tout notre sang ému par le cœur mâle du soleil 30
ceux qui savent la féminité de la lune au corps d'huile
l'exaltation réconciliée de l'antilope et de l'étoile
ceux dont la survie chemine en la germination de l'herbe !
Eia parfait cercle du monde et close concordance !

Écoutez le monde blanc 35
horriblement las de son effort immense
ses articulations rebelles craquer sous les étoiles dures
ses raideurs d'acier bleu transperçant la chair mystique
écoute ses victoires proditoires trompeter ses défaites
écoute aux alibis grandioses son piètre trébuchement 40

Pitié pour nos vainqueurs omniscients et naïfs !

Eia pour ceux qui n'ont jamais rien inventé
pour ceux qui n'ont jamais rien exploré
pour ceux qui n'ont jamais rien dompté

Eia pour la joie 45
Eia pour l'amour
Eia pour la douleur aux pis de larmes réincarnées.

et voici au bout de ce petit matin ma prière virile
que je n'entende ni les rires ni les cris, les yeux fixés sur cette ville
   que je prophétise, belle,
[donnez-moi le courage du martyr]² 50
donnez-moi la foi sauvage du sorcier
donnez à mes mains puissance de modeler
donnez à mon âme la trempe de l'épée
je ne me dérobe point. Faites de ma tête une tête de proue
et de moi-même, mon cœur, ne faites ni un père, ni un frère, 55
ni un fils, mais le père, mais le frère, mais le fils,
ni un mari, mais l'amant de cet unique peuple.

Faites-moi rebelle à toute vanité, mais docile à son génie
comme le poing à l'allongée du bras !
Faites-moi commissaire de son sang 60
faites-moi dépositaire de son ressentiment
faites de moi un homme de terminaison
faites de moi un homme d'initiation
faites de moi un homme de recueillement
mais faites aussi de moi un homme d'ensemencement 65

faites de moi l'exécuteur de ces œuvres hautes
voici le temps de se ceindre les reins comme un vaillant homme –

Mais les faisant, mon cœur, préservez-moi de toute haine
ne faites point de moi cet homme de haine pour qui je n'ai que haine
car pour me cantonner en cette unique race   70
vous savez pourtant mon amour tyrannique[3]
vous savez que ce n'est point par haine des autres races
que je m'exige bêcheur de cette unique race
que ce que je veux
c'est pour la faim universelle   75
pour la soif universelle

la sommer libre enfin
de produire de son intimité close
la succulence des fruits.

Extract from *Cahier d'un retour au pays natal*

Paris nègre

The *Cahier* stages the birth of a historical consciousness in the colonised, and though it was first published in a fairly obscure journal, *Volontés*, in Paris in 1939 and remained unnoticed due to the historical circumstances, it went on to play a significant part itself in this birth after the war. Césaire often said that he discovered Africa in Paris in 1931, first in the person of his fellow student Léopold Sédar Senghor (1906–2001), who had arrived from Senegal two years earlier, and became his mentor and friend. Then, in what they called their 'ardent years', Césaire not only immersed himself in classical Western culture but also read and met writers, artists and political thinkers who fervently debated the idea of a Negro or African identity. A multiplicity of factors had made it a compelling theme. First, hopes of full citizenship for the subjects of France's empire in the African colonies had faded even though the colonial troops who had fought in France during the First World War had paid a heavy price. This led to the beginning of a politicisation of those who had stayed, mostly as workers, waiters, servants and dockers. Lacking a true anti-colonial perspective, the French Communist Party failed to capitalise on the situation in the twenties, and pan-Africanism started to appear as a historical alternative to assimilation as well as to class struggle.[4] Second, the fascination of the French intelligentsia for *art nègre* had reached a peak. It had been initiated by artists, notably the Cubists and then the Surrealists, and reinforced by the popularity of jazz brought to France by African American troops. More generally the celebration of magic and the unconscious, of image and rhythm and of whatever seemed to oppose the previously dominant ideology of rational progress, occupied the intellectual scene.

Third, extraordinarily influential thinkers of the time, such as Péguy (1873–1914) and Bergson (1859–1941) had initiated a rebirth of spiritualism, in politics and history as well as in metaphysics and epistemology. In 1941 Césaire published a celebration of Péguy in the first issue of his journal *Tropiques*.[5] Later Senghor repeatedly acknowledged his debt to Bergson's philosophy of time, which questioned the reducibility of experienced time to the mechanisms constructed by science.[6] Fourth, social anthropology was becoming one of the dominant social sciences. The well-publicised ethnographic expedition Mission Dakar-Djibouti took place in 1931–3. The 1931 Exposition Coloniale (which attracted thirty million visitors) celebrated the achievements of colonisation, but could also be seen as the greatest celebration of difference ever. Its organisers represented an intellectual current that had moved French colonial thought towards separate development, and away from the assimilationism that had dominated until the 1920s (and remained the hope of most of the colonised at the time).[7] A significant figure in this transformation had been a colonial administrator, Maurice Delafosse, who had written several volumes on Negro arts and cultures and was read and highly praised, for instance, by African American writers of the 'Harlem Renaissance'.[8] There was political opposition to the Exhibition, and the Surrealists and Communists jointly held an Anti-Colonial Exhibition, but *La Revue du Monde Noir* praised it because it showed that traditional societies had civilisations. The *Revue* was published in 1931–2 by the Nardal sisters from Martinique, who held a salon in Clamart attended by all the Caribbean, African and African American writers of the period. Finally, one should mention the influence of the German anthropologist Leo Frobenius whose work was also published by Aimé and Suzanne Césaire in *Tropiques*. Frobenius saw Africa as a supremely orderly and aesthetic society. He thus violently opposed the dominant idea of the barbarity of the continent.[9] Among the morphologies of cultures he outlined, Frobenius confronts civilisations that had an antagonistic relationship to the earth with those ('Ethiopian' as well as 'Germanic') that were linked to plants and the germinative cycle and aimed for a fusion, the first being civilisations of space, the others of time.[10]

Composition of the *Cahier*

Writing the *Cahier*, a poem seventy pages long, was for Césaire so intense (bringing him close to madness, according to Senghor) that he had to convalesce after this experience. This process of painful metamorphosis of the self through writing is not just what this poem narrates but also what it is about, at two levels, personal and collective.

At the personal level, it can be read as a sequence of three moments, each inhabited by a contradiction:

(a) Dismay at the bleakness of colonial reality, pictured as fragmentation in space and decay in time, and general insignificance, as opposed to what Césaire calls 'éclaboussement d'or / des instants favorisés'. The development of images is what shapes meaning in Césaire and in this case the image/matrix of the first aspect, repeated over many stanzas, is that of the island as a disparate wreckage ('échouage hétéroclite'), seen in the cold light of a bleak dawn, portrayed as end rather than rebirth: 'au bout du petit matin'. Space is fragmentation and time is either the mechanical repetition of labour or the organic process of corruption. The opposite image is not about extension and repetition but intensity: the childhood memory of an extraordinary creole Christmas, a single moment in time, but rich with intensities of sounds and tastes. The young poet's hope is to reflect such intensities and bring meaning to this people through his writing, and to finally discover 'la terre où tout est libre et fraternel, ma terre'.

(b) But the alienation of this colonised people, 'cette foule qui ne sait pas faire foule', is such that no collective consciousness seems possible. The only solution is escape from the island and in this second moment two fundamental scenes are opposed again: first the vision of a miserable 'nègre', seen in a tramcar, presumably in Paris, described through the degradation produced by abject poverty, and as an animal (a 'pongo', an ape). The effect of this vision on the aspiring poet is an ethical awakening: he realises suddenly that he had shared the gaze and the derisive smile of the other passengers of the tram. The counter-image is an astonishing reversal, opposing the immemorial, 'native' sense of belonging to the world of the 'nègre' to the unhappy detachment of the colonisers' consciousness. This is where our text is situated and where *négritude*, defined not racially, but as a trait of civilisation, is first introduced and celebrated.

(c) This elicits a third moment and a new stance: creating a poetry that participates in life. In an extraordinary prayer, the poetic voice assumes the long history of the suffering and oppression of the fundamental race which is like the genesis of a new poetic voice: 'je te livre ma conscience de chair'. Soon the prayer turns into its opposite, a prophetic vision. The poetic voice will produce the consciousness of a new people, who will discover in *négritude* their hidden identity: 'et le grand trou noir où je voulais me noyer l'autre lune / c'est là que je veux pêcher maintenant la langue maléfique de la nuit en son immobile verrition !'[11]

At the same time, the *Cahier* can be read not just as the performative of an individual spiritual trajectory but also as the expression of a collective historical phenomenon: the transformation of the consciousness of the colonised. It had been deeply alienated and was unable to define its values other than by reference to those of the coloniser. This is what, for Césaire, distinguished the colonial situation from 'simple' exploitation. Here, subjectivity is not just constrained, it is also emptied out from the inside, devoid of autonomy, a phenomenon the Martiniquais psychiatrist and political thinker Frantz Fanon described meticulously in his *Peau noire, masques blancs* (1952). Like Césaire, Fanon considered that racism, as the main instrument of alienation, was consubstantial with colonialism. The *Cahier* expresses a revolt, no longer asking for the respect of the universal human rights that had been alleged to justify Europe's 'mission civilisatrice', but rather in the name of a collective identity.

Sartre, in 1948, explained this process through the myth of Orpheus. In order to regain the soul they had lost, the colonised had to explore the darkest areas of themselves and history, and learn to celebrate their identity by defiant opposition. Then they would be able to return to the light of the universal on their own terms. He noted that revolution always produces a new subjectivity, and he saw in that subjectivity a 'rapport de soi-même avec soi, source de toute poésie.'[12] The orphic poetry of negritude was therefore for him the only revolutionary poetry of the time.

Négritude and the prophetic stance

Our excerpt stages the crucial transition between the second and the third moments of the *Cahier*. It starts with a third-person celebration and ends with a first-person prayer:

> ô fraîche source de la lumière
> ceux qui. . .
> . . .
> et voici au bout de ce petit matin ma prière virile. (l. 48)

The first moment is the revelation of *négritude*, the second expresses the desire for a transformation of the poet into a prophet. *Négritude* is defined as a particular attitude towards the earth and a relationship to the elements of the world, made of belonging in space and acceptance in time. Its opposite is the technological stance of the white world: separation and effort. The second moment translates in historical terms what the first revealed in cosmological ones; it is a prayer for reconciliation but of the self with his people, the poet's voice becoming the repository of this people's inheritance of suffering and authenticity. It prays to be able to predict and elicit a future:

> faites de moi un homme de recueillement
> mais faites aussi de moi un homme d'ensemencement (ll. 64–5)

In the first moment, the main quality of the images is synaesthesia: light comes from a fresh spring (l. 2), the day is clamour (l. 10), the sky ardent flesh (l. 14), dawn is tepid (l. 29), the moon's body oily (l. 31). This sets the scene for the emphasis on the mystical relationship of these people to the world: 'Eia parfait cercle du monde et close concordance !'[13] Perceptions based on separation (in sight and hearing) are now physically linked to their objects via traditional associations of colour and touch: not only is the (African) soil red like flesh, but the sky too is red and not translucent blue, because it is ablaze with the fire of the sun, 'chair *ardente*' (l. 14). Red is the colour of *négritude*. Blue will be the colour of the white world's steel: 'ses raideurs d'acier bleu transperçant la chair mystique' (l. 38).

128

This experience of fusion allows Césaire to turn a historical opposition into an ethical and then metaphysical one. The bearers of negritude are first defined by what they never did: *inventer, dompter, explorer* – actions which suppose a distancing of the self from the world it maps and upon which it acts, often violently (gunpowder and compass). This instrumental or technological relationship to the earth is probably what made history possible,[14] but there were other values, other than *domptage* or domination: those of people who belong to their domain of action, and are the product of what they do. In space, *négritude* is compared to a 'silo' (the deep underground grain reserves of traditional societies), or a 'Gibbosity', a hump, an inflection on the spine of the earth, where it 'plunges'. As for their relationship to time it is one of abandonment: '*saisis* par le mouvement de *toute* chose', an allusion to mythological thought. A whole web of images expresses visually this opposition of values. For instance, the (military) tower and the cathedral of the colonisers, in their verticality, symbolise the detachment of men from the earth and thus its desertion (l. 7), and while the White world rends and pierces the mystical flesh, or is described as blind and stone-deaf, *négritude* sees life even in the inanimate.[15]

These visual associations are in turn supported by a multiplicity of syntactic and metrical means. For instance, there is a subtle transition from the objective and collective to the subjective and personal through appositions, a technique often used by epic poets: 'ceux qui', 'gibbosité', 'silo', 'ma négritude'. 'Gibbosité' (l. 7) and 'silo' (l. 9) are pivotal points. The closure of the sentence starting with 'ceux qui' is delayed by a series of subordinate clauses, so that when we reach these points, highlighted by their position and unexpected technicality, we feel that they celebrate 'ceux'. But there is no punctuation and we soon discover that they also start a new sentence and qualify 'ma négritude'. Retrospectively then, 'ceux qui. . .' is read as qualifying 'lumière'. It is as if waves of text overlapped rather than succeeded each other. In the process, from the multiple ('ceux') through the general ('silo') we finally reach the personal, and later on the first-person plural, in a similar way: 'Sang ! Sang ! tout *notre* sang'. . . / ceux qui' (l. 30).

Africa is not named here[16] and *négritude* is not defined racially (it is not opposed for instance to 'les blancs' but to 'le *monde* blanc' (l. 35)). Rather it is a mode of belonging to a world. So this is not just a great ecological celebration, but the attempt to overcome a metaphysical loss – that of the *presence* of the world to men. It is marked in the text by the passage from 'terre' to 'monde' (which ends each line from 22 to 28) and by the addition to earth of the elements of traditional ontologies: 'souffles', 'eaux' and 'feu'. In this mythical, primary civilisation ('fils aînés du monde') 'exaltation' is 'réconciliée' and *eros* ('cœur mâle du soleil' and 'fémininité de la lune' (ll. 30–1)) is an instance of the general concordance.

We are now in a better position to understand the final prayer, where the poet mirrors this stance of acceptance, fusion and exaltation, but this time in his relationship to his people: 'je m'exige bêcheur de cette unique race' (l. 73) 'de produire de son intimité close / la succulence des fruits' (l. 79). It is also clear why *négritude* is not racial hatred but hatred of hatred (l. 69). A similar analysis of the structure of images and syntactic tools can then easily be carried out. But the comparison between the two moments highlights additional tools that Césaire uses: sounds and rhythm. Sound is often linked to meaning here. For instance the arthritis ('articulations rebelles' (l. 37)) of the white world is echoed by a proliferation of harsh consonants, while in the previous stanza, emotion is celebrated by a multiplicity of 'm' and 'n'. Repetitions of similar sound patterns over the long duration of the text show how the poet works on words as acoustic material. In addition, Césaire noted that in his poetry, 2+2 equalled 5, meaning that, as in African music, it was not measured by default in equal units. So here, the lengths and rhythms of the lines mimic the phases of the consciousness they express. For instance, phases of exaltation correspond to lengthening lines and accelerating rhythms (ll. 1 to 7 through 8, or 23 to 28 and then 29). In the second phase (ll. 48–79) we find a much more regular pattern. The imperative dominates the prayer, a certainty has already been gained, and both affects and voice are stabilised. The object was the process of a transformation of consciousness, so here again there is concordance of form and content.

Césaire's prophetic tone has been criticised and may be hard to relate to nowadays. To understand it, one needs to bear in mind the astonishing inner transformation and assertion that this assumption of an African identity meant for a Martiniquais at the time. It is useful to bear in mind, as well, the historical function poetry can assume in the constitution of a potential community under conditions of oppression. Deleuze and Guattari wrote of minority cultures:

> c'est la littérature qui produit une solidarité active, malgré le scepticisme; et si l'écrivain est en marge ou à l'écart de sa communauté fragile, cette situation le met d'autant plus en mesure d'exprimer une autre communauté potentielle, de forger les moyens d'une autre conscience et d'une autre sensibilité.[17]

In the prophetic, and in particular the apocalyptic voice, the self disappears into its vision. This astonishing poem turned out to be the programme of Césaire's life.

Notes

1 The poem was written in 1939 and revised several times. From the 1956 edition onwards, this stanza is detached from the preceding text. The text presented here is based on the edition of the *Cahier* published in Aimé Césaire, *La Poésie* (Paris: Seuil, 1994), checked against the bilingual edition of Clayton Eshleman and Annette Smith, *Notebook of a Return to the Native Land* (Middletown, CT: Wesleyan University Press, 2001). I thank A. James Arnold and Alex Gil who have graciously given me access to their electronic edition of all the published versions of the *Cahier*.

2 This line was only present in the 1939 edition.

3 1939 edition: 'catholique' instead of 'tyrannique'.

4 See Philippe Dewitte, *Les Mouvements nègres en France, 1919–1939* (Paris: L'Harmattan, 1985). In 1919 a Pan-African Congress was organised in Paris by the African American writer and activist W. E. B. Du Bois, the Senegalese deputy Blaise Diagne and the deputies from Guyana and the Caribbean. On the chronic incapacity of French communists to deal with colonialism in Africa, see Césaire's *Lettre à Maurice Thorez* (Paris: Édition Présence Africaine, 1956).

5 Aimé Césaire, *Tropiques* (Fort-de-France, 1941–5, reprint Paris: Éditions Jean-Michel Place, 1978).

6 See Souleyman Bachir Diagne, 'Senghor and Bergson', in special thirtieth anniversary humanities conference, 'Canonical Works and Continuing Innovation in African Arts and Humanities', Accra, 17–19 September 2003, available at: www.codesria.org/Links/conferences/accra/humanities.htm (accessed October 2009).

7 Except for intellectuals such as Césaire who wrote that from the outset the very idea of 'assimilation' seemed to him 'l'aliénation, la chose la plus grave'. Aimé Césaire, *Nègre je suis, nègre je resterai, Entretiens avec Françoise Vergès* (Paris: Albin Michel, 2005) p. 28.

8 See Benoît de l'Estoile, *Le Goût des autres: de l'exposition coloniale aux arts premiers* (Paris: Flammarion, 2007). The polemic between Delafosse and René Maran is symptomatic of the transformations of the time. In 1922, Maran, a colonial administrator from French Guyana who worked in Africa, was the first black man to win the Goncourt prize for his novel *Batouala*, an event widely celebrated by the African American press in the United States. Its preface violently attacked colonialism and the novel itself drew an equally unflattering picture of the colonisers and the colonised. The scandal was such that Maran had to resign. Delafosse violently attacked Maran for having no real understanding of African cultures and judging them from a European point of view.

9 On Frobenius's 'Germanic' vision of Africa, see Christopher L. Miller, *Theories of Africans: Francophone Literature and Anthropology in Africa* (Chicago: University of Chicago Press, 1990).

10 Christopher L. Miller noted the importance German 'mysticism' had for Senghor. A. James Arnold analysed the ideological influence of Frobenius and Péguy on Césaire in 'Beyond Postcolonial Césaire: Reading *Cahier d'un retour au pays natal*', *Forum for Modern Language Studies*, 44(3) (2008), pp. 258–75.

11 On the meaning and translation of 'verrition', see Jean Khalfa, 'The Discrete and the Plane: Virtual Communities in Caribbean Poetry in French', in *Mantis, A Journal of Poetry and Translation*, vol. I available at: http://mantisjournal.stanford.edu/M1/Mantis1.html, December 2000 (accessed October 2009).

12 Jean-Paul Sartre, 'Orphée noir', preface to Léopold Sédar Senghor, *Anthologie de la nouvelle poésie nègre et malgache de langue française* (Paris: Presses Universitaires de France, 1948), p. xv.

13 'Eia' means 'Courage!' in classical Greek. A concordance is an index but also a reconciliation of all the apparent contradictions between and within the books of the Bible.

14 A theme Césaire probably encountered in Latin poetry, in Rousseau, in the contemporary renewal in spiritualism and vitalism, and perhaps in the recently imported philosophy of Martin Heidegger.

15 On Césaire and life in the mineral, see Jean Khalfa, 'Césaire volcanique', *L'Esprit créateur*, 14(2), (Summer 2005), pp. 52–61.

16 Though it is evoked through the red soil, the antelope and the royal cailcedra (a Senegalese tree endowed with medicinal properties and mythological associations, as a tree that forbids lies).

17 Gilles Deleuze and Félix Guattari, *Kafka, pour une littérature mineure* (Paris: Les Éditions de Minuit, 1975), pp. 31–2.

Further reading

Arnold, A. James, *Modernism and Negritude: The Poetry and Poetics of Aimé Césaire* (Cambridge, MA: Harvard University Press, 1981).

Césaire, Aimé, *State of the Union*, trans. Clayton Eshleman and Dennis Kelly (Bloomington, IN: Caterpillar Press, 1966).

Return to my Native Land, trans. Emile Snyder (Paris: Présence Africaine, 1968).

Return to my Native Land, trans. John Berger and Anna Bostock (Harmondsworth: Penguin Books, 1969).

Collected Poetry, trans. Clayton Eshleman and Annette Smith (Berkeley, CA: University of California Press, 1983).

Non-Vicious Circle: Twenty Poems of Aimé Césaire, trans. Gregson Davis (Stanford, CA: Stanford University Press, 1984).

Lyric and Dramatic Poetry: 1946–82, trans. Clayton Eshleman and Annette Smith (Charlottesville, VA: University of Virginia Press, 1990).

Confiant, Raphaël, *Aimé Césaire* (Paris: Écriture, 2006).

Gregson, Davis, *Aimé Césaire* (Cambridge: Cambridge University Press, 2008).

Kennedy, Ellen Conroy (ed.), *The Negritude Poets* (New York: Thunder's Mouth Press, 1989).

Kesteloot, Lilyan, *Aimé Césaire* (Paris: Seghers, 1989).

Le Brun, Annie, *Statue cou coupé* (Paris: Jean-Michel Place, 1996).

Leiner, Jacqueline, *Aimé Césaire: le terreau primordial* (Tübingen: Narr, 1997).

Munro, Martin, *Shaping and Reshaping the Caribbean: The Work of Aimé Césaire and René Depestre* (Leeds: Maney, 2000).

Scharfman, Ronnie Leah, *Engagement and the Language of the Subject in the Poetry of Aimé Césaire* (Gainesville: University of Florida Press, 1987).

Suk, Jeannie, *Postcolonial Paradoxes in French Caribbean Writing: Césaire, Glissant, Condé* (Oxford: Clarendon Press, 2003).

14 Francis Ponge, 'Le Volet, suivi de sa scholie'

PHILIPPE MET

Le volet, suivi de sa scholie

Volet plein qui bat le mur, c'est un drôle d'oiseau qu'un volet. Qui ne s'envole mie. Et se désarticule-t-il ? Non. Il s'articule. Et crie. Par les gonds de son aile unique rectangulaire. Et s'assomme comme un battoir sur le mur.

Un drôle d'oiseau cloué. Cloué par son profil, ce qui est plus cruel ou qui sait ? Car il peut battre de l'aile. Et s'assommer à sa guise contre le mur. Faisant retentir l'air de ses cris et de ses coups de battoir.

Vlan, deux fois.

Mais quand il nous a assez fatigués, on le cloue alors grand ouvert ou tout à fait fermé. Alors s'établit le silence, et la bataille est finie : je ne vois plus rien à en dire.

Dieu merci, je ne suis donc pas sourd ! Quand j'ai ouvert mon volet ce matin, j'ai bien entendu son grincement, son cri et son coup de battoir. Et j'ai senti son poids.

Aujourd'hui, cela eut plus d'importance que la lumière délivrée et que l'apparition du monde extérieur, de tout le train des objets dans son flot.

D'autres jours, cela n'a aucune importance : lorsque je ne suis qu'un homme comme les autres et que lui, alors, n'est rigoureusement rien, pas même un volet.

Mais voici qu'aujourd'hui – et rendez-vous compte de ce qu'est aujourd'hui dans un texte de Francis Ponge – voici donc qu'aujourd'hui, pour l'éternité, aujourd'hui dans l'éternité le volet aura grincé, aura crié, pesé, tourné sur ses gonds, avant d'être impatiemment rabattu contre cette page blanche.

Il aura suffi d'y penser; ou, plus tôt encore, de l'écrire.

Stabat un volet.

Attaché au mur par chacun de ces deux *a*, de chaque côté de la fenêtre, à peu près perpendiculaire au mur.

Ça bat, ou plutôt stabat un volet.

Stabat et ça crie. Stabat et ça a crié. Stabat et ça grince et ça a crié un volet.

Stabat tout droit, dans la verticale absolue, tendu comme à deux mains placées l'une au-dessous de l'autre le fusil tenu par deux doigts ici, deux doigts plus haut, tenu tout près du corps, du mur, dans la position du présentez-armes en décomposant.

Et on peut le gifler, même le plus grand vent : Stabat.

Non, ce n'est pas le mouvement du pendule, car il y a *deux* attaches : beaucoup moins libre.

Attention ! J'atteins ici à quelque chose d'important concernant la liberté – quelle liberté ? – du pendule. Un seul point d'attache, supérieur. . . et il est libre : de chercher son immobilité, son repos. . .

Mais le volet l'atteint beaucoup plus vite, et plus bruyamment !

(Ce ne doit pas être tout à fait cela, mais je n'ai pas l'intention de m'y fatiguer les méninges.)

Le volet aussi me sert de nuage : il suffit à cacher le soleil.

Va donc, triste oiseau, crie et parle ! Va, mon volet plein, bat le mur !

. . . Ho ! Ho ! mon volet, que fais-tu ?

Plein fermé, je n'y vois plus goutte. Grand ouvert, je ne *te* vois plus:

VOLET PLEIN NE SE PEUT ÉCRIRE
VOLET PLEIN NAÎT ÉCRIT STRIÉ
SUR LE LIT DE SON AUTEUR MORT
OÙ CHACUN VEILLANT À LE LIRE
ENTRE SES LIGNES VOIT LE JOUR.

(Signé à l'intérieur.)

SCHOLIE. – Pour que le petit oracle qui termine ce poème perde bientôt – et quasi spontanément – de son caractère pathétique, il suffirait que (dans ses éditions classiques) il soit imprimé comme suit:

VOLET PLEIN NE SE PEUT ÉCRIRE
VOLET PLEIN NAÎT ÉCRIT STRIÉ
SUR LE LIVRE DE L'AUTEUR MORT
OÙ L'ENFANT QUI VEILLE À LE LIRE
ENTRE SES LIGNES VOIT LE JOUR.

C'est en effet la seule façon intelligente de le comprendre (et de l'écrire, dès que le livre est conçu). Mais enfin, il ne me fut pas donné ainsi. Il n'y avait pas tant un livre, dans cette chambre, que, *jusqu'à nouvel ordre*, ce LIT.

L'oracle y gagna-t-il en *beauté* ? Peut-être (je n'en suis pas sûr. . .) Mais en ambiguïté et en cruauté, sûrement.

Pas de doute pourtant: fût-ce aux dépens de la beauté, il fallait devenir intelligent le plus tôt possible : c'est-à-dire plus modeste, on le voit.

On me dira qu'une modestie véritable (et la seule dignité peut-être) aurait voulu que j'accomplisse le petit sacrifice de mes beautés sans le dire et ne montre que cette dernière version. . . Mais sans doute vivons-nous dans une époque bien misérable (en fait de rhétorique), que je ne veuille priver personne de cette leçon, ni manquer d'abord de me la donner explicitement à moi-même.

. . . Et puis, suis-je tellement sûr, en définitive, d'avoir eu, de ce LIT, raison ?

From *Pièces*

Articulating the window shutter

More often referred or alluded to by critics than properly analysed or glossed, enriched with idiosyncratic features such as an unusual double-barrelled title which immediately suggests a diptych-like composition, the prose poem entitled 'Le Volet, suivi de sa scholie' is yet arguably an exemplary encapsulation of Pongian poetry and poetics, as well as of their inextricable linkage.[1] A brief look at the history of the text, from both a biographical and an editorial standpoint, should provide us with a first entry point into the layered texture and complex architecture of the work.

'Le Volet' was originally part of a group of texts (including 'La Terre', 'Les Olives', 'La Cruche' et 'L'Ébauche d'un poisson') under the heading *Cinq sapates*. As a staunch proponent of 'une rhétorique par poème' (or to each poem its own rhetoric), Francis Ponge was particularly fond of unearthing obsolete genres, rejuvenating forgotten practices, and recharging outdated terminologies (*momon*, *proême*, etc.), all of which also inspired some memorable coinages (*eugénie*, *objeu* et *objoie*). Defined by *Littré* (a veritable treasure trove of the French language in the eyes of the author) as a munificent present hidden inside a mundane or insignificant gift (e.g. a lemon containing a huge diamond), the *sapate* has therefore all the appearances of a fairly short, seemingly trivial and uninteresting text. Once prised open, however, it will reveal a wealth of potentialities, subtleties and lessons for the reader's enjoyment and enlightenment.

In his *Entretiens avec Philippe Sollers*, Francis Ponge revealed that the 'real' point of departure of his text was a one-panel, solid shutter fitted onto the window of a room he occupied in Coligny from late 1942 to mid-1944. If the time period might prompt the reader to suspect that 'Le Volet' is rife with ideological over-tones or generally, albeit obliquely, reverberates with a distressful zeitgeist, it more largely corresponded for the poet with an increasing experimentation in processual poetics. This frequently resulted in open-ended, unfinished – indeed, 'unfinishable' – dossiers, ruminative works in progress, or genetic notebooks (notably in texts later collected in *La Rage de l'expression*), which did not entirely forego the chiselling of deceptively glittering gems or the execution of osten-sibly prosaic miniatures where, as in *Le Parti pris des choses*, brevity and closure, density and volatility are prime values and can turn into insidious vehicles for social critique or political statement. As Ponge confesses to Sollers, 'ce volet m'avait ému': 'Il battait assez fort; enfin c'était un objet qui exigeait impérieuse-ment d'être pris en considération . . . il fallait que je le fasse taire en le *couvrant* de mes propres paroles.' As often with Ponge, the poem originates in an emotional shock or response (of an aesthetic or visceral, rather than intellectual or abstract nature), semantically emphasised here by the verb *battre* (which refers to the *banging* of the shutter whilst implicitly linking it to the *beating* of the poet's heart), which literally sets the writing process in *motion*. If the object's *call* has typically to be answered (by the poet's *calling*, in a sense), the call emanating from the shutter is unusual in that it appears to be more akin to a call for recog-nition (in the sense also of having to be reckoned with) than for self-expression. As an ambassador of a voiceless world, which is how Ponge once defined his role, speaking/writing on its behalf and championing its cause, the poet also usually shows himself to be an 'enabler' – one who allows or enables inanimate objects and inarticulate creatures alike to express themselves and make them-selves known for what they truly are (including, albeit not exclusively, through the rhetorical device of prosopopeia). In the case of 'Le Volet', an object that sig-nalled its own presence through sonorous disruption, Ponge's initial objective seems for once to have been to silence the object rather than let it speak (out), to suppress its voice rather than restore it, to drown out its obstinate cry (for help? of rebellion?) with his own words ('en le *couvrant* de mes propres paroles' – Ponge's emphasis).

And yet the central issue about the *volet* does seem to be one of *articulation* – both in the linguistic and mechanical sense, as the opening paragraph of the poem makes clear. The staccato rhythm, the dislocated syntax, the various effects of recurrence ('se désarticule' and 's'articule', precisely linked together through a question/answer pattern; 'battoir' echoing 'bat', the anaphoric 'et') all contribute to a mimetic rendition of the incessant, insistent, unnerving banging and squeaking of the shutter – of its idiosyncratic articulation. The reader should

keep in mind that through or beyond the 'analogical magma', Ponge is searching to isolate the 'differential quality' of any given object. The bird metaphor,
however incongruous it might appear on cursory view, is thus established from
the outset and will serve as a main thread through the rest of the poem. More
importantly, however, not only is it introduced by sudden irruption (an anaco-
luthic first sentence bookended by the lexeme 'volet'), immediately qualified
and singularised ('qui ne s'envole mie' – the discordance of the archaic negation
calling attention to this peculiarity), but it revitalises, or remotivates, an idiomatic cliché: 'un drôle d'oiseau' – a literally apt phrase for an indeed strange
bird – designates an odd customer in common parlance, much in the way
'battre de l'aile' in the next paragraph overtly refers to the flapping of a bird's
wing while covertly subverting an ossified idiom for floundering or being on the
wane. In this way, the lure of anthropomorphic fallacy that Ponge, an avowed
admirer of La Fontaine's *Fables*, was once wrongly accused of falling prey to by
some critics, is also kept at bay.

In the second paragraph, although still a major concern, articulation per se
tends to take a temporary back seat to repetition and amplification. The semantic and imagistic web that the spider-poet (cf. 'L'Araignée' composed in the same
period and later included in the same volume, *Pièces*) had started to spin in the
opening lines keeps going through the same points again while expanding.
'Un drôle d'oiseau', 's'assomme[r]' and 'cri[s]' are all picked up again, and, as a
freshly minted analogon, 'battoir' (a washerwoman's beater) is a derivative of
– and therefore clearly echoes – 'battre'. On the other hand, a soon-to-become-
prominent component, the biblical contextualisation of the 'Passion' of the
volet, is here foreshadowed by the notion of nailing: emphasised via anadiplosis
('Un drôle d'oiseau cloué. Cloué par son profil. . .'), it can be construed retrospectively and symbolically as a form of Crucifixion. At this point in the poem
and on a more rhetorical level, the emergence of 'clouer' might also be secretly
motivated by a hidden or latent matrix, a present/absent feature not uncommon
in Ponge's texts according to certain semiotics-oriented readings, notably in the
form of wordplay, e.g. the literalisation of a figurative, proverbial or set phrase.
In the present instance, colloquial French for shutting someone up, 'clouer le bec
(à quelqu'un)', would nicely connect the nailing action both to the bird imagery
and the idea of reducing an opponent to silence, serving to us as a reminder of
the author's (later) statement about blanketing the shutter out with his own language. The aptness of this obfuscated correlation does not simply lie in its *muteness*: in an almost concrete sense, securing the 'avian' shutter into place – nailing
it, literally – also directly results in silencing it, or 'nailing its beak'. One may
note in passing that such covert punning would be more improbable in English,
if only because of the all too obvious derivational linkage between 'shutter'
and 'shut (up)'. As for the half-veiled, loaded or ironic allusions to a religious
framework, they might be traced to other expressions present in the text. In the
light of Christ-like suffering, the seemingly paradoxical wording 's'assommer *à*

sa guise contre le mur' (my emphasis) seems to trivialise obliquely (possibly into masochistic impulse) what could have potentially been read as self-sacrifice or martyrdom, as a gallant or defiant, albeit poignant, last stand. One may likewise suspect that the idiomatic, now semantically unmarked expression, 'Dieu merci' (see two paragraphs down), is not entirely devoid of antiphrastic derision. Before the death of the Son of God on the Cross is even explicitly evoked, the 'drôle d'oiseau cloué' might be taken to recall even more ancient superstitious or conjuratory rites such as, in early Rome, the nailing of an owl to the door of a house in order to ward off evil.

The next paragraph continues to hit the nail on the head, so to speak, mostly in terms of bipolarity or binarity, as we might have expected from the brief, exclamatory *articulation*, 'Vlan, deux fois': opened v. closed, silence v. noise, visibility v. invisibility, sayability v. unsayability. More telling, however, is the slippage from a mainly impersonal mode of description-definition to a subjective agency through the modulation of personal pronouns: 'nous', 'on', and finally 'je', concluding with another *battement* or oscillation of the literal and the figurative whereby the letter of a common phrase is reactivated and the connection between vision and writing foregrounded: 'je ne *vois* plus rien à en *dire*' (italics added). This syntagm adumbrates the final assertion before the oracle, in the form of an emphasised direct address this time: 'Plein fermé, je n'y vois plus goutte. Grand ouvert, je ne *te* vois plus.'

All of this leads logically to the ensuing paragraphs which develop and exacerbate those various elements – more particularly, the personal narrative as well as the appearance–disappearance duality. The former aspect is in a way encapsulated by a deceptively banal statement like 'quand j'ai ouvert mon volet ce matin'. The possessive adjective *mon* actuates the shift from the notional essence of an anonymous object (to be defined and reduced to its core qualities, or distinctive features)[2] to a subjective, indeed sensory, experience, complete with a surprisingly heightened, almost intimate, sense of physicality or corporeality ('j'ai senti son poids'), about a specific individual (at once representative of and distinct from its class), which will subsequently turn 'mon volet' into a quasi-term of endearment: 'Ho ! Ho ! mon volet, que fais-tu ?' A seemingly minimal or insignificant temporal coordinate is added to the deixis ('Aujourd'hui, cela eut plus d'importance'), soon to be symmetrically opposed to other days ('D'autres jours, cela n'a aucune importance') and finally oxymoronically conflated with 'eternity'. What might be at first glance perceived as an incoherence or an impossibility is in fact closer to a form of circular pattern of closure. From (the) window shutter as a rather opaque artefact that a single metaphor, no matter how diversified or complexified, cannot quite seem to capture or fix, to a particular *volet* 'caught' in a deictic, *hic et nunc* context and part of a sympathetic, if not empathetic, rapport, and on to the atemporal, universal essentialising of the object, the wheel has come full circle (or, to put it in a more Pongian fashion, the shutter-bird has folded back its singularly single wing): 'voici donc qu'aujourd'hui, pour l'éternité, aujourd'hui dans l'éternité le volet aura grincé'. The overemphatic grandiloquence of the statement should alert us to the partly tongue-in-cheek nature of the passage and its repeated, ironic use of the Christian lexicon. Eternity is thus to be understood in a secular (immortality) rather than in a religious (the hereafter) sense, unless Ponge has more specifically in mind Spinoza's *sub specie aeternitatis* (i.e., under the aspect or from the point of view of eternity), which serves to designate what is universally and eternally true. More importantly, perhaps, and half in jest, half in earnest this time, the process of immortalisation is here less concerned with the object proper – be it that of the poet's desire (the beloved one), as in the love poetry of yesteryear (in that sense, the emphasis on 'aujourd'hui' might be seen as an indirect reference to the *carpe diem* trope, in its original Horatian stoicism rather than in the Ronsardian vein), or that of his investigative scrutiny (here, the shutter) – than with the lyrical subject and, above all, the text itself.

That said, the three elements are now inextricably linked, as the use of the first-person possessive adjective in 'mon volet' can now be interpreted as a marker not only of *ownership* but of *authorship* of a text-object. In other words, we are presented with an original artefact '(signed on the inside)' (an interiority typographically visualised or reduplicated by the parentheses that frame it), as will be specified at the end of the oracle, in lieu of the customary inscription of the actual name of the poet/artist, as at the close of *Le Pré*, for example. Signing is an all-important and complex issue in Ponge's writings, as Derrida has shown.[3] In the case of 'Le Volet', the signature per se can be dispensed with insofar as the author's name has already been mentioned in a feigned ceremonious fashion: 'et rendez-vous compte de ce qu'est aujourd'hui dans un texte de Francis Ponge'. More fundamentally, the stele-like, upper case, punctuation-free, octosyllabic oracle that concludes the pre-scholium section of the poem is a perfect example of the ideal Pongian text-as-object or object-as-text: one that, patterned after Roman lapidary writing (monuments, stone inscriptions, etc.) and emulating a Malherbian paradigm that Ponge (re-)constructs *after* Lautréamont, can stand on its own in perpetuity, braving and resisting the ravages of time (or the weather); one that will prove to be simultaneously crystal clear and enigmatic, predictive and ambiguous, accessible and authoritative, elementary and elemental, idiosyncratic and anonymous; one that will foreground *le propre* or *le particulier* (peculiarity, ownness, idiosyncrasy, singularity, subjectivity) as the only basis of, and even guarantor for, *le commun* (commonness, universality, generalness or genericity, proverbiality, popular wisdom, impersonality).

The opening of the shutter ('j'ai ouvert mon volet ce matin') was already reminiscent of an increasingly common practice – more strategic than contextual or ritualistic – in Ponge's *écriture* in the 1940s: the opening of a notebook.[4] A pivotal moment in this allegorical process is when the conflation of the two planes (including in a geometrical sense since in both cases we are dealing with surfaces) is, if not quite completed, explicitly signalled, as the window shutter is 'impatiemment rabattu contre cette page blanche'. Textuality and referentiality will henceforth coincide, the page being quite literally written under the shutter's *imprint*. In that respect, the introduction of the *stabat* sequence is not the mere continuation or re-injection of a previously noted biblical isotopy (the nailing of the window shutter); it also furthers the textual dimension of the object: the shutter is now hooked to the wall by the 2 *a*'s of *stabat*,[5] the latter being paronomastically, albeit belatedly (for an enhanced surprise effect), linked to 'ça bat', thus referring us back to the *incipit*. More generally, the entire passage is rhetorically saturated, from anaphora ('stabat' repeated, mantra-like, at the beginning of numerous sentences) to epanalepsis ('stabat' opens and closes the section, thereby bookending it) via anastrophe (which results in a systematic *rejet* of 'volet', each time accenting it at the end of a sentence). All this is typical of Ponge's processual, palimpsestic modalities of writing, characterised as they are by reiteration and self-correction, variation and amplification. The fourth indented line is a case in point: 'Stabat et ça crie. Stabat et ça a crié. Stabat et ça grince et ça a crié un volet.' Through this process of over-determination and dissemination, the language of the shutter, or the shutter-as-language, is truly swinging on its own hinges, against or with the written page.[6]

The fact remains that the syntagm 'Stabat un volet' (and its variants) cannot but tacitly reference a religious and iconic intertext: *Stabat mater dolorosa* ('the sorrowful mother was standing') are the opening words of a liturgical hymn from the Roman Catholic ritual, referring to the suffering of Mary during the Crucifixion of her son. If, as we have mentioned, this source illuminates *a posteriori* the nailing-of-the-shutter moment (another example of that delayed revelation or deferral effect favoured by Ponge, at the risk sometimes of turning his texts into erudite riddles or endless treasure hunts), the dual process of radical truncation and reappropriation/reconfiguration secularises the empathetic piety and sentimentality of the original citation, most noticeably by the erasure of the tormented maternal figure. It recontextualises them into an objectal being-thereness (*Dastehen* rather than *Dasein*) or possibly an exemplary fabular trope:[7] 'Stabat un volet', or *Il était une fois un volet*. Furthermore, an earlier passage had already staged a subterranean subversion or de-spiritualisation of a sacred archetype in the form of a strictly mechanistic epiphany (which should not be surprising, coming from a self-confessed devotee of Lucretian materialism like Ponge). The actual opening of the window shutter as a purely sensorial, bodily experience takes precedence (in every sense) over what it opens onto – be it a *deus absconditus*, or the sign of a divine presence ('lumière délivrée') hidden in the landscape à la Jaccottet, or even a phenomenal reality ('l'apparition du monde extérieur'). No theophany or ontophany here. What is at stake, however, is a much more mundane paradigm shift: centring one's interest on a single item pertaining to our quotidian realm of existence, and as such largely unnoticed, if not invisible.[8] In lieu of some grand, sweeping vista on the sensible world, or of a *fiat lux* that would create, conjure up, or disclose the real, a more modest shift in perspective and focus is liable to enable us to actually seize and see an object such as the shutter. Failing which, as is the case on other days, when the poet is 'un homme comme les autres', hopelessly blind and deaf to his immediate environment, the shutter on the window is 'rigoureusement rien'. This applies, by extension to the world of man-made, proximate objects, with a predilection for the most common or 'médiocre' (e.g. 'La Cruche'), the most maligned or insignificant (e.g. 'Le Cageot'), if not the most ungraceful of them: with the help of paronomasia, one might say that the 'volet' *grince* because it is lacking, aesthetically and spiritually speaking, *grace* – or is it *graisse* (*grease*)? All or nothing, double or quits: such a categorical dichotomy manifestly reinscribes the fade-in/fade-out rhythm of the 'volet'.

If Ponge next introduces a cursory, contrasting look at the pendulum, this is not simply a renewed conative gesturing towards the differential propriety or the specific set of attributes of the object under scrutiny. The rest of the poem (excluding the oracle) conspicuously *oscillates* between abstract notions and concrete, even anecdotal, details, between seriousness and flippancy. For instance, no sooner is a discussion about free will (defined as 'an important point') initiated than it is abruptly dismissed with cavalier detachment. It soon leads up to a brief snapshot of fictional narrative which seems to perform a coincidence of diegesis and mimesis through an unmediated, informal apostrophe inciting the window shutter to self-expression and verbalisation – 'in real time'. This, one may note, stands in contra-distinction to the author's initial objective, as stated in his conversations with Sollers, of talking the *volet* down, and therefore bears testimony to the dramatic evolution of the rapport between subject and object. Surprisingly, for a poet who has long professed an anti-Valéryan stance vis-à-vis any worldview privileging the intellect ('Ideas are not my forte', he declared at the beginning of *My Creative Method*, defiantly turning the *incipit* of *Monsieur Teste* on its head), and a mocking distrust of the 'grrrands métaphysicoliciens', one of the intended functions of *sapates* such as 'Le Volet' is precisely to cleanse the reader of such intellectual approaches;[9] yet, unsurprisingly, in an openly self-reflexive, metadiscursive development, philosophical considerations largely prevail in the 'Scholie', at least nominally and not without a degree of irony. They could easily be rearranged as a chain of binaries: cognition or rationality ('intelligence') v. aesthetics ('beauté') (this quasi-Kantian duality being displaced in the final, self-doubting sentence by the idiomatic use of 'reason': *avoir raison de*, or 'to get the better of'); dignity or modesty v. pathos and authenticity; formal perfection v. semantic ambiguity and cruelty.

According to the poet himself, there seems to be a practical 'lesson' to be learned in that coda. The scholium is yet another obscure and antiquated rhetorical form that has now all but fallen out of usage outside of mathematical treatises, which is here rescued by Ponge who, after all, early coveted the title of scientist rather than poet. In line with the original philological practice, it is here presented as a gloss, or 'tentative d'explication', as the author defined it to Sollers. Mallarmé's *scolies* (cf., for instance, *Igitur*) are thus both referenced and held at bay (as the difference in spelling might indicate): far from being a mere variant or draft appended as raw material, the Pongian *scholie* appears to be a both ludic and scrupulous effort towards hermeneutic analysis via self-correction. Regardless of whether the reader will indeed first find it illuminating or, on the contrary, confusing, it is essentially a postscript or addendum (a 'note après coup', to borrow from the subtitle of 'La Mounine') highlighting a specific, concrete, factual – indeed (auto)biographical – detail that pertains not to the genesis of the text as a whole (the *scholie* never addresses the extended description-representation of the *volet*), but to the allegorical crystallisation of the oracle. While reinforcing the overlapping of text and shutter (the lines of verse on the page are homologous to the slits in the shutter, and one can equally *see the light* between the former and through the latter), as well as of text and paratext (the scholium), the motivated inclusion and articulation of the two oracular versions blurs all operative distinctions between *texte* and *avant-texte*, thereby bypassing, if not undermining, the efforts of genetic criticism by seemingly providing readers with a 'turnkey' textual construction.

This, however, does in no way imply that a fixed, pre-determined meaning is assigned to, or built into, the poem-cum-critical-apparatus: as soon as the shutter can no longer exercise its free will or free play – its *jeu*, as both play and slack – by swinging around its hinges, it becomes invisible and therefore unutterable, unwritable. Either it defies fixity or it resists language. Similarly, albeit in a different context, the unusual act of textual self-censorship presented in the scholium potentially suggests that an exposed residual meaning can conceal another. By definition, muzzling oneself or keeping things under wraps, as much as letting a coded subtext show through, is not a neutral or insignificant gesture in the charged context of occupied France. Without adhering to the 'contrebande' style of a poem like 'Le Platane' (a half-veiled allegory of endurance and national identity in times of adversity, ending with a barely disguised call to join the Resistance), the combined notions of censorship (in the writing process), freedom of expression or móvement (as personified by the shutter), subordination of truth and beauty to the pragmatism of a 'new order', are definitely susceptible to political or ideological interpretation. Be that as it may, not only is an appreciable amount of interpretative leeway left to the reader, but the latter acquires a key role in the production and perpetuation of the poem in either version of the oracle. Outwardly paronymous in nature, the revision of 'lit' into 'livre' might also be based on an untold correlation: the idea of *coucher* (lying down) links the (death)bed as couch to the book as that which is couched in writing. Underscored by typography and inverted syntax alike ('d'avoir eu, de ce LIT, raison'), the reprise of *ce lit* (this bed) in the closing sentence should alert us to a possible homophonic echo with *se lit* (is read). In a sense, the epitaphic oracle should indeed be read as an alpha and omega micro-narrative – not so much the compass of human existence, however, as the condensed story of the creative-critical process structured around three key moments: the death of the author or scriptor (a construct that should perhaps be viewed less as a precursor of Barthesian and post-structuralist tenets than as a throwback to the potential elocutionary vanishing of the poet behind words according to Mallarmé); the birth of the poem ('voir le jour' amphibologically refers both to coming into the world and seeing daylight through the shutter slits); and the reader as heir or legatee (on the condition that he or she be able to crack the text – elicit its potentialities or decode its plural meaning – by 'reading between the lines').

If the processual *mise-en-scène* or performance of the shutter – its animation or articulation – moved from opposition and imposition (the shutter making its physical presence felt forcefully while resisting any external attempt to comprehend, assimilate or reduce it) to interposition (between the gazing subject and the phenomenological reality) and superposition (of referent and text), the self-referential, metapoetic oracle completes and exemplifies the core of Pongian poetics par excellence: not simply the con-fusion but, to plagiarise Claudel, the *co-naissance* of object and text as authorial epitaph. 'Volet plein naît écrit strié'.

Notes

1 Francis, Ponge, *Pièces* (Paris: Gallimard, 1962), pp. 103–6.
2 The article is elided before 'volet' at the start of the poem as if this were a dictionary entry. Although unsystematic, this is a device that Ponge is wont to use. See, for example, the spectacular opening of 'Le Cheval' where this elision of articles is disseminated through an entire sentence and coupled with antepositioned qualifiers for greater defamiliarising effect.
3 See, in particular, Jacques Derrida, *Signéponge* (Paris: Seuil, 1998).
4 See the texts later collected in *La Rage de l'expression* (Paris: Gallimard, 1976), notably 'Le Mimosa': 'Comme c'est un sujet très difficile il faut donc que j'ouvre un cahier' (p. 76).
5 In Philippe Sollers, *Entretiens de Francis Ponge avec Philippe Sollers* (Paris: Gallimard, 1970), Ponge further points out that the vertical lines of military rifles held in the 'present arms' position, mentioned in the final paragraph of that section, mimologically represent the two *t*'s of *stabat*.
6 See in the previous section: 'le volet aura . . . tourné sur ses gonds'. See also in 'Ébauche d'un poisson', which immediately precedes our poem in the volume *Pièces*, the definition of the 'tournoie' as a 'poisson de l'épaisseur d'un volet' which sometimes 'tourne sur ses gonds' (pp. 99–102).
7 Ponge often expressed his desire to emulate the great French fabulist, Jean de La Fontaine.
8 Defined as 'un de ces objets dont, bien qu'ils se rapportent directement à eux, ils [i.e. les humains] ne se rendent habituellement pas le moindre compte', the *lessiveuse* is but one of numerous examples of our neglect and inattention, courtesy of a jaded perception (*Pièces*, p. 72).
9 *Pages bis, V*, in *Le Parti pris des choses: Proêmes* (Paris, Gallimard: 1978), p. 193.

Further reading

Beugnot, Bernard, *Poétique de Francis Ponge: le palais diaphane* (Paris: Presses Universitaires de France, 1990).

Collot, Michel, *Francis Ponge: entre mots et choses* (Seyssel: Champ Vallon, 1991).
  La Matière-émotion (Paris: Presses Universitaires de France, 1997).

Derrida, Jacques, *Déplier Ponge: entretien de Jacques Derrida avec Gérard Farasse* (Villeneuve d'Ascq: Presses Universitaires du Septentrion, 2005).

Farasse, Gérard, *L'Âne musicien: sur Francis Ponge* (Paris: Gallimard, 1996).

Gleize, Jean-Marie, *Francis Ponge* (Paris: Seuil, 1988).
  (ed.), *Ponge, résolument* (Lyon: ENS Éditions, 2004).

Higgins, Ian, *Francis Ponge* (London: Athlone Press, 1979).

Met, Philippe, *Formules de la poésie: études sur Ponge, Leiris, Char et Du Bouchet* (Paris: Presses Universitaires de France, 1999).

Ponge, Francis, *Méthodes* (Paris: Gallimard, 1988).
  Selected Poems, ed. Margaret Guiton, trans. Margaret Guiton, John Montague and C. K. Williams (London: Faber and Faber, 1998).
  Soap, trans. Lane Dunlop (Stanford, CA: Stanford University Press, 1998).

Sartre, Jean-Paul, *Situations I* (Paris: Gallimard, 1947).

Schwenger, Peter, 'Words and the Murder of the Thing', *Critical Inquiry* 28 (Autumn 2001), pp. 99–113.

Veck, Bernard, *Francis Ponge, ou le refus de l'absolu littéraire* (Liège: Mardaga, 1993).

Part III

Poetics of presence

15 René Char, 'Gravité'

ROGER CARDINAL

Gravité

L'emmuré
S'il respire il pense à l'encoche
Dans la tendre chaux confidente
Où ses mains du soir étendent ton corps.

Le laurier l'épuise,
La privation le consolide.   5

Ô toi, la monotone absente,
La fileuse de salpêtre,
Derrière des épaisseurs fixes
Une échelle sans âge déploie ton voile !

Tu vas nue, constellée d'échardes,   10
Secrète, tiède et disponible,
Attachée au sol indolent,
Mais l'intime de l'homme abrupt dans sa prison.

À te mordre les jours grandissent,
Plus arides, plus imprenables que les nuages qui se   15
    déchirent au fond des os.

                        *

J'ai pesé de tout mon désir
Sur ta beauté matinale
Pour qu'elle éclate et se sauve.

L'ont suivie l'alcool sans rois mages,   20
Le battement de ton triangle,
La main-d'œuvre de tes yeux
Et le gravier debout sur l'algue.

Un parfum d'insolation
Protège ce qui va éclore.   25

From *Fureur et mystère*

147

The poetic writings of René Char are characterised by a gnarled terseness which shuns ornamentation. Travelling beyond its origins in the spontaneity of Surrealist automatism, the mature work aspires to a measured alertness and austerity. Char has the reputation of being elliptical and abrupt. His idiom thrives on wilful contradiction and startling paradox, with nodes of urgent, compressed meaning set amid stretches of more relaxed evocation. Imbued with a strong philosophical strain and stripped of redundancy, his poems tend to assume an impermeable hardness, as if they had been hammered out on an anvil and tempered in icy water.

Char's poetry is oriented to a range of aesthetic, emotional and moral concerns, and his instinct is always to face up to challenging extremes. His search for expressive fulfilment is often at the expense of mental stress. 'Beauté, je me porte à ta rencontre dans la solitude du froid', he writes, as through gritted teeth, in the poetological sequence 'Afin qu'il n'y soit rien changé'. This bold stepping forth, in defiance of discomfort, implies confidence and a concomitant refusal of vagueness. Yet there is a lingering hesitancy, a fringe of wordless implication about Char's declaration: for the time being, we may infer, not quite everything has been said, and what still remains unsaid may not altogether be sayable in commonplace speech. Accordingly, the poet must settle for being a *magicien de l'insécurité*, never an infallible lawmaker or formulator of absolutes. This is why, when we read Char, we should not expect each and every dictum to yield meaning effortlessly.

Let us examine the verse poem 'Gravité'.[1] As readers coming fresh to these lines, we need to settle a few immediate questions. Who is speaking here? To whom? And under what circumstances? If we are prepared to accept that there must be more to this textual unit than a disjointed jumble, then we can begin by spelling out a few reasonably straightforward inferences. We can safely assume that the addressee (*tu*) is female, given that her qualities are voiced through feminine adjectives (e.g. 'nue', 'secrète'). She is being addressed by a first-person speaker (*je*) whose tone is sufficiently passionate to indicate the voice of a (presumably male) lover. (In strict fact, the pronoun *je* occurs only in the second part of the poem, but in the first we can take *je* as the implied speaker. *Tu*, of course, occurs in both parts.) It remains to identify a third-person male protagonist (*il*), who is absent from the second part of the poem. However, it is not difficult to make a small leap of interpretation and to conclude that the *il* of the first part of the poem and the *je* of the second signify the selfsame person. This hastens a more compact reading, and heralds coherence, given that there are now only two protagonists to consider. Moreover, we are beginning to grasp that the poem is delivered in two instalments. In the first phase of the text, the lover seeks to articulate his predicament in objective terms, while the second represents a more personal outpouring of his impassioned desire. The phrases 'mains du soir' and 'beauté matinale' are indications of a distinct shift between the two phases: from the nocturnal to the diurnal, or from darkness to light.

Thus far, the poem seems to be about a lover's fascination with a female addressee (*tu*), whose attributes are laid out as a sequence of feminised adjectives and past participles. These generate a flurry of metaphoric associations suggestive of an exceptional and exciting presence.

> Tu vas nue, constellée d'échardes,
> Secrète, tiède et disponible,
> Attachée au sol indolent

The reader is invited to visualise a female creature, unclothed yet hard to see because of her 'constellation of shards' – we might try to make sense of this image in terms of the effect of splintered light cast across her body. This makes her seem enigmatic ('secrète'), though she is still accessible to understanding and contact ('disponible'). The warmth ('tiède') of her nakedness seems a function of her nonchalant sauntering across the earth. That phrase 'sol indolent' can be taken as a transferred epithet, for it may be supposed that it is in fact the woman who is indolent, or rather who becomes indolent to the extent that she is attached to the earth and is thereby recognisable as a fully corporeal being, subject to the law of gravity ('attachée au sol'). This reading offers a firm handhold to support our further steps of construal.

Let us return to the title of the poem. If the word 'Gravité' is our first clue as to how the poem is to unfold, then we may begin with the expectation that the text has to do with an issue of some weight, a situation of some gravity. Knowing Char's reputation, we may want to prepare ourselves for a prospect of interpretative difficulty or 'heavy going'. The subtitle '*L'emmuré*' confirms and compounds this prospect in its suggestion of confinement, at which point, we may begin to posit a confrontation within the space of the poem of two contrary impulses: one conducive to heaviness and inertia, the other to buoyancy and euphoria. That we are listening to a male prisoner who is trapped within torpor seems a reasonable inference; the female presence then emerges as the conduit of energy and zestfulness.

If we set the text aside for a moment, we can bring into play certain insights arising from supplementary knowledge of Char's work. It is worth clarifying the context in which 'Gravité' first appeared, namely the poetic sequence *Le Visage nuptial*. Of the five poems therein, 'Gravité' was the first to be written, probably in early 1937. It was published in May 1938, in Char's last pre-war collection *Dehors la nuit est gouvernée*. The other four poems were composed in the spring and summer of 1938, but the completed set was not published until after the war, in February 1945, in the volume *Seuls demeurent*. This was then re-issued, along with the wartime notebook *Feuillets d'Hypnos* and other material, in Char's most important collection, the 1948 compendium whose title can be taken as his watchword: *Fureur et mystère*.

As a sequence, *Le Visage nuptial* unfolds with increasing poetic and emotional intensity, Char's customary pithiness giving way to lyrical fluency. Notably, the third poem, 'Le Visage nuptial' – which gives its name to the whole sequence and follows immediately after 'Gravité' – is a celebration in verse of a magical female who equates to a pagan goddess, mediating flux and governing the movement of impulses throughout the natural world. It is known that Char was reading the pre-Socratic philosopher Heraclitus at the time of writing this poem, and we may take the Greek thinker's cosmology as a legitimate framework of understanding. It posits a space of flux in which opposing forces constantly clash yet resolve into harmony.

Furthermore, biographical information about Char's great love of the Vaucluse region, where he grew up, allows us to situate these ideas and images within an actual setting. Once we learn that Char particularly treasured the slow-moving River Sorgue, which crosses this area, it suddenly makes sense to read the lines about a secret female 'attached to the indolent earth' as a half-hidden reference to that stream, its exposed surface shimmering with speckled light ('constellée d'échardes'). Admittedly, Char does not develop this riverine theme any further, except in the phrase 'Et le gravier debout sur l'algue'.

Whether as woman, goddess or river, Char's beloved is being presented to us in a vision determined by the resources of the poetic process. By this token, she participates in a general allegory of creativity and loveliness. Indeed, Char's symbolic scheme in this poem is almost certainly underpinned by a character-istic association whereby the beloved woman represents poetry itself. It is a fact that many modern poets, such as Yves Bonnefoy, Jacques Dupin and Octavio Paz, have repeatedly exploited the tropes of love and eroticism as fuel for metaphoric extrapolation in their poetry and a means to introduce secondary (metatextual) observations about writing itself. In like fashion, Char draws on the lexicon of amorous desire to articulate a pattern of meanings relative to his personal poetics. It would make perfect sense to say that the woman addressed in the poem *is* the poetry: that is, she is synonymous with the semiotic inter-weaving proposed by the poet's intellect and imagination. A splendid mirage, she nonetheless inhabits a verbal fabric which fervently seeks to summon up a palpable presence.

'Gravité' presents this mythic creature through a rich, exclamatory saluta-tion:

> Ô toi, la monotone absente,
> La fileuse de salpêtre,
> Derrière des épaisseurs fixes
> Une échelle sans âge déploie ton voile !

The excited and intimate address 'Ô toi !' at once conveys the emotional arousal of the speaker and seems rather at odds with the third-person reference which follows – 'la monotone absente' – an epithet that seems to reduce her to an object of indifference: for we may suppose that, if she is 'monotone', she can hardly inspire interest, while if she is 'absente', then she is beyond reach anyway.

It is certainly hard to picture such an ambiguous being – a woman at once there and not there. She is acknowledged as an enigma insofar as she wears a veil ('ton voile [déployé]'), and is hidden ('derrière des épaisseurs fixes'). Yet she is also a 'fileuse de salpêtre', a fairytale figure capable of spinning (and thus producing malleable fabric) – albeit the crystalline substance, saltpetre (potassium nitrate). What she has chosen to spin is strictly non-malleable and potentially dangerous (saltpetre is the principal ingredient in gunpowder). These intriguing yet vexing lines are of course not the only ones that will tax our patience and elude full illumination.

If much of what is being said about this desirable female in the first section of the poem partakes of the imaginary, its last lines do herald a sense of the physical, and indeed do so through a violent image: 'À te mordre' introduces an idea of direct and indeed aggressive contact. And once we come to the second section, with its switch to an explicit and assertive *je*, the actuality of a woman's beauty is realised in an abrupt and sensual spasm.

> J'ai pesé de tout mon désir
> Sur ta beauté matinale
> Pour qu'elle éclate et se sauve.

Whereas they were somewhat sluggish in the first section, the advances of the male lover are now accelerated and fulfilled, the past tense underlining an indisputable sense of consummation. Possession of the beloved woman represents both a wideawake response to her 'beauté matinale' and a stimulus to its swift bursting-forth ('éclate') and no less swift dispersal ('se sauve'). We cannot escape the fact that, at the literal level, these lines delineate an erotic encounter. In allegorical terms, the poet may be boasting that he has grasped the essence of the poetic and known the triumph of definitive expression. As the critic Jean-Pierre Richard has observed, Char often muses upon encounters, both euphoric and stormy: 'Et de fait quelque chose d'orageux, de dangereusement électrique précède toujours et entoure pour Char les jonctions heureuses.'[2] In 'Gravité', the erotic coupling has the character almost of a clash of combatants – we recall the earlier allusion to biting ('À te mordre'). In their lapidary formulation, these lines offer a glimpse of, as it were, a singular climactic wound. Yet, if it countenances a destruction, it is one which, paradoxically, generates a fresh order. Within the logic of the poetic, the shock of collapse becomes pivotal – a dangerous embrace at once modulating into its opposite. As Heraclitus might have said, darkness necessarily gives rise to light.

The twinning of darkness and light is indeed a thematic constant in Char's work, and is reflected in his enthusiasm for the Renaissance artist Georges de la Tour, one of whose paintings, dating from around 1640–5, depicts a woman with a candle visiting a prisoner in his cell. Char had come across the picture in 1934, at an exhibition held in the Orangerie in Paris. At the time, it bore the title *Le Prisonnier*. (It is now commonly identified as *Job et sa femme*, but Char

151

ignores the biblical reference.) Proof of the poet's attachment to the work is to be found in entry 178 of *Feuillets d'Hypnos*, the prose notebook he kept during his highly fraught career as a guerrilla leader in the *maquis*. Char relates how he pinned a coloured postcard on the whitewashed wall of his command post and how he and his fellows drew solace from the figure dispelling darkness with her candle flame. The radiant orange of her robe dominates the picture; as she bends to speak to the huddled prisoner, clad in rags and barefoot, so her hand seems about to smooth his hair. Char imagines her speaking: 'Le Verbe de la femme donne naissance à l'inespéré mieux que n'importe quelle aurore'. It is clear that the poet militant, during the dark night of conflict, envisages the woman as a promise of liberation, while the association of freedom with daybreak points back to the pre-war poem 'La Liberté'. These various allusions and echoes mark the poet's effort to formulate a Resistance credo through an efficacious symbolism. (Further, one could see his iconic female as consonant with the traditional personification of France as Marianne.)

It is worth noting that the explanatory subtitle *'L'emmuré'* (the incarcerated one) was inserted into 'Gravité' only in 1945, when the poem was finally lodged within *Le Visage nuptial*. The relatively abstruse past participle makes an explicit link with the same entry in *Feuillets d'Hypnos*, where we find the sentence 'La femme explique, l'emmuré écoute'. To apply this to 'Gravité' is to confirm a relationship, for the beloved addressee is there described as 'l'intime de l'homme abrupt dans sa prison'. Now much of our text can be legitimately understood as the reverie of a long-term prisoner, eking out 'les jours. . . arides' of captivity with erotic images.

> S'il respire il pense à l'encoche
> Dans la tendre chaux confidente
> Où ses mains du soir étendent ton corps.

These lines indicate that the man draws breath at the thought of a groove or slit ('encoche') cut into the whitewashed wall of his cell; we may suppose that he has scratched an image of the desired body ('ses mains. . . étendent ton corps') into that hard surface, which at once becomes 'tendre' (sensually yielding) and 'confidente' (complicit, intimate). I take this to be an index of the capacity of the prisoner to refute captivity through a vision shaped by amorous longing. The immured lover embraces an incarnation of the desirable, just as the poet finds beauty and hope in the idea of light overcoming darkness.

We have now come to see Char's agitated text as the condensed and fervent telling of a multifaceted allegorical tale. In a compelling act of the imagination, a protagonist who is at once lover, poet, prisoner and combatant manages to transcend his predicament and to transform his narrow prison – and the constraints of ordinary consciousness – into what, to borrow a phrase from Gaston Bachelard, may be termed an 'immensité intime'. Char's title may now be construed as a dual index, first of the poet's insistence upon a deeply committed approach to the poetic enterprise, and second of the need for weightiness, for a commitment to earthly priorities – a refutation of idle make-believe. For Char, as both poet and freedom-fighter, it is vital that things be real.

There is, of course, no denying that we still have a devious and fitful residue on our hands. A laurel tree, spun saltpetre, a ladder, a veil, torn clouds, alcohol, the Magi, a throbbing triangle, sunstroke – how can such a miscellany of signifiers hold together? Even if enunciated with authority, Char's pronouncements can remain baffling. I might guess that 'Un laurier l'épuise' could translate as 'the prisoner is disheartened by facile praise' (the laurel crown being a mark of acclaim); and that he prefers to be left to his own devices ('La privation le consolide'). But I can find little satisfaction in the final couplet: 'Un parfum d'insolation / Protège ce qui va éclore'. Such pockets of resistance float like debris on the tide, and we just have to tolerate them, hoping at least to have caught the main drift. The critic Georges Poulet has observed Char's tendency to transmit 'une vision morcelée et déchiquetée',[3] but contends that the very fragmentation of his discourse creates a force-field of energies, a dissemination of impulses which recharge our imaginative hold on a widening space. The poet Jacques Dupin sees Char's writing in similar terms as 'un éclatement qui se perpétue',[4] an explosion of gunpowder, so to speak, which never ceases to reverberate. This could be taken to mean, as Char's text itself allows, that strong poetic writing gives rise to a beauty 'qui éclate et se sauve' – such beauty comes in an amazing outburst and then disperses, so as to mark the world with meanings that are puzzling yet indelible.

Notes

1 René Char, *Fureur et mystère* (Paris: Gallimard, 1962), pp. 56–7.
2 Jean-Pierre Richard, *Onze études sur la poésie moderne* (Paris: Seuil, 1964), p. 96.
3 George Poulet, 'René Char: de la constriction à la dissémination', *L'Arc*, 22 (Summer 1963), p. 45.
4 Jacques Dupin, 'René Char', in Georges Raillard, *Jacques Dupin* (Paris: Éditions Seghers, 1974), pp. 157–8.

Further reading

Cardinal, Roger (ed.), *Sensibility and Creation: Studies in Twentieth-Century French Poetry* (New York: Barnes and Noble, 1977).
Caws, Mary Ann, *The Presence of René Char* (Princeton, NJ: Princeton University Press, 1976).
Char, René, *Poems of René Char*, trans. Mary Ann Caws and Jonathan Griffin (Princeton, NJ: Princeton University Press, 1976).
   Selected Poems of René Char, trans. Mary Ann Caws and Tina Jolas (New York: New Directions, 1992).
Fourcade, Dominique (ed.), *René Char* (Paris: L'Herne, 1971).

Greene, Robert W., *Six French Poets of our Time: A Critical and Historical Study* (Princeton, NJ: Princeton University Press, 1979).

Lawler, James R., *René Char: The Myth and the Poem* (Princeton, NJ: Princeton University Press, 1978).

Mathieu, Jean-Claude, *La Poésie de René Char, ou, Le Sel de la splendeur* (Paris: José Corti, 1984–85).

Michel, Laure, *René Char: le poème et l'histoire, 1930–1950* (Paris: Champion, 2007).

Minahen, Charles D. (ed.), *Figuring Things: Char, Ponge, and Poetry in the Twentieth Century* (Lexington, KY: French Forum, 1994).

Mounin, Georges, *La Communication poétique, précédé de Avez-vous lu Char?* (Paris: Gallimard, 1969).

Soulé, Yves, *René Char, une géologie talismanique* (Paris: L'Harmattan, 2006).

Veyne, Paul, *René Char en ses poèmes* (Paris: Gallimard, 1990).

16 Yves Bonnefoy, 'Rue Traversière'

VICTORIA BEST

Rue Traversière

Quand j'étais enfant je m'inquiétais beaucoup d'une certaine rue Traversière. Car à une de ses entrées, pas trop loin de notre maison et de l'école, c'était le monde ordinaire, tandis qu'à l'autre, là-bas. . . Cependant que ce nom troué de feux m'assurait qu'elle était bien le passage.

Et je regardais donc de tous mes yeux à droite et à gauche quand nous la prenions, car cela nous arrivait, à des jours, et même pour aller jusqu'au bout, comme si c'eût été une rue quelconque, mais je parvenais là fatigué, un peu endormi, et c'était soudain l'espace bizarre du grand jardin botanique. – Est-ce ici, m'étais-je dit à plusieurs moments, que là-bas commence ? Ici, dans cette maison dont les volets sont fermés? Ici, sous ce lilas ? Et dans ce groupe d'enfants qui jouent, au cerceau, aux billes, sur le trottoir déjointé par l'herbe, l'un n'est-il pas déjà de l'autre bord, ne touche-t-il pas les mains des petites filles d'ici avec des doigts de ténèbre ? Notions certes contradictoires, fuyantes. D'autant que ces pavillons, ces voûtes d'arrière-cour, ne se distinguaient nullement de beaucoup d'autres de notre ville, on n'y sentait, on n'y respirait jusqu'aux dernières portes de tôle peinte que le surcroît de torpeur des banlieues un peu potagères. Ah, que ce qui importe a peu de visage ! Arrivé au jardin, qui a des noms inscrits sous chaque arbre, dans l'odeur autre, je partais en courant, soudain réveillé, je voulais aller loin, entrer ailleurs, mais les allées bordées de petits arceaux devaient bien tourner, dans l'ombre du buis, et se renouer à leur origine, car je me retrouvais vite au point de départ, cette fois encore.

Quel bien m'a fait ce nom de rue Traversière ; et ce jardin des essences ; et ce latin végétal dans les soirs de chaleur humide !

Il y a cinq ans, quand ma mère fut soignée à l'hôpital qui est auprès du jardin, je suis passé à nouveau, deux ou trois fois, à des

155

heures d'après-midi, rue Traversière. Je retrouvais simultanément, après tant d'années au loin, la ville de l'enfance presque oubliée et cette rue qui ouvrait à un autre monde.

Et c'était toujours la même prudence, ou même paix ; toujours cette odeur mouillée des salades devant les portes, ces vieilles qui cousent l'infini dans des linges décolorés aux fenêtres, toujours ces paons byzantins affrontés dans la broderie des rideaux de salle à manger, dont l'un parfois bouge, une seconde. Et la craie tuffeau qui se délite à l'angle des murs, encore. Et ces enfants silencieux. Non, la rue Traversière n'avait pas changé. Et pourtant. . .

Comment dire ? Il me semble qu'ici, où j'étais, et là, où j'allais, c'était tout ensemble ce qu'autrefois je ne situais qu'aux confins, dans l'invisible.

From *Rue Traversière et autres récits en rêve*

Yves Bonnefoy's *Récits en rêve* are marked by a fascination with the elasticity of experience and its capacity for metamorphosis.[1] As their name suggests, the ability of phenomenological, lived experience to reorganise itself into narrative and (or in the process) deform itself into the world of the dream becomes the very source of the poetic. As such, Bonnefoy's prose poems often explore experience as a kind of unfolding into any number of parallel universes, in which similar events find themselves replayed and subtly distorted in the realm of memory or fantasy, or in the acts of analysis that promise, but do not necessarily deliver, the gliding of meaning. 'Rue Traversière', the titular poem of the collection, shows itself to be concerned, in exemplary fashion, with the kind of intriguing confusion that clings to the most intense and significant experiences. It seeks to explore the impossible, unverifiable dimensions of a place that has been of uncanny importance, for its coordinates have become as much emotional and psychic as they are spatial. And it inhabits the split perspective of the adult redeploying the viewpoint of the child, in which reality becomes infinitely more flexible and fantastic, more alive to an alternative realm of rich possibility than in the quotidian rationality that restricts later life. Fundamentally, it is a poem about the profound and unexpected relationship between an individual and the *genius loci* and the way that inhuman geographical spaces come to impinge in a meaningful manner on our sense of self.

'Quand j'étais enfant je m'inquiétais beaucoup d'une certaine rue Traversière', Bonnefoy's confiding, autobiographical voice tells us. 'Car à une de ses entrées, pas trop loin de notre maison et de l'école, c'était le monde ordinaire, tandis qu'à l'autre, là-bas. . .' As his voice trails off, so his perspective opens up, and the simple passageway, a connecting street between the comfortably familiar child's kingdom of school and home and an unknown, unspeakable world of otherness, becomes a route into the twilight zone. In fact, the street discharges him into the botanic gardens but not before moving him through a different kind of dimension, one that leaves him disorientated and suspicious, fatigued as if enchanted, in which the information of his sight is insufficient to inform him of his real situation. 'Est-ce ici, m'étais-je dit à plusieurs moments, que là-bas commence ? Ici, dans cette maison dont les volets sont fermés ?' The difference between 'here' and 'là-bas' with its rather demonic, chilling connotations might well be understood as a perpetual problem for the child, whose nascent object relations leave him stitched into his context, unable always to locate stable boundaries and helplessly porous to all external influences, but Bonnefoy's haunting evocations of the house with closed shutters and the child stretching out 'des doigts de ténèbre' seem to indicate a more extreme disjunction between vibrant vitality and a stealing deathliness, a menacing supernatural underside. But just as the far side of rue Traversière is never properly reached, so the characteristics of its fantastic regions are never fully explored. The power of the street's exotic otherness resides in thoughts and sensations that are 'contradictoires, fuyantes', and its threat is wholly without clear location, subsumed into the ordinary indistinguishableness of its houses and 'le surcroît de torpeur des banlieues'. The charm, the thrill and the terror of rue Traversière are all bound up in the paradox of space it represents; the ability for one place to be many different places at once, without any visible change occurring.

As such the poem 'Rue Traversière' fits neatly, if unwittingly, into the concept of psychogeography, as defined by Guy Debord for the Situationist movement.[2] In his 'Introduction to a Critique of Urban Geography', written in 1955, Debord proposed that: 'Psychogeography could set for itself the study of the precise laws and specific effects of the geographical environment, consciously organised or not, on the emotions and behaviour of individuals. The adjective psychogeographical, retaining a rather pleasing vagueness, can thus be applied to the findings arrived at by this type of investigation, to their influence on human feelings.'[3] For all that he describes a fairly nebulous interaction between identity and environment, Debord had something wholly practical and scientific in mind: a new way of understanding and mapping the city that would pay specific attention to 'The sudden change of ambience in the street within the space of a few metres; the evident division of a city into zones of distinct psychic atmospheres; the path of least resistance which is automatically followed in aimless strolls (and which has no relation to the physical contours of the ground); the appealing or repelling character of certain places – all this seems to be neglected.'[4] In fact it would continue to be neglected, as notoriously few psychogeographical accounts of the city followed out of Debord's prescriptive theories, despite the fact that he had adopted a method of experiencing the city known as *la dérive*: a method that had in earlier times resulted in some of the finest experimental French writing. The *dérive* is a kind of aimless wandering, 'a technique of transient passage'[5] involving 'playful-constructive behaviour and awareness of psychogeographical effects; which completely distinguishes it from the classical notions of the journey and the stroll.'[6] At first sight it is hard to know how to distinguish the *dérive* from the citywide meanderings of the Baudelairean *flâneur*, or the erotically driven urban escapades of Breton and Aragon. But there is a basic knowingness and purpose to the *dérive*, for all that it is supposed to be without destination. It is undertaken with the specific intention of open receptiveness to the cityscape, as a scientific experiment whose results must be meticulously noted in order to produce a new kind of emotional cartography.

Bonnefoy's 'Rue Traversière' provides an intriguing variation on the theme of the *dérive*. His is undoubtedly a transient passage through varied ambiences, but the wandering takes place in the realm of memory rather than in the physical world. Bonnefoy's imaginative travels here aim to remap accurately a section of the city in terms of its emotional and psychic resonance for him, but they do so across an unboundaried stretch of time that works to problematise ever further the already uncertain *points de repère* of here and there. Debord intended the *dérive* to be a politically subversive gesture, 'a reconnaissance for the day when the city would be seized for real'.[7] As Merlin Coverley describes it, 'The *dérive* takes the wanderer out of the realm of the disinterested spectator or artistic practitioner and places him in a subversive position as a revolutionary following a political agenda. The *dériveur* is the foot soldier sent out to observe enemy territory.'[8] Bonnefoy's psychogeographical wanderings up and down the rue Traversière are certainly free of any military agenda, but they remain playfully and powerfully subversive; not subversive politically, but subversive existentially, for the way they locate the 'enemy' of solid, palpable, stable reality as always already within and barely visible. Yet the otherness that infuses rue Traversière and fascinates Bonnefoy is far from negative. There is a sense of shuddering delight that accompanies the child poet's journeys down this street, a delicious kind of fear that heightens his sensory experience and transforms his passage into one of wide-eyed engagement with the unknown, and introduces him to a superimposed world of indistinct, intransigent, unarticulated meaning that will later become the poetic realm. But for now rue Traversière becomes a psychogeographer's dream – or possibly nightmare – in its concentration of intense and conflicting ambiences within a space that is at once distinct but almost entirely without location. 'Ah que ce qui importe a peu de visage!' (*RT*, p. 68) the poet exclaims. For in the complex interaction of space and subjectivity, how are we to plot the coordinates of those dramatic alterations in ambience? In which elements of the landscape, geographical, architectural, or corporeal, do they reside?

'[W]hen a memory comes to mind it exposes a desire or impulse, it has designs on us; when we choose to remember, we act on the past's residues, altering their configurations by the kind of pressure we exert.'[9] In the first half of this poem, the poet's cherished memory is explored for the designs it has on him, for the simultaneously pressing but featureless power of rue Traversière's internal difference from itself. The street becomes the figure of inexplicable transition itself, of the lack of geographical location, of significant change. When Bonnefoy returns to the street as an adult, he finds it, inevitably, both similar and different. His visit coincides with his mother's illness and so the deathliness of rue Traversière is subsumed elsewhere; on this occasion the surreality of the street remains the uppermost of its shape-shifting qualities. What catches his eye this time is the coded presence of the fantastic in 'ces vieilles qui cousent l'infini dans des linges décolorés' or in 'ces paons byzantins affrontés dans la broderie des rideaux de salle à manger, dont l'un parfois bouge'. Whereas for the child the impression overwhelmed the details, now as an adult the details point to the presence of the street's excessive strangeness that is literally embroidered into its textile landscape. It is a strange and faintly unexpected trick of the rue Traversière to remain constant in its uncanny passage from the familiar to the fantastic, despite the poet's own transition from childhood to maturity, and yet if this place does not reveal the poet's otherness to himself, as the return to spaces incubated in memory so often does, then it reveals instead the sophistication of otherness as the adult is now capable of experiencing it. The culmination of his experience that ends this poem is the paradoxical acknowledgement that 'ici, où j'étais, et là, où j'allais, c'était tout ensemble ce qu'autrefois je ne situais qu'aux confins, dans l'invisible'. What the rue Traversière has to tell the poet is that the marginal and the invisible are inevitably central, that in the manner of Rome, all roads lead to them. What might seem to hover on the very edges of existence, what might seem to be defined by its status on the boundary, can deploy the ability of space to fold in on itself, to produce a tuck which brings the corners of the known universe together.

This unusual attribute of space is more readily encountered in the dream world, where all constraints of space and time are rewritten. Indeed, the dream is the place where we might also expect to find the most exotic and intriguing of mental *dérives*. The space of the dream, with its startling associative meanderings, and its comfortable embrace of the most bizarre and outlandish locations, is a journey of impossible leaps and bounds, interspersed with the experience of symbolic cul-de-sacs. Bonnefoy's remembered street appeals to the dream in its open-ended significance, in its magical, unarticulated power, in its vivid fragmentariness, and in its unmoored, floating location in the mind. The notion of the *dérive* as part of the dream is expounded by Barthes, who suggests that 'Le rêve serait . . . un texte aux guillemets incertains, aux parenthèses flottantes (ne jamais fermer la parenthèse, c'est très exactement: dériver)'.[10] This image of the brackets that never close around the dream sentence functions as an intriguing analogy to Bonnefoy's dream narrative that never quite manages to locate the beginning and the end of his significant passageway. But Barthes's drifting text also shows how the writing of the dream offers analogies to the writing of the poem, in which meaning insists without achieving any kind of lucid articulation. The poetic representation of the street is frayed at the edges, uncertain and drifting; the notions of 'here' and 'there' float over the visual image of the street without attaching themselves to distinct locations, just as the peacocks in the curtains retain the fundamental mobility to shift backwards and forwards across them. On both literal and figurative levels, the elements of the poet's street waver and oscillate, drifting on the tide of memory images. This instability affects the signifying level of the prose poem, which travels towards meaning without ever quite making it there, without ever quite finding definitive, bracketing end points that would allow for meaning to be ascertained. Without any proper *points de repères* we cannot in all certainty say what this street means for the poet, or what the fantastic experience of the street means per se.

We might make a useful return at this point to the figure of the *dérive* as it appears across Barthes's criticism, and in so doing plot the drifting significance of Bonnefoy's street from the psychogeographical to the experimental and poetic. For what begins as the plotting of subjective experience is rapidly overlaid with an enigmatic interrogation of the location of meaning. Andrew Brown, in his brilliant analysis of the Barthesian figure of the *dérive*, points to the fundamental instability of the sign in what Barthes terms writing: writing for Barthes indicating the kind of text that was more alive to the open-ended play of signification. The Lacanian ideogram of the signifier over the signified is developed by Barthes 'in somewhat fluid ways, to construe signifiers as being able to free themselves from their signifieds: to float away from one meaning, to remain in a state of suspense – and then, perhaps inevitably, to be attracted down again to form an equally unstable liaison with a new signified'.[11] Bonnefoy's signifier, 'Rue Traversière', performs a similar poetic function, floating in a state of suspense in the poet's representation, tied briefly to his early childhood memories and then again to the later, adult ones, although without gaining any sense of definition from these engagements. What Bonnefoy refers to, in his complex, ambiguous and perpetually disorientated descriptions of rue Traversière, is never wholly clear. This drift from the evocative geographical to the richly subversive psychogeographical is subject to a further act of radical destabilisation. The wandering *dérive* of Bonnefoy's poetry returns to this placeless location once again in another poem, 'Seconde rue Traversière', in which it turns out that the street Bonnefoy remembers so clearly is now no longer to be found on a map and, indeed, appears not to exist at all.

In this poem, a chance conversation with an interlocutor who had read Bonnefoy's description and recognised the street concerned, indicates that Bonnefoy has been mistaken in his location of it. When he returns home he gets out his map and sees that his interlocutor is correct; the rue Traversière is in the rich quarters in the east of the city, an area which he knew well as an adolescent, but not the district where he thought that the original rue Traversière of memory was to be found. And indeed no street on the map seems to correspond to that original memory, even though only a few years have passed since he last walked down it. Bonnefoy is deeply perplexed: are there two rue Traversière or none at all? The psychological has become so deeply enmeshed in the geographical here, that Bonnefoy's obligatory shuffle of the cards of memory threatens to undermine his unified sense of subjectivity. Who was he, when he walked down a street that seems to have vanished? It is entirely in keeping with the spirit of these prose poems that Bonnefoy leaves his questions as rhetorical ones and locates the heart of his poetry in the enigma itself:

> Quelle carte faut-il placer sur quelle autre, quelle sans figure, et d'une seule couleur, pourpre gris, aveugle, ai-je déjà posée sur quelle trop significante, à moins qu'elle ne remonte du jeu remué comme, irrésistible, dernière, non l'annulation du sens, mais le sens ? J'ai beaucoup de souvenirs incertains, ouverts, à déchiffrer encore, je le vois bien. Toute une rue Traversière à porter loin parmi mes premiers hasards, mes premiers lieux mal compris, mes affections mal vécues, jusqu'à l'origine à la fois absolue et indifférente. (*RT*, p. 73)

This beautiful passage illustrates both the significance of the psychogeographical for Bonnefoy and also the writing of the *dérive* that helps him achieve his poetic effects. Bonnefoy drifts from the image of his shifting superimposed maps to the play of meaning, the labyrinthine structures of the city miscegenated with the neurological patternings of the mind; from there he glides to the analysis of his dream-like memory fragments; and from this unboundaried arena he floats into the old slippage of the signifier rue Traversière over its new potential field of significance, as metaphor for the journey of self-discovery bound up in the retrospective tracing of his old steps through the shifting scenery of experience. The destination of this journey is ultimately that of certainty – the absolute place of the real – but it is no surprise that it should be described as indifferent, when it is wholly eluded in the space of poetry. Poetic meaning lies not in the absolute, but in the unexpected shifts and drifts of significance that veil it. Andrew Brown suggests that for Barthes the use of *la dérive* in his language produced a series of 'narratives of emergence',[12] in which the properly subjective and the properly subversive unfold delicately and subtly out of the refusal to allow meaning to fix and stagnate. Bonnefoy's poetic rites of passage through an elusive street similarly create a narrative of emergence, in which the psychogeography of his soul is repeatedly troubled by the addition of new layers of uncertainty. Whilst the absolute that lies at the end of the road recedes ever further into the distance, so the poetry of the very impossibility of cohering the self across time and space is intensified. Bonnefoy's *dérive* through lost but evocative states of being is a masterful example of why it is always better to travel than to arrive.

Notes

1 Yves Bonnefoy, *Rue Traversière et autres récits en rêve* (Paris: Gallimard, 1992), pp. 66–7. In all subsequent page references it will be abbreviated to *RT*.
2 The Situationist International (1957–72) was a small group of international political and artistic agitators influenced by Marxism and the early European avant-garde.

Its journal was edited by Guy Debord whom some saw as giving the movement necessary definition and clarity, and others as exerting dictatorial control. The group was fraught with divisions from its earliest days and split into a number of different groups in the 1960s before disbanding for good in 1972.

3 Guy Debord, 'Introduction to a Critique of Urban Geography' in Ken Knabb (ed.), *Situationist International Anthology* (Berkeley, CA: Bureau of Public Secrets, 1981), p. 5.
4 *Ibid.*, p. 6.
5 From 'Internationale Situationniste', in Knabb, *Situationist*, p. 45.
6 Guy Debord, 'Theory of the Dérive', in Knabb, *Situationist*, p. 50.
7 Simon Sadler, *The Situationist City* (Cambridge, MA: MIT Press, 1982), p. 81.
8 Merlin Coverley, *Psychogeographies* (Harpenden: Pocket Essentials, 2006), p. 97.
9 Michael Sheringham, *French Autobiography: Devices and Desires* (Cambridge: Cambridge University Press, 1994).
10 Roland Barthes, *Roland Barthes par lui-même* (Paris: Seuil, 1975), p. 110.
11 Andrew Brown, *Roland Barthes: The Figures of Writing* (Oxford: Oxford University Press, 1992), p. 14.
12 *Ibid.*, p. 7.

Further reading

Acke, Daniel, *Yves Bonnefoy essayiste* (Amsterdam: Rodopi, 1999).
Bonnefoy, Yves, *New and Selected Poems*, ed. John Naughton and Anthony Rudolf (Chicago, IL: University of Chicago Press, 1995).
Buchs, Arnaud, *Yves Bonnefoy à l'horizon du surréalisme* (Paris: Galilée, 2005).
Caws, Mary Ann, *Yves Bonnefoy* (Boston, MA: Twayne Publishers, 1984).
Finck, Michèle, *Yves Bonnefoy, le simple et le sens* (Paris: José Corti, 1989).
Finck, Michèle, Lançon, Daniel, and Staiber, Maryse (eds.), *Yves Bonnefoy et l'Europe du vingtième siècle* (Strasbourg: Presses Universitaires de Strasbourg, 2003).
Gagnebin, Murielle (ed.), *Yves Bonnefoy, lumière et nuit des images* (Seyssel: Champ Vallon, 2005).
Greene, Robert, *Searching for Presence: Yves Bonnefoy's Writings on Art* (Amsterdam: Rodopi, 2004).
Jackson, John E., *Yves Bonnefoy* (Paris: Seghers, 2002).
Lallier, François, *Avec Yves Bonnefoy, de la poésie* (Vincennes: Presses Universitaires de Vincennes, 2001).
Leuwers, Daniel, *Yves Bonnefoy* (Amsterdam: Rodopi, 1988).
Naughton, John T., *The Poetics of Yves Bonnefoy* (Chicago: University of Chicago Press, 1984).
Née, Patrick, *Rhétorique profonde d'Yves Bonnefoy* (Paris: Hermann, 2004).
    Yves Bonnefoy, penseur de l'image ou Les Travaux de Zeuxis (Paris: Gallimard, 2006).
Née, Patrick and Lançon, Daniel (eds.), *Yves Bonnefoy, Poésie, recherche et savoirs* (Paris: Hermann, 2007).
Thélot, Jérôme, *Poétique d'Yves Bonnefoy* (Geneva: Droz, 1983).

André du Bouchet, 'Accidents'

EMMA WAGSTAFF

Accidents

J'ai erré autour de cette lueur.

Je me suis

déchiré, une nouvelle fois, de l'autre côté de ce mur,

comme l'air que tu vois,

à cette lueur froide.   5

De l'autre côté du mur, je vois le même air aveuglant.

Dans le lointain sans rupture,

comme l'étendue même de la terre entrecoupée que,

plus loin, je foule, nul ne sent la chaleur.

Nous serons lavés de notre visage, comme l'air qui   10

couronne le mur.

From Dans la chaleur vacante

Dans la chaleur vacante, from which 'Accidents' is taken, was published by Mercure de France in 1961 and was the first collection by André du Bouchet to gain widespread critical notice.[1] He began writing in the 1940s and continued until shortly before his death in 2001. Along with several poets of the same generation, such as Yves Bonnefoy and Jacques Dupin, du Bouchet is known for his rigorous investigation of 'la réalité rugueuse', to use Rimbaud's expression. Turning away from Surrealism, with its insistence on the marvellous, dream, and the internal resources of the imagination, these poets attempted to evoke an experience of the real world around them. In many cases, this meant focusing on apparently inhospitable landscapes rather than expressing the thoughts and feelings of an individual. Du Bouchet's poetry is often considered difficult to access because it does not narrate, offer neat conclusions or develop extended metaphors. Although poems may be voiced by a 'je', readers are given no information about this subject that would enable them to understand its personality or life as an individual. It is far from the expressive subject of Romantic poetry.

Nevertheless, the language that du Bouchet uses is not difficult in itself. He generally employs simple vocabulary, but the minute attention he pays to the forms and combinations of words means that no choice is arbitrary, and words can carry several implications simultaneously. Equally, while his writing is not explicitly about people's lives, it is always about human experience: of space, of place, of time, of perception and of the body.

'Accidents' is exemplary because it explores the elemental landscape through the sensations experienced by the subject. The setting is the air, 'l'air que tu vois', and the earth, 'la terre. . . que. . . je foule', bright light, 'je vois le même air aveuglant', and cold, 'à cette lueur froide'. The phrase 'nul ne sent la chaleur' is rather different, as 'nobody' is said to feel the heat. This produces an uninhabited environment, but it does so by reference to the sensation of heat, or bodily perception. There are no details to distinguish the scene as any particular landscape, but the poem is literally set, or embedded, in a physical environment.

Of course, the poem still appears hermetic because it is often impossible to visualise its images. How does one wander around light, or even tear oneself? How is one washed of one's face? But rather than developing surreal images, which would require an unexpected juxtaposition to be grasped by the reader, here du Bouchet is simply offering a verbal exposition, as precisely as possible, of the actions taking place.

The subject is engaged in the landscape, whose overwhelming feature appears to be its brightness, but its position is far from comfortable. 'Accidents' proposes several instances of tearing, in which the integrity of a person or thing is violated. The subject is torn, for example, and the earth on which it tramps is broken up; the image of ploughed earth is frequent in this collection.

Broken earth is contrasted with the view into the distance, which is 'sans rupture'. However, instead of setting up the contrast by a term implying opposition, du Bouchet chooses 'comme', which would normally be employed to compare objects that share some characteristic. Du Bouchet's use of 'comme', which is typical of his poetry, distances the term from its role in the classic simile, because he does not make an obvious comparison, nor does he propose one term as a referent, with the other as a term of comparison. In the last section, 'we' are divested of our face, 'comme' the wall is crowned by the air; there is no obvious similarity in image, and both 'nous' and the wall are equally present in the scene. And yet a connection is produced between the two actions by the word 'comme'. In addition, the self is torn 'comme' the air. Again, neither the self nor the air is a secondary, absent, term of comparison, but both undergo the same process. Air is normally considered to be invisible, or made up of individual particles, but not to be a substance that could be torn as a single entity. Du Bouchet, on the other hand, implies that it has a solid materiality that can be breached.

Air is as thick a substance as the earth. They are both contrasted with the image of a wall, which acts as a surface that is opposed to the depth and volume of the elements. The wall is an object that produces a beyond in distinction to immediate space, 'de l'autre côté de ce mur', and to the prospect of uninter-rupted space evoked by 'le lointain sans rupture'. The top of the wall is sur-rounded by air, so, although it is a man-made construction in an otherwise natural environment, it is not the only object in empty space; it is given equal consistency with the usually overlooked element, the air.

If the wall creates closeness and depth, near and far, these are concepts that can be understood only from the perspective of an observer, so that although the subject appears to be somewhat at the mercy of the landscape, perception governs the way in which the scene appears. 'De l'autre côté' has to be perceived from the point of view of a person who occupies a particular position. However, this subject is not a stable entity. In the very first line, it is torn, both in the image 'je me suis / déchiré', and by the positioning of that image, a reflexive verb that operates over the line break. Enjambement separates the pronouns and auxiliary from the participle, thereby enacting the division described. This is a repeated occurrence, signalled by 'une nouvelle fois', and indeed du Bouchet employs repetition in order to produce the impression that the actions taking place do so time and again. He repeats nouns, 'mur' and 'air', but also employs the technique of repetition with variation, so that the reader has the sense both of similarity and of slight difference. 'De l'autre côté de ce mur' becomes 'de l'autre côté du mur', and 'l'air que tu vois' becomes 'je vois le même air'. The result is subtle change, with reference back and forth in time, rather than stasis.

Once the 'je', who appears twice in the first two lines of the poem, has been torn, two other figures appear: 'tu' and 'nous'. These are equally ill-defined, and no relationship between those whom they designate can be discerned except what is provided grammatically; that is, the 'tu' is the other to the 'je', and the 'nous' includes the 'je', and probably also the 'tu'. Once again, the figures are perceived from the perspective of the speaking subject.

The move from 'je' to 'tu' to 'nous' can be seen as a progression. First, the coherence of the 'je' is disrupted. Then the introduction of a 'tu' figure links the speaking subject to another; they both see the air. In the third section, the subject is connected to the earth through the action of tramping on it, and, finally, the 'nous' emerges. It is not clear whether this designates the 'je' and the 'tu' together, but the action that takes place happens to a collective per-sonal pronoun. It might seem paradoxical that this newly found joint identity is undergoing the action of having its face removed, because the face could be seen as the marker of identity. But perhaps du Bouchet is suggesting that it is by leaving behind individual identity that the subject is able to achieve a closer link with others and with the pure matter that is air.

Du Bouchet's use of tenses also reinforces the impression that the poem enacts a progression. It begins in the perfect tense: 'j'ai erré', 'je me suis déchiré'. It then moves into the present: 'je vois', 'tu vois', 'je foule', 'nul ne sent'. In the last section, the surprising phrase 'nous serons lavés' enacts a change to the future. Through the use of the passive voice, the phrase produces a sense of the future perfect, the time of anticipated past action, which is frequently used by du Bouchet. It allows him to conjure up the moment when a future action has just taken place. In this way, it does not so much project forward as produce movement that must always be understood in relation to the immediate future and the immediate past. There are no isolated actions; instead, everything that takes place does so within a larger progression. That, of course, is the essence of poetry. Each line or phrase of a poem is created, and read or heard, in relation to those that precede and follow it, be this through the medium of traditional rhyme and metre, or in the rhythm and echo that is more typical of much contemporary poetry.

'Accidents' gestures to prosodic devices, with echoes such as 'fois', 'vois' and 'froid', or the surface of the wall, 'mur', linked to the breaching of surfaces: 'rupture'. It includes several phrases of six syllables, some of which could be combined into alexandrines, as well as three octosyllables and two decasyllables. But there are several clauses that consist of seven or nine syllables, which are highly irregular. The poem appears to take account of traditional metre and rhyme, but to move away from them, producing instead its own particular marriage of rhythm and space.

It is clear from a glance at the poem that du Bouchet is very attentive to the aspects of writing that distinguish poetry from prose. While he might not employ regular line length, he is far from writing prose. Instead, the spacing of the text on the page is of paramount importance. Reproductions of du Bouchet's manuscript poems show that his corrections do not only involve changes to words and phrases, although he does make minute corrections and alterations on this level. In addition, he often moves words and phrases a fraction to the right or the left, and increases or decreases the amount of space between sections of text. 'Accidents' is laid out in such a way that the first section includes gaps between phrases, which serve to fragment them and emphasise the rupture that is being evoked, much as the enjambement that interrupts the phrase 'je me suis / déchiré' produces the action. In the second and third sections, on the other hand, the lines may be uneven, but there are no spaces to separate them, so they allow for greater coherence. This corresponds well to the image of extensive uninterrupted space that is described, and to the new connection found with the earth and with others.

Du Bouchet's careful use of the space of the page, combined with the sense of progression that he creates, serves to link time and space in movement. The action of walking is central to many of his texts. Here it is present in the phrase 'la terre entrecoupée / que, plus loin, je foule'. The addition of 'plus loin' takes the action and poem forward through the present of walking. In other poems it emerges even more clearly, through images of taking steps, crossing rough terrain or breathing cold air. In the action of walking, du Bouchet emphasises the close involvement of the self with its surroundings, in which it is necessary to experience the feeling of the ground beneath one's feet, the temperature and movement of the air and the brightness or darkness that affect visual perception. He also finds in walking an analogy to poetry, which requires rhythm, as well as a sense of the space over which the action, the writing and the reading unfold: time and space are inseparable.

Although 'Accidents' has little recognisable plot, there is plenty of action. It evokes an experience of the immediate present, but also movement and change, and projection forward into the future that does not involve forgetting what has gone before. Du Bouchet creates the sense of the poem as an event in itself. The shifts in tense and pronoun, the almost repeated phrases, and the use of rhythm, echo, enjambement and spacing to enact what it evokes, ensure that the poem takes place, rather than describing or referring mimetically to an occasion beyond its own existence. In other words, as in all poetry, the form of the text is inseparable from its content, and it would not be the same poem if it were expressed in different words. As Jacques Roubaud argues, a poem is a piece of writing that cannot be paraphrased.[2]

That might go some way towards explaining the mysterious title. The noun 'accident' has various meanings in French.[3] Most obviously, it refers to a chance event, sometimes an unfortunate one. The emphasis is on contingency rather than on a clear reason for an event occurring. It also has the more specialised musical meaning of 'accidental', a mark that raises or lowers a note by half a tone. While music and poetry are, of course, often related, music is unlikely to be a major factor in du Bouchet's choice as there is no other reference to sound; in fact, the scene is a notably silent one, as is often the case in his writing. In French, it is also possible to speak of 'accidents du langage', or unusual ways of expressing oneself, which could be applied to the initially 'difficult' aspects of du Bouchet's writing, and even to poetry more generally. Most striking, however, is the meaning of 'accident' as an unexpected detail that ruptures the uniformity of the whole. That sense is vital, not only to this poem, but to much of du Bouchet's writing, in which he explores the interaction between surface and depth. Fissures in the immediate surface of things reveal glimpses of what lies underneath or behind, both in the literal sense of the ground or walls, and in du Bouchet's determination to make the reader look more closely at the surroundings he or she might normally pass through without paying them much attention. Details that rupture uniformity, or 'accidents', are the singular events, words and perceptions that enable his poetry to reveal the world in a changed light.

André du Bouchet is sometimes said to exemplify the solitary poet, and at first sight texts such as this one would seem to confirm that view: here is a work inspired by lonely walking in an elemental landscape, written by a poet who patiently works on words until their multiple meanings and combinations set off new constellations of images. However, it emerges even in this short text that the speaking subject is seeking connections with others, and with the world around. The resulting poem is an event in itself, rather than a descriptive text or self-reflexive musing on personal experience.

Although du Bouchet refused to propose any theoretical underpinning to his work, as did many of his contemporaries, his poetry can be understood in terms of a phenomenology of presence: the human subject is embedded in its surroundings: in time and in space. Poets of du Bouchet's generation were influenced by Heidegger, via a meeting that took place between Heidegger and René Char, whose own poetic investigations of landscape and Being were important to du Bouchet and others.

Through Heidegger's later writing, they also became acquainted with the work of the German Romantic poet Hölderlin, and with what Heidegger considered his unveiling of Being through poetic language.[4] Du Bouchet was among those who translated Hölderlin into French, and he used Hölderlin's texts as the basis of his own reflections on the act and implications of translation, and on ways in which the writing of poetry might be analogous to translating, in texts such as *Notes sur la traduction*.[5]

Du Bouchet's writing was not undertaken in isolation. Despite the apparent impersonality of many of his texts, he engaged in dialogue with others in various ways. He was a prolific and adventurous translator from English and Russian as well as German. The influence of the great poets who inspired him, such as Pierre Reverdy, is clear in texts such as *Matière de l'interlocuteur*, in which Reverdy's words mingle with his own and are reread by him. He was a founding editor of the review *L'Éphémère*, and worked on its editorial board with Dupin, Bonnefoy and des Forêts, among others.[6] *L'Éphémère* published writing by young poets, foreign language poetry in translation, and drawings, etchings and engravings by past and contemporary artists. Du Bouchet's own links with visual artists were very strong. He worked with friends and contemporaries including Alberto Giacometti and Pierre Tal Coat to create some of the major *livres d'artistes* of the late twentieth century, and wrote thoughtful, exploratory texts on the artists' work. Some of these are collected in *Qui n'est pas tourné vers nous*, on Giacometti, and in *Peinture*.[7] Du Bouchet's writing, as well as involving a rigorous investigation of language and the place of the self in the world, is evidence of a writer's close engagement with aspects of the literature and art of the European tradition, and of the second half of the twentieth century in particular.

While these interests may not be evident in his poetry, close reading of the poems reveals a determination to explore the position of the human subject in relation to the world around. In 'Accidents', this emerges above all through the bodily sensations that are evoked. The poem produces 'accidents', or ruptures in our perception of the surface of things, which cause us to see the world, and language, in slightly altered ways.

Notes

1 Republished in André du Bouchet, *Dans la chaleur vacante, suivi de Ou le soleil* (Paris: Gallimard, 1991), p. 42.

2 Jacques Roubaud, *Poésie, etcetera: ménage* (Paris: Stock, 1995), p. 77.

3 See *Le Grand Larousse de la langue française*, 7 vols. (Paris: Larousse, 1989).

4 Martin Heidegger, *Erläuterung zu Hölderlins Dichtung: Gesamtausgabe*, vol. IV (Frankfurt: Klostermann, 1981).

5 André du Bouchet, 'Notes sur la traduction', in *Ici en deux* (Paris: Mercure de France, 1986), n.p.

6 *L'Éphémère* (1967–72). For more information, see Alain Mascarou, *Les cahiers de 'L'Éphémère' 1967–1972: tracés interrompus* (Paris: L'Harmattan, 1998).

7 André du Bouchet, *Qui n'est pas tourné vers nous* (Paris: Mercure de France, 1972), and *Peinture* (Saint-Clément: Fata Morgana, 1983).

Further reading

Bishop, Michael, *Les Altérités d'André du Bouchet* (Amsterdam: Rodopi, 2003).

Collot, Michel (ed.), *Autour d'André du Bouchet* (Paris: Presses de L'École Normale Supérieure, 1986).

Depreux, Jacques, *André du Bouchet ou la parole traversée* (Seyssel: Champ Vallon, 1988).

Du Bouchet, André, *Where Heat Looms*, trans. David Mus (Los Angeles: Sun and Moon, 1996).

Met, Philippe, *Formules de la poésie: études sur Ponge, Leiris, Char et du Bouchet* (Paris: Presses Universitaires de France, 1999).

Wagstaff, Emma, *Provisionality and the Poem: Transition in the Works of du Bouchet, Jaccottet and Noël* (Amsterdam: Rodopi, 2006).

18 Jacques Dupin, 'Commencer'

MARY ANN CAWS

Commencer comme on déchire un drap, le drap dans les plis duquel on se regardait dormir. L'acte d'écrire comme rupture, et engagement cruel de l'esprit, et du corps, dans une succession nécessaire de ruptures, de dérives, d'embrasements. Jeter sa mise entière sur le tapis, toutes ses armes et son souffle, et considérer ce don de soi comme un déplacement imperceptible et presque indifférent de l'équilibre universel. Rompre et ressaisir, et ainsi renouer. Dans la forêt nous sommes plus près du bûcheron que du promeneur solitaire. Pas de contemplation innocente. Plus de hautes futaies traversées de rayons et de chants d'oiseaux, mais des stères de bois en puissance. Tout nous est donné, mais pour être forcé, pour être entamé, en quelque façon pour être détruit, – et nous détruire.

From *Moraines*

It's up to us

Once, long ago, a prose poem struck me with all the force of a revelation. It was brief, containing only about ten lines of description, action and resolution. Having read this poem, 'Commencer' in the volume *Moraines,* I then began to read and care about, immensely, the writing of the contemporary poet Jacques Dupin.[1]

Moraines: 'an accumulation of earth and stones, carried and eventually deposited by a glacier'. So a glacial chill is there from the beginning, in this early prose poem. Already, then, the poet clearly states his refusal of any romanticism, even in a forest walk, that could have had a Rousseauist tinge to it: but it does not. No 'solitary walker', rather a community of logs split to let the light and air into the text, in its central action, an image of the poem itself. These prose poems are, then, like so many residual traces of an original glacier, and the traces will be equivalent to writing.

They are, it seems to me, peculiar acts of poetic courage. They have that feeling of irregularity that earth and stones would force upon the text, as it is carried along, as it is deposited, as it is received. Each serves as a manifesto of the poetic act.

Earth, then, for the ongoing text, and stones for the hard-core sayings that permeate the rest. The amalgam works. In my view, the prose poems of Jacques Dupin are his masterpieces in the written genre: his work on the artists Joan Miró, Alberto Giacometti, Saul Steinberg and others occupies the imagination of the visual, as his poems do that of the verbal. Except that the latter do both, in their intense visuality.

Take this poem that begins with the word 'Commencer. . .'. To begin a poem with the positive word 'to begin' is already an act of daring. To end it with destruction, the word 'détruire', is no less daring.

Here's the odd thing: the opening of the poem is impersonal 'Commencer comme on déchire un drap, le drap dans les plis duquel on se regardait dormir.' It then moves through the writing act, rupture and burning and displacement, and subsequently the act of betting – betting everything one has: 'toutes ses armes et son souffle'. Still the impersonal: no one has entered. 'Rompre et ressaisir, et ainsi renouer.' The break and the tearing lead to a regrasping, a holding, and a re-knotting, a re-linking to the universe of the poem included in this one paragraph.

And now appears the personal: 'Dans la forêt nous sommes plus près du bûcheron.' We have come in, but as the collective, not as ourselves. Then a statement of what there no longer is: no innocent contemplation of anything, no more romantic strolls in the forest with sunbeams and birdsongs: only the potential of future logs for the building of fires – that is, towards destruction. Ironically, the poem ends with forcing, cutting into something, and that destruction already declared. But here, as in the forest, I am not alone. I am not actually in this poem, except as part of a common experience.

Significant beyond words, precisely; beyond ordinary words even as the poem uses the ordinary; of course. In the very centre of the poem, there is a taking up again after the break, there is a linking. It occurs precisely before the offer made to us and the negative slicing of it, like firewood, into so many bits. 'To destroy us' – never a single I here, no individual, only the collective of a community.

In a sense, this condensed credo of a poem links up with another poem by Dupin, beginning 'Même si la montagne', also from the volume *Moraines*. This poem, situated in the country of the 'even if' – 'Même si la montagne se consume' – is about (partly, as all Dupin's poems are partly about this or that) 'happiness, indestructible happiness', and describes itself as vigil and vow: 'vigils on the promontory' and the promise 'Not to go down'. 'Ne pas descendre. Ne plus se taire . . . Bonheur. Indestructible Bonheur.' This whole drama takes place on the heights. From where we can look down.

Let me look at the poem beginning with beginning once again. As if we were re-beginning. 'Commencer comme on déchire un drap . . . L'acte d'écrire comme'. The triple echo of 'commencer comme . . . comme' already signals another drama, like *the trois coups* in the theatre, announcing the opening of the play. Once we see how the impersonal 'on' commences, and then how the collective persona 'nous' takes its stance with the final destructive impulse, the simplicity of the framing words seems to set up the central discovery: 'renouer'. This poem is in no way exclusive of happiness – it is, in fact, about a restitution, about how the torn sheet and its dreams can lead to a new discovery.

Dupin, splendid in his spacing, dense in his statements and manifestos – of which this is surely one – has spent his high and poetic life on the grounds of poetry and of meditation on writing as a positive/negative motion. Such a beginning and ending sum up and contain much beyond themselves. This is the poetic act, in all its singular and collective network and profound play.

Finally, let us look at what the choice of such a poem might mean as an image of a poet's work as a whole. Could we not take it as a fractal representation of a life overall? It moves from outset to end, from displacement to replacement, with a central rethinking of the entire vision, in the crucial word: 'renouer'. To be sure, witness the various translations into English of that word in this poem, it can be several things at once. The distance between the literal 'to re-knot', and the imaged extension into 'to renovate' (a near cognate) or 'to renew' is not a great one, but an important one all the same. I now think the re-knotting is the point and the anchor of the poem as act and life.

First act. The poetic process which is, in this case, life, begins with the objective and general 'on', the you who undoes the pleats you saw yourself as sleeping in, like an ex-plication seen as a drastic unfolding. It is a cruel involvement, the rupture and the series of breaking apart being as necessary and as positive as the decision to begin. To be born, that is, fully to the poetic act. Or rather, in it, in its rip tide and its conflagration.

Second act. A personal engagement: you have to bet your whole everything, throw it down with all its weapons and expose your whole respiration and self, as if it did not matter whatever comes next, without knowing exactly what that is to be. You just do it, as part of the global thing, realising that your complete giving of yourself will not even be noticed. The result? When you have broken with all the links you had, you seize new ones, and in that way you are a re-part of the whole, renovated in yourself and renewed in your vision. This is the summit of the life poem.

Third and last act. Not a lovely lonely walk, free of commitment and full of what we think of as beauty, but a re-beginning with a woodcutting task sensed as cruel (as in the initial 'engagement cruel de l'esprit' – that sense of necessity Antonin Artaud had in his theatre of cruelty), in order for the rebuilding to take place. The displacement or 'déplacement', result of the rupturing of the dream of passivity, was leading all along to this replacement of empty and lyric Romanticism by something else that can be started, broken into – 'entamer' as in a seemingly negative form of 'commencer' – destroyed but only 'en quelque façon' – in one sense only. Sure enough, we will be destroyed, but we knew that. We knew that was what life is and was about. All the same, the poem and the act are about beginning. And waking.

A few years ago, right after the event we call 9/11, I had to go to Dublin to speak about contemporary French poetry. So clear in my mind were the recent events in New York, where I am writing this now, that they formed the inescapable background to all my thoughts. I found myself talking about the poets, the three French poets of our days, with whom I would have chosen to walk through the ruins: René Char, Yves Bonnefoy and Jacques Dupin. The kind of drastic understanding their works display explicitly and contain implicitly seemed and now still seems to me the guarantee of how poetry can speak in the worst times. It speaks, like this one short text, of what is central, crucial and enduring even from the beginning to the end, and speaks in a continuum from the impersonal and universal 'on' to the very personal involvement of the self in a poetic community signalled by the 'nous'. We are the poem.

Note

1 In Jacques Dupin, *L'Embrasure* (Paris: Gallimard, 1971), p. 146.

Further reading

Brophy, Michael, *Voies vers l'autre, Dupin, Bonnefoy, Noël, Guillevic* (Amsterdam: Rodopi, 1997).

De Julio, Maryann, *Rhetorical Landscapes: The Poetry and Art Criticism of Jacques Dupin* (Lexington, KY: French Forum, 1992).

Jacques Dupin (Amsterdam: Rodopi, 2005).

Dupin, Jacques, *Jacques Dupin, Selected Poems*, selected by Paul Auster, trans. Paul Auster, Stephen Romer and David Shapiro (Newcastle upon Tyne: Bloodaxe Books, 1992).

Fetzer, Glenn W., *Palimpsests of the Real in Recent French Poetry* (Amsterdam: Rodopi, 2004).

19 Philippe Jaccottet, 'L'Ignorant'

L'Ignorant

Plus je vieillis et plus je croîs en ignorance,
plus j'ai vécu, moins je possède et moins je règne.
Tout ce que j'ai, c'est un espace tour à tour
enneigé ou brillant, mais jamais habité.
Où est le donateur, le guide, le gardien ?   5
Je me tiens dans ma chambre et d'abord je me tais
(le silence entre en serviteur mettre un peu d'ordre),
et j'attends qu'un à un les mensonges s'écartent :
que reste-t-il ? que reste-t-il à ce mourant
qui l'empêche si bien de mourir ? Quelle force   10
le fait encor parler entre ses quatre murs ?
Pourrais-je le savoir, moi l'ignare et l'inquiet ?
Mais je l'entends vraiment qui parle, et sa parole
pénètre avec le jour, encore que bien vague :

« Comme le feu, l'amour n'établit sa clarté   15
que sur la faute et la beauté des bois en cendres . . . »

From *L'Ignorant*

In 'Le Livre des Morts'[1] Philippe Jaccottet declares: 'only unknowing persists' ('Seule demeure l'ignorance'). The theme of the poet's lack of knowledge is absolutely central to his work. It is a theme that is related to Rilke's concept of 'poverty', and is also linked to such neighbouring themes as mortality, fragility, reserve and seclusion, obliteration, numb fear and terror, to create the portrait of a poet which is as discreet as it is troubled, a portrait deeply scored by marks of doubt and disquiet.

A sharpened sense of his own limitations throws a dark shadow over the poetic experience, restricting his language; incapable of performing feats and wonders, poetic language stands accused of deceptive tricks and deficiencies. The outcome is a poetics of *the least said*, in which nothing is ventured without circumspection and modesty.

Though the poetry moves towards an inscription of death, at the end of the text mortality is nonetheless presented clearly as the precondition of love, language and beauty. It is indeed solely 'the ending' which 'is illuminating'. The paradox is only superficial: the states of unknowing and being finite cross-pollinate, burgeon and bear fruit. Poetry exists because human beings know nothing about their own end: it takes up residence in the space created by that lack of knowledge. Poetry is born out of the very nature of the divided self; it springs from the search for self-knowledge and the lack of self-mastery.

What will strike the reader in this particular poem, which also provides the title, *L'Ignorant*, to one of Jaccottet's earliest collections, is the proliferation of questions. Parentheses, antitheses, paradoxes and repetitions also abound; they are all indications of the self-questioning at work in the poem, drawing us into an inner monologue which is its core. The key word introduced in the title sets in motion a resonant sequence of sounds ('mourant', 'vraiment', 'cendres') and is echoed twice over in the words 'ignorance' and 'ignare', as well as being present in the empty moulds of figures whose absence is stressed: the 'donateur', 'guide' and 'gardien'.

Hence the poem traces a line of rhetorical and meditative thought which leads to a conclusion in the form of a quotation resolving the tensions and contradictions woven into the text. At the same time, the reader is witness to a twofold transformation from speech to silence and from the oral to the auditory. Under threat, speaking changes into attentive listening. Reflection thus takes shape, almost surreptitiously, through a process of poetic counterpoint.

This is something that we might call 'the labour of unknowing': ignorance constituted as both a principle and a process of knowledge; it brings us to an awareness of the paradox that, first of all, ignorance must know itself. The poet's foremost desire is to succeed in being right. He is searching for truth rather than knowledge.

As regards the formal structure: the poem 'L'Ignorant' consists of sixteen lines following the alexandrine pattern but without end rhymes. Since a tone of familiarity, arising from the poet's questioning voice, predominates, sentences take precedence over lines of verse and hence the capitals which normally distinguish the beginning of each line are lost.

The main body of the poem is made up of a series of questions which are at first posed abruptly and in apparent distress ('Où est ?', 'Que reste-t-il ?'); later the questions seem counterbalanced by surprise, or even by a kind of internal knowledge which reacts spontaneously to the questioning which the poet is undergoing (ll. 10–12). Between these two different kinds of questions, the poet has situated a scene which has the air of a ritual: writing is staged in terms of a period of watchfulness, of meditation, receptiveness and interrogation. Taken together, they constitute the heart of the poem (ll. 5–12).

The central body of the poem is preceded by four lines in which the subject matter is dominated by a preoccupation with the themes of retrenchment and dispossession. Expressed at first in terms of a paradox (l. 1), then through antithesis (l. 2), the poet selects images which engender coldness, an icy expanse (which might suggest a blank page) where he seems to anticipate a coming into being. This creates a feeling of suspense, which is sustained by the questions that follow.

The poem culminates in a moment of responsive listening, a moment when speech and light appear in harmony: entering simultaneously with silence, the light of day provides its own answer – or perhaps even its own wisdom. The two lines which close the text link beauty to lack and illumination to mortality.

The first line presents us with an unexpected equation: it affirms that to grow older is to grow in ignorance, although old age is normally understood as the sum of accumulated experience. This concept is reiterated in *La Semaison*: 'Il reste l'ignorance croissante' (what is left is growing ignorance).[2] This is clearly a paradox, succinctly expressing ever-growing deficiency and doubt, yet the verb 'to grow' also implies that ignorance bears fruit. Not to have knowledge or understanding of something, considered a reprehensible condition (in Christian writings the Latin word *ignorantia* was used to designate those who had no knowledge of God), might in this context mark the paradoxical beginnings of a kind of wisdom. Let us not forget that only a simple circumflex divides *croîs* from *crois*. It will take a second reading of the text, however, in order to reach this level of meaning which remains hidden in a preliminary encounter with the text. For the moment, the repetition of 'plus' (the more) signals the inescapable, fatal, almost mechanical nature of this loss of familiarity and knowledge: as the self ages, so he becomes more and more aware of how vain and empty is our knowledge of the world: increasingly, he has to come to grips with questions to which there are no answers.

In the second line, the words 'plus j'ai vécu' reiterate the theme of ageing, but in the past tense, as if to mark the speeding up of time passing and herald its termination: thereby a strange weighting, even imbalance occurs between the wealth of accumulated experience and the feeling of dispossession. The power to control has also been abandoned ('moins je règne'), so that the classical motif of the old king who is as wise as he is wealthy is now being challenged, inverted, at the expense of a violent antithesis between the past and the present.

In the third line, 'Tout ce que j'ai' is a symmetrical reprise of 'moins je possède' in order, this time, to conjure up an image – which is deliberately left unde-fined – of the poet's mental space, designated as cold, bright and empty. The 'je' does not seem to have found anywhere to be but in this state of endless, desolate waiting, by turns cold and radiant, yet always shattering, motionless, fundamental.

The impression of loneliness evoked in the preceding lines is emphasised in line 5 by a question which has three complementary aspects. The master is absent. There is no benefactor – no one who might bestow the gift of meaning, beauty or poetry. There is no guide to lead us through this terrain and render it familiar, no guide we may follow as we traverse our human condition to its mortal end. There is no-one to stand guard and defend or define the limits of these uncharted waters. All three aspects collude to imply a failure to achieve transcendence. At the very least, here we have to contend with an unrelenting interrogation (three different expressions of the same idea) echoing the ontological loneliness of one who does not know.

The questioning is momentarily abandoned in line 6, though it emerges again in lines 9 to 12, in order to make way for the depiction of an inner state in which choosing and being resolutely determined upon a course of action means that the 'je' re-acts or replies for the first time to the absence of a master figure. Michaux's advice, passing on one of Buddha's teachings, was: 'Tenez-vous bien dans votre île à vous' (stay on your own island). Here the preferential treatment given to being within one's own space is emphasised five times by the use of first-person pronouns and a possessive adjective (je, me, ma, je, me). The room welcomes writing as it embraces intimacy: 'Je me tiens dans ma chambre' (I stay in my room) means 'je me tiens en moi-même' (I keep to myself). 'Je me tiens', 'je me tais', 'j'attends'; these three verbs, following one another, determine the steps which make up the poet's behaviour (characterised by outward passivity). First he moves into a state of inner tranquillity, then he establishes one in which he can embrace silence.

In line 7, the servant coming to tidy the room, which is the poet's inner world, is an allegory of silence. In a sense, the servant moves into the place left vacant by the benefactor. When meaning is not supplied and guaranteed by a higher power, silence must take on the task of providing a truthful or accurate relationship to language. Silence makes it possible to access what Jaccottet calls 'language reduced to its very essence' ('le langage réduit à l'essentiel').

The overriding desire to achieve a precise balance is foremost for 'L'Ignorant', and line 8 makes this explicit: here poetic writing consists mainly in seeking to eliminate, to purify, to pare things down to the bone. The 'mensonges' in their turn take on the role of people whose presence is unwanted. The theme of lying, as we know, is one to which Jaccottet insistently returns in his work. In *La Semaison*, for example, he writes: 'Pour moi, de plus en plus, j'entends le mensonge des paroles, ce qui me paralyse. Je voudrais que la misère les dénudât.'[3] ('I personally have become more and more aware of the mendacity of words, which paralyse me. I wish despair would strip words of their lies.') The poet sees his main task as authenticating what truly constitutes human existence.

Line 9 signals the beginning of a series of questions seeking to find what might remain when there is no benefactor, guide or guardian. The poet addresses the question of basic survival: if we cleanse the world of its lies and illusions, what is left to make life worth living? Providing an answer to this question is one of the vital tasks of poetry. In Jaccottet's terms it is a task that requires perseverance. Surprisingly, as a further example 'ce mourant' is brought into play by means of a demonstrative adjective ('ce') which accords this dying man a dominant role, emphasised dramatically by the repetition of the question 'que reste-t-il ?'

What we are dealing with here is surely a double or avatar of the 'ignorant' – the unknowing self, representing the poet himself, but now radically reduced to its ontological state when faced with death. We might go so far as to say that silence has stripped him of his title and his position, and he has to abase himself as deeply as possible. What is left of a human being once he has put aside all the lies is 'un mourant': someone in the process of dying. Yet there is something which still connects this dying man to life, and which forces him to keep on expressing himself.

In lines 10 and 11 the poet raises fundamental questions about the will to live and to continue to speak, even though he is imprisoned within the four walls of mortality. The answer to this question is delivered (metaphorically) in the last two lines of the poem. For the time being, however, it remains in a state of suspense, as if the speaking poet were placed within the frame of his own self-expression: a text which talks of a 'je' telling itself to be silent, whilst questioning what enables him to speak. And thus the character of the 'ignorant' gradually becomes more complex.

The final question in line 12 again takes up the theme of unknowing, and thereby intensifies it: 'moi l'ignare et l'inquiet', but this time unknowing is harnessed to anxiety, which is an interrogative state, marked by the absence of tranquillity, a spiritual feverishness. It puts the finishing touches to a self-portrait located in a negative space, a mould without content, which is to be seen in its entirety through an opaque lens rendering knowledge impossible. In Jaccottet's work we often come across what I would call a 'poésie de la prétéri-tion' (paralipsis), indicated by the poet 'saying that he does not express what he nonetheless expresses' ('[qui] dit qu'il ne dit pas ce que néanmoins il dit'), or rather speaking only to criticise the shortcomings of language. In calling himself in this instance 'l'ignare' (ignoramus), the poet is adding weight to the theme of not knowing, since the term itself is used pejoratively to describe a person who knows nothing at all.

At the point where the text reaches its conclusion, the dying man takes over, speaking for himself in a way that is both piercingly accurate and deliberately vague. From the 'je me tais' ('I keep silent') of line 6 the text leads us through to: 'je l'entends vraiment qui parle' ('I truly hear the one who is speaking') (line 13); which means that having been suppressed, speech is reinstated. What is more, speech itself is now in a different position, and, one might almost say, in a different mouth: from the mouth of the unknowing poet it has been transferred to the mouth of the dying man who does know (the voice altering its tone from feverish anxiety to the more peaceful notes of one who has come to terms with mortality). The speaking subject has become an auditory one, listening to his own voice which has become that of another (perhaps the voice of the dying man he at first refused to be?); depersonalised by this point, it merges with the early morning light, a light which transmits an awareness of the presence of death. Such a testament could only be made in a voice as vague and as true as this. We cannot escape the feeling of witnessing a strange double act in which the 'ignorant' is at one and the same time the man who does not know and the man who is dying, the speaker and the listener, the teacher and his disciple. Unable to be the bearer of knowledge, he is, above all else, a conscious mind.

The two lines which end the poem stand apart, in quotation marks. This technique of delegating thoughts or their expression to a third party is one which Jaccottet employs quite often. On the surface, these two lines are not easy to understand: instead of giving clear and direct expression to a thought, they encrypt it in an image, as if reserving judgement upon it and calling for us to reflect upon it. The image which represents the thought is based on the classical comparison between love and fire. Yet fire here is also meant in the literal sense, if it is a metaphor: it is for the burning up of time, or for some vital energy, rather than for emotion. Both fire and love illuminate something only as they consume it. If we were to sum up the meaning of these two lines, it could best be done by quoting from another poem: 'L'Effraie': 'Que la fin nous illumine' ('May the end throw light on us'). Quite simply, in order to exist we must accept the presence of death. Something must be extinguished so that something else may radiate light. Moreover, there is another aspect of this image which is both precise and complex. The poem speaks of 'la faute et la beauté' of the 'bois en cendres' ('the fault and the beauty' of the 'woods in ashes'). The word 'faute' comes as a surprise in this context; it is probably appropriate here to understand it in the sense of something missing rather than a mistake or a trespass of some kind.

Thus Philippe Jaccottet defines two positions in this text which interlock: the poetic and the existential, a moral code of writing and an ethics of the individual. He maps out the extent of the shadows cast by death on poetic experience as well as those cast by misgivings over language itself, its lures and disappointments.

Poetry brings speech closer to death. At the end of the passage mortality is clearly shown to be the precondition of beauty, of speech and of love. It is only the end, and nothing else, which illuminates. 'Cette splendeur semble avoir sa source dans la mort, non dans l'éternel ; cette beauté paraît dans le mouvant, l'éphémère, le fragile' ('This splendour seems to arise from death, and not from the eternal; this beauty is visible in what is not still or stable, but in what is fragile') wrote Jaccottet in *La Promenade sous les arbres*.[4]

Translated by Michèle Lester

Notes

1 Philippe Jaccottet, 'Le Livre des morts', in *L'Ignorant, poésie 1946–1967* (Paris: Gallimard, 1977), p. 90.
2 Philippe Jaccottet, *La Semaison* (Paris: Gallimard, 1984), p. 96.

3 *Ibid.*
4 Philippe Jaccottet, *La Promenade sous les arbres* (Lausanne: Mermod, 1957), p. 38.

Further reading

Brunel, Pierre, *Philippe Jaccottet, cinq recueils* (*L'Effraie, L'Ignorant, Leçons, Chants d'en bas, À la lumière d'hiver*) (Nantes: Éditions du temps, 2003).

Cadi, Andrea, *Measuring the Visible: The Verse and Prose of Philippe Jaccottet* (Amsterdam: Rodopi, 1992).

Chauvin, Danièle, *Viatiques: essai sur l'imaginaire* (Grenoble: Presses Universitaires de Grenoble, 2003).

Dumas, Marie-Claire (ed.), *La Poésie de Philippe Jaccottet* (Geneva: Slatkine, 1986).

Ferrage, Hervé, *Philippe Jaccottet, le pari de l'inactuel* (Paris: Presses Universitaires de France, 2002).

Giusto, Jean-Pierre, *Philippe Jaccottet ou le désir d'inscription* (Lille: Presses Universitaires de Lille, 1994).

Jaccottet, Philippe, *Words in the Air: A Selection of Poems by Philippe Jaccottet*, trans. Derek Mahon (Oldcastle: Gallery Press, 1998).

Jossua, Jean-Pierre, *Figures présentes, figures absentes: pour lire Philippe Jaccottet* (Paris: L'Harmattan, 2002).

Mathieu, Jean-Claude, *Philippe Jaccottet: l'évidence du simple et l'éclat de l'obscur* (Paris: José Corti, 2003).

Onimus, Jean, *Philippe Jaccottet: une poétique de l'insaisissable* (Seyssel: Champ Vallon, 1982).

Richard, Jean-Pierre, *Onze études sur la poésie moderne* (Paris: Seuil, 1964).

Steinmetz, Jean-Luc, *Philippe Jaccottet* (Paris: Seghers 2003).

20 Édouard Glissant, 'Pour Mycéa'

JEAN-PASCAL POUZET

Pour Mycéa

[1]

Ô terre, si c'est terre, ô toute-en-jour où nous sommes venus. Ô
plongée dans l'éclat d'eau et la parole labourée. Vois que tes mots
m'ont déhalé de ce long songe où tant de bleu à tant d'ocre s'est
mis. Et vois que je descends de cette nuit, entends

*

[2]

Si la nuit te dépose au plus haut de la mer
N'offense en toi la mer par échouage des anciens dieux
Seules les fleurs savent comme on gravit l'éternité
Nous t'appelons terre blessée ô combien notre temps
Sera bref, ainsi l'eau dont on ne voit le lit
Chanson d'eau empilée sur l'eau du triste soir
Tu es douce à celui que tu éloignes de ta nuit
Tel un gravier trop lourd enfoui aux grèves de minuit
J'ai mené ma rame entre les îles je t'ai nommée
Loin avant que tu m'aies désigné pour asile et souffle
Je t'ai nommée Insaisissable et Toute-enfuie
Ton rire a séparé les eaux bleues des eaux inconnues

*

[3]

Je t'ai nommée Terre blessée, dont la fêlure n'est gouvernable, et
    t'ai vêtue de mélopées dessouchées des recoins d'hier
Pilant poussière et dévalant mes mots jusqu'aux enclos et
    poussant aux lisières les gris taureaux muets
Je t'ai voué peuple de vent où tu chavires par silence afin que terre
    tu me crées
Quand tu lèves dans ta couleur, où c'est cratère à jamais enfeuillé,
    visible dans l'avenir

*

[4]

J'écris en toi la musique de toute branche grave ou bleue
Nous éclairons de nos mots l'eau qui tremble
Nous avons froid de la même beauté
Le pays brin à brin a délacé cela qu'hier
Tu portais à charge sur ta rivière débordée
Ta main rameute ces rumeurs en nouveauté
Tu t'émerveilles de brûler plus que les vieux encens

*

. . .

*

[6]

L'eau du morne est plus grave
Où les rêves ne dérivent
Tout le vert tombe en nuit nue
Quelle feuille ose sa pétulance
Quels oiseaux rament et crient
Dru hélé de boues mon pays
Saison déracinée qui revient à sa source
Un vent rouge seul pousse haut sa fleur
Dans la houle qui n'a profondeur et toi
Parmi les frangipanes dénouée lassée
D'où mènes-tu ces mots que tu colores
D'un sang de terre sur l'écorce évanoui
Tu cries ta fixité à tout pays maudit
Est-ce ô navigatrice le souvenir

*

. . .

*

[8]

Je n'écris pas pour te surprendre mais pour vouer mesure à ce
plein d'impatience que le vent nomme ta beauté. Lointaine, ciel
d'argile, et vieux limon, réel
Et l'eau de mes mots coule, tant que roche l'arrête, où je descends
rivière parmi les lunes qui pavanent au rivage. Là où ton sourire est
de la couleur des sables, ta main plus nue qu'un vœu prononcé en
silence

*

[9]

Et n'est que cendre en brousses tassée
N'est qu'égarement où le ciel enfante
L'eau d'agave n'apaise pas la fleur timide
Les étoiles chantent d'un seul or qu'on n'entend
Au quatre-chemins où fut rouée la sève
À tant qui crient inspirés du vent
Je hèle inattendue errance
Tu sors de la parole, t'enfuis
Tu es pays d'avant donné en récompense
Invisibles nous conduisons la route
La terre seule comprend

From *Pays rêvé, pays réel*

In the second half of the twentieth century, francophone poetry took up again with landscapes, not as mere picturesque backgrounds but as substance and *dramatis personae* – as, for instance, the writings of Yves Bonnefoy, Philippe Jaccottet, Jacques Dupin or André du Bouchet diversely attest. The work of Édouard Glissant partakes of the celebration of their new visibility which is felt everywhere.[1] Yet Glissant writes of American territories that 'La poétique du paysage . . . n'est pas directement confondable avec la *physique* du pays' (Glissant's emphasis). It is a difference that unfolds an obligation to memory and discourse shared by both landscape and language: 'Le paysage garde mémoire de ses temps. Son espace est ouvert ou clos sur des signifiés.'[2] 'Pour Mycéa' is the seventh of nine sections in a collection of poems that precisely offers itself as poised between the exact physicality of 'pays réel' and a total poetics of the 'pays rêvé'.[3] Since the collections belonging to the earliest periods of activity, however, *Le Sang rivé* (1947–54), *Un champ d'îles* (1952) and *La Terre inquiète* (1954) – which the sections of *Pays rêvé, pays réel* revisit to a large extent – these forms of discrepancy and tension have been brought into what Pierre Reverdy (with whom Glissant shares essential Modernist conceptions) called an 'effervescent contact of the mind with reality'.[4] Wedged in between two indissoluble versions of an Antillean 'pays', 'mon pays' [6] in search of expression, the poem sets itself the difficult task of being this significant space of encounter between 'réel' and 'rêvé'.

The title of the seventh section, 'Pour Mycéa', indicates that it is in the rhetorical form of a dedication, a feature it shares explicitly with only one other section (section 5, 'Pour Laoka'), but also with the epigraphic inscription heading the whole collection, 'à merveille qui ne se dit / à liberté qui fleure en souches'. Judged from a narrow perspective, the dedicatee might seem an elusive figure, perhaps like a simple immanence of the 'pays rêvé'. But the beginning of the poem instantly invites an identification of Mycéa with the earth – though with concessive modality: 'Ô terre, *si* c'est terre' [1]. In similar hesitation as to the tangible and conceptual reality of land in stanza XXX of *Les Indes* (in 'Le Voyage'), the fixity of naming re-enacts the risk of blurring, or even undoing the connivance between land surveying and idiom for this land of invasion 'où nous sommes venus' [1], as conquerors (name-givers) or slaves (those named). Furthermore, the Protean recurrence of Mycéa throughout Glissant's oeuvre, in the company of Papa Longué, Thaël (the 'nom de proximité' of Raphaël Targin), Mathieu Béluse, and Marie Célat, establishes it/her as one of the familiar overarching figures inhabiting the whirling *Tout-monde*. Some of these figures (together with some 'key notions') are apparently 'explained' with a gloss in the section at the end of *Pays rêvé, Pays réel* called 'Tracées' – an organic constituent of the collection, especially as one recalls the importance of *la Trace*, the rhizome of 'Trails', in Glissant's works.

Willed by a poet who is far from being averse to the force of concept, this ninth and final section is a complex machinery calling forth a reminiscence of a pregnant structure of Western medieval thinking with which Glissant is familiar: the text/gloss pattern. Largely unprecedented in Antillean writing, its tripartite structure, divided into 'Glose', 'Légende' and 'Réel', may owe something of its design and of the consummate subtlety of its content to such sophistication as, for instance, that of the three-layered regime of 'texte' 'glose' and 'allégorie' devised by Christine de Pizan in *L'Epistre d'Othéa* – exemplifying an inventive empowerment of the vernacular text as it was wrenching itself away from the exclusiveness of Latinate culture in the early fifteenth century.[5] Here, in similar vein, the written poem testifies to a liberation of the 'pays' expressed through the resilient violence of the pervasive image of roots and uprooting – the second part of the dedication of *Pays rêvé, pays réel* is 'à liberté qui fleure *en souches*'. Amidst the network of words expressing an image otherwise constant throughout Glissant's poetry, from the 'mélopées *dessouchées* des recoins d'hier' [3] to 'La ravine où je dors est un brasier qu'on *souche*' [7], and the preternatural, countercyclical, if *quasi*-alexandrine, melody – or, more pointedly, 'chanson d'eau' [2] or 'mélopées' [3] – of 'saison *déracinée* qui revient à sa source' [6], Mycéa registers and conveys the *labour* of *oral* poetic *parole* ('la parole *labourée*' [1], both 'tilled' and 'laboured') and *écriture* ('J'écris en toi. . .' [4]; 'Je n'écris pas pour te surprendre mais pour vouer mesure. . .' [8]), through to its/her own final liberation from the realm of speech whose bounds the earth finally exceeds: 'tu sors de la parole, t'enfuis' [9] – a gesture of exile in which the end of the section is also adumbrated. The final 'Tracées' serve, less to stabilise improbable definitions than to avoid referential stability in land and language and to highlight the verbal elusiveness of Mycéa 'Insaisissable' [2], one of the three figures classified under 'Réel': '*Mycéa*. Celle dont le poète est enchanté, qu'il nomme à chaque ventée. Mais dont les mots ne rendent compte'. Mycéa challenges attempts at a deeper-rooted form of referential 'fixity' which, when evoked, makes her surge up as either the 'cri' of 'terre' in the face of 'pays' ('tu cries *ta fixité* à tout pays maudit' [6]), or as the antecedence of 'pays d'avant' [9], teeming with gestures begun yesterday and carrying 'le souvenir' [6] – 'cela qu'hier / Tu portais à charge sur ta rivière débordée' [4]. The impossibility of *reviewing* Mycéa in words, her will not to commit herself and 'planer dans un entour sans référence' ('to hover around with no reference'), effectively inflect the energies of the lyrical subject towards a 'langage d'images et de flottaisons', as Glissant writes in *Tout-monde*.[6]

Indeed the poetic first person is embarked on a drift across the 'pays' expressed essentially through Aeolian and nautical imagery, in the course of which the activity and passivity of surveying and naming are in dialogic correspondence, and often in empathetic exchange with a lyrical second person. By virtue of a dynamic matrix which may be a partial legacy of the Rimbaldian *descente* 'des fleuves impassibles', every impulse to lead and to name ('je *descends* de cette nuit' [1]; 'Nous t'*appelons* terre blessée' [2]; 'j'ai *mené* ma rame' [2]; 'je t'ai *nommée*' [2] (twice); 'je t'ai *nommée*' 'et t'ai vêtue' [3]; '*dévalant* mes mots', '*poussant* aux lisières' [3]; 'j'*écris* en toi' [4]; 'où je *descends* rivière' [8]; 'Je *hèle* inattendue errance' [9]; 'nous *conduisons* la route' [9]) almost always matches a secret acquiescence in being led and fashioned ('tes mots m'ont *déhalé*' [1]; 'Si la nuit te *dépose* au plus haut de la mer' [2]; '**je t'**ai nommée / Loin avant que **tu m'**aies *désigné* pour *asile et souffle*' [2] which deploys the reciprocation of 'elective affinities' through chiasmus; '*tu chavires* par silence afin que *terre tu me crées*' [3]; '*dénouée lassée* / D'où *mènes*-tu ces mots que tu colores' [6]). Moreover, the proliferation of formulae *around* Mycéa-the-earth launches out into a two-dimensional, simultaneous exploration of landscape as much as of language: both diving, or delving into the thickness ('dru' [6]) of things, and delineating *lignes de fuite* for the rhizomatic 'pays'. Mycéa-the-earth is '*plongée* dans l'*éclat* d'eau et la parole labourée' [1]; the gravel is '**enfoui** aux grèves de minuit' – in a contrast with the adjacent figure of the 'Toute-**enfuie**' which is highlighted by paronomasia [2]. Typically, 'éclat' is a Glissantian notion expressing the glittering presence of (is)lands, their feminine fulguration, their 'musique' [4] and their 'couleur' [3], most particularly as in *Un champ d'îles*. The navigation of *Pays rêvé, pays réel* 'entre les îles' [2] likewise steers its course with 'inattendue errance' [9] amidst a series of 'zones of *éclat* or brilliance', in which 'the word *éclat* is to be taken here in the double sense of illumination [here once more nudging Rimbaud, perhaps] and explosion', and thanks to which the celebrated 'Poetics of the Relation makes itself most visible'.[7]

However, the explosive dimension of 'éclat d'eau' reverberates not only across 'l'eau qui *tremble*' [2], but also in a wound that is not easily staunched – with the subsequent spilling of 'sang' [6] and 'sève' [9] – and in the *ungovernable* 'fêlure' [3] of the 't/Terre blessée' [2, 3]. A possible source is the influence on Glissant of Bonnefoy's *Du mouvement et de l'immobilité de Douve* which was perceptible as soon as published (1953); in a later essay the Martiniquan poet described his compelling vision of the organic 'corps de Douve' as 'shattered multiplicity' ('multiplicité fracassée'). This object of poetic knowledge ('Douve qui promet la connaissance') which is tugged and torn about ('*écartelée* secrète connaissance, et qui se *rompt*'),[8] is to be related to Glissant's 'À toute géographie tourmentée' – the famous dedication of *Le Sang rivé* – and here to a number of operations which maintain the dolorous dynamism of verbal processes: the earth is 'blessée' (an epithet used twice); 'la parole' is 'labourée' [1]; the 'chanson d'eau' is 'empilée sur l'eau du triste soir' [2] and monotonous melodies are 'dessouchées' [3]; your laughter 'a séparé' [2]; the crater (yet another potential signifier of explosion) is 'à jamais enfeuillé' [3] (a phantasmal displacement of 'endeuillé'?); the river is 'débordée' [4]; 'mon pays' is 'hélé de boues' ('hailed by muds') [6]; the season is 'déracinée qui revient à sa source' [6] (in a typical movement of 'retour amont', as René Char wrote); 'tu' is 'dénouée lassée' ('unbound wearied') [6]; ash is 'tassée' ('stacked up'), sap was 'rouée' [9] (an image of flogging, as in the French phrase 'rouer de coups'). The residual violence of those past participles, some characteristically employed as adjectives in Glissant's idiom, ties in with the intensity of verbal forms ('N'offense' [2]; 'tombe' [6]), nouns ('échouage' [2]; 'fêlure' [3]; 'égarement' [9]), the adjective 'maudit' [6], the negativity of 'n'a profondeur' [6], 'n'apaise pas', 'on n'entend' [9]; or with the meticulous stubbornness of 'Le pays *brin à brin a délacé* ('unlaced straw by straw') cela qu'hier / tu portais à charge' [4]. 'Pour Mycéa' is an *arena* (literally, 'aux *grèves* de minuit' [2], and 'de la couleur des *sables*' [8]) where poetic diction confronts the apotropaic sacredness and essential mystery (or *opacity*) of nomination, definition and (in) vocation. On the one hand Mycéa-the-earth is hemmed in by a multiplication of formulae – 'Nous t'appelons terre blessée' [2]; 'Je t'ai nommée Insaisissable et Toute-enfuie' [2]; 'Je t'ai nommée Terre blessée' [3]; 'Tu es pays d'avant donné en récompense' [9] – to the point of semantic depletion: '*n*'est *que* cendre', '*n*'est *qu*'égarement' [9], and, in correlation, 'la houle qui *n*'a profondeur' [6]. The allocutive power of invocation, with 'Ô' as the time-hallowed marker of lyrical *adnominatio*, is also summoned: 'Ô terre', 'ô toute-en-jour' [1]; 'ô navigatrice' [6]; and is flanked by votive gestures: 'je t'ai voué peuple de vent' [3]; 'vouer mesure' [8]. On the other hand, this proliferation of babble, 'ces rumeurs' which your hand 'rameute' ('rounds up') [4], is countered by a propensity to silence, solitude, evanescence and transmutation which is often aided or *inspired* by wind ('à tant qui crient *inspirés* du vent' [9]), or marked by blood or the colour red: 'Je t'ai *voué* peuple de *vent* où tu chavires ('capsize') par *silence*' [3]; 'Un *vent rouge seul* pousse haut sa fleur' [6]; a '*sang* de terre' is 'évanoui' [6]; 'ce plein d'impatience que le vent nomme ta beauté' [8] is immediately followed by the appositive feminine 'Lointaine' in the next sentence; the singing of stars 'd'un *seul* or' [9] is not heard, and your hand is 'plus nue qu'un *vœu prononcé en silence*' [8]. Such an apparently oxymoronic balance, also carried out between 'mon pays' and 'à tout pays maudit' [6], between '*long* songe' [1] and 'ô combien notre temps / sera *bref*' [3], is further materialised in the vernacular 'quatre-chemins' [9] (the

Martiniquan word for 'crossroads'), and above all in the watershed between 'eaux bleues' and 'eaux inconnues' brought forth by the 'rire' of Mycéa-the-earth [2].

But what precisely begins as a *quasi*-metaphysical blazoning of the earth ('Ton rire' [2], 'ta main' [twice: 4, 8], 'ton sourire' [8]) finally *overflows*, like the 'rivière débordée' [4], the drifting dreams (they 'dérivent' [6]) and all that is 'enfuie' [2], 'délacé' [4] or dénoué' [6], all that is 'déhalé' [1] or 'dévalant' [3]. This baroque 'démesure' of '[dé]mesure' as poetic *tekhne*, which is so dear to Glissant,[9] reinstates an organic justification for the scarcity of punctuation – some marks are still clinging to the more prose-looking sections [1] and [8], thus marking off ambiguously the conjunctive segment 'tant que roche l'arrête', which *may or may not* stem the flux of 'l'eau de mes mots' [8] (since 'tant que' superimposes implications of 'until' and 'as long as . . . not'); and there is the rare, though integral medial comma in [2], [3] and [9]. Such fluency of locution and syntactic open-endedness, probably some of the most influential prosodic lessons of poetry since Apollinaire (recall 'Zone', for instance), enlarge the circulation of a 'souffle' which is imparted by 'tu' ('avant que *tu* m'aies désigné' [2]), the pronoun of Modern lyrical address par excellence – here anaphorically present in several lines, including the last three of [4]. The difference between 'pays rêvé' and 'pays réel' is thus made more fluid, and the substances of earlier poems – 'le sang rivé', 'le sel noir' – may leak into the synaesthetic colour of 'branche . . . bleue' [4], 'vent rouge' [6], and colouring of words with 'un sang de terre' [6]; the rising of Mycéa-the-earth 'dans ta couleur' [3]; or the mixture of the dream 'où tant de bleu à tant d'ocre s'est mis' [1]. And the words which haul the speaker out of his long dream, this apparently smooth *enjambement* (syntactically most perceptible in [2] and [6]) from 'rêves' [6] to 'réel' [8], and from 'hier' [3, 4] and 'avant' [2, 9] to what is 'visible dans l'avenir' [3] – through a dominance of the indicative present tense, alongside a significant proportion of 'passé composé', in terms of verbal aspect a form of present in which the past is *subsumed* – may also facilitate the exposure of deeper secrets which *'seules* les fleurs savent' [2], and over which the acquiescence evoked earlier may also hold full sway. Indeed, in natural counterpoint to flow, drift and flight, a recurrence of images of effort in conveyance (*'poussant* . . . les gris taureaux muets' [3]; 'Un vent rouge seul *pousse* haut sa fleur' [6]), and most particularly of heaviness, gravity and depth (earth which the night *'dépose'* [2]; 'chanson d'eau *empilée'* [2]; 'tu *portais à charge'* [4]) is heard, as if compulsively, in the extensive paronomasia-*cum*-polyptoton around **'grav-'** which insinuates itself: 'Seules les fleurs savent comme on *gravit* l'éternité', *'gravier* trop lourd' and the *'grèves* de minuit' where it lies buried [2], 'toute branche *grave* ou bleue' [4], and again with 'l'eau du morne' declared to be 'plus *grave*' where dreams drift not [6]. This absorption and resurgence of natural and geographical coordinates may betray signs of an absolute fusion of real and intimate topographies, *also* to the extent that the poet's earliest apprehension and personal charting of Martiniquan landscape began as a maternal piggyback ride from the hilly, inland Morne Bezaudin (the poet's birthplace) to the coastal Cohée du Lamentin – a foundational experience and a 'mythe d'enfance' which Glissant has rewritten several times, and of which both the fluidity of 'inattendue errance' [9] and the gravity of 'tu portais à charge' are apposite figurations [4]. Moreover, the 'chanson d'eau' is 'douce', and this is perhaps one of Glissant's own melodies of the 'pays', not unlike (if not secretly reminiscent of) 'Une chanson douce', the love song, in the form of a modern lullaby-*cum*-fairytale, so memorably performed with bitter–sweet lyricism by the late Antillean/Parisian singer-songwriter Henri Salvador.[10] The combinatory musicality – as it were – of Glissant's poetry is heard everywhere, for instance in the repeated encounter between the liquid, flowing quality of the alveolar lateral [l] and the more compact, though muffled, hissing of the two sibilants in 'asile et souffle' [2], or the alliterative flux of inextricable dentals, nasals and approximants in 'Ta main rameute ces rumeurs en nouveauté' [4]. Furthermore, the figuration of musicality is at the heart of the fulguration of synaesthetic metaphor, with the 'chanson d'eau empilée sur l'eau du triste soir' [2], the 'mélopées dessouchées' [3], and 'la musique de toute branche grave ou bleue' [4], as if the strength of affective tension inherent in this effort of imagery were pressed into service to touch the irreducible elusiveness of the earth, which may or may not eventually 'raccorde[r] le pays de mer et le pays de terre', and 'rassembler le partage';[11] and to touch also the personal/collective myths contained therein.

Both this primeval 'musique' and the 'mélopées' – however *anti-atavistic* their *uprooting* from 'les recoins d'hier' [3] – may also allude to the pure *radicality* of taking stock of earlier forms of creation merging *unpredictably* into later ones.[12] Indeed, in addition to the multivalent figure of Mycéa which has been familiar since *La Lézarde* (1958), *Pays rêvé, pays réel* has an earlier, shorter namesake of an Urtext in prose written in December 1967 and inserted in *L'Intention poétique* (first published in 1969).[13] Though more overtly political (concerning governmental responsibilities in the aftermath of a hurricane hitting Martinique at full blast at the end of 1967), this 'description d'une île' already contains themes and words which have seeped into the later collection, and this is of course perceptible in 'Pour Mycéa': one may note the aphoristic, injunctive interplay of 'réel' and 'rêvé' ('Ne te sers pas du réel pour justifier tes manques. Réalise plutôt tes rêves pour mériter ta réalité'); the tremor of earth and water, and the mingling of colours; the importance of 'cri', 'profondeur' (which 'n'est pas au mystère; pour nous, elle tient toute à la continuité'), and 'beauté'; the hermeneutic link between the collective self of 'nous', 'paysage' and 'terre' ('Savoir ce qu'en nous il [le paysage] signifie. Porter à la terre ce clair savoir'); and the intimacy of wounds and words, as the 'description' leads 'jusqu'à la secrète fêlure que tout homme souffre, et dont – hors ses rêves non souvenus – il ne suit la trace qu'avec le *doigt des mots*' (Glissant's emphasis). With a melodious variation on the same themes across years, the full sway of reminiscences in creative *répétition* and *ressassement* may yield and express a 'circular' form of nomadism in thoughts, through which the vocation of 'mesure' also brings words to extremes of conveyance, 'jusqu'aux enclos', like subservient cattle – and, likewise, the 'gris taureaux *muets*', an animal (totemic?) image running in syntactic parallel to the 'mots', are themselves goaded towards the limen of expressivity, 'aux lisières' [3]. *Through words*, the creative unpredictability of chaos (the 'chaos-monde' of the 'Tout-monde') can merge with the soothing force of the muteness of things, with 'silence', 'sang de terre . . . évanoui' [6], and 'merveille' of the landscape whose unsayability (the 'merveille qui ne se dit' of the dedication) is foregrounded by the *realisable* outcomes of novelty through *Relation*: the rounding up of rumorous babble is 'en *nouveauté*', immediately followed by the more intense burning of which 'Tu t'émerveilles' [4]. This expressive sense of marvel is a source of liberty: there is no forcing of 'mots' or 'paroles' out of silent entities, but a respect of their immanent presence (the 'muteness' of bulls). It is only by virtue of a 'mild' form of prosopopoeia – for instance 'parmi les frangipanes / d'où mènes-tu ces mots' (comparable to Derek Walcott's perception of cabbage palms as reciting Saint-John Perse)[14] – that a devolution of the power of utterance and 'parole' may happen, to those which consent to speak. Only thus can words be at one with the seemingly contradictory facts of natural poetry: the antinomies of gesture inherent in 'quelle feuille *ose* sa pétulance' [6] v. 'la fleur *timide*' [9], in 'vêtue' [3] v. 'délacé' [4]; the difference in density between the compactness of '**délacé**' [4] and its apparent *dilation* in '**dé**nouée **lassée**' [6] through paronomasia; the hailing of 'mon pays' by muds (an inflexion of 'terre'), or the outcry of 'oiseaux' and 'Tu'-Mycéa [6], or 'les étoiles' which 'chantent' [9]. There is also the mystery of the red wind which 'pousse haut sa fleur' in the 'houle' which has no depth [6], with the syntactic ambiguity of 'seul' (is the red wind *alone*, or is it the *only* entity which does this?), and the agentive valency of the verb 'pousser' which the possibility of semantic contamination in context (with 'la fleur pousse') can bring to a surprising twist: not only does the wind *push up* its flower, but it may also *grow* it. This, allied to 'Seules les fleurs savent comme on gravit l'éternité' [2] and 'la fleur timide' [9], leads to floral imagery as a medium of aphoristic expression not at so many removes from the 'minute particulars' of William Blake's *Proverbs of Hell* ('To create a little flower is the labour of ages'), or the formulae of René Char.

If poetry can thus aim to become formulaic or aphoristic, it is because the space of the poem, with emotional continuity and resilience, revivifies and brings together a community of 'mots' within landscape: the words of Mycéa-the-earth ('*tes* mots') which 'm'ont déhalé' [1] ('have hauled me out') and '*ces* mots que *tu* colores' [6]; those of the lyrical subject ('*mes* mots' [3], 'l'eau de *mes* mots' [8]); and those of an inclusive – though ambiguous as to who exactly is concerned – first-person plural: 'Nous éclairons de *nos* mots l'eau qui tremble' [4], this 'nous' which is regularly present in 'Pour Mycéa' ('nous sommes venus' [1]; 'nous t'appelons', 'notre temps' [2]; 'Nous avons froid de la même beauté'

[4]; 'nous conduisons la route' [9]). The organic fusion within 'nous' is aesthetic, with a view to this chilling 'beauté' – perhaps an archaeological reminiscence of Baudelairean *Spleen et idéal* (with the communicative mineral frigidity of 'rêve de pierre' in 'La Beauté'); otherwise possibly lodged in such alexandrine, musical perfection as the chiasmus of '**Lointaine**, *ciel d'argile*, et *vieux limon*, **réel**', which is the qualification of 'ta beauté' evoked immediately before [8]. The interlacing of personal pronouns ensures a form of lyrical sharing subsumed in the collective 'parole', but also extinguished in the final flight ('Tu sors de la parole, t'enfuis'), as the earth may exceed words. The thematic presence of words is elemental (water: 'chanson d'eau' [2] and 'l'eau de mes mots' [8]; earth: 'parole labourée' [1] and 'ces mots que tu colores / d'un sang de terre' [6]; air: 'ce plein d'impatience que le vent nomme ta beauté' [8] and 'À tant qui crient inspirés du vent' [9]), and it is notable that the element of fire is perhaps that which *consumes and exhausts* them most: from 'Nous *éclairons* de nos mots l'eau qui tremble' [4] to 'Tu t'émerveilles de *brûler* plus que les vieux encens' [4], through to 'La *brûlure d'eau* où nous posons les mains' [5], 'les *mots* me font *brûler*' [7], and finally to 'Et n'est que *cendre* en brousses tassée' [9]. However, the overarching persistence of synaesthesia and zeugma ('la musique de toute branche grave ou bleue' [4]; 'l'eau de mes mots' [8]) also means a form of consent of words to the sacrificial enigma of landscape, which is the promise of true knowledge.

In constant celebration of 'opacité' and 'relation', Glissant's poetic language avoids 'comprehension' in a narrow conceptual sense which is hierarchical and reductive, but seeks to impart an understanding and respect of knowledge which is shared and expansive. In this light, the verb 'comprendre' in the final line of 'Pour Mycéa' ('La terre seule comprend' [9]) can be taken to sway from 'comprehend' to 'embrace' – only she ('seule') can undertake the *highest* form ('*au plus haut* de la mer' [2]; 'un vent rouge seul pousse *haut* sa fleur' [6]) of the intellectual fused with the physical, of landscape encountering and *realising* 'toutes les différences du monde' within the lyrical corporeality of the voice. In this respect, 'Pour Mycéa' exemplifies the extent to which any of Glissant's texts or poems is an echo chamber of this 'alchemy' – that of writing blending through 'rhythmic accumulation' with 'the metallic brilliance of oral rhetoric'; in this process, words and themes whirl about and reverberate everywhere in *Tout-monde*, conveying an idea of poetry as 'ethnotechnology'.[15] But the *ethnotechnology* of Mycéa, or Mycéa as *ethnotechnology*, is an operation of trembling fervour: 'l'eau qui tremble' [4] may materialise 'la pensée du tremblement' recently evoked by the poet, by virtue of which 'l'être comme étant *frémit* pour nous'.[16] The quivering of poetic idiom may well set selected words ablaze – 'Il est des mots qui brûlent en leur lieu, ils ne servent qu'à une fois'.[17] Yet through words Glissant's 'sensibilité chérissante d'un pays' ('cherishing sensitivity to a land') is fully expressed,[18] and poetic knowledge is 'irrepressible'.[19]

Notes

1 See Michel Collot, *Paysage et poésie du romantisme à nos jours* (Paris: José Corti, 2005), which includes a chapter on Glissant, 'L'Ouverture au(x) monde(s)', pp. 371–92, simultaneously published in Michel Collot and Antonio Rodriguez (eds.), *Paysage et poésies francophones* (Paris: Presses Sorbonne Nouvelle, 2005), pp. 43–61.

2 Édouard Glissant, *Le Discours antillais* (Paris: Seuil, 1981; repr. Paris: Gallimard, 1997, 2002), p. 449.

3 All references to Glissant's poems are to *Poèmes complets (Le Sang rivé, Un champ d'îles, La Terre inquiète, Les Indes, Le Sel noir, Boises, Pays rêvé, pays réel, Fastes, Les Grands Chaos)* (Paris: Gallimard, 1994); *Pays rêvé, pays réel* is pp. 287–350. 'Pour Mycéa' has 9 stanzas in all, of which stanzas 5 and 7 are omitted here for reasons of space. For ease of reference, original stanzas are preceded by bracketed numbers used in the essay. Unless otherwise indicated, all characters in italics and bold type denote my emphases. All translations are mine.

4 Quoted by Georges-Emmanuel Clancier, 'Mémoire de Reverdy', in *La Poésie et ses environs* (Paris: Gallimard, 1973), pp. 159–63 (p. 161). See Édouard Glissant's essay on Reverdy, 'Purs paysages' in *L'Intention poétique (Poétique II)* (Paris: Seuil, 1969; repr. Paris: Gallimard, 1997), pp. 73–9. My thanks to Hugues Azérad for bringing the Modernist connection between Reverdy and Glissant to my attention.

5 Gabriele Parussa (ed.), Christine de Pizan, *Epistre d'Othéa* (Geneva: Droz, 1999). European medieval culture is an important constituent of Glissant's thinking, as formulated notably in 'Au commencement du temps "universel" occidental', in *Traité du Tout-monde (Poétique IV)* (Paris: Gallimard, 1997), pp. 92–103, and in *Les Entretiens de Baton Rouge* with Alexandre Leupin (Paris: Gallimard, 2008).

6 Édouard Glissant, *Tout-monde* (Paris: Gallimard, 1993; repr. 1995, 2002), p. 404: 'Mycéa concentrée sur sa volonté de ne pas paraître vivante ni engagée dans les accrochages du jour: elle ne désirait que de planer dans un entour sans référence. Mathieu qui suivait la pente, adoptant peu à peu ce langage d'images et de flottaisons, auquel Mycéa l'inclinait.'

7 Édouard Glissant, 'Beyond Babel', *World Literature Today*, 63 (4) (1989), pp. 561–3 (p. 561).

8 Édouard Glissant, 'Du corps de Douve', in *Traité du Tout-monde*, pp. 141–7 (p. 143; the words in italics are quotations from Bonnefoy's poems by Glissant); see also pp. 224–9 of 'Par l'astre le plus lointain', in *L'Intention poétique*.

9 See Édouard Glissant, *Introduction à une poétique du divers* (Paris: Gallimard, 1996), pp. 92–5.

10 'Une chanson douce', also known as 'Le Loup, la biche et le chevalier' (1950), is the collaboration of Maurice Pon (lyrics) and Henri Salvador (tune).

11 Édouard Glissant, 'Bezaudin', in *Tout-monde*, pp. 207–8.

12 'Anti-atavistic' alludes to Glissant's distinction between 'cultures ataviques' and 'cultures composites', on which see *Introduction à une poétique du divers*, in particular pp. 33–6 and 59–60.

13 'Pays rêvé, pays réel', in 'Offrande', second of two sections in 'Intention et Relation', last movement of *L'Intention poétique*, pp. 237–41.

14 Derek Walcott, *What the Twilight Says* (London: Faber and Faber, 1998) p. 78: 'when I see cabbage palms moving their fronds at sunrise, I think they are reciting Perse . . . At last, islands not written about but writing themselves! At last! The royal palms of Guadeloupe recite *Éloges* by heart.'

15 Glissant, 'Beyond Babel', p. 561 (for the 'alchemy'), and p. 563 for 'the idea of an ethnotechnology, through which the means of evolution can be adapted to the real needs of a community, to a landscape preserved in its entirety. The promotion

of languages is henceforth the first axiom of this ethnotechnology. We know too that, in the field of knowledge, poetry has always been . . . the ethnotechnology par excellence. The defense of languages also passes through poetry.'

16 Édouard Glissant, 'Philosophie du Tout-monde', seminar of the Institut du Tout-monde with Paris 8, Paris, 30 May 2008, digitised at www.tout-monde.com (accessed 15 September 2009).

17 Glissant, 'L'Eau du volcan', in *Les Grands Chaos*, p. 465.

18 Régis Antoine, 'Les Sources de l'émotion chez l'écrivain Glissant', in *Poétiques d'Édouard Glissant*, ed. Jacques Chevrier (Paris: Presses de l'Université Paris-Sorbonne, 1999), pp. 33–42 (p. 40).

19 Yves Bonnefoy, 'Igitur et le photographe', in *Sous l'horizon du langage* (Paris: Mercure de France, 2002), p. 233.

Further reading

Britton, Celia, *Édouard Glissant and Postcolonial Theory: Strategies of Language and Resistance* (Charlottesville: University of Virginia Press, 1999).

Crowley, Patrick 'Édouard Glissant: Resistance and Opacité', *Romance Studies*, 24 (July 2006), pp. 105–15.

Dash, Michael, *Édouard Glissant* (Cambridge: Cambridge University Press, 1995).

Fonkoua, Romuald, *Édouard Glissant: essai sur une mesure du monde au XXe siècle* (Paris: Champion, 2002).

Gallagher, Mary, *Soundings in French Caribbean Writing since 1950: The Shock of Space and Time* (Oxford: Oxford University Press, 2002).

Hallward, Peter, *Absolutely Postcolonial: Writing between the Singular and the Specific* (Manchester: Manchester University Press, 2001).

Nesbitt, Nick, *Voicing Memory: History and Subjectivity in French Caribbean Literature* (Charlottesville: University of Virginia Press, 2003).

Part IV

New voices, new visions

21 Michel Deguy, 'Le Métronome'

BÉATRICE BONHOMME

Le Métronome

Qui bat là
Une phrase de langue
Au vent du jeu

Neume du mètre
Le balancier confie   5
Le temps à la diction

Rythme seuil il faut
Qu'une porte en mots
soit ouverte et fermée

Longue brève et pause   10
Le temps passe
Il repassera

Il y a du comme dans l'être
Un air de famille un air de rien

Le courant d'airs   15
tourne les pages
ça ne fait pas un pli
mais six

Encore un instant
Monsieur le lecteur   20
Le temps d'un mot nu
Entre deux tournes

Ce qui me chante
             se plie
Aux calibres des couleurs   25

From *Aux heures d'affluence*

How can we prevent the poem itself from becoming a thing, when the poem is like a canon, a ritornello, a nursery-rhyme; a poem which plays with popular forms out of context, and seems unburdened by theory; a poem situated halfway between a passing breeze and the painter's palette? The most important question for Michel Deguy appears to be: in speaking of things, how can we prevent life from becoming dead matter if it ceases to renew itself? Naming things petrifies them – this we must flee. We should paint not the thing itself but the effect it creates; paint not the things themselves, but the space between them. Then we may show that the thing which is written continues to move, and thus continues to renew its perpetual quest. Verse turns and returns: advances, halts, begins again. It constantly returns; like a ferret retracing its tracks, drawing, withdrawing and then erasing its traces: 'Le temps d'un mot nu / Entre deux tournes'.[1] Once a line is completed, we see the poet anxious to return and start again as if for a completely new beginning: 'Le temps passe / Il repassera'. The fact that the poem revolves does not mean that it simply returns, but rather that it simultaneously disappears and remains. The poet speaks, withdraws what he has said, and speaks again: 'Le courant d'airs / tourne les pages'. What remains is created by this constantly withdrawn and renewed progression, as every line potentialises the one which precedes it: 'ça ne fait pas un pli / mais six'. In the halfway house created by poetry it is possible to tap into forces which generate a playful connection between the theory of poetry and poetry itself: 'Sans cesse soutenue par l'ouvrage du poème, autant que par la réflexion philosophique et par un faisceau d'actions annexes convergeant vers le langage . . . cette interrogation constitue l'axe essentiel d'une œuvre que réévalue obstinément le pourquoi et le comment de la poésie en son extrême contemporain'.[2] The poem as experience and the poem as the language of that experience are not two different things: 'Il n'y a pas philosophie d'un côté, poésie de l'autre.'[3] The bridge that links poetry with reflection on poetry remains firm, even if occasionally frail and seeming to tremble *au vent du jeu*, in the draught of a half-open door.

The poem 'Le Métronome'[4] follows 'Légendes sur un livre-bouquet composé par le peintre Dorny', and thus is strongly connected to painting and takes its place in the chapter 'Travaux pour un rectangle', composed of texts dedicated to Bram van Velde, Pignon and Bertrand Dorny. This asserts the affinity between the plastic and poetic arts – a complicity which gives rise to hybrid works such as those in 'Donnant donnant' (*AF*, p. 168). Perhaps, since this is so, we should allow ourselves to be transported by the poem's mobility, by its rhythmic sense and beat, so as to see the full beauty of the poetic emerge, forming a single whole in texture and shape, in sound and image. This text plays games with us and itself: here, openings, palpitations and hesitations reminiscent of Valéry are used with irony, are dramatised, de-dramatised. The rhythm can immerse us in its atonal colours and irony. On the other hand, 'Le Métronome' immediately precedes a meditation on 'Le Rapt du RAP', and its own title at once shows it to be linked to the musical domain. Lastly, the poem offers an evocation of the book as object, 'Le courant d'airs / tourne les pages' and the Mallarméan fold, 'ça ne fait pas un pli / mais six' – an allusion to Mallarmé and his ever-absent bouquet, already seen in the captions composed for the painter, Dorny:

Comme des *fleurs les mots*
Sont mis en pots . . .

Artifice, ô définition
fais la fleur !
Une fleur sans pétale à qui manquent les tiges. . .
C'est le bouquet ! (*AF*, p. 171)

The solution is as Mallarméan as 'l'absente de tout bouquet'. To paint between the things, to say the thing even while denying it, is to evoke it magically in words: 'Le poème ne décrit pas, il absente la fleur d'un bouquet. É-voquer, dit Mallarmé, arracher par la voix à la cueillette réelle'.[5]

'Il y a du comme dans l'être'. In German, the French 'comme' is translated by two very different words: *als* and *wie*. The first is 'apophatic', in that it signals the thing in itself, the second 'hermeneutic', in that it subjects the thing to conflicting interpretations and places it at the confluence of metaphors (*PPS*, p. 88). The first is the philosophical invariant, the second, the poetic 'comme', the 'comme' of creation. In this sense, 'Le Métronome' affirms from the outset that 'la poésie n'est pas seule'; it dances with rounds and popular songs, but also with the circle of the Muses: 'Je préfère voir les choses en rond, en ronde avec. Tout est acolyte, accompagnement' (V). It is composed 'comme la peinture' since it is concerned with painting, and equally, it is 'comme la musique'. It is indeed the fundamental nature of poetry to desire, since poetry is lacking what it needs in order '[d']être comme ce qu'elle désespère de ne pas être': philosophical thought, the matter of the senses themselves, which it abstracts, the evocative power of music and the song of the human voice. Thus it will become 'as if' ('comme') philosophical, sensory and musical, a complex intermedial intertext, underlying the poet's vast enterprise:

Il y a du comme dans l'être
Un air de famille un air de rien

Or again, 'Il y a du comme dans l'air' (*PPS*, p. 52). And poetry 'ne manque pas d'air', since we need air to breathe and without it everything stops. It is air that lets things breathe and ensures that there is breath in the poem and in life. Air provides space and spaciousness, makes the poem move and tremble and prevents it from becoming frozen within constraints, calibrations or any other kind of metrics. Air, 'C'est le respirable, l'envisageable, et c'est ce qui maintient la mélodie. L'air, la poésie, mettent du côté du commun partage' (V). Poetry's strength comes precisely from the fact that it forms a bridge – woven from liana and breezes – between these realities. Here the 'comme' is clearly shown to be sidestepping the pitfalls of identity. In the dance of the arts – painting *and* music *and* poetry – the poetic acts as syncretist at the mid-point of the *and*, where song and dance pass from one art to another, 'donnant forme à' and 'informé par' painting, music, poetry. *Comme* is at the crossroads of words and things. *Comme* transforms, runs, aerates, decants into language phrases and creates doorways out of words. In this sense, poetry is also a voice 'as if'. Comparison allows poetry to give birth. *Comme* is reflected, reciprocal and reversible, each element receiving its sense of being as the other, which in turn defines it within the round of words. Might this community of comparison have any connection with imitation, mimesis – reduplication through the looking glass? In fact, we understand only too well that it is the complexity of crossed and antagonistic connections which prevents this particular reduplication from being imitation in the negative sense, for imitation would cause things to freeze into a deceptive solidity. In this poetry, then, mimesis must be understood as the invention of the mediating seme, where each object, poem, painting, piece of music or philo- sophical thought finds at once both its other and the possibility of being itself. Mimesis between two terms does not signify their mirror-reproduction, but that they are both, as it were, a third term. Poetry passes in between, in the space or interval between two *turns*:

> La pensée poétique, l'écriture, si vous préférez, hésite. En général c'est l'hésitation prolongée qui est la bonne formule du lieu, que Valéry faisait osciller entre son et sens. Disons: entre prose et vers, poème en prose et prose en poème, ou entre poésie et philosophie, entre une langue et une autre, entre signification et sens, entre. . .[6]

The 'between' (*l'entre*) constitutes that zone of transit and exchange, the place where what is common in *comme* materialises. This place is neither simply dis- junctive nor solely conjunctive: it *converts*: 'Longue brève et pause' (in music: long, breve and pause). Nothing is truly far and nothing truly near. The 'com- munity' acts primarily to preserve differences and such sacrifices are essential in understanding a work that flowers in the 'between' or interval. The work moves from one 'comme' to another, and this passage, this displacement – this draught of air – allows the thing itself to remain unfixed, whilst continuing to vibrate within it. Stability has no place in interval theory. The 'between' in Michel Deguy opens out into the alchemic cave of his poetic sleight of hand 'au vent du jeu' – and all in the flash of a present moment: 'ce qui m'intéresse, c'est évidemment le présent. Mais la question, c'est: qu'est-ce que le présent, ou bien, ce qui revient au même, qu'est-ce que la présence et comment faire avec la présence'.[7] The 'tourne' is the setting in motion of creation: 'Mais par quoi est déclenchée l'émotion sinon par une mise en tableau, une sorte de mise en scène déjà prédisposée qu'il s'agit de remarquer? Autrement dit, il y a un cercle et c'est tout ça que j'appelle l'expérience au sens artistique. Il y a une mise en cercle de l'émotion et du ce devant quoi c'est de l'émotion' (SB).

> Encore un instant
> Monsieur le lecteur
> Le temps d'un mot nu
> Entre deux tournes

This is, of course, addressed to the reader of the poem, but it is also aimed at the viewer of Dorny's work. The pleasure of seeing now becomes the pleasure of showing. The eye of the reader–viewer is creative; it makes the poem exist. The poet enables us to see. Establishing an internal reader helps the real reader to identify with the virtual reader/author. Reading travels primarily through the prism of the reader's eye, the reader becoming the author's accomplice; in this way the poet is transformed into a projectionist of the world.

Similarly, the materiality of the writing process, the way the lines are 'turned', the processes of manufacture and creation all reveal its secret underground workshop: 'dans ses tours de main, dans son savoir-faire, dans ses habitudes, la poésie n'est pas seule' (V). The writing drifts from word to word and offers the reader the illusion of seeing the text gradually take shape. These processes alert and focus the attention of the reader, who meticulously reconstitutes his or her fabric of images from beginning to end. Making things visible is no easy matter: it implies constantly subverting the process of seeing both as act and as experience. It does not imply a showing of the obvious. Making visible is inherently divisive and subversive, and this brings the readers themselves into play. The text's game of hide-and-seek disturbs both the vision and the viewer. Michel Deguy wraps his readers inside the poem's canvas, casting them as decoders. From intertextuality to intertextuality, the text overflows the pages of the book. Between all these realities, poetry is ultimately like a 'pendulum', a 'metronome', but alive rather than mechanical – it is a pulsation, a rhythm between poet and reader: 'cherchant l'essence du rythme là où on ne s'attend pas qu'il soit question de lui, songeons à un phénomène de battement – au pouls d'un phénomène' (*PPS*, p. 45). Thus the poem's metrics are evoked, only to be transcended:

> Neume du mètre
> Le balancier confie
> Le temps à la diction

In order to speak of the relationship between form and meaning in a poetic text, Paul Valéry earlier suggested the rhythm of a pendulum, whose oscillating movement would never stop:

> Pensez à un pendule qui oscille entre deux points symétriques. Supposez que l'une de ces positions extrêmes représente la forme, les caractères sensibles du langage, le son, le rythme, les accents, le timbre, le mouvement, en un mot la voix en action. Associez d'autre part, au point conjugué du premier, toutes les valeurs significatives, les images, les idées, les excitations du sentiment et de la mémoire, les impulsions

> virtuelles et les formations de compréhension – en un mot tout ce qui constitue le fond, le sens d'un discours. Observez alors les effets de la poésie en vous-même. Vous trouverez qu'à chaque vers, la signification qui se produit en vous, loin de détruire la forme musicale qui vous a été communiquée, redemande cette forme.[8]

We see that rhythm is a movement 'between' two times, an openly contradictory 'between-ness' swinging from past to future. The optical paradoxes of the temporal image actualise the potential and potentialise the actual:

> Plutôt que le mètre, le rythme . . . Il ne s'agit plus de mètre, mais il s'agit quand même toujours de rythme, puisque nous sommes tous héritiers du siècle littéraire précédent, héritiers de l'histoire de la littérature. Dans le rythme, il y a la rémanence audible de formules anciennes, par exemple de métriques anciennes . . . Il y a de la hantise dans la littérature. La littérature hante la littérature. La formule de pieds française, parce que je n'aime pas parler en termes syllabiques de mètre: c'est là que le dispositif est très complexe: diérèse, e muet, quantité, accent. . . Tout cela, ce serait un rythme. La formule ancienne est toujours là à faire entendre. Dans une incrédulité, si l'on veut, un faire comme si, qui continue (SB).

> Longue brève et pause
> Le temps passe
> Il repassera

Michel Deguy, then, defines poetry as *seuil*. The *seuil* or threshold is a major term of discourse; it is the margin or border, signalling disconnection and connection:

> Rythme seuil il faut
> Qu'une porte en mots
> soit ouverte et fermée

This threshold is the threshold of language, whose pulse turns language into a door which can allow us to pass through and accede to the world outside. Its rhythms are the rhythms of the heart and the sea, its pulse those of blood and the wind:

> Qui bat là
> Une phrase de langue
> Au vent du jeu

The poet encourages things to coincide. He strays on the margins. Indeed it is boundaries and junctures that define the specific function of the poet. Each thing is close to another, but the extent of the things and their relationship must be defined. Thus on every threshold beats another threshold: a notion which arises from the logic of the fold. Each line tends towards infinity, while the folds follow divergent connections and intersecting networks; and reality becomes reconstituted through the random encounters of folds, following their salient points. All these folds, pleats and creases cross and intersect, making the potential return to its origins:

> Le courant d'airs
> tourne les pages
> ça ne fait pas un pli
> mais six

Chuang Tzu's apologia – in fact quite similar to Plato's – in which the butcher never sharpens the blade of his knife because he always directs it precisely where the membrane divides the two pieces of flesh, casts light on Michel Deguy's theory of poetry. Here too it is not so much a question of cutting as of following the joints. Along the articulations of reality the outline of a fold is sketched. The incision, however respectful and delicate, is, and will always remain, butchery of a kind, if in the course of its action it does not allow a reversal. The incision is well directed when one knows how to pull back from it, at the very point where the joint is articulated, at the spot where two elements meet and join. With each new incision, a new fold reveals an unsuspected angle. It is in the nature of a fold to be intersected by countless further folds, which triggers an infinitely accelerating movement back and forth – in a process of lightning encounters – which in turn gives rise to a never-ending reduplication of folds.

This encounter of folds, then, creates the poetic event, where something new and unforeseeable arises between each and every fold, after which our mathematical notion of the 'fractal' becomes a philosophical notion of the heuristic, since every meeting of lines produces points of return, germination and resonance. Such an aesthetic of resonance and germination recalls the composition of a musical line, a structure which simultaneously opens and closes. The rhythm, the beating of language, the (diastolic-systolic) expansion and contraction, the *sumbolé* and *diabolé*, combine to produce the pulse of poetry: poetry is linked to rhythm, a figure of flux, a stable form of flux. Poetry is exchange, a coming and going, an ebbing and flowing in metaphorical elasticity: 'Le rythme pour apparaître passé par son affinité avec la vague, son être-comme-flot, soit l'image de la houle' (*PPS*, p. 47).

Compensating for these fractures, seeking a return to unity, can only be achieved through a fragmentary hiatus in continuity, in the dance of words beating in a draught of air. In verse the word becomes new-born; it is above all a new word, a '*mot nu*'. The poem thus confronts us with infinity, but in all its immanence: 'Encore un instant / Monsieur le lecteur': 'Just one more minute, please!', as spoken to the executioner. This symphysis between macrocosm and microcosm finds expression in the overflowing immanence of the poetic fold, enlarged to encompass the world, these phrases borne on the wings of playfulness (*le vent du jeu*), as my heart and my language fancy. The spaciousness of this poetry-between-open-and-closed-doors is founded on all the oscillations and to-ings and fro-ings possible in all places and at every moment, thus permitting the binding and unbinding of folds, in order to produce 'l'amplification à mille joies de l'instinct de ciel en chacun', as Mallarmé puts it. In returning to set expressions, proverbs or clichés, Deguy gives them a twist, a shake of the stereotypes: the poet becomes a juggler of words in a crystalline structure of rhythm, subverting the rule of the metronome – which so easily takes on the guise of constraint, imprisonment or threat – in order to advance towards the stumbling rhythms of true freedom:[9]

> Ce qui me chante
>> Se plie
> Aux calibres des couleurs

Translated by Jane Yeoman

Notes

1 Translator's note: the author probably has in mind a familiar French children's song here, 'Le furet du bois', which refers to the coming and going of the ferret: 'Il court, il court, le furet . . . Il est passé par ici . . . Il repassera par là', etc.
2 Jean-Michel Maulpoix, 'Michel Deguy, pourquoi la poésie?', available at: www.maulpoix.net (accessed September 2009).
3 Interview with Maud and Arnaud Villani, *Nu(e)*, 8, 5 May 1997 (unpaginated) (henceforth V).
4 In Michel Deguy, *Aux heures d'affluence* (Paris: Seuil, 1993), p. 172 (henceforth *AF*).
5 Michel Deguy, *La Poésie n'est pas seule* (Paris: Seuil, 1987), p. 164 (henceforth *PPS*).
6 Michel Deguy, *L'Impair* (Tours: Farrago, 2001), back cover.
7 Interview with Stéphane Baquey, also in *Nu(e)*, 8, 5 May 1997 (unpaginated) (henceforth SB).
8 Paul Valéry, 'Poésie et pensée abstraite', in *Œuvres*, vol. I (Paris: Gallimard, 1987), pp. 1314–39.
9 Deguy's poem, in itself a Valeryan intertext, could also be alluding to Ezra Pound's famous *mot d'ordre*: 'As regarding rhythm: to compose in the sequence of the musical phrase, not in sequence of a metronome', in *A Retrospect* (1918), in John Cook, *Poetry in Theory. An Anthology 1900–2000* (Oxford: Blackwell, 2004), p. 84.

Further reading

Bishop, Michael, *Michel Deguy* (Amsterdam: Rodopi, 1988).
Deguy, Michel, *Given Giving: Selected Poems*, trans. Clayton Eshleman (Berkeley: University of California Press, 1984).
    Recumbents, trans. Wilson Baldridge (Middletown, CT: Wesleyan University Press, 2005).
Loreau, Max, *Michel Deguy: la poursuite de la poésie tout entière* (Paris: Gallimard, 1980).
Mouchard, Claude (ed.), *Michel Deguy* (Paris: Larousse, 1999).

Moussaron, Jean-Pierre, *La Poésie comme avenir: essai sur l'œuvre de Michel Deguy* (Grenoble: Presses Universitaires de Grenoble, 1992).

—— (ed.), *Grand Cahier Michel Deguy* (Coutras: Le Bleu du ciel, 2007).

Rueff, Martin (ed.), *Michel Deguy: l'allégresse pensive* (Paris: Belin, 2007).

22 Bernard Heidsieck, 'Poème-partition B2B3 (Exorcisme)'

JEAN-PIERRE BOBILLOT

première voix	deuxième voix avec écho
oui oui	
voilà	
voilà	
. . . la mobilisation. . .	**ton pouls**
voyez-vous	**poulet bleu rat lapin minet gris**
. . . la mobilisation d'une créance	**ton pouls**
née sur l'étranger, consiste en une	**poulet bleu rat lapin minet gris** **à se mordre nos sexes à se tordre**
avance sur factures ou sur traites,	**nos corps colibri singe et puce** **(P.P.R.)**
simples ou documentaires, à vue	**pierres briquettes** **pierres**

ou à usance.	**briquettes briques**
	    fixes fermes en file
	silence ni clac tac et nuit
	       toc

Elle bénéficie de la Banque de	**droite gauche**
France, à court ou moyen terme,	**toc**
d'un taux de rescompte privilégié,	**rien**
la négociation de l'effet correspon-	**glisse une heure**
dant, créé à quatre-vingt dix jours	**feux phares**

(cut)

BIEN

                                     ROOOôôôôôôôôôôôôôôôme

  BIEN   (P.P. D3Z)

    BIEN   vole vole survole vole voussh fixe et

      bien   déferle vole pèse gris ouf souffle

      bien   pesant sol sil menaces lence sol

       bien   passe suspendu imminence sta-

        bien   tique air passe sol sol indices et sol

                              air pré- sages -mices gris fulguran-

            bien   ce schwartz air air immaté immémo

            bien   sol gris black

             bien   (P.P. J)

              bien

                         niveau-nique-méca-matique-ticket-

                         manette-mais-oui-mardi-au même-

              bien   clavier-bordereau-credi-rivé-credi-

                         classant-classé-dre-di-rivant-

                         samedi-contribue patati-hagard-

                         participe-unifor-jeudi-for-formé-

                         ment-HIER-UNIFOR-AVANT-HI-CE

                         GESTE-JOURD'HUI-NI MOINS-QUI

                         ÉGALE-TOUT AUTANT-SI DRÔLE-SI

                         PEU-INUTI-JEUDI-UTILEMENT UN

                         PEU-DEMAIN-DOUTEUX-POUR SUR-

de plus...   INVERSE-OUQUI FUT-ET QUI FUT

                         QUI EST-LUNDI-DILUN-DRE-DI-

                         IMPERCEPTI-A JAMAIS-ÉTI-

                         QUETTES-SAMEDI-VENDRE-SINON-

                         ET POURTANT-LUNDI-MAR-

     DE PLUS . . .   (P.P. K)

                              Août-Octobre 1962

                              Extract from *Partition V*

Poème-partition B2B3, composed by Bernard Heidsieck between August and October 1962, was the first poetic work ever produced to be based entirely on the superimposition of two different 'texts'.[1] One, contained in the left-hand column, is intended for live, on-stage reading by the poet (who stands, and is seen by the audience clearly holding the typed pages); and the other (column on the right) is transmitted from off-stage – it should be synchronised with the reading, and is therefore pre-recorded.

The result of this method of composition, which achieved a synthesis between *theatrical poetry* (voice + action or *performance*) and *recorded poetry* (voice + sound technology – or *phono-techne*) was inaugurated during the 'Domaine poétique' evenings on 18, 21 and 22 May 1963, in Paris. In the same year, *B2B3* was published on a 45 rpm vinyl disc (mono), and distributed with the eleventh issue of *KWY revue*; in 1964 it appeared in book + vinyl disc form, with the aid of Paul-Armand Gette and Gianni Bertini of Castel Rose publishers in Paris: this represented the first (private) discographic publication of a work by Bernard Heidsieck.

As such, sound poetry is primarily intended for public reading by the poet him/herself; its recording – which then provides private listening – is of secondary concern. In the final tape-recording (subsequently reproduced on disc), the two 'texts' are recorded in parallel and synchronically superimposed on one another throughout the poem's duration. On listening they are thus inseparable and effectively constitute one single text. As with a printed page, on the typed page each column appears to constitute two autonomous 'texts': but as read, is not the poem.

Indeed, the sound poem's written 'text' is not the *text*. As Heidsieck's title indicates, the text provides the score alone: more specifically, its verbal components, arranged on the page according to a particular typographic layout, with perhaps (as here), instructions or stage directions regarding the recording, the reading itself, and any accompanying 'action':

> Lorsque ce texte a été donné en public, j'ai toujours lu, ou dit, sur scène, – style très anonyme de conférence – l'exposé de technique bancaire qui en constitue l'une des deux parties, l'autre partie, sur bande, étant retransmise par les haut-parleurs, simultanément.[2]

Heidsieck himself readily contributed additional 'Notes' regarding background: political, ideological, technical, or (particularly the case here) aesthetic – even biographical concerns. Strictly speaking a work of sound poetry exists only in – and through – its performance, whether staged or discographic.

In that it is theatrical *and* discographic, Bernard Heidsieck's 'sound poetry' or 'action poetry' draws on several different historical strands (until now largely unrecognised as such), and offers a synthesis which is both original and bold:

- The history of theatrical poetry, which one may trace back to the joyous and rowdy sessions of the 'Hydropathes' Club, founded in Paris in 1878 by Émile

Goudeau, and the place where Marie Krysinka and Maurice Rollinat achieved their renown. In 1881 the club was succeeded by the famous 'Chat noir', created by Rodolphe Salis.

• The history of recorded poetry, which may be traced back to the phonographic sessions of December 1913 – fifty years before Heidsieck's *B2B3* – directed by Ferdinand Brunot for the 'Speech Archives' ('Archives de la Parole') at the Sorbonne in Paris, with poets such as Apollinaire, Verhaeren and René Ghil. As early as February 1914, in the article 'Nos amis les futuristes' ('Our Friends the Futurists'), which appeared in his own review, *Les Soirées de Paris*, Apollinaire himself declared:

> Avant peu, les poètes pourront, au moyen des disques, lancer à travers le monde de véritables poèmes symphoniques. Grâces en soient rendues à l'inventeur du phonographe, Charles Cros, qui aura ainsi fourni au monde un moyen d'expression plus puissant, plus direct que la voix d'un homme imitée par l'écriture ou la typographie.[3]

• The history of simultaneous poetry, in which the above two strands meet, can be traced back to the rehearsal of Jules Romains's poem, *L'Église*, at Apollinaire's house in 1908 or 1909, where, as he later reported, it was performed with several voices. As early as June 1914 ('Simultanisme-librettisme', again in *Les Soirées de Paris*), Apollinaire made a direct link between the future of the newly born simultaneous poetry, indeed the future of poetry generally, with the *creative* use of phonographic recording, then also taking its first unsteady steps:

> Comme si le poète ne pouvait pas faire enregistrer directement un poème par le phonographe et faire enregistrer en même temps des rumeurs naturelles ou d'autres voix, dans une foule ou parmi ses amis?[4]

Sound and action poetry next travelled by way of Marinetti's 'futurist' evenings (from 1910); the sessions at the 'Cabaret Voltaire', founded in Zurich in 1916 by Hugo Ball (with, among others, his own 'verse without words', *Karawane*, and Tristan Tzara's 'poèmes simultans' *L'Amiral cherche une maison à louer*); through Pierre Albert-Birot's *Poème à crier et à danser* and his poems 'à deux voix' or 'à 3 voix simultanées' (1916–18); the 'dramatistes' theories of Henri Martin Barzun (1913) and the simultaneous readings of 'Art et Action' theatre (1917–); the danced 'phonetic poems' by Raoul Hausmann (1918); Kurt Schwitters' performance of 'W' (Weimar, 1922) and *Ursonate* (1921–32); Marinetti's (1924, 1928–), Schwitters's (1925, 1932), and Fernand Divoire's phonographic recordings (1931); the radiophonic 'simultanéistes' pieces by Carlos Larronde (1931–), etc.

Diversifying and multiplying, sound and action poetry pursued its path after the Second World War, with the 'lettristes' readings of Isidore Isou and the group which rapidly formed around him (1946), then through Antonin Artaud's radiophonic piece, *Pour en finir avec le jugement de dieu* (1947), the 'crirythmes' ('screamrhythms') of François Dufrêne (1953), the 'audio-poèmes' of

Henri Chopin (1955?), the 'permutations' of Brion Gysin (1959), and his own 'poèmes-partitions' (1955–).

In that it is performed on the stage *and* uses electro-acoustic equipment, Bernard Heidsieck's 'sound poetry' also approaches recent and contemporary experiments in the fields of 'musique concrète' – Pierre Schaeffer (1948–50) – and 'musique électronique' (1950–): Schaeffer/Henry in Paris, Eimert/Beyer in Cologne, Ussachevsky/Luening in New York, as well as Berio, Maderna, Xenakis and Stockhausen, and 'event' art, which was practised and gradually developed by George Maciunas and the other 'Fluxus' artists in New York, then in Wiesbaden and across Europe. Shortly after completing *B2B3*, Heidsieck was one of the few spectators at the Paris 'concerts' – given during the European tour, *Festum Fluxorum* – of 3–8 December 1962. It was from then on that he preferred to use the term 'poésie action' ('action poetry').

On one side, then ('track 1', left-hand column), a text smoothly unfolds without interruption or special effects of any kind: it is spoken in an opaque and studied voice: 'serious', 'detached' and with all the gravity required of a 'professional' – a text which is highly and explicitly *prosaic*, and which in detailed bureaucratic language describes, 'some methods of financial banking'. While not in itself constituting a 'found poem', this is essentially a *found text* (or *ready-made* text). In counterpoint (or, as the author himself has suggested, in 'counterweight') ('track 2', right-hand column), several sequences taken from previous 'Poèmes-partitions', duly musicalised, are spoken in a voice which amplifies and anamorphoses the 'resonances' and 'natural echoes' – employing shouts, cries, silences, accelerations and growlings of every kind – sometimes linked, sometimes not, now retreating, now vehemently invading. Even if these sequences do not appear to be authentic citations, they no less effectively form a collection of *quoted (recontextualised) poems*.

Here we should note that the seemingly serious and the strictly informative nature of the dry banking description, delivered in predictable rhetoric, is at once demystified: obviously from the exterior, through the flurries of phonemes which arrive, as it were, in impetuous waves, to claw and tear apart the reassuring, the overly facile gloss; but also – even prior to the phonemes' introduction and therefore before any superimposition – by a preliminary and less than imposing, 'oui oui . . . voilà . . . voilà'/'yes yes . . . that's it . . . that's it', followed, straight after the very first words of the banking presentation itself, '. . . la mobilisation . . .'/'. . . the raising of a loan. . .', by a 'voyez-vous'/'you see', quickly followed and effaced by the repetition of the initial sentence in its entirety: 'la mobilisation d'une créance née sur l'étranger'/'the raising of a loan-fund sourced from abroad', etc.

In the same way, the final sentence of the presentation follows symmetrically and incongruously, with a stream of 'chevilles' ('padding', meaningless words) marking, as we imagine it, the embarrassment of the speaker (the fictional 'character', or the poet who lends his voice and appearance to him), at the

closing moment, 'évidemment . . . évidemment . . . enfin . . . BIEN BIEN BIEN
. . .'/'of course . . . of course . . . well . . . GOOD GOOD GOOD good good good
good good good good good good (all this very quickly, then followed by:) 'de
plus . . . DE PLUS . . .'/'and furthermore . . . and FURTHERMORE. . .' – the flow
of 'chevilles' strongly resembling a sequence in the other track. Through this
hesitant introduction and unexpected interruption, the 'technical' part, apparently imperturbable, becomes somehow *contaminated* from the inside, by the
irruption, first sporadic, then systematic, of the spoken (overly 'prosaic'?) which
superficially then irreparably disturbs the still linearity, the presumed univocal –
in the same way as, from the exterior, and far more weightily, the coincidence,
indeed *concurrence*, of the musicalised (overly 'poetic'?)

Inversely, these sets of words – most often short (monosyllabic), sometimes
distorted (through vocal lengthening), liberally repeated, truncated, and as a
result, onomatopoeic ('[très vite:] tape bondit . . . tape bat . . . bondit rebon-
dit bat bat BAT . . . BAT')/('[very quickly:] taps leaps . . . taps beats . . . bounds
rebounds beats beats BEATS . . . BEATS') among the onomatopoeia ('[très vite:]
ROCHES PUK . . . PEP . . . PETITES pites ITES brung . . . KLATAF . . . pierres pierres
. . . POK')/('[very quickly:] ROCKS PEAKS . . . PESKY . . . PETTY pikes YIKES brong
. . . KLATTA . . . stones stones . . . STUK') together with the breathy ('hhweui
wfuou hhweui wfuou hhweui wfuou hhweui wfuou' [hooey fooey hooey fooey
hooey fooey]) – which constitute the musicalised parts, most often turn out to
be linked, if one listens attentively (or reads the 'text' on the score), to various
aspects of everyday life (thus linked in the same way as they are to the banking
presentation) and in particular to its *rhythms*: physiological ('ton pouls'/'your
pulse') or socio-economic ('JAMAIS-ÉTIQUETTES-SAMEDI-VENDRE-SINON-ET
POURTANT-LUNDI-MAR')/('NEVER-PRICE-TAGS-SATURDAY-SUNDRY-IF NOT-
AND NEVERTHELESS-MONDAY-TUE'). In the same way, yet quite differently.

Throughout his life, Bernard Heidsieck worked for the Banque Française du
Commerce Extérieur (BFCE). And if he still maintains an attitude of wise reserve,
of tactical segregation, towards that professional life, and still takes care not
to open too widely, indeed to even half-open the bank's doors to poetry, it is
because he understood very early that such poetry was on principle excluded, as
not quite 'serious'. Conversely, however, he did not hesitate or delay in warmly
welcoming into his own poetry (as he had immediately done with the *everyday*), banking, money, the economy – their language so serious and, a priori,
so unpoetic ('mais tout compte fait, écrit-il, il est de ces préjugés' – (but taking
everything into account, he wrote, this is mere prejudice)): but all this balanced
with references to almost all the activities – serious or not – which occupy our
daily lives. In others words, in place of a reciprocal ignorance, institutional and
sterile, of a deep-rooted distrust, every bit as sterile, Heidsieck preferred confrontation – 'dialogue'; and to counter the idea of exclusion, he offered 'exorcism',
from which comes the subtitle of *B2B3*.

It is certain that if 'the structure of the poème-partition' – of which the most important component and, as it happens, most remarkable innovation, is 'the juxtaposition of two texts' – also serves quite different ends, a firmly established and equally lasting practice was the risky confrontation of two kinds of discourse which were known to be different in every way, even mutually antagonistic. One, strictly codified, functional, 'transitive', able to be immediately shared (by those it addresses): thus eminently, even imperiously, communicational; the other, apparently spontaneous, gestural, 'intransitive', irreducibly singular (in not addressing itself to anyone in particular): but irresistibly communicative.

This juxtaposition is also reflected in the confrontation of two 'I's, both diametrically opposed by the said as much as the saying: the one, conforming to the *sociolect* – the dominant discursive practice – and thereby colluding with the machinery of a society which, on principle, mistrusts 'extremes' (which it uses itself to normalise); the other, enclosing itself in its *idiolect* – marked by a treatment highly differentiated from common language – and thereby refusing any compromise and distrusting, on principle, the 'means', were they to be required for an even minimal mutual understanding.

In fact, the poetic is not necessarily (by nature or vocation) biased towards the extremism of wild subjectivity, unbridled musicalisation, the absolute exception, the fundamental anarchism of desire: it does not necessarily come out of the disruption of all rationality and coherent discourse, all communicability. But certainly since Rimbaud, Verlaine, Laforgue and others, the poetic has been partially linked to all of this, and loses a lot if we neglect it; thus, apropos of Verlaine's *Sagesse* (in a letter from November 1883), Jules Laforgue spoke to his friend and future editor, Gustave Kahn, of his admiration for 'true poetry', which he recognised as: 'des vagissements, des balbutiements dans une langue inconsciente ayant tout juste le souci de rimer'.

In the poems, Bernard Heidsieck had already pushed experimentation very far in that particular direction; and the re-recording that he then specially organised in the Roman cellars in Reims – a unique performance, in advance of later public readings – further accentuated the role of phonic spontaneity. With *B2B3*, the poem (that is to say, the *text*) is created in listening to the confrontation, never before heard, of the two 'texts', which resulted, as we have described, from their simultaneous unfolding: a dialectic (in actuality), bringing together – battling – two modalities of language and subjectivity (two 'I's), without doubt diametrically opposed, but not without complicity and mutual influence, and both equally implicated in the general functioning of language and the speaking subject.

On the one hand, then ('first voice'), there is a speech, largely in keeping with the social exigencies of performance and mutual understanding; but no less with the requirements – as much dogmatic as basic – of individual lucidity and cohesion; and on the other ('second voice'), there is the anonymous and unrepresentable stirring of depths – the organic and/or symbolic underside of language – inexhaustible and in Freudian terms irrevocably doomed to 'censor-ship', and no less, to 'repression'.

Let us stress: each of these 'texts' was simultaneously borne, the one by the first, the other by the second of the two 'voices', and the two becoming con-fused; each 'voice' the result of a particular treatment of the same and unique *real voice*: that of the poet, grappling here with the everyday. From the collision (occasionally the collusion) between these two entities – these two *voice-texts* – resulted, in uncertain manner at the outset, the *text* of this 'poème-partition' – which overall is characterised by, according to a commentary by Bernard Heidsieck, 'son aspect de rêve interne-externe'.

The poem is a demonstration – as realistic as it is lyric and as permanent as it is original and which paradoxically was enabled by a return to the *phono-techne*'s cold objectivity – of that dual language, at once 'la langue de l'Autre' and 'm'langue' (to borrow from Jacques Lacan and Jean-Pierre Verheggen respectively), where the cleft subject, 'moi/je', emerges and is indeed created. It is a demonstration with no rhetoric other than that (equally indirect) of the banking 'text', of that 'double postulation', of that double pragmatics at work in language and through which, for better or worse, the human being is consti-tuted – emerges – as 'speaking being': 'parlêtre' (to use Lacan's term).

It is a brilliant embodiment and spatialisation of the subject's intimate strug-gle with the overwhelming appeal of the driven and the organic, and a submis-sion, both comforting and anaesthetising, to the dull and arrogant jargon of the inauthentic. From that point on, one could easily accept that this double prag-matics was nothing but the two dynamics, which according to Freud are at work in our 'psycho-somatic make-up': in other words, the two particular phenomena which constitute subjectivity, concurrently the 'primary' and the 'secondary' processes. But no one is obliged to accept this connection.

As early as 1963, Heidsieck himself signalled ('Notes on poèmes-partitions h1 and h2 or "Quatrième Plan", versions I and II') the paradoxical and intimate link which established itself between the particular capacity – as much cognitive as pragmatic – of the *phono-techne* to offer something of objective reality *and* to provide access to some part of subjectivity, which otherwise would remain unseen, or silent:

> Quant à la machine (le magnétophone) . . . son usage procède de l'approche précisément nouvelle, et sous un certain angle plus exacte, de la Réalité, qu'elle autorise. Ses possibilités permettent en effet d'éveiller, de réveiller d'autres couches de la sensibilité, d'atteindre ou de mettre à nu d'autres horizons ou dimensions de la conscience. Car par le jeu ou une manipulation des vitesses, découpages, intensités, superpositions, confrontations, associations. . . peuvent être obtenus, en effet, une photographie, un calque, plus fidèles des mouvements, sortilèges, entrelacs, rythmes, flous, raccourcis, interférences de la conscience, tant individuelle que collective.

[With respect to the machine (the tape-recorder) . . . its usage comes out of the new, precisely, and in one sense, more exact, approach towards Reality, which it enables. Indeed, its potential allows for the possibility of alerting or awakening different levels of sensibility, and of attaining or uncovering further limits or dimensions of consciousness. Through the play and manipulation of speed, cutting, intensity, superimposition, confrontation, connections. . . might indeed be produced a photograph, an exact copy, which is more faithful to movement, tricks, interweaving, rhythm, soft focus, short cuts, interferences of consciousness, as much individual as collective.]

This was a possibility, of course, scarcely dreamed of fifty years earlier, but one which was just discernible as being the voice of the poet/reader, such as he himself could subsequently hear it, as reconstituted by a stuttering machine. Thus, André Salmon, witnessing his first-hand experience of that recording, in the company of Apollinaire, declared:

Il s'écoute, non sans stupeur. Ses amis le retrouvent, mais il ne se reconnaît pas! Il est en effet des organes profonds de perception auditive dont nous ne jouissons que grâce au phonographe . . . lorsqu'il nous renvoie cette propre voix qui étouffe, quand nous parlons, lesdites perceptions profondes, trop délicates; les voix intérieures, eût dit Hugo qui eût aimé l'invention du professeur Brunot. Ainsi à l'audition seconde nous entendons-nous, somme toute, pour la première fois, d'où une assez vive surprise. Après Guillaume Apollinaire, nous connûmes cette émotion, ce trouble, en entendant chanter notre double.[5]

[He listens to himself in some amazement. His friends recognize him, but he doesn't! It is only thanks to the gramophone that we can rejoice in the fundamental organs of auditory perception . . . when it returns to us our own voices, which when we speak stifle such profound, overly delicate, perceptions: the internal voices, Victor Hugo would have said, who himself would have appreciated Professor Brunot's invention. Thus on the second hearing, we hear ourselves, when all is said and done, for the first time, which is quite a surprise. After Guillaume Apollinaire, we ourselves have recognised that emotion, that unease, when we heard our double sing.]

Would this 'double' not be precisely the person we hear throughout *B2B3*? This was what Heidsieck suggested, when, apropos of the voiceover, he conjured up the emergence:

d'un personnage second, d'un Double, physiquement présent cependant, particulièrement capital, insistant et charnel, mais incontrôlable-incontrôlé, abondant, désordonné, réceptif, impressionnable.
D'une substance fondamentale, originelle.

Personnage imparfaitement cerné, assumé, donc. Sa voix, jaillis-
sante ou ramasseuse, spontanée, toute à trac, roulant, fusant, herbier
où puiser.

Force motrice ou mise en cause. Alternativement.[6]

[of a second character, a Double, nevertheless physically present, particularly dominant, persistent and carnal, yet uncontrollable/uncon-
trolled, profuse, disordered, receptive, impressionable.

Of a fundamental and original substance.

A character, as such indistinctly defined and thus assumed. His voice
invasive or welcoming, spontaneous, out of the blue, rolling, binding,
a herb garden from which to pluck.

Driving force or questioning. Alternately.]

Translated by Jane Yeoman and Peter
Collier

Notes

1 Bernard Heidsieck, in *Partition V* (Bordeaux: Le Bleu du ciel [1973] 2001), pp. 38–48.
2 *Ibid.*, p. 38.
3 Guillaume Apollinaire, *Œuvres en prose complètes*, vol. II, ed. Pierre Caizergues and Michel Décaudin (Paris: Gallimard, 1991), p. 971.
4 *Ibid.*, pp. 976–7.
5 André Salmon, 'Plus de livres . . . des disques!', *Gil Blas*, 25 December 1913.
6 Heidsieck, 'Notes to *B2B3*', in *Partition V*, pp. 51–2.

Further reading

Bobillot, Jean-Pierre, *Bernard Heidsieck poésie action* (Paris: Jean-Michel Place, 1996).
    Trois essais sur la poésie littérale (Romainville: Al Dante, 2003).
    Poésie Sonore: éléments de typologie historique (Reims: Le Clou dans le fer, 2009).
Bohn, Willard, *Modern Visual Poetry* (Newark, NJ: University of Delaware Press; Associated University Presses, 2001).
Jackson, K. David, Vos, Eric and Drucker, Johanna (eds.), *Experimental, Visual, Concrete: Avant-garde Poetry since the 1960s* (Amsterdam: Rodopi, 1996).
Noland, Carrie, *Poetry at Stake: Lyric Aesthetics and the Challenge of Technology* (Princeton, NY: Princeton University Press, 1999).
Wheeler, Lesley, *Voicing American Poetry: Sound and Performance from the 1920s to the Present* (Ithaca, NJ: Cornell University Press, 2008).
www.ubu.com/sound/heidsieck_p.html (accessed September 2009). Ubu Sound is a website dedicated to sound art, where an excellent collection of recordings of Heidsieck and of many other artists can be found.

SUSAN HARROW

L'Incorrigible

Le chaos suburbain, sa magie équivoque,
J'ai cru sincèrement que je ne les aimais
Plus : je vous recherchais, Vallée Heureuse. Mais
On ne se refait pas. Qu'est-ce qui me convoque ?

Alors aussi longtemps qu'un reste de vigueur   5
Me gardera le pied vaillant sur les pédales,
Je recommencerai d'aller par ces dédales
Entre les boulevards qui traînent en longueur.

Tout change sans arrêt ; une faible mémoire
Me fait revoir à neuf ce qui n'a pas changé,   10
Et souvent l'inconnu me semble un abrégé
Des figures peuplant le morne territoire

Où pourtant je m'enfonce encore, jamais las
De vieux murs décrépits, de couchants qui s'éteignent
Au fond de potagers en friche dont la teigne   15
Disparaît en avril sous un flot de lilas.

Comme le vers repart et tourne dans la strophe,
En prenant pour pivot la rime sans raison,
Je vais d'un coin de rue à l'autre : ma prison
Adhère à l'infini constamment limitrophe.   20

Mais soudain les cloisons s'envolent : on atteint
Un rebord où le ciel embrasse tout l'espace.
Dans leur intimité sans mouvement, je passe
Et repasse, à la fois convive et clandestin.

Comme dans la clarté qui pénètre le rêve   25
Où je reconnais tout (mais tout est surprenant)
Tout fait signe, et je vais comprendre, maintenant,
Ou bien dans un instant qui dure, qui m'élève.

Et je roule sans poids, je lâche le guidon :
Voici le vrai départ, qui clôt la promenade,   30
Le vrai monde – son centre est cette colonnade
Qu'on voit au loin depuis une gare, à Meudon.

From *L'Incorrigible: poésies itinérantes et familières*

Pivotal poetry

'L'Incorrigible' is at once the title poem and the epilogue of Jacques Réda's collection of verse poems, subtitled *Poésies itinérantes et familières (1988–1992).*[1] The poem is an urgent, capacious reflection on what it is to be a contemporary poet and, more particularly, what it is to be *this* poet. Réda is the freewheeling explorer of quotidian urban and suburban spaces, whose relishing of the poeticity of the particular and the material catalyses forms of metaphysical desire and a yearning for a sublime glimpsed beyond the debris of the everyday. Across the eight stanzas of this poem we journey with a writer impelled by the interstices of the city, alert to the acoustic murmurs and visual eruptions of daily life, and seized by the imponderability of the real and its epiphanic potential. In 'L'Incorrigible' Réda scrutinises the material sources and the resources of his poetry, and reflects on the rhythmic and kinetic energies he harnesses and deploys in his real-time, imaginary and textual excursions.

The competing pressures and pleasures of the everyday and the sublime are played out in the pliant prosody and varied tonality of Réda's poetry. In 'L'Incorrigible', the formal constancy of alexandrines (set in quatrains of *rimes embrassées*) is offset by a radical, fracturing enjambement, and the metaphysical rise is checked by deflationary colloquialism ('On ne se refait pas', l. 4). In this concluding poem of the collection, the sole occupant of the section entitled 'Retour aux environs', metapoetic intention spurs autobiographical desire as the poet speculates on what draws him back to the familiar, messy, chaotic suburbs and their uncertain magic.

'Le chaos suburbain, sa magie équivoque': with this suggestive parataxis, the poem opens. The absence of a syntactic connector between these perfectly balanced hemistiches invites readerly speculation as the caesural comma performs a tantalising pivot: does ontological chaos (whether acoustic, visual or haptic in origin) actively nourish equivocal magic, or is magic uncertain because it is rarely, barely discernible behind the chaos of the everyday? Is there magic *because of* – or *in spite of* – the material pressures of the here-and-now? As we travel from the evocation of the everyday, in the first hemistich, to the intimation of 'magie équivoque', in the second, we experience something of the *stretch* of the poet's desire as it strains, impossibly, to possess what eye, ear, hand and word can only skim. Whether the relationship between everyday materiality and equivocal magic is apprehended (by poet, by reader) contrastively, contiguously or causally, the movement of the incipit enacts the yearned-for ceding of quotidian chaos to a more profound, metaphysical order: just as the first hemistich impels the second, so chaos precipitates the desire for magic, both verbal and transcendental.

The (deceptively) straightforward, summative 'chaos' of line 1 compresses the topoi – concepts and objects – that Réda unfolds across his urban and suburban poetry. Inchoateness, debris, vestiges, contingency and cacophony generate an experiential grammar which the poet declines materially and metonymically in his work as photographs, walls, leaves, murmurs, monuments, fabrics, cries, colours, bricks, fences, paths, factories, and alleys. Here 'le chaos suburbain' condenses those myriad materials into a single nominal instance which concentrates, as it inevitably elides, the lightness, density, volume, texture, colour and sheer multifariousness that other texts – earlier and later in Réda's corpus – unfold.

Material unevenness and metaphysical uncertainty, which Réda condenses in the pure nominalism of the incipit, are expressed here in the equipoise of the hemistiches whose rhythmic equality (6/6) imparts the idea of affective equality. As 'chaos' conjures up a teeming, tumultuous materiality and intimates something of the metaphysical reach of Réda's poetry, it introduces – and formally induces – a fracture and the memory of a *fausse piste*. Here, the poet briefly revisits the site of a crisis: a moment of writerly equivocation when he almost succumbed to an Arcadian dream – or cliché as the mock-precious apostrophe to the 'Vallée Heureuse' suggests (l. 3). The totemic upper-case letters monumentalise the idea(l) of a literary Arcadia, a vision dismantled just as quickly as it is anthropomorphised. The search for that 'Vallée Heureuse' is, happily, consigned to the past, but the imperfective memory ('je vous recherchais') underscores the (past) persistence of that search for creative solutions which are too pacific, too smooth and too aligned with forms of lyricism that habit has codified and rendered obsolete. Such forms are antithetical to this poet (so antithetical as to call into question the authenticity of the poet's search for lyrical *contentment* and the sincerity of the confession).

The opening quatrain replays the moment of crisis thematically and formally: the disjunction of the elements of negation in the enjambement 'je ne les aimais / Plus' (ll. 2–3), and the terminal 'Mais' (l. 3) place a disruptive frame around the false idyll, whose definitive relegation relaunches the poet and the reader on a familiar track. Just as the pace slowed to conjure up the un-Rédean valley of aesthetic self-contentment, so now the rhythm rips with a tip-of-the-tongue colloquialism ('On ne se refait pas' – 'to start all over again').

Quickened style brings a quickening of desire. Prosaic concerns with ageing and the brief temptation of inwardness are dispelled by a new sense of poetic urgency and the magnetic solicitation of a metaphysical agency that resists naming and definition: 'Qu'est-ce qui me convoque ?' The interrogative provokes a sudden loosening and rushing of the consciousness; it precipitates a leap into speculation that is figured by the blank space between the stanzas, betokening a perpetual postponement of closure. The return to the question of what impels him is deferred (until stanzas 3 and 4) as stanza 2 interrupts now with a more autobiographical line that will lead to a reaffirming of the poet's commitment to a poetics of the city.

Anticipating a feature of Réda's more recent writing, the second stanza reprises the preoccupation with ageing that surfaced in the truncated 'on ne se refait pas [à cet âge]' of line 4. The creative project will be sustained just as long as corporeal strength is maintained: 'le pied vaillant sur les pédales' is a metonym of the poet's trademark physical activity (Solex-riding, cycling and walking). The kinetic project (em)powers the poet in his research *sur le terrain*: 'Je recommence-rai d'aller par ces dédales / Entre les boulevards qui traînent en longueur'. The internal rhyme stresses the shift from '<u>Vall</u>ée' to 'dé<u>dal</u>es' and to spaces thicker, deeper and more compellingly intractable, which are accessible to the active, applied poet pressing on his literal and metaphoric 'pé<u>dal</u>es'. Displacing the idea of irresistible magnetism ('Qu'est-ce qui me convoque ?') is the poet's inten-tionality expressed in the form of something approaching, if not a manifesto, at least a promise made to the reader, to himself, to poetry: 'aussi longtemps qu'un reste de vigueur / Me gardera', 'Je recommencerai'. In this poetic *serment*, the quester qualities of tenacity and vigour, curiosity and *engagement* are not simply evoked, but actively summoned by the twice-iterated future tense. The future is the default tense-time of the *incorrigible*, whose writerly recidivism commits him always to plunge in again, opening up new prospects in a familiar topography. Writing poetry and writing the self are projects which are indelibly linked: the poet is 'incorrigible' precisely because he rewrites (transposes, transforms, meta-phorises) the indelible memories and desires that form him; he is the author of a mental script which cannot be overwritten ('on ne se refait pas'). Indeed, in the years following the publication of the collection *L'Incorrigible*, Réda has contin-ued to immerse his writing – poetry and narrative – in the currents of the city, extending his poetic *périple* to provincial France, Ireland, Italy, Turkey, England, and Syria.

The 'incorrigible' identity dovetails with those anti-heroic identities for which Réda is known. 'Clandestin' (l. 24) – like 'furtif' and 'hérétique' – is a recurrent sobriquet in his writing, at least from *Les Ruines de Paris* (1977). The surreptitious explorer interacts rarely with other *citadins*, but it is with constant empathy that he observes and records the local and small-scale. The dual outsider–insider identity is captured in the oxymoronic naming of self as 'convive et clandestin' (l. 24).

Interstitial spaces draw in this latter-day Daedalus, inviting him to scrutinise the inscrutable, to chart an alternative topography in the *impasses*, back streets, wildernesses and shadowlands. Infiltrating real and imaginary *dédales*, the con-temporary poet takes forward – now in a suburban landscape – modern poetry's investment in the 'plis sinueux des vieilles capitales' (Baudelaire, 'Les Sept vieil-lards'). Just as the forced diaspora of the lower classes under the Second Empire's

Haussmann project offered intriguing interstices for Baudelaire, so the post-Second World War suburban mazes lure Réda. In topographico-poetic terms, Réda is a continuer of Baudelaire, arrested by an intoxicating mix of mystery and banality, and oscillating between ecstasy and *ennui*: '*Entre* les boulevards qui *traînent en longueur*' (l. 8, my emphasis), with its five slow, terminal syllables seems to mimic the boredom induced by the suburban flatlands.

Ephemera-induced weariness is cancelled by a surge of delight at what gives itself to be appraised *now*, in the syncopated rhythm of 'Tout / chan/ge / sans / a / rrêt' (l. 9): here an echo of Baudelaire's 'Le Cygne' can be heard. It is not the senses but his own precarious memory which reinvigorates the poet, spurring him to envision the familiar afresh ('une faible mémoire / Me fait revoir à neuf', ll. 10–11) and leads him to metamorphose (metaphorise) the materially inert. And thus, by a series of imaginative leaps, Réda takes us to the Baudelairean heart of the poem: to the *inconnu*, whose apprehension provides an oblique contour to the rhetorical interrogative of line 4, the poem's founding question.

The tension between the populated impersonality of the suburbs' 'morne territoire' and the poet's invigorated plunge into hidden recesses and depths generates a structuring oxymoron of this poem and of Réda's poetry more generally: any view may be insipid, but the poet seeks to apprehend the richer, deeper potential of what appears superficially depleted (precisely because it is ordinary; precisely because he has scrutinised it many times before). Anaphoric echoes of earlier suburban rambles in *Les Ruines de Paris* and intimations of *L'Adoption du système métrique* (e.g. 'Éloge de la brique') shape the mental and physical landscape of stanza 4:

> jamais las
> De vieux murs décrépits, de couchants qui s'éteignent
> Au fond de potagers en friche dont la teigne
> Disparaît en avril sous un flot de lilas.

The poet's vision – parsing that of nature itself – is transformative: the lingering trace of 'la teigne' (a type of moth) is abolished semantically and rhythmically by the efficacious *rejet* ('Disparaît'). The second hemistich brings metamorphosis where the blossoming exuberance ('sous un flot de lilas'), borne by the marine metaphor, fills the end of the line and spills over into the space of the interstanza. Here Réda challenges the nature/culture dichotomy: the (sub)urban poet, he demonstrates, is always already a poet of nature. Singularly attentive to birds, plants, trees, and pebbles, he seizes the quick and the still of the city.

As the florescence subsides, so space is produced, in stanza 5, to create an enfolded reflection on rhythm and repetition, corporeal and metrical:

> Comme le vers repart et tourne dans la strophe,
> En prenant pour pivot la rime sans raison,
> Je vais d'un coin de rue à l'autre. . .

Now the poem comments on its own rhythmic and rhyming pattern, as it limns the movement of the poet. The *gérondif* 'en prenant' (l. 18) provides a hiatus before the resurging of the first-person agency of the poet and the relaunch of movement: 'Je vais d'un coin de rue à l'autre'.

Notions of corporeal and writerly pliancy pivot on a *rejet* whose thrust is at once kinaesthetic and poetic where the anaphoric 'je passe / Et repasse' is lifted into the rhyme and the rhythm of this supple, self-defining iteration. The poet is poised, scrutinises and then turns to launch his quest in another place.

Such supple lines put to work the notion of corporeal and poetic pliancy. The poem is equally performative in its conscious investment in the theme and the practice of return: there is the willed return to the theme of suburban chaos, the reprise of *rimes embrassées* (which feature prominently across the *poésies itinérantes* of this collection), and the iteration of a series of gestures, actions, and movements which form the relief map of the poet's material-metaphoric itinerary. Peripatetic pliancy is carried over into the patterned flexibility of prosody with *rimes embrassées*, which take forward the idea of the poetic pivot, this time at the level of stanza-embedded rhyme (abba). A kinetic analogue to the movement of the *vers*, the movement of the poet involves constant looping from one street corner to the other, as from one end of a line and a rhyme to the next, as unpredictable *rimes riches* cause the prosaic to cede to the mythic ('pédales' / 'dédales'), or the metapoetic to be jostled by the everyday ('strophe' / 'limitrophe'). Réda's itinerary is consciously, simultaneously peripatetic and prosodic.

Paradoxical desire invested in tumultuous, equivocal suburban beauty drives the poem forward. Thus, an ironic and salutary counterpoint to the disenchanting Happy Valley (l. 3) is the cherished space of 'ma prison' (l. 19). Just as the poet had resisted Arcadian charm, now he embraces constraint and limitation in the space of creativity which he alone defines. Each value, material and metaphysical, counterbalances the other: 'l'infini constamment limitrophe' (l. 20) is a reminder that the return to the real is inevitable and necessary if poetry is to replenish itself in the everyday. The juxtaposing of the language of the metaphysical and the discourse of the urban surveyor ('limitrophe') articulates a Freudian *fort-da* sense of pleasure and unpleasure, tension and release, which intensifies the poetic charge. The experience of ecstatic revelation, as constraints are miraculously lifted, is as intense as it is instantaneous: 'Mais soudain les cloisons s'envolent' (l. 21). Now the sibilants impart the sudden hush induced by awed vision.

The alliterative stream and the cascading inner rhymes of 'le ciel emb**rasse** tout l'es**pace** . . . je **passe** / Et **repasse**' (ll. 22–4) produce a concatenation of sound similarities suggestive of the perpetual shifts and returns as the poet's desire moves between the external world and the metaphysical dimension, which draws the poet and holds him off in a continuation of that *fort-da* play.

Then comes the surprised recognition (stanza 6) that the poet's pursuit of alertness and his power of exquisite receptivity can make every sign meaningful ('tout fait signe', line 27), an echo of Baudelaire's 'Correspondances'. The solicitation of signs is an invitation to apprehend the metaphysical, even if understanding is only ever prospective: 'je vais comprendre, maintenant / Ou bien dans un instant qui dure, qui m'élève' (ll. 27–8).

The desire for understanding, expressed transpositionally in line 28, is lifted into metaphors of weightlessness. The resolution of the competing pressures between the material and the metaphysical is glimpsed in the final miraculous *envol*: 'je roule sans poids, je lâche le guidon' (l. 29). The anaphoric loosening induces a rolling movement ('le vrai départ', 'le vrai monde', ll. 30–1), which invites contemplation of the fresh virtualities that might exist beyond this poem and this collection. The poem is properly performative, for it transports the reader into the moment of revelation, an experience which distils material, corporeal and metaphysical implications with the reminder that every closure brings a new opening: 'Voici le vrai départ, qui clôt la promenade'.

Rapture contours the epiphanic moment which this poem – and every poetic act – strives to envision. The drawing upwards, the volatilising of the self and the yearning for a higher space precipitate images of sublime imponderability. Yet, for all the enraptured lightness of being, there is a countervailing intensity and urgency here, and the line impels the poet and the reader onwards. The lift into another space, another time, is desired, its promise glimpsed beyond the world's hard edges, represented here by Meudon's liminal colonnade.

The eight stanzas of 'L'Incorrigible' effect a compression of Réda's poetics as they unfold the defining qualities of his verse and prose collections: *Les Ruines de Paris* (1977), *Châteaux des courants d'air* (1984), *Beauté suburbaine* (1985), *Accidents de la circulation* (2001); *L'Adoption du système métrique* (2004) and *Ponts flottants* (2006). Each successive stanza of 'L'Incorrigible' acknowledges and enacts Réda's will to poetry: that is, that the marvellous discernible in material and everyday formations may be held, however tenuously, in the metamorphoses and reversibilities of poetry. As each stanza expands and elicits the next, so in turn each of Réda's signature preoccupations is addressed: the lure of the city, the active charm of its interstices, the desire to revisit and to reappraise, the conjunction of kinetic and metric suppleness, and the precarious vision of an *ailleurs* whose luminosity comes suddenly, urgently to language.

Note

1 Jacques Réda, *L'Incorrigible: poésies itinérantes et familières* (Paris: Gallimard, 1995).

Further reading

Harrow, Susan, *The Material, the Real, and the Fractured Self: Subjectivity and Representation from Rimbaud to Réda* (Toronto: University of Toronto Press, 2004).
Joqueviel-Bourjea, Marie, *Jacques Réda: la dépossession heureuse* (Paris: L'Harmattan, 2005).

Micolet, Hervé, *Lire Réda* (Lyon: Presses Universitaires de Lyon, 1994).

Réda, Jacques, *The Ruins of Paris*, trans. Mark Treharne (London: Reaktion, 1996).

   Treading Lightly, Selected Poems 1961–1975, trans. Jennie Feldman (London: Anvil Press Poetry, 2005).

Richard, Jean-Pierre, *L'État des choses* (Paris: Gallimard, 1990).

24 Bernard Noël, 'Les états de l'air'

ANDREW ROTHWELL

Les états de l'air

nous n'avons que la vue
les parois de vent
ce vide est le pays

ici la profondeur renverse
le regard sur soi   5
elle nous fait sauter dans nos yeux

toujours le va-et-vient
le vu et le non-vu
la greffe du pas-là
sur ce qui est là   10

tant de passages
en nous-même s'ouvrant
en nous-même passant
et l'œil à travers
s'enroule au bâti d'air   15

chaque chose se tient dans ce qu'elle est
plus de centre
mais du central

tout le corps voit
et la feuille est derrière la vue   20
comme le dos derrière soi

un chemin d'air
semé de cailloux d'encre
et la porte dedans
la porte qui s'en va   25

miroir vous êtes
notre tête au-delà
on y rentre chez soi
par la pupille
cette petite lune noire   30

au ciel de papier
une part d'air
page pour battements
quand la pensée s'envole

buée de traces   35
buée parmi laquelle
chacun retourne au tout

les écailles limpides
le dessous planté d'os
puis l'obscur   40

partout du seuil
et le même partir
l'étonnement suffit
rien n'arrête l'ouvert
sauf sa propre surface   45

chaque limite appelle
le regard s'y dépasse
la tête est ce là-bas
où elle le rejoint

alors dans l'œil allé   50
le corps se voit venir
où le mental s'aère

mais voici l'Autre en Vous en Lui
la rencontre affrontée
le doublement du monde   55
un philtre d'air
l'in-fini

et ce mur de rien
où la langue s'entête
puis se noie dans les yeux   60

From *Poèmes 1*

This is a poem about looking and seeing, complex acts that we generally take for granted. Its occasion was a modest art exhibition held around Easter 1982 at the Galerie Jeanne Bucher in the Quartier Latin (53, rue de Seine), for which Bernard Noël, a poet with a deep interest in contemporary art, had been invited to write the catalogue preface. The pictures to which he was asked to respond – recent works by Brazilian artist Maria Helena Vieira da Silva (1908–92) – were small to medium-sized, largely monochrome, abstract drawings in oils, charcoal, Indian ink and tempera on various types of paper. We might imagine him encountering these works for the first time, contemplating each in turn and letting their visual substance imprint itself on his perception, observing his own reactions and wondering how best to write about them.

The drawings already had intriguing titles, one group hinting at cosmic, historical or mythological themes ('Présage', 'Dédale', 'Tancrède', 'Les Deux Lunes', 'L'Observatoire', 'Mercure', 'Les Êtres'), another referring to artistic techniques and genres ('Perspectives', 'Paysage suspendu', 'Intérieur russe', 'Contrechamps', 'Projet pour Ledoux', 'Épure') and a third with more abstract referents of space, movement and vision ('Mirage', 'Parlance', 'Déplacement', 'Cadence'). The exhibition's title, 'Perspective labyrinthe', embraced all three types of theme: 'Perspective', in addition to being the foundational technique of post-Renaissance realism, also suggests open prospects and receding views, 'labyrinthe' (synonymous with 'dédale', from Daedalus, builder of the Cretan labyrinth in which the Minotaur was imprisoned) connotes enclosure, complexity and claustrophobia. Both thematise space, pictorial and existential, a common preoccupation of da Silva's images, with their multiple vanishing points and reticulate construction: the viewer's gaze is drawn into the picture by a sense of depth, then caught up in intricate cellular networks which it tries in vain to interpret representationally, until it finds itself engaging fundamentally with space itself.

Although written to accompany the exhibition, 'Les états de l'air' is not a *poème de circonstance* restricted to a transient context now preserved only in the catalogue.[1] When it was republished in Noël's *Poèmes 1* the following year,[2] only the dedication 'à Vieira da Silva' remained to link it to the drawings on display for those few weeks, while in the most recent republication, in *Les Yeux dans la couleur* which brings together his poetry about art,[3] even this dedication has disappeared – yet the text continues to resonate on its own. Nor is it primarily an example of ekphrasis, or *transposition d'art*: an attempt to recreate the original drawings in a different, verbal, medium. In fact, beyond a basic description of materials and visual lineaments of the kind attempted above, it is not obvious what form such a *transposition* might take in the case of abstract images without forms or colours drawn from the real world: in the absence of such visual anchors the referential function of words might be expected to be either frustrated or misapplied in the search for merely speculative analogies. This raises a more fundamental question: how do we actually look at and appreciate pictures which so knowingly deflect our instinct to see them as representations of the world? And what might that tell us about our looking more generally? 'Les états de l'air' develops a richly minimalist reflection on these broad issues, while remaining sensitive to the specific qualities of Vieira da Silva's drawings.

In the exhibition catalogue and in *Poèmes 1*[4] the poem is distributed over four pages, each containing 15 lines grouped into four stanzas, two of three lines and one each of four and five, in varying order (the importance of particular numbers, including 15, and of numerological compositional constraints, has been acknowledged by the poet and partially investigated by critics).[5] Though this might suggest reading each page as a separate 'meditation', strong thematic continuities run through the poem as a whole, with key words falling into three main lexical groups:

- **vision**: *vue, regard, vu, non-vu, œil, voit, miroir, pupille, buée, yeux* (significantly, the final word in the poem);
- **space**: *parois, vide, pays, profondeur, bâti, centre, central, dos, derrière, chemin, porte, dedans, au-delà, ciel, air, le dessous, l'obscur, seuil, l'ouvert, surface, limite, doublement, l'in-fini, mur;*
- **movement**: *renverse, sauter, va-et-vient, passages, s'ouvrant, à travers, s'enroule, s'en va, rentre, battements, s'envole, retourne, partir, s'y dépasse, là-bas, rejoint, allé, venir, s'aère, rencontre, affronté.*

Even before we engage with the poem's detailed articulation, its lexis thus establishes seeing as a dynamic process figured in terms of spaces and boundaries, openness, enclosure and transition. These lists (and one smaller group relating to the body: *tête, corps, langue*) actually enumerate a high proportion of the words in the text – an indication of its density and thematic overdetermination, suffused throughout with the figural *air* of the title.

A first reading of the opening stanza may identify an unfamiliar image of the way that vision works, but it can equally be interpreted as the initial reaction of a gaze encountering the spatial enigmas of Vieira da Silva's drawings:

> nous n'avons que la vue
> les parois de vent
> ce vide est le pays

Strikingly, that gaze belongs not just to the poet but also to the reader, who is implicated from the first word (*nous*, not *je* or *on*), as if the poet were inviting *us* to 'see' the drawings in the same way that he does and accompany his vision of them (and of vision itself) as the text sets out along its narrative path. The visual sense which gives us our feeling of belonging to the world (all the rich associations of *pays* are active here) is at first an empty, three-dimensional space intangibly bounded by airy walls as we await the emergence of something to feed our gaze. The observer is not separate from this 'invisible box' but intimately involved in it, as a remark from 1976 in Noël's *Journal du regard*[6] confirms: 'Le regard est une mise en boîte, qui fait de nous l'un des côtés du monde. Tout le visible est là, dans la boîte; quant à l'invisible, c'est le dos de l'horizon et tout ce qui est derrière notre dos' (*JR*, p. 22).

It is because we are part of the perceptual *boîte* that we feel at home there, and this spatial configuration also defines existential horizons – external but also personal – which will become important later in the poem. For Noël the fundamental mechanism of perception is a folding inwards of the visual into an analogous *mental* space where our impressions are formed, in the geometrical manner of light passing through a lens (here, in the eye): 'Le visible, en se renversant dans nos yeux, devient l'invisible dont s'alimente notre mentalité. Le sentiment d'intériorité n'est-il pas le simple report, derrière l'œil, du volume du regard?' (*JR*, p. 24).

This spatial model of mental experience is mediated throughout Noël's work by a play of variations on the figure of *air*, a material but invisible substance which surrounds (and so interlinks) external phenomena, but also offers a telling analogy for our conceptual relations: 'Tout espace n'est-il pas de l'air, y compris analogiquement sous le crâne? Ce que l'on voit mentalement n'est nulle part, et pas même dans les yeux. . .' (*JR*, p. 89). Whereas the perception of everyday phenomena works as a one-way transfer ('simple report') of *air* from world into head, art has the unique property of instigating a reciprocal relationship with the viewer. This turns our looking back onto ourselves and, as the poem's extraordinary sixth line puts it, 'nous fait sauter dans nos yeux' – plunging us not into the *air* of some pictorial view, but back into the space of our own gaze that the work (particularly abstract ones such as these) opens up. There, a reciprocating, questioning movement of exchange ('toujours le va-et-vient') is set up between picture space and mental space in which the mental (the *non-vu* and the *pas-là* of stanza 3) becomes 'grafted on' to the physical, tangible marks made by the artist on the paper (*le vu, ce qui est là*). As we gaze at the drawing and try to interpret visual 'passages' through its abstract, airy labyrinth, corresponding pathways open in our inner, mental space (stanza 4), while our gaze, in a metaphor that fuses the physical with the mental and the abstract with the concrete, 'twines around' the airy scaffolding that it discovers (one of the few direct allusions in the poem to the visual structuring of the drawings).[7]

These interactive, reflexive metaphors are developed further in the second group of four stanzas, which opens with an assertion of the need to look afresh at each aspect of reality, rather than simply recognising it within our conventional conceptual system (as in a realist aesthetic). While this may deprive our perceptions of any natural *centre* – a privileged perspective coded in a mimetic representation by vanishing-point perspective – when we look in this new way, each feature of what we see acquires in compensation a new *centrality* which magnifies and enriches our visual experience. Now as we gaze at the picture it takes on a spatial correspondence with our corporeal self, the visual relationship in which it engages us (*la vue*) expanding out from the paper to fill the space between it and us, 'backed' by the paper. Looking is now an activity that engages our whole physical existence ('tout le corps voit'), as we are lured into our own inner *dédale* by seeking to explore the pictorial one with which we are confronted. Like Le Petit Poucet (Tom Thumb) in Perrault's fairytale, we follow a 'chemin d'air' through the mental forest-labyrinth, marked out not by white pebbles but by 'cailloux d'encre' (the visual traces contained in the drawings, but also the words of Noël's poem which is becoming their analogue), a white/black inversion which parallels the literal/figurative one of the intertextual reference. In the same stanza the paper of the drawing undergoes a further metamorphosis, becoming a door onto a space beyond the picture surface (depth now extending behind rather than in front of the picture plane); then in the eighth stanza this is reconfigured again as a mirror. While an ordinary mirror shows us the (laterally inverted) image of our physical appearance, the metaphorical 'mirror' of the drawing (and the poem) contains 'notre tête au-delà', a projection of our mental space into which we can cross by the vertiginous process of staring, as in a real mirror, into our own pupil (this 'black moon' representing a further visual inversion, as of a photograph and its negative). Thus the picture engages us in a *mise en abyme* of our own consciousness, as looking at it, we see ourselves seeing ourselves looking. This rapid sequence of figural transformations (paper – labyrinth – door – mirror) finally comes full circle, as the moon/pupil image expands into an equation between drawing and sky, a 'ciel de papier' in which the observer's mental processes can take wing, like a bird. Such mental liberation, here re-grounded in the material existence of the picture after the figural detours by which the to-and-fro of his engagement has been developed, represents for Bernard Noël an important ethical as well as existential function of art.[8]

In the following (tenth) stanza, the 'mirror' of the pictorial surface becomes misted as the invisible vapour (air-borne breath, *pneuma* or *souffle*) of the observer's thinking gaze 'condenses' on it, at once becoming visible, even tangible, but also blurring the image and rendering its 'traces' indistinct – a metaphorical materialisation of the 'grafting' or superimposition of mental onto physical attributes that seeing brings about. Significant art, for Noël, presents us with challenging objects which appeal to what is universal in our humanity, so that by perceiving the pensive *buée* whose precipitation they cause, 'chacun retourne au tout' – a further reason for the inclusive *nous* of the poem's narrative voice. This universal reality is that all our emotional and intellectual responses, indeed the whole of our mental life, are rooted in the body, to which the eleventh stanza now returns in a movement inwards which balances the earlier metaphors of outward projection and exchange. Starting from the physiological surface, the 'écailles limpides' of the skin (now metaphorically translucent), the poet's gaze penetrates down past the skeletal 'dessous planté d'os' into the 'obscur' of his (and our) most unknown physiological workings. As the following stanza suggests, however, in acting as an invitation to explore concealed depths, our own 'seuil' (skin) is also analogous to the surface of the drawing, and the revelatory 'étonnement' which results allows us, by another analogical *renversement*, to perceive the picture itself as having a somatic foundation, an imagined 'body' beneath the 'skin' of the paper, manifested in the physical gestures of its creator to which the pictorial *traces* bear witness.

The last four stanzas of the poem open up rich new possibilities of spatial interaction whose underlying mechanism, the creation-perception of a visual-mental 'image', is defined in a note of 1975 in *Journal du regard*: 'L'œil contient le vu et contient le regard. L'œil réfléchit l'image et il en est la réflexion. Je pense en moi, mais je pense également hors de moi dans un renversement perpétuel du dedans et du dehors, du projeté et du réfléchi, dont le croisement[9] produit cet objet mental: l'image' (*JR*, pp. 17–18).

When in stanza 13 the poet's gaze probes beyond the 'limite' of pictorial and bodily surfaces, his mental space becomes translated into an external projection in and beyond the picture (where *la tête* goes to join, or catch up with, *le regard*). This projection establishes not only a new mentality but also a revitalised perception of the body from which it emanates and which, in turn, it now 'aerates' with mental life:

> alors dans l'œil allé
> le corps se voit venir
> où le mental s'aère

At the same time ('mais voici', stanza 15), it also introduces 'l'Autre' into the self, since the image being observed is the imprint of the physical–mental processes of the artist who created it. This relational alterity, generalised by the use of capitalised pronouns ('Vous', 'Lui'), is a second ethical imperative of art, an opportunity for the exchange of thought and experience, through the mediation of the gaze, with a person remote in space and time.[10] The resultant 'doublement du monde' is not just an index of reciprocity and reflexivity, it is an enrichment of our lives, a (punning) 'philtre d'air', or mental magic potion promising always new, always open-ended relations ('l'in-fini').

By the time it reaches the final stanza the poem has constructed an 'airy scaffolding', a lacunary but interconnecting edifice of figural equivalences, inversions and perspectives around the twin themes of vision and art, deftly picking a narrative pathway through a *dédale* of connections and reflections between artist, image and viewer, surface and depth, the mental and the physical. In doing so, it has taken its cue, without ever seeking to reproduce them, from the visual materials of Vieira da Silva's drawings, and it is fitting that it should return at the end to this starting point, the pictorial 'mur de rien' around which the text has been constructed. *Rien* because, except for some marks on pieces of paper, there really is nothing 'there'; just as the gaze interprets depth on the basis of cues inscribed on a plane surface, so the poet's *langue* (tongue and language, concrete and abstract) has, by dint of stubborn persistence, worked away at this figural wall to open up the mutually informing, reflexive spaces of vision and the mental–physical life that it conveys. By writing his own self-questioning perceptions in metaphorical form, Noël has been able to communicate the 'états de l'air' (never *d'esprit*, a word banished from his vocabulary for its historical dualist presuppositions) of artist and onlooker as mediated by the space of the drawings, linking himself with Vieira da Silva and us also, through him, with her. The verbal labyrinth which he has invited us to explore is thus a performative recreation in another medium of the drawings as 'machines for seeing' – which gives the poem an ekphrastic function after all. Now, in a closing pirouette, the *langue* writes itself out of the text, first disappearing back (in another pun of its own making) into the virtual *tête* of its own projection, then finally dissolving its effort to express and leaving behind only the poem's original instigator – the embodied gaze.

Notes

1 Vieira da Silva, *Perspective labyrinthe, dessins* (Paris: Galerie Jeanne Bucher, 1982), n.p. The exhibition ran from 20 March to 30 April 1982.
2 Bernard Noël, *Poèmes 1* (Paris: Flammarion, 1983), pp. 299–304.
3 Bernard Noël, *Les Yeux dans la couleur* (Paris: P.O.L, 2004), pp. 29–32.
4 But not in *Les Yeux dans la couleur*, presumably for reasons of space.
5 See Jean-Luc Bayard, 'B. N. rit du rien: une lecture de *Bruits de langues*', *Faire-Part*, 12–13 (1989), pp. 159–64 (special issue on Noël) and Andrew Rothwell, 'Introduction' to Bernard Noël, *La Chute des temps/Time-Fall* (Halifax, NS: VVV Editions, 2006), pp. 24–30.
6 Bernard Noël, *Journal du regard* (Paris: P.O.L, 1987) (henceforth *JR*). Cf. two related notes from 1978: 'Tout regard est une boîte' (p. 41); 'le visible, également, est une boîte: le regardeur en est l'un des côtés; les murs, l'autre' (p. 42).
7 This image is also reminiscent of Baudelaire's 'Le Thyrse' (*Petits poèmes en prose*).
8 Cf. 'Le Dehors mental', a poetic preface of 1978 composed for another exhibition at the Galerie Jeanne Bucher with the title 'Regard en demeure', which also featured pictures by Vieira da Silva alongside works by Louise Nevelson and Magdalena Abakanowicz: 'L'espace de l'œuvre est analogue au trajet de l'aile, / qui n'inscrit pas son vol tout en le traçant. / Cet espace est la mentalité, / qui n'inscrit pas sa présence tout en étant présente'. (*Les Yeux dans la couleur*, pp. 13–21; p. 19). In the same text Noël observes that art contains 'un air dont la trace ne trace rien mais nous monte à la tête' (*ibid.*).
9 This hybridisation looks back to 'la greffe' of stanza 3.
10 'Le regard oublie qu'il est la substance même de la rencontre: substance aérienne qui est réciproquement l'air de la tête et l'air du monde' (*JR*, p. 37).

Further reading

Bishop, Michael, *The Contemporary Poetry of France: Eight Studies* (Amsterdam: Rodopi, 1985).
Carn, Hervé, *Bernard Noël* (Paris: Seghers, 1986).
Kelley, David and Khalfa, Jean (eds.), *The New French Poetry* (Newcastle upon Tyne: Bloodaxe, 1996).
Wagstaff, Emma, *Provisionality and the Poem: Transition in the Works of du Bouchet, Jaccottet and Noël* (Amsterdam: Rodopi, 2006).
Wateau, Patrick, *Bernard Noël ou l'expérience extérieure* (Paris: José Corti, 2001).
Winspur, Steven, *Bernard Noël* (Amsterdam: Rodopi, 1991).

Jacques Roubaud, 'Dès que je me lève'

MERYL TYERS

Dès que je me lève

Dès que je me lève (quatre heures et demie, cinq heures), je prends mon bol sur la table de la cuisine. Je l'ai posé là la veille, pour ne pas trop bouger dans la cuisine, pour minimiser le bruit de mes déplacements.

Je continue de le faire, jour après jour, moins par habitude, que par refus de la mort d'une habitude. Être silencieux n'a plus la moindre importance.

Je verse un fond de café en poudre, de la marque ZAMA filtre, que j'achète en grands verres de 200 grammes au supermarché FRANPRIX, en face du métro Saint-Paul. Pour le même poids, cela coûte à peu près un tiers de moins que les marques plus fameuses, Nescafé, ou Maxwell. Le goût lui-même est largement un tiers pire que celui du nescafé le plus grossier non lyophilisé, qui n'est déjà pas mal en son genre.

Je remplis mon bol au robinet d'eau chaude de l'évier.

Je porte le bol lentement sur la table, le tenant entre mes deux mains qui tremblent le moins possible, et je m'assieds sur la chaise de cuisine, le dos à la fenêtre, face au frigidaire et à la porte, face au fauteuil, laid et vide, qui est de l'autre côté de la table.

À la surface du liquide, des archipels de poudre brune deviennent des îles noires bordées d'une boue crémeuse qui sombrent lentement, horribles.

Je pense : « Et l'affreuse crème / Près des bois flottants / . »

Je ne mange rien, je bois seulement le grand bol d'eau à peine plus que tiède et caféinée. Le liquide est un peu amer, un peu caramélisé, pas agréable.

230

Je l'avale et je reste un moment immobile à regarder, au fond du
bol, la tache noire d'un reste de poudre mal dissoute.

From *Quelque chose noir*

In memory of Ruth Bagnall[1]

The poet's mourning coffee

Jacques Roubaud's *Quelque chose noir*[2] is a poem cycle whose autobiographical
subject, approached in many ways, is the untimely death, apparently from
cancer, of his wife Alix Cléo. The indelible image of the dead body of his wife
and his immediate reactions in the days and months following is interwoven
with memories of her and of their life as a couple, often prompted by contemplating photographs she took which festoon their apartment now empty of her
physical presence.

Quelque chose noir concentrates chronologically on the period 1983–5, seemingly from Alix's death until shortly before the book's date of publication,
although this 'real-time' presence is diluted by memories of other times, and
some date details remain unclear. Although the poems can state specific facts
and dates baldly, they operate more generally in a register of ambiguity that
enables the individual experience to speak to a wider audience while preserving
some of the exact details for the poet alone.

As a reader, one rarely feels personally addressed: rather, the reader is a
privileged, occasionally voyeuristic, witness to private dialogues and scenarios
inside the poet's own head as he debates with himself, often in philosophical
exchanges that recall medieval idiom, or as he reminisces with his dead wife
through her photographs. 'Dialogue' (p. 124) notes: 'Un poème se place toujours dans les conditions d'un dialogue virtuel', but goes on to make clear in
how many ways this dialogue can be mediated, and between which entities it
can be conducted.

Many of the poems enact or describe Roubaud's faltering attempts to speak of
Alix's death when his most natural form of self-expression – language, and in
particular poetry – appears to be totally defeated, even prohibited, by the enor-
mity of his loss, a muting which finds its most explicit expression both in '1983 :
janvier.   1985 : juin' (p. 33) and in 'Aphasie' (pp. 131–2):

Devant ta mort je suis resté entièrement silencieux.

Je n'ai pas pu parler pendant presque trente mois.

Je ne pouvais plus parler selon ma manière de dire qui est la poésie.

All too often, then, the poet finds himself hardly able to write at all: words become sparse and the white space of the page creeps into his lines.

Roubaud can be an artful poet of place: *La Forme d'une ville change plus vite, hélas, que le cœur des humains* (1999) contains his own quirky, neatly formal enumerations of Paris's streets; and individual poems in *Quelque chose noir* revolve around topographical reference points that have a special resonance for Roubaud and his wife, whether in Paris or elsewhere. 'Un jour de juin' (p. 47) mentions looking out towards the Île de la Cité; others refer, for instance, to the poet's trip to meet his wife after her recuperative stay at La Bourboule and a walk along the Dordogne ('Roman, III'), or to 'Christmas shopping in Manchester' (*ibid.*); or they mention more restricted localities such as the John Rylands Library ('Portrait en méditation'), or Wittgenstein's grave near Cambridge ('Ludwig Wittgenstein'). Such evocative memories of 'elsewhere' are grouped around the same section of the text while those of Paris and the couple's corner of it (the flat, seemingly in the Marais) recur more widely. In 'Dès que je me lève', the outside world is referred to on a small scale, the poet noting that he buys his coffee at the Franprix supermarket opposite the Saint-Paul metro station: the outside world is also rejected, as the poet sits with his back to the window, staring at the kitchen's mundane furnishings.

However, *Quelque chose noir* is no piece of ripely comforting flight into the past or the elsewhere. In many cases, the writing exists in the moment in which the poem is being written, and past and future seem equally amputated, especially so in the first and last 'bookend' sections which contain some of the most austere poems.

'Dès que je me lève' is the first poem in the second section of *Quelque chose noir*, which is arranged in nine numbered sections each of nine poems, with a single untitled poem ('Ce morceau de ciel' is its first line, p. 147) forming a tenth section headed 'Rien' and dated 1983. Thus, there are eighty-two poems in all, a number which may reflect one of the significant dates of Roubaud's mourning. In such a tightly patterned arrangement, 'Dès que je me lève' is hard to dissociate from the fabric in which it lies embedded; parts of many of the poems re-echo each other, and this one finds its own sketchy shadows in apparently throwaway lines from the bleak 'Au matin' (p. 35): 'Dans mon bol des archipels de boue noire   qui fondent / / Je bois tiède'.

There is a legitimate and perfectly obvious question here: is this a poem? Plenty of its neighbours are in blank verse, and several seem to be fragments of memoir-narrative; but few require such close attention from the literary police to tease out their legitimate identity. In my view, its context qualifies it, followed by its echoic qualities and the occasional flights from the banal to the highly charged. In wine-tasting terms, it has a 'mouth-feel', and there are also visual clues which put it out of the ranks of normal prose. Finally, there is its pared-down quality, conveying a lot with a little, which gives it the layers and distillations we associate with poetry. I do, though, class its subdivisions as paragraphs rather than stanzas or lines, and others may disagree with my argument to allow more than a little poetic licence as to its identity.

Style

'Dès que je me lève' is a poem whose style deliberately underlines its content. Both are markedly prosaic, and convey the listless banality as well as the hope-lessness of life during grief. Few poetic 'tricks' if any can be discerned (unlike, for instance, the comically banal repetitions of 'C.R.A.Pi.Po.: Composition rythmique abstraite pour pigeons et poète', pp. 43–4). The reader feels the heaviness at the end of each sentence, as the paragraphs seem to wind down, lose steam prematurely, or fail to connect with any more meaningful train of thought. Then we notice that almost every paragraph begins baldly with 'je' plus a main present-tense verb, apart from the sixth and the first, which nonetheless begins with a subordinate clause containing this pronoun. There is none of the expected literary French style, loading of drama to ends of sentences, front-loading of subordinate clauses, syntactic complexity or density.

In both flow and phraseology, then, the paragraphs of this poem are strikingly inelegant: some are clunky, while in others language seems to drift away from meaning, anchorless; and no paragraph echoes another by word choice, rhythm or any kind of syllabic countability (hence, in my view, no stanzas). They might be called Flaubertian, in the sense of that author's capacity for prosodic bathos, seen at the end of *Hérodias*, 'Et ils la portèrent alternativement' where the adverb has been noted for its heaviness, so noticeable in French where a semantically weak but clumsily heavy element such as a one-word adverb would not normally be placed in so prominent a position. Paragraph 6 ends similarly, not only with a heavy adverb but then a disconnected adjective whose initial glottal syllable clashes with what precedes: '[des îles noires] qui sombrent lentement, horribles.'

Is there a tiny poetic ring in those three successive syllables assonating in 'ent', one of which is visible but unpronounced? If so, it shows the compressed, subconscious scale on which poetry is allowed to scrape an existence within this poem. But if style, content, punctuation and syntax here are almost exclusively prosaic, this does not mean they are unintended, any more than the ringing of almost imperceptible poetic chimes.

Deprivation

We are thrown into a world deliberately muted. No spoon is mentioned for the coffee (no wonder it does not dissolve). We speculate about any noise the tap might make, or running water, but they are not mentioned. The given time of night ensures we imagine a dead silence.

The dead-of-night waking also indicates sleeplessness, which conveys a feeling of solitude and desperation whatever cause is responsible. Is the poet insomniac, or his sleep interrupted, or is the early hour normal for this writer?

The poet's coffee bowl is carried, but not described: we are deprived of texture and colour in the description of most of the poet's surrounding objects. We imagine the barely tepid contents hardly sensuous: temperature is muted to a lukewarm *tiédeur*. From its use in other poems here, the 'tiède' can connote only desolation and horror. In 'Méditation de la certitude' (pp. 13–14), when Roubaud discovers the body of his wife, it is on the livid colour and fading warmth of her hand that he compulsively focuses: 'Tiède. tiède seulement. tiède encore'.

If the poet had only used a spoon, we would benefit at least from the imagined crunch of it into the jar of powder, but the poet is intent on depriving his actions of all sound, all texture.

Escape

After the opening gloom of hollow rituals, the third paragraph is full of glaring juxtapositions and awkwardnesses, and forms one of the strange highlights of this poem.

Here we suddenly veer into a very different, if equally alienated, mode from that underlying the poem generally. Locations, brand names, weights and exact assessments of the degree of awfulness of supermarket own-brand instant coffee are specified. Clunky brand names, rendered nearly meaningless (Zama, Nescafé, Franprix), two of them in capital letters to retain their fully alienated perception by the poet and his reader, disrupt the dull flow of anti-poetry.

What the reader at first identifies using notions of descriptive colour, even local colour, is on examination not connected at all with literal hues but something more abstract: a jangling explosion of words on the page. With their bold geometries of shape in the choice of 'marques' using 'x' and 'z', with their capitals pumping up the volume, and with what might be termed barbaric typography and terminology, 'ZAMA' and '200' being the boldest, 'FRANPRIX', 'Nescafé', 'Maxwell' and 'lyophilisé' slightly less so, these strange syllables present us with what passes for colour in commerce, the drama-on-the-cheap of the supermarket brand, pushing forward the full implications of the phrase 'rapport qualité-prix'.

All these odd-shaped building blocks piled on each other throw out a sonorously chewy, visually angular set of verbal defences in the face of any attempt by the reader to discern relief, beauty or lyricism in the poet's apparent escape from the claustrophobic confines of his interiority. If he seems trapped in his mind, his home and his poemless prison, then this window on the outside world proves the alternative to be no better: a harsh world in which the exact words for and measures of what passes for real life offer no comfort. The words that come to him are black and white and geometric; even pushed to extremes, as here, they cannot or may not evoke colours, dimensions or emotions. The normal relationship between words and reality is consumed by the hollowness of grieving as a moth is by a flame.

The coffee has been judged: it tastes about a third worse than the famous brands, and is about a third cheaper. A sort of just symmetry of judgement is brought to bear here: the complete accuracy of objective measurement makes the offhanded subjectivity of 'pire' and 'pas mal' incongruously vague, and even lugubriously comic.

The placing of paragraph 3 within the poem indicates that these highly precise views of largely unremarked things, the decision to buy the coffee that tastes a third worse, the type of supermarket and location, form a temporary nerve-wrenching distraction from the eternities of the empty home, the dead-of-night waking, and the kitchen's comfortless atmosphere with its ugly, empty chair.

One mention of the external world anchors the text in Paris: the Saint-Paul metro. It brings with it whiffs of the ancient, the Marais for which this is one of the principal metro stops being one of the oldest parts of the city. It furnishes a small link with the rest of *Quelque chose noir* in which the view out of the Roubauds' apartment window, with its specific church roof, trees and skyscape, is stated as a theme and modified through many iterations.

Subject–Verb–Scandal

The dull plainness of mood, the sensorially deprived texture of the poet's world, is reasserted in paragraph 4: a small bubble of linguistic play, hinting at the poet's customary *joie de vivre* in language, has rapidly burst.

Paragraph 4 is a simple subject–verb–complement sentence. With its austerity of expression, it seems crafted for drama, yet the content is bathetic as well as potentially shocking – depending on the reader's attitude to the proper enjoyment of coffee. To reinforce the poem's many scandalous acts (its lack of pattern, rhyme, rhythm, poetic sensibility), it brings the reader up short with its plain description of an act normally associated with sensual pleasure – the rituals and scents of the day's first coffee – making this beverage with deliberately inferior coffee powder and tepid water straight from the hot tap.

Colours

True colours in imagery only surface in the colours of the coffee powder, minutely observed as it turns from dark brown to black (paragraph 6), 'des archipels de poudre brune deviennent des îles noires bordées d'une boue crémeuse'.

In the final paragraph, the browns, blacks and muds of the poem's palette, set off by one or two hints of cream, are echoed once more by a 'tache noire' of badly dissolved powder remnants, suggesting also the typographical sign of the full stop that will come to close this apparently stillborn poem.

The 'tache noire' figure is present throughout *Quelque chose noir*, signifying everything from a full stop, literally and metaphorically, to the dark triangle of Alix Cléo's pubic hair, evoking the poet's still-vivid sexual attraction to his lover and the centrality of eroticism to his memories of her ('Pexa et hirsuta', p. 64; many mentions of the 'point vivant du ventre' associated with ideas of surrounding darkness). This darkness is set off by frequent mentions of whiteness and light, in monochrome photographs, in the notion of photography as painting with light, and elsewhere. Apart from some vivid splashes of red, black and white are the prevailing colours of the poem cycle.

The 'tache noire' is therefore, in the context of *Quelque chose noir*, both a tiny jot and a hugely central motif, echoing in the ambiguous grammar of the poem cycle's very title. And so in this one small brushstroke Roubaud, at the end of such a bleak, comic, sad, dis-pleasurable non-poem, awakens the reader to a sense that all along, 'Dès que je me lève' has belonged in its context, and does share the hidden literary drive of the poems alongside which it lies.

Taste

Against the dullness established in the opening paragraphs, any hint of sensuality stands out amidst the surrounding abstinence. As the poem builds, the sense of taste at least is not ignored, but seems to grow in unpleasantness as it receives closer focus: we first conceive of it during the prolonged description of how the coffee is chosen in paragraph 3; then the anticipation of its taste grows as we are diverted via paragraphs 4 and 5 into descriptions of how it is made, seating arrangements and the liquid's appearance, all hardly designed to thrill. Finally, after an enigmatic quotation that seems to occupy what ought to be the paroxystic place, the climax of the drama, the poet drinks his coffee on the downswing from this moment, and it proves as anticlimactic as we had long expected: 'à peine plus que tiède et caféinée', 'un peu amer, un peu caramélisé, pas agréable'. There is none of the digestive comfort, cheer, camaraderie, consolation that our instincts tell us ought to follow. On the small canvas of the poem, this is attributable to the lamentable way in which the coffee is made: but what is more comfortless – this deplorable procedure, or the gaping loss that is the unspoken background and reason behind it?

However, we have passed over the climactic line, 'Je pense : "Et l'affreuse crème / Près des bois flottants / ."'' This is a slight misquote of Rimbaud's 'Les Amis', part of 'Comédie de la soif', from *Vers nouveaux*. And thus opens another broad window off the text, forming a counterweight to paragraph 3 in its release of claustrophobia, but different in offering an exit into the expansive landscape of the literary imagination.

Unlike the earlier point of escape, this one is adumbrated in a one-line paragraph of quotation – but the view from this window promises much more. Conjured up before the poet's mind we may suddenly imagine a world of beautifully arranged words and citations, the metatextual implications of the presence of Rimbaud, the wit of a link to a 'comedy of thirst' in this poorly caffeinated scene. It links us to Roubaud's normal persona: polymathic and prolific. It hints that some of the refusenik quality of 'Dès que je me lève' may be inspired by this one fleeting glimpse of Rimbaud's all-consuming teenage rebelliousness against life, the universe and the dictates of the poetic rulebook. 'Les Amis' features higgledy-piggledy rhythms and seems to descend, in the two final lines quoted by Roubaud, from tipsiness into drunken depression:

> J'aime autant, mieux, même,
> Pourrir dans l'étang,
> Sous l'affreuse crème,
> Près des bois flottants.[3]

We may start to discern the presence of a drunken boat in Roubaud's images of sinking island shipwrecks ('des îles noires . . . qui sombrent') and strange archipelagoes. The drab gloom, the use of 'horribles', 'boue' and dark assessments of the mundane ('fauteuil, laid et vide', 'un peu amer', 'mal dissoute') now recall Rimbaud's thesaurus of displeasure. The referential broken couplet itself morphs into a 'floating island' like those of the previous paragraph, an undissolved coffee ground against the backdrop of the poem. Somewhere in the cascade of tastes and colours of paragraphs 6 and 7, do I also detect the incongruous sweet pleasure of 'îles flottantes'? I suppose that, being compelled to bear witness to such total sensory cheerlessness, the poem has provoked a moment of sheer escapist fantasy.

Yet, despite all this potential for colourful, broad diversion into pleasure, a tonic for the sensory and literary imagination, what the poem actually offers us is the massive compression of these positives into a small moment, one single line. Nothing is made of the flickering of this single poetic neurone. We return at once to the disappointment we have been awaiting, and the bleakness of the poet's world as we are observing it.

We can read all sorts of emotional colourings into this one line of quotation – self-awareness, self-deprecation, awkward wistfulness for the rich poetic seams from which Roubaud feels cut off. What we are faced with is what faces the poet: that reality says no to these pleasures, and even to the desire for them: 'Je lis de la prose inoffensive', 'Je ne parviens pas à ouvrir un seul livre contenant de la poésie' ('1983 : janvier. 1985 : juin'). To change his drear habits and seek access back to his world of self-expression would be to seek a way out of grief: to do that would be to accept grief, and hence to accept the loss of the person for whom he grieves, which is unthinkable, for then the vivid presence of her life to him will begin to change. This is why his coffee ritual must remain the same: 'Je continue de le faire, jour après jour, moins par habitude, que par refus de la mort d'une habitude' (paragraph 2). The final two paragraphs spiral downwards, and the inconclusive ending finds the poet's gaze trapped in his bowl, contemplating the lone speck of coffee that remains.

In 'Dès que je me lève', there is no overt reference to the main theme of *Quelque chose noir*. However, the atmospheric clues woven through the poem give more away about its place in a book of grief. The focus on a time of day when the human system is at its lowest; the monastic hush maintained; the complete lack of gustatory pleasure; the deliberate reinforcement of unease, displeasure, un-love for the process, the coffee and its drinker, sing out clearly to a greater melancholy.

The poet seems to have pared away all his instinct for beauty, precision, formality. His waking presents him with a series of flavourless minutiae into which he incorporates two brief forays into a more ingenious menu; the irregular chiming of 'je' initiating each paragraph recalls his barely wandering imagination to the bald prose of his empty ritual.

And yet – not. The reader is intrigued and provoked to close attention, knowing what the poet knows, that his writing cannot help but be read as artefact, and that in the end, less will be more. The first reading will trouble us with its minute details and ugliness; then we discern deep and genuine sadness in the unlovely phrases as we connect them with fathomless loss. Finally, longer scrutiny makes us examine our own responses: are we fighting off the inappropriateness of finding this poem droll, even charming? Can we be so unsympathetic as to find its anatomisation of time fascinating? Is the black, brown and cream colour scheme of the one paragraph that stands out for not beginning with 'je' trying to remind us of a painting we have seen? Or, more basically, are we rather relieved that we can escape from the poet's lost world, and are we now itching for a fix of *grand crème* properly made?

The structure of *Quelque chose noir* is heavily 'arranged', patterned with quite calculated precision, in a way familiar to readers of the other work of Roubaud the mathematician, philosopher and medievalist. However, for me and others, *Quelque chose noir* stands out in its touching pain, its need and (hence) its accessibility. Its poetic and emotional diction of loss ranges from small subtleties of punctuation and typography, like a musical score of different values of silence, to our greater sense of the whole as a complex topography of grief.

The poem cycle explores familiar paradoxes of literature: the expressibility of the inexpressible, the presence of absence, and the allowability of artistic endeavour as a response to a real tragedy, whose weaving into accepted reality via the distorting prism of art should be somehow impermissible. And yet it explores these nostrums with a fresh edge, prompted by a loss close to home, and quietly records a gamut of fine-tuned emotional modes – among them gentleness, humour, anger, meditation, longing, and finally literary self-assurance.

Who else could have expressed the extent of grief, the depth of disconnection from the simple gustatory pleasures so central to a sensual and basic sensory connection, than a Frenchman describing making his breakfast coffee with instant granules and water from the hot tap? And who else than this poet in complete command of all the poetic palette could speak with such unforced and touching ineloquence to express the tragic banality and profound bleakness of grief?

The reader, looking on human distress helplessly and perhaps feeling that fascination is yet another wrong response, is eventually persuaded, by the poems' content and their arrangement, that he/she has witnessed the poet living through not only the death of his poetic personality but its rebirth in what may be a new form. This is crystallised in the final, haunting poem, in which the poet frames and dedicates a square of the sky that will always belong to Alix Cléo.

Notes

1 Ruth Bagnall died in 2004: she was a brilliant Cambridge contemporary of Meryl's who introduced her to Roubaud.
2 Jacques Roubaud, *Quelque chose noir* (Paris: Gallimard, 1986). 'Dès que je me lève' can be found on pp. 27–8.
3 Arthur Rimbaud, *Poésies: Une saison en enfer. Illuminations* (Paris: Gallimard, 1973), p. 104.

Further reading

Davreu, Robert, *Jacques Roubaud* (Paris: Seghers, 1985).
Montémont, Véronique, *Jacques Roubaud: l'amour du nombre* (Villeneuve D'Ascq: Presses Universitaires du Septentrion, 2004).
Poucel, Jean-Jacques, *Jacques Roubaud and the Invention of Memory* (Chapel Hill, NC: University of North Carolina Press, 2006).
Roubaud, Jacques, *Some Thing Black*, trans. Rosmarie Waldrop (Urbana-Champaign, IL: Dalkey Archive Press, 1990).

26 Marie-Claire Bancquart, 'Essentiel'

SHIRLEY JORDAN

Essentiel

Huiles de l'abandon
ensembliers à modifications très douces.

Vœux joués
sur gamelang des pluies.

Tu dis en vain   5
je suis
le plus petit rond d'humidité sur la table
quand on a bu et que l'enfant
frotte le bois les convives s'étant éclipsés.

Tu dis moins :   10
je suis
un faîtage oublié par les relevés d'architecte.

Ton morceau de route
est seul dans la forêt qui marche pour son compte.

                              *
                         *   *

Désertés   15
nous marouflons un peu de discours humain sur le ciel
parmi d'aveugles nuits.

                              *
                         *   *

Nous crions l'ombre des mots vers la terre.

Nous marquons d'ongles des photographies.

Nous proclamons c'est nous   20
qui n'aimions pas les mouches la filasse
la sciure les pommes de pin éclatées.

240

Il passe des loirs sur les pierres.

On se tait enfin.

Alors la nudité superbe de l'amour   25
trouve du répondant aux souches.

From Opportunité des oiseaux

What is 'essential'? This poem, taken from Marie-Claire Bancquart's *Opportunité des oiseaux*,[1] explores the question and exemplifies the art of paring down. Both spare and rich, it gives voice, succinctly, to some of the poet's essential themes. The collection of which it is part, remarked upon by Michael Bishop as representing 'an exquisite provisional peak of accomplishment' within Bancquart's work,[2] is articulated in six sections, each with its own preoccupations but with a strong overall wholeness of vision. Section titles – 'Journal des eaux', 'Exils, célébrations', 'À l'enseigne du monde', 'Inclusions', 'Habitations', 'Alliance' – suggest at a glance the volume's concerns. These include attentiveness to nature; reflections on spirituality; the uneasy status of humankind between belonging and exile; a concern with construction, dwelling (including dwelling in poetry) and rootedness; and the intuition of affinities between humans and the material world. Bancquart's 'Choses sans maîtres et muettes'[3] with their 'Exhortation massive'[4] recall Francis Ponge's emphatic endorsement of the importance of simple objects, while her strong sense of journeying, and of our residing 'À la porte du dérisoire'[5] evoke, as we shall see, the tenor of André Frénaud's poetry. Bancquart's characteristic density and deftness of line inform all the collection's poems, and the emotional control and intimacy of her poetic voice, which soothes even as we share her starkest, most difficult musings, are constant throughout.

Situated within the section entitled 'Exils, célébrations', 'Essentiel' explores exile within a celebratory context. It is about existence and death, solitude and separation, and our place in nature. It is about what is left when the babble of the daily round is stripped away. It is also, self-referentially, about poetry and language. In it the speaker takes great pleasure in essential matter (oils, rainwater, wood, words) and in concentrated forms of expression (the notes of a gamelan gong; a vow; a photograph). Each stanza, often no more than one or two lines long, is the essence of a musing or perception; each resonates with affect and meaning. This is a meditative poem into which Bancquart injects space and silence. Lines range from the markedly clipped (two or three syllables) to the extended (twelve, thirteen or fourteen syllables), the shortest and longest sometimes being juxtaposed to great effect as a halting meditation abruptly unfurls. To read 'Essentiel' is to trace a sequence of images which surface and coalesce like stepping stones across the current of the speaker's thought.

The first two stanzas, each of two lines, are concentrated image groups sealed with a full stop and surrounded by silence. They are calming and evoke subtle pleasures of touch and sound. In them the speaker seems to be searching for an adequate metaphorical evocation of something: of poetic language, perhaps? or more simply, of words? First, the theme of abandonment is launched in an enigmatic opening line which suggestively confers upon this abstract noun some materiality, implying that its essence may be distilled like an oil. It is not yet clear, however, whether the abandonment referred to is that of sensual enjoyment or of loss. The mysterious 'ensembliers' (assistant set designers or interior decorators) introduced in the following line help to 'set the scene' and are a fitting image for words: rich distillations of sense and feeling, especially in a poetic context, words work alongside the poet, gently inflecting messages.

In the following stanza the soft percussion of raindrops as they land on various resonant surfaces evokes a gamelan xylophone, the notes of which bear the speaker's wishes. The sonorous, rhythmic dimensions of language are thus highlighted. At the same time the peculiar sounds of the gamelan, its harmonies and disharmonies which remain exotic to the occidental ear, are consistent with the heightened and unfamiliar use of words in poetry. This image in turn marks the commencement of an ongoing meditation on the degree of mastery the speaker is able to exercise over life, language and the irrevocable order of things. Far from her 'conducting' affairs, we will see that some of them seem to take place around or even without her, and that what remains for her to celebrate is the partial control which constitutes her sense of being-in-the-world. She collaborates as best she can with the richly imperfect, wilful matter of language: the rain falls at its own rhythm and makes its own percussive statements; the assistant set designers go about their work and modulate the environment whilst she looks on.

The play of pronouns in the following three stanzas, each of which is addressed to an unspecified *tu* whom we assume to be the poet, marks this as a poem of self-situation. Stanzas 1 and 2 refer to her use of language; stanza 3, in a familiar existential metaphor, refers to the short stretch of path that is her life. The first person recurs frequently in Bancquart's poems and is one of the features that lends them their intimate dimension. Her *je* is often explicitly feminine, a poet, and occasionally even bears the author's name: one poem in *Opportunité des oiseaux* indeed begins 'Je Marie-Claire',[6] thus apparently conflating author and narrating voice. Locating the lyric *je*, however, leads more readily in Bancquart to considering what it shares with the general lot, rather than to notions of a particular autobiographical self, as this poem will go on to show. The first person characteristically stands outside the self, her identity rapidly merging into others'. In this part of the poem the self is already somewhat dislocated, at one step removed and apostrophising itself as poetic persona.

The first two stanzas follow the same scheme. In both the speaker responds to the unspoken question 'What am I?' by proffering and assessing a metaphor to encapsulate her essential sense of self. Both stanzas demonstrate the earnestness and care of this meditation; both frame the self through hesitant negation. In both the mere commencement of a definitional phrase – 'je suis' – stands alone on a line, teetering between a bald assertion of existence and a fuller portrayal. The first metaphor is elaborately extended and is held in exquisite tension within a stanza that dismisses it, even before we read it, as being uttered 'in vain'. With humility it suggests that the speaker's essence is located in solitude, silence, the insignificant and the everyday. 'What am I?': a mere residue; a droplet of moisture; a 'rond', not even a 'goutte', fragile and ephemeral enough to be wiped away by a child's rapid gesture. As an image for annihilation this is remarkable for its gentle domesticity. Notable too is the view of the self as fluid and as belonging to the life-giving element of water. Finally, Bancquart's invocation of conviviality requires interpretation: the 'convives' of the recently dispersed gathering may well be readers, guests in the refreshing act of sharing poetry, or more broadly they may represent the gathering that is life itself.

In the following stanza a more assertive self-image is fleetingly explored: that of a ridge-tile, an essential structuring component of the summit of a roof. From a fantasy of self-erasure in which the *je* was barely perceptible, the speaker shifts to consider her self as a key strengthening item within an edifice and the play with scale which is one of the features of this poem (from the microscopic to the imposing; the human to the divine; the infinitesimal to the cosmic) continues. Connecting the poetic self with shelter, Bancquart crafts an image which evokes poetry as habitus: in other words, poetry is both a (building) activity and a human dwelling as fundamental as any physical structure. In this case, however, the image of the poetic self as a structuring feature on which all else hangs is doubly foreclosed. First, this particular ridge-tile is forgotten, left off the plans of a negligent architect. Second, this is a relatively uncongenial self-image to the speaker who sees herself less in this light ('Tu dis moins') than in the former unassuming image. The poet as 'faîtage' evokes an outdated notion of the poet's privileged vision and elevated status. It was fitting perhaps for a Hugo or a Rimbaud, but not for the humbler practitioners of the late twentieth and early twenty-first century, many of whom consider themselves artisans of matter rather than visionaries.

In the subsequent two-line stanza the speaker shifts from her (unfulfilled) task of self-definition to another ontological issue: the 'morceau de route' which is an individual life. In a surprising twist which abruptly dislocates the freshly forming image in line 1 of an individual walking, line 2 presents the surreal concept of a route walking itself or being travelled without the traveller. How can our path walk on without us? Such an image once again raises issues of volition, power and presence. The speaker's lack of control over time and destiny is stressed not only through this odd personification which sets her outside the current of life, but also through this line's distinctive rhythmic qualities, for here Bancquart's formally unsettled free-verse poem settles into a line of recognisable cadence. Imposing itself by its brief evocation of implacable regularity, its four solid beats suggesting a determinedly steady walking pace, this line alludes to the irrevocable march of time (and does so whether or not we pronounce the mute '*e*' at the end of 'marche', thereby forging for ourselves a classic alexandrine). A final point: in terms of our spatial appreciation of the poem, we see at a glance that each of these three stanzas is shorter than the last, the whittling from five to three to two lines following the poem's overall thematic and structural emphasis on paring down.

The next, interim section which stands between the two longer parts of the poem is a three-line stanza which the poet has taken care to separate graphically from the rest, already suggesting that there is something distinctive about its tenor and taking no chances with the quality of our attentiveness. All at once the speaker's train of thought shifts to an unspecified collective: the *nous* which will be the subject of the remainder of the poem and whose various activities will be charted. Who exactly belongs to this undefined pronominal group? We may speculate that it is humankind in general, poets more particularly, or both. Whatever the case the assessment of the sum of human activity and of our place in the universe is, for the moment, extremely starkly rendered. Bancquart has stated her admiration for and attachment to the poetry of André Frénaud[7] and this poet's difficult insistence upon hopeful unhope, his uncompromising poise between negation and faint affirmation, find their echo here. The same unsensationalised statement of persistence in the certain knowledge of absurdity is present. No context of religious faith sustains us; no supreme being, no 'architect' includes us in a master plan; there is no guide through the forest. We are 'in the dark', 'blind' and 'deserted'. Such images are common coinage within poetic and philosophical visions which question religious 'certainties', and Bancquart does not labour them. The question of (but not the quest for) the divine has been important since her very first poems, typically leading to composed, clear-sighted assertions about our lack of ontological guy-ropes, delivered without anguish or sentimentality. Here a religious context is clearly evoked ('désertés'; 'ciel'), but the poem is at the same time void of any sense of God, and 'Dieu' is not alluded to.

A one-word poetic line can be fiercely powerful and the impact of 'Désertés' which opens this unit of meditation is immense. Like stanzas 3 and 4, this one begins in a spirit of negation. It goes on to contribute to the poem a particularly hard-nosed assessment of the human condition and pursues the theme of language, asserting in line 16 that speaking is our primary method of fending off despair, whilst it instantly undercuts the efficacy of speaking. The verb 'maroufler' holds together a group of ideas concerned with consolidating, gripping, glueing ('la maroufle' is strong glue) and attaching backing or lining substance to flimsy material in order to make it more robust. This concrete image is linked to the metaphor of the missing ridge-tile and reinforces the theme of flawed attempts to shore up our security. We try, asserts the speaker, to perform the very concrete human-scale operation of 'marouflage' on the vastly intangible – the atmosphere, the sky. This attempt at saving-through-speaking (and note that Bancquart chooses the word 'discours' not 'écriture' here, emphasising the provisional and ephemeral nature of spoken language) is at once determined and derisory. Here perhaps is Bancquart's domesticated, feminised alternative to Camus's image of Sisyphus rolling his rock. We cut, paste, sew and use the homespun elements available to us as we try repeatedly to hold together and repair what is fragile, to give it contour and strength, and it is language that lends (a little) shape to the amorphousness of life. This is a statement of near futility, yet there may well be some small effectiveness in the act. In graphic terms, the pagination provides a visual confirmation of this stanza's bleak assessment: its three lines stand in stark isolation, floating between tiny constellations of asterisks.

The first three fragments of the poem's remaining section (two single lines then a three-line stanza) draw our attention to the *nous* whose shared activities they delineate. A painful thematic of separation and loss emerges as the group seems not to be earthbound but exiled and other-worldly. Framed here as reluctant absentees, as distant as the dead from the living, they seek acknowledgement and attempt vigorously to communicate across time and space. Their determined efforts to be taken into account – to count – are vain: their voices project only weak and shadowy echoes of words; spectre-like, they leave traces of fingernail dents on photographs: a haunting image of lost contact. The intensity of their desire for self-affirmation ('crions', 'marquons', 'proclamons') is sadly out of proportion with the meagre results of their efforts. It is worth dwelling here on Bancquart's enigmatic and uneasy reference to photographs. If the *nous* are fascinated by photographic images and keen to imprint upon them the marks of their presence, this is because of the peculiar, haunting status of photographs as documents which stand in a complex relation to time and which bear witness, with the click of a button, to the fundamentals of the human condition. We take photographs in order to firm up our sense of existence. They mark our significance as we fill their frames with our activities and our presence; they mark our insignificance as the moment of their taking is always already past. They chime with Bancquart's persistent awareness of time, provisionality and the weight of the present moment. They also reactivate the idea expressed earlier in this poem that our sense of being is reinforced through 'pasting' our language on to the void: in the same way, we paste photographs into albums to shore up and verify self-knowledge. Photographs stud our route like (retrospective) milestones, illuminating and conferring sense upon our past lives – illusory markers of orientation which console briefly as we walk forward in the void.

A final bid for recognition comes with a call to memory as the *nous* list some of the distinctive traits by which they were known. Three features of this proclamation strike us: first, the use of the imperfect tense which suggests that these individuals have long been exiled from those they seek to contact; second, the peculiarly negative strategy of defining the self by enumerating dislikes; third, the idiosyncratic nature of the items listed: flies; coarse and broken hemp ready for spinning; sawdust; splintered pine cones. Apart from an implied preference for wholeness emerging from the last three elements, and perhaps an intolerance for imperfection, it is difficult to interpret this list. What is clear, however, is the futility of these clamouring voices, as yet incapable of embracing the reality of their condition.

The poem's concluding section, again composed of three distinct parts, slips away from these urgent cries for recognition. The poet abruptly turns our attention to an image of other lives simultaneously running their course: somewhere, oblivious to our existential plight, dormice are quietly scurrying over stones. The human drama is once again put into context, our small and transitory nature accepted, as the poem moves on with another inclusive pronoun: 'On se tait enfin'. Silence reigns. And in that silence emerges, as the final stanza tells us, the naked essence of love. This pure abstraction is fleetingly embodied in the image of a powerfully beautiful naked body which surfaces in the penultimate line, evoking love's beauty and vulnerability. Its awesomely uplifting grace is an ultimate counterweight to the bleakness that momentarily holds sway in the poem's second section. Love is affirmed with a quiet joy. If language and even poetry itself are earlier called into question as potentially vain, love is not, and the signs of it are everywhere in the natural world, even in humble pared-down tree stumps, for it is in the unremarkable wonder of the everyday that love is housed. This is Bancquart's culminating affirmation.

'Essentiel', then, provides an essential taste of what poetry in the best cases can do: halt us in our tracks, sharpen the quality of our attentiveness to things and words, and lead us to take, from time to time, our most fundamental bearings. Poised between celebration of the simple and perturbation at the troubling enigma of our existence, this poem is, like all Bancquart's communications, a 'Faire-part des difficultés'.[8]

Notes

1 Marie-Claire Bancquart, *Opportunité des oiseaux* (Paris: Pierre Belfond, 1986).
2 Michael Bishop, *Contemporary French Women Poets*, vol. I: *From Chedid and Dohollau to Tellermann and Bancquart* (Amsterdam: Rodopi, 1995), p. 136.
3 'Choses', in *Opportunité des oiseaux*, pp. 19–20 (p. 19).
4 'Paroles du monde', *ibid.*, p. 35.
5 'Énigme', *ibid.*, pp. 39–40 (p. 39).
6 'Tentée', *ibid.*, p. 50.
7 Marie-Claire Bancquart (ed.), *André Frénaud, la négation exigeante* (Cérisy-la-Salle: Actes du Colloque de Cérisy, 2000).
8 From the cover of Bancquart's prizewinning *Mémoire d'abolie* (Paris: Belfond, 1978).

Further reading

Bancquart, Marie-Claire, *Enigma Variations*, trans. Peter Broome (Halifax, NS: VVV Editions, 2004).
Broome, Peter, *In the Flesh of the Text: The Poetry of Marie-Claire Bancquart* (Amsterdam: Rodopi, 2008).

Nguyên Hoàng Bao Viêt, 'Anne Frank'

THANH-VÂN TON-THAT

Anne Frank

Tenant par le bras l'âme de la défunte
Victime d'une mort douloureuse et injuste
Inlassablement je chemine, silencieux.
Jamais je ne me suis senti si solitaire
Trois générations de vies humaines   5
Par troupes incessantes, sont noyées sans pitié
Dans une mer de sang !
Aucune étoile dans la voûte céleste
N'est donc plus minuscule que moi.

Ainsi, je vais en quête de l'Amour humain   10
Non encore manifesté
Sur les lèvres, par le sourire, dans les regards.
L'humanité
N'imaginez pas que ce soit une chaumière délabrée
Et abandonnée   15
Là, je n'aimerais pas me précipiter, pour y trouver refuge.
L'humanité
Regardez comme elle est dessinée !
Par la voûte dorsale de la Terre embrasée de feu
Par Varsovie écrasée et détruite   20
Ces wagons bondés de déportés
Ce portrait d'Hitler
Six millions de Juifs et compagnons de route disparus
Ayant succombé aux travaux forcés
Dévêtus, asphyxiés ou assassinés.   25
La peste du siècle
La candeur des enfants innocents
La médaille militaire. L'oraison funèbre
L'ultimatum irrévocable
La Croix-Rouge plantée sur le canon   30

La famine en quarante-cinq
L'enfer de feu, Hiroshima.
J'ose le dire sans réserve
L'humanité a besoin d'être protégée
Comme la bien-aimée   35
Autant en pleine lumière que dans l'obscurité profonde
Mes compagnons, mes amis, ont péri
Avant même de dépasser leurs vingt ans.

À chacun, soucieux du destin de la future génération
Le séjour des morts est prévu   40
Comme l'autobus, à son terminus.
Pourquoi le corps encourt-il, toute sa vie, des supplices ?
La conscience en proie à des tourments et remords
À chaque rappel des camps d'Auschwitz et de Bergen-Belsen ?
Parmi les derniers beaux jours, les derniers mois bienheureux   45
Qu'avec tendresse, je me suis attaché à retenir
De tous mes efforts
Comme une fillette, plongée dans son sommeil profond
Persistait à étreindre, avec soin, sa poupée

Il est impossible de douter de la présence d'Anne Frank.   50

From *L'Empreinte du Phénix*

Nguyên Hoàng Bao Viêt presents himself as a universal poet endowed with a mission ('je me suis attaché à retenir / De tous mes efforts'), using a tone which is lyrical but overshadowed by history, and particularly that of the twentieth century. He addresses his readers directly, calling on them as spectators and witnesses of their century, as well as confidants of the writer expressing himself as a lyrical 'I' but opening up the perspective of a new fraternity ('Mes compagnons', 'mes amis') which overflows into political and religious concerns, traversing national and temporal boundaries. Speaking in the present tense of a past which remains painfully alive in people's memories, he denounces war in all its forms ('J'ose le dire sans réserve') as it represents evil transformed into hell on earth. He resuscitates a fragile and poignant figure, a veritable tutelary saint of literature: that of Anne Frank (1929–45), without any sentimental personification but rather resorting to a poetic diction of invocation and incantation. This is not merely a personal homage to one specific person, even if she is known everywhere. The tragic destiny of this young girl and her family who lived in hiding in Amsterdam before being arrested and deported is circumscribed by historical circumstances and the conditions of a private life that we have all discovered on reading *The Diary of Anne Frank*, published after her death by her father (1947), who alone survived.

This phoenix of a poem[1] carries on from where the diary left off, amplifying and universalising its written record. The innocence and purity incarnated by the young girl are reborn from the ashes of wars (the plural is important), in spite of her trial by iron and fire, like Joan of Arc burned at the stake. Indeed the poet constructs around her a network of historical images, and knits unexpected connections between periods and worlds which initially seem disconnected. These places and characters, the executioner (Hitler) and his victim (Anne Frank, whom the poet rejuvenates and whose childish innocence he underlines by calling her a 'fillette' (little girl), along with the symbol of the doll which reflects the image of a torn and reified human nature, a suffering body, a corpse in waiting) intersect, miraculously borne by a fragile speech act surviving both wars and death, with this paradox of a contemporary Vietnamese poet evoking a young girl lost more than sixty years ago in a European concentration camp. The poem reads as a saga of violence and horror, a historical trajectory (the Second World War to the Vietnam War), and a geographical one between Europe (Hitler's Germany, Poland murdered during the insurrection of the Warsaw ghetto in 1943 and the setting up of the extermination camps) and Asia (Japan represented by the sacrificial city of Hiroshima, Vietnam incorporated into the poet's words and the lost voices of his companions). The text moves beyond good and evil, since yesterday's victors, liberators of the prisoners of European concentration camps are today's executioners, guilty of atrocities in Asia. We know how this parallel applies to the French heroes of the Resistance and Liberation who went to Indochina to fight another war. The poet is more discreet and modest when he evokes a tragedy that affects him more intimately. For the Vietnam War is present only in an implicit, allusive fashion, and we are not even told whether it concerns the war with France or with the United States or both, for no place name (Haïphong, Hanoï, Saïgon) and no date (1946, 1954, 1975) appears, unlike those relating to other countries.

The poet and the dead girl at first form an unlikely couple, an Orpheus and Eurydice for modern times. Anne Frank is at once the 'bien-aimée', the companion, a sister in exile, suffering, and a child in need of protection. The poet 'silencieux', 'solitaire', 'Tenant par le bras l'âme de la défunte / Victime d'une mort douloureuse et injuste', 'chemine' (wanders) – as did Victor Hugo seeking his dead daughter at the start of 'Demain dès l'aube' – 'en quête'. In search of the mystery of this earth turned to hell, it evokes from line to line the spasms of the tortuous, tortured twentieth century. In this song of the 'mal-aimé'[2] spurned by country, friends, family and love itself, echoing the 'bien-aimée', the exiled poet is torn from his past and his native land. But his Odyssey is long over and no Penelope is waiting for him. At the end of his desert crossing, the only homeland that awaits him is that of the poetry of language and the dead.

Landscapes, instead of recording the historical and geographical reality of war, take on symbolic and cosmic dimensions ('mer', 'étoile', 'voûte céleste'). We feel an almost Pascalian disproportion between the 'minuscule' poet, depicted wandering in search of an Infinite which is not that of Divine love but that of a non-transcendental 'Amour humain' among the great family composed by humanity. This discovery is experienced in terms of a painful revelation, when the moment of poetic enlightenment spills over into the horrifying image of the end of the world and a universal cataclysm ('la terre embrasée de feu'). Our planet seems naïvely 'dessinée' and offered up for the contemplation of the reader-spectator, but this is no innocent drawing à la Saint-Exupéry, for it is ravaged and almost abandoned. Does the visionary poet lead us to imagine, without wishing to describe them in detail, the rased cities, the lunar landscapes ravaged by the atom bomb, the land-mined paddy fields, the napalm-scorched forests? One war may hide another, and speaking even of a war with no name will raise the shadowy ghosts of all other wars.

The only date mentioned is 1945, paradoxically presented not as the year of victory but as the year of famine. The 'Trois générations de vies humaines' drowned in a 'mer de sang' may well allude to the generations of Vietnamese stricken by a succession of wars, lasting for nearly thirty years from 1946 to 1975. Might we note the similarity with the thirty years which separate the two World Wars (1914–45) or is this mere coincidence? The 'mer de sang' is also a hyperbolic and metaphorical way of representing the ravages of global wars, with the Pacific bleeding from battles between the United States and Japan and the oceans criss-crossed by 'boat-people' after the end of the Vietnam War in 1975. The poet's allegorical reverie continues with the impossible vision of the 'chaumière délabrée et abandonnée', a symbol of the hearth and home deserted and destroyed, the ruins of an Ithaca impossible to find, impossible to reconstruct. The disappearance of the original homeland is a nightmare rather than a fairytale. It is the vanquished and the innocent who are massacred. The shadows of famine and deportation roam, all flee on the road towards nowhere. And yet strangely, humanity is metonymically associated with real places, before being personified at the end of the poem. The poem plunges into the reality of war, using commonplace references seemingly taken from contemporary newsreels ('Juifs . . . dévêtus et asphyxiés', 'La Croix-Rouge plantée sur le canon') or from a history textbook with its real people and place names (Auschwitz, Bergen-Belsen, Warsaw, Hiroshima).

Hypotyposis looms, as we approach the spectacle of history having become literally monstrous, accumulating hyperbolic and unbearable dimensions. To show is to condemn. There can be only connivance with the reader, who can but acknowledge, who can but empathise. Despite all the distances and differences in political context and circumstance, the poet takes the risk of bringing together on the same stage these episodes which share the extermination of human life and a collapse into inhumanity; he commingles images whose horror is resumed by a few names with their evocative and macabre resonance (Hitler, Auschwitz, Hiroshima), just as he uses the name of Anne Frank as a symbol. He selects 'Varsovie écrasée et détruite', personifying it as an emblem of a human, rebel, martyred city. He lists images of deportation ('Ces wagons bondés', 'Six millions de Juifs' delivered up as a sacrifice to the modern Moloch, whose effigy is displayed: 'Ce portrait d'Hitler') which are also clichés of history in both senses of the term – both snapshots and commonplaces. The verbless, laconic phrases which form the rest of the enumeration establish a terrible legacy, mingling horror with biblical resonance ('peste', 'famine', 'L'enfer de feu') and the simplicity of abstract plainsong with specific determinants: the pleonastic 'La candeur des enfants innocents' contrasting with the 'médaille militaire. L'oraison funèbre').

The spatial allegory, those places of memory, give way to the personification of humanity suffering in its universal dimension, compared to the 'bien-aimée' of the start of the poem, which confers a cyclical aspect to the poem. The end moreover is more peaceful in the relative euphoria of renewed hope with the expression 'beaux jours' and 'mois bienheureux'. Femininity (the character of the young girl who recalls the sacrificial figures of Antigone, Cassandra, Electra, or the city of Warsaw as allegories of humanity) is figured here on the side of peace and suffering with the creation of this new myth. Light and darkness are metaphors for the phases of history, whose periods of happiness are blank pages, as Hegel once said. The last part of the poem is devoted to the poet's wartime Vietnamese memories which are evoked in abstract and general terms, as if silence and discretion were more effective than wailing and mourning. It renders a surreptitious homage to comrades lost too young ('compagnons', 'amis', 'avant . . . vingt ans') who share with Anne Frank their loss of life and innocence at the moment of maturity. We detect a certain resignation ('Le séjour des morts est prévu') faced with the outcome of individual fates (is this a Buddhist view of existence?), but yet without nostalgia, for its intent is resolutely focused on the future of the survivors ('destin de la future génération') and the dead. Moreover, 'Le séjour des morts est prévu' is a formula which echoes a Vietnamese proverb: 'La vie est un séjour, la mort est un retour.'

Poetic language is performative, and the path of initiation followed by the poem leads us to a luminous conclusion: 'Il est impossible de douter de la présence d'Anne Frank.' Suffering is expressed as understatement, without exaggeration or pathos. In an inversion of values, death becomes seen as rest and sleep, whereas life on earth becomes hell ('supplices', 'tourments', 'remords'). The names of the 'camps d'Auschwitz et de Bergen-Belsen' weave an onomastic tissue with the other sites of the tragedy of our history (Warsaw, Hiroshima), in a written text which confronts and superimposes realities apparently distant in space and time. Thus it invites the reader to share in this suffering, to identify with the speaker in a movement of salutary and cathartic empathy.

This poem is rooted in simplicity and sobriety; it is both realistic and allegorical. It projects the images and the phantoms of our modern history, as both tragic and banal, in a poetic vision of the world, which is not content merely to denounce, but which tears from the depths of the void a final beauty. The poet struggles with forgetfulness but intends to overcome this 'douleur' by reviving it in words, rather as Marguerite Duras tried to exorcise hers in her book *La Douleur* (1985). The low-key comparison with the bus station is unexpected and recalls metaphors of travel (reminding us of the terrible trains of deportation) while modernising them. The poet tries to grasp some moments of pure time, as in childhood; he identifies with a frightened little girl, he invokes the name of Anne Frank in order to awaken our awareness and conscience in that state of half-sleep, half-wakening where we try to banish the repetitive nightmares of the past; for even among us today, 'life is a dream'.

Translated by Peter Collier

Notes

1 This poem was originally written in 1959 in Vietnamese. It was subsequently revised by the poet and translated into French by Hoàng Nguyên in 1980, and it is this version that is analysed here. This French version of the poem has recently been published in *L'Empreinte du Phénix, Poèmes*, trans. Hoàng Nguyên (Paris: Éditions Ban Van, 2008).
2 A reference to Guillaume Apollinaire's 'La Chanson du mal-aimé', in *Alcools* (1913).

28 | Claude Esteban, 'Ils sont riches, mon père / et ma mère'

ROBERT W. GREENE

Ils sont riches, mon père
et ma mère

ils n'ont pas voulu que je descende
comme une mendiante

ils ont mis sur ma poitrine beaucoup   5
d'or, un homme a dit

je peindrai son image
sur le bois le plus précieux, choisissez-vous

le cèdre ou le sycamore, puis je passerai
deux couches de cinabre   10

au-dessus de ses paupières, elle sera
belle pour les dieux longtemps

c'était mon père et ma mère, ils pleuraient
comme des pauvres, ils

n'écoutaient plus.   15

From *Fayoum*

for Claude Esteban (1935–2006) *In memoriam*

The elegiac reach

Possible initial impressions of slightness notwithstanding, Claude Esteban's brief, untitled poem, 'Ils sont riches, mon père / et ma mère', first published in his chapbook *Fayoum*,[1] fairly throbs with muted, plangent power, as subsequent readings of the text, I believe, attest. In what follows, I shall examine the poem's sombre radiance from several directions. I shall begin with a word about Esteban's corpus before 1999, as a way to situate 'Ils sont riches' within the poet's practice. That discussion will lead to a consideration of the themes of loss, grief and mourning in Esteban's poetry, and of the elegiac strain that appears

253

to have darkened and redirected it since the late 1980s. I shall then attempt to show how the text in question functions as a poem, and how its prosody, rhetorical figures and diction collaborate to create its overall effect of (what one might call) stalwart melancholy.

Alert as he is to the philosophical and ideological cross-currents of the age, Esteban never assumes that his task as a poet will be an easy one. As his 1985 collection *Le Nom et la demeure* makes clear, he is as aware as Francis Ponge of the problematic relationship of words and things, of poetry and the world (see, e.g., Ponge's *Nouveau Recueil*),[2] and is as conscious as Samuel Beckett of the artist's 'obligation to express' in spite of the absurdity of any endeavour along those lines (see Cronin).[3] Also, like many French poets since Rimbaud's time, Esteban seems equally at home in verse and prose, and as ready as any of his contemporaries to let theoretical concerns inform his practice, whether in verse or prose.

A brief untitled text from 'Espèces de romances', a sequence of poems in verse from the section of *Le Nom et la demeure* called 'Paroles d'eau, paroles d'air', typifies Esteban's art. What one can and cannot do with words never seems far from the poet's concerns. What are the limits of verse, he seems to be asking. That he poses such a question in a song, a love song at that, a 'romance', scarcely diminishes the seriousness of his query. Nor should the poem's plain language and simple structure be read as merely the conventional features of a song. For, rather than treating a standard theme of the lyric (e.g. lost love), his text foregrounds the challenge facing poets who would meet each new dawn with the right words for articulating that ineffable encounter:

> Rien encore
> dans le jour.
>
> Même aurore
> que toujours.
>
> Nulle fête
> pour les yeux.
>
> Dans la tête
> les mots vieux.
>
> Tout reprendre
> seul à seul.
>
> Rien ou dire
> le jour tel. (p. 171)

In twelve three-syllable lines, rich or sufficient rhyme locks the first eight lines into place, while near or consonantal rhyme performs that function in the last four. Also, the poet adheres strictly to the law, in French verse, of alternating feminine and masculine end rhymes. Moreover, if the twelve three-syllable lines are compressed, with terminal mute e's held mute, that sturdiest of all rhythms in French verse, the alexandrine, sets the pace for the three new lines so formed. Finally, the first word of the first stanza ('Rien') is repeated as the first word of the last stanza, a reprise or recursion that demarcates the poem as a poem. As regards some of the most basic conventions of French prosody, the poem thus conforms to tradition. Esteban quickly turns tradition upside down, however, by informing 'Rien encore' with themes that are bare of sentiment, and that are more at home in other kinds of texts: themes of nothingness, sameness, uselessness, the necessity of always starting again, aloneness. Esteban enriches his romance by asking the following questions: Can utterance carry meaning? Is even the most gifted poet struck dumb by the experience of dawn? Must nothingness – that is, the ultimate failure of expression – always prevail? Or can that supreme instance of both dawn's glory and the poet's will to capture it, Rimbaud's 'Aube', inevitably recalled here, inspire the poet to keep chasing 'le jour tel' in spite of everything?

Now comes the turn towards darkness in Esteban's poetry. About a year after *Le Nom et la demeure* was published in 1985, on 19 September 1986 to be exact, the poet's wife, the painter Denise Esteban, died from the injuries she suffered in an accident while cycling near the house they shared on the Île d'Yeu, offshore from Nantes. The death of his life partner devastated the poet and had a profound effect on his poetry.

Elégie de la mort violente (1989) comprises the poet's first formal responses, in verse and prose, in French and fragmentarily in Spanish, to this horrific, pivotal event in his life. A haiku-like verse fragment in 'Images peintes', the second section of *Élégie de la mort violente*, evokes the paintings that Denise Esteban will never execute:

Dans cette main
que tu n'as plus, le pinceau
neuf, la courbe du soleil
intacte. (p. 61)

The artist's most essential capacity, that of resuming work, has been lost. Henceforth brush and shape will remain untouched, untried, with the very possibility of creation denied.

Esteban's next major collection of poetry, *Morceaux de ciel, presque rien*, appeared in 2001. It consists of five verse sequences, all written since *Élégie de la mort violente*, including a series of twenty-seven texts entitled *Fayoum*, a chapbook first published in 1999 (*Morceaux de ciel*, pp. 133–61). In *Fayoum*, more overtly than in the other parts of *Morceaux*, yet with utter tact, the poet reprises the lamentation he had begun a decade earlier. Now, however, Esteban has, in a sense, fused his wife's painterly art with his own craft as a poet. To see that fusion, one must know what a Fayoum is.

El Fayoum is a region of Egypt located in the Nile river valley about 130 kilometres south of Cairo. The place name has also become an art historical term, designating the funeral portraits that were unearthed by Western archaeologists at this site, as well as elsewhere in Egypt, in the late nineteenth century. The Fayoum portraits, numbering in the hundreds, thus constituting the largest ensemble of paintings surviving from classical antiquity, are found today in major museums around the world. Supposition has it that they were executed by Greek or Greek-trained artists living in Egypt in the period extending from the first to the fourth century CE.

Although we cannot be certain about the conditions under which the Fayoum artists laboured, at least one scholar, Jean-Christophe Bailly, believes that the subjects of the portraits sat as models for the painters; hence that we are looking not at death masks but at pictures of living human beings. Be that as it may, male or female, young or old, Levantine or Nubian in aspect, all are finely attired, bespeaking the wealth of the families able to engage the services of a painter-for-death. The frank gaze emanating from the portraits, the startlingly intense, individuated faces, and our awareness that the works were meant to be seen only by the gods, never by us, support the theory that the subjects were alive when painted, even if in some sense they must have been getting ready for death when they sat for their portraits. The title alone of Bailly's study of the Fayoum portraits underscores their haunting presence, and their power to address us as if from beyond the grave: *L'Apostrophe muette*.[4]

That Esteban has distilled his (and our) mourning to its essence in *Fayoum* is palpable throughout the chapbook, but especially in 'Ils sont riches, mon père / et ma mère.' The poet's grief, turned now into a searing but subtle mini-drama, becomes the fate of all who have outlived loved ones.

The first voice we hear is that of the dead daughter, the miraculously eloquent subject of the Fayoum portrait. She tells us that her father and mother are rich and that they did not want her buried like a beggar. The second speaker, the painter, in offering the parents his sales pitch, describes how he will make their daughter 'belle pour les dieux longtemps'. Then we hear the daughter again. No longer are we in the present, the future or the compound past, but in the imperfect, in the remote time of story and fairy tale ('il était une fois'), and thrice over in scarcely three lines.

As it must eventually do – and the sequence of tenses in the poem shows us this – the ever receding past prevails over the present and the future. The voracious maw of the gone, devourer of all links to the now and the next, causes the living and the dead to drift apart, which may be the ultimate sorrow of death. The inexorable fading of grief, the gradual transformation of the agony caused by the death of a loved one into something quieter, no doubt causes us the most intense anguish.

The poems in *Fayoum*, we appreciate early on, belong to the broad category of elegy, which teaches us, among other things, that we can endure the pain of loss if we suffer, as does Roquentin at the conclusion of Sartre's *La Nausée*, 'en mesure, sans complaisance . . . avec une aride pureté'. [5]As unexpected as the Sartre–Esteban connection may appear, Roquentin's illumination, as formulated by Sartre, seems particularly apt as a description of what Esteban achieved when he transformed his suffering into art in his Fayoum poems. Sartre's protagonist attains his illumination, we recall, after losing both his mistress and his vocation as a historian, while listening to a recording of 'Some of These Days', with its haunting blues melody, for the hundredth time.

In just such a way, Esteban achieves his elegiac effects by means of repetition and insight. The references to wealth and poverty that frame 'Ils sont riches, mon père / et ma mère' occur at its outset and just before its end. We observe, however, that the opposition of wealth and poverty means nothing here, since everyone stands equal before the law of laws. All parents, rich and poor alike, mourn the death of a beloved daughter.

Esteban appears at his most controlled in the structure that he has given his poem. Its fifteen lines (or line fragments) fall into three parts, with part 1 consisting of three two-line stanzas, part 2 likewise, and part 3 one two-line stanza followed by a single line. The resulting segmentation, symmetrical and deliberate, is thus 6, 6, 3. And inasmuch as free verse characterises the poem's rhythm, its patterning must spring from sources other than the regular recurrence of an identical syllable count.

As already intimated, speaker and verb tense collaborate to divide the poem. The voice of the daughter and the present tense ('Ils sont') shape part 1, the voice of the artist and the future ('je peindrai') part 2, the voice of the daughter again and the imperfect ('c'étaient') part 3. A further mark of the poem's tripartite structure: yellow ('beaucoup / d'or') dominates part 1, red ('deux couches de cinabre') part 2, while no colour is associated with part 3.

What strikes readers of Esteban's text most vividly, however, is not the divisions that set off its constituent parts, but rather its indivisible wholeness. And in the end the poem's oneness trumps its dividedness.

The unity of Esteban's text derives from the dazzling deployment of enjambement within it. The device is used unobtrusively in the poem's first stanza, where the coordinating conjunction 'et' at the beginning of the second line ties it securely to the first. Something comparable might be said about the second stanza, where 'comme une mendiante' seems such a natural analogical completion of the previous line's thought that we hardly think of the phrase as a *rejet*. Also, the end rhyme 'descende' / 'mendiante' distracts us from the enjambement.

The third stanza differs from the first two by its more blatant use of enjambement. We notice immediately that the words 'beaucoup' and 'd'or' appear on successive lines rather than following each other on the same line, as we would expect to encounter them in traditional verse. We also observe, of course, that by isolating 'd'or' in the *rejet*, the poet has thrown into relief the value and brilliance of the material that has been placed on the breast of the laid-out figure.

The third stanza's second, even more daring enjambement ties it directly to the next stanza (ll. 6–7), hence to the poem's second part. I am alluding to the stanza's last words, 'un homme a dit', which introduce the painter and his patter, the poem's second voice.

Before concluding our survey of the formal aspects of the poem's first part, we should note that its three stanzas constitute three separate and distinct statements: 'Ils sont riches'; 'ils n'ont pas voulu'; 'ils ont mis'. The statements follow one another paratactically, without explicit connectors to link them, beyond the fact that 'ils' always refers to the speaker's parents. By contrast, as we shall now see, the poem's second part moves smoothly from its beginning to its end, thanks primarily to its bold enjambements.

Indeed, enjambement rules the poem's second part, both within the stanzas and among them. In a flash, the Fayoum painter's entire arsenal is conjured up. And with three futures ('je peindrai', 'je passerai', 'elle sera'), plus an ambiguous locution, either a command or a question ('choisissez-vous'), the painter utters his promises casually but swiftly. Each line runs on into the next and each stanza flows into the one following it. It is as if the painter is delivering his speech in a single breath, to keep the parents from pondering their decision. Enjambement makes this effect possible.

When we reach part 3 of the poem, we see that Father and Mother have been relegated to the past, weeping, no longer even listening. We hear Daughter's voice again, but we know that it comes to us from a time irretrievably lost. Enjambement still rules, binding together lines 13 and 14, then lines 14 and 15, but a gap has opened up in the text. What in the text gives us a sense that it breaks or turns at this point?

If we rethink the painter's promise, we realise how modest it was. He assured the parents that he would make their daughter beautiful for the gods for a long time, not forever. The poet's diction at this critical juncture (in final position within the text's second part), his choosing 'longtemps' over 'toujours', adds immeasurably to the poignancy of the parents' grief. Their precious daughter has been taken from them forever and they are proffered extended but not permanent beauty as recompense, a shabby bargain in any culture, including that of late ancient Egypt. The word 'longtemps' marks the place in the poem, the gap, where reality intrudes to reassert its dominion over the parents' hearts, where the soothing *legato* created by the enjambements is interrupted. The devices of art may ease or gloss over human suffering, but only for a while.

Inspired by Egyptian funeral portraiture practised in late antiquity, Esteban, a French poet of the late twentieth century, adapted Fayoum art for lyric poetry so as to convey his grief a dozen years after the death of his beloved wife Denise, a distinguished painter. As a form, the Fayoum gave the poet what he now needed to memorialise and share with others his fully absorbed suffering: a way to write (of) his suffering 'en mesure, sans complaisance . . . avec une aride pureté'.[6] Maybe finally, if only temporarily, through his work, he could repel the forgetfulness that threatened his widower's desire to recall everything about his deceased life partner, most of all her genius for creating durable yet finite beauty, hence her kinship with the Fayoum painters. Maybe finally Esteban could perform a ceremony of anamnesis through his writing.

What comfort can art, a painter's or a poet's, offer us for the loss of a loved one? Esteban's poem seems to suggest that, at least for the duration of our experience of them, certain works of art can carry us across our bereavement to a momentary respite or reprieve. In its total integration of form and feeling, of craft and pain, in its extraordinary elegiac reach, Esteban's 'Ils sont riches, mon père / et ma mère' may be such a work of art.

Notes

1 *Fayoum* (Tours: Farrago, 1999). Other volumes of poetry by Esteban quoted in this chapter are *Élégie de la mort violente* (Paris: Flammarion, 1989); *L'Immédiat et l'inaccessible* (Paris: Galilée, 1978); *Morceaux de ciel, presque rien* (Paris: Gallimard, 2001); *Le Nom et la demeure* (Paris: Flammarion, 1985).
2 Francis Ponge, *Nouveau Recueil* (Paris: Gallimard, 1967).
3 Anthony Cronin, *Samuel Beckett: The Last Modernist* (New York: HarperCollins, 1996), p. 398.
4 Jean-Christophe Bailly, *L'Apostrophe muette: essai sur les portraits du Fayoum* (Paris: Éditions Hazan, 1997).
5 Jean-Paul Sartre, *La Nausée* (Paris: Gallimard, 1938), p. 245.
6 *Ibid.*

Further reading

Esteban, Claude, *Transparent God*, trans. David Cloutier (San Francisco: Kosmos, 1982).
  Conjuncture of Body and Garden: Cosmogony, trans. James Phillips (San Francisco: Kosmos, 1988).
Vilar, Pierre (ed.), *L'Espace, l'inachevé*, Cahier Claude Esteban (Paris: Léo Scheer, 2003).

29 Gérard Titus-Carmel, 'Or battant . . .'

MICHAEL BISHOP

Or battant en brèche les promesses de l'aube comme mourir nous sied
Nous abandonnons les mots au fort courant que la bouche entraîne
Et délivrant ces fleurs de première brassée avouant au dernier pétale
Je n'ai fait que passer j'ai ridé l'eau de ma nage sans mesurer
Mes efforts j'ai inscrit bord pour bord ma traversée dans cet instant   5
Du monde qui ravive sur ma joue la blessure dormante jamais fermée
D'un ancien affront ah quand cesserons-nous donc de prétendre
Que parcourir cette distance émeut le corps que la rive est à portée
De lèvres et que c'est à ce prix seul que s'ouvre en nous le jardin car
L'immobilité a plombé nos membres à jamais nous singeons le squale 10
Géant mais les flots se sont usés sous nos ventres et nous découvrent
Vains & amers raclant les grands fonds l'utopie fidèle au cœur
Et la mort en balance qui leste tous nos rêves de sa large ombre plate
& souriante dans le miroir irrédimée & souriante toujours recommencée

From *Seul tenant*

The poem with which we compactly and intensely engage here is the seventh
of twenty-four numbered sonnets in roman font which, interlaced with twelve
other italicised sonnets forming an equally numbered sub-suite titled *Recitativo
obbligato*, and twelve other rather more aerated and parenthesised seven-line
poems, constitute the central eponymous *volet* of the tripartite *retable* (altarpiece) that is Gérard Titus-Carmel's 2006 collection *Seul tenant*.[1] This, initially
and minimally, situates 'Or battant. . .', but also implicitly reminds us that,
beyond the immediate context of the sonnet's embedding in the structural
and mathematico-rhythmic intricacies of its own forty-eight-unit panel, and
the latter's pivotal positioning between the opening forty-eight-poem panel
titled '*Je ne serai pas confondu pour toujours*. . .' and the third and closing panel,
'*Je suis ici où j'ai posé mon ombre* ' (equally composed of forty-eight poems with
their strophic, metric and other harmonies), there lie contexts inevitably vaster
and more complex. These contexts resonate to a greater or lesser extent with
the formal, emotional and ontological features of, arguably, every word in the
sonnet at hand: the twenty or so other collections of poetry Titus-Carmel has
published since the 1987 *La Tombée*, down to *Ici rien n'est présent* (2003), *Manière*

de sombre (2004), *Jungle (non-lieu)* (2005) and, of course, *Seul tenant*; a similar
number of books such as *Notes d'atelier* (1990) and *Épars* (2003) and others
offering studies and meditations on Picasso, Chardin, Bonnard or Goya, Roud,
Reverdy, Vargaftig or Bonnefoy; the serenely swarming universe of a plastic
production that has made him one of the greatest artists of his time, honoured
by Jacques Derrida, Alain Robbe-Grillet, Denis Roche, Yves Bonnefoy, Patrick
Casson, Alfred Pacquement, Marie-Claire Bancquart and countless others; and,
last but by no means least, the numerous collaborations and accompaniments
Titus-Carmel has engaged in to celebrate and acknowledge the work of, for
example, Jacques Dupin, Pascal Quignard, Philippe Jaccottet or Jean Frémon.
It is, of course, beyond present feasibilities to interweave into the close reading
of 'Or battant. . .' all of the threads of such an exquisitely delicate and ever
consciously created tapestry which the above represents. But it is good to bear
in mind such rich implicitness and to understand the breadth and depth of the
teeming interpenetrations and interpertinences we often can only allude to in
the analysis that now follows.

The first three lines of 'Or battant. . .' offer a characteristic opening, uncon-
textualised, plunging us into some ongoing meditative logic doubly suspended
via line 1's present participle floating in the pure nowness of time and argument and the parenthesis of the somewhat disquieting subordinate clause
('comme mourir nous sied'). Already in this first line we sense the metaphoric
and structural density of Titus-Carmel's consciousness, clear and firm though
its syntactic articulation may be said to be: the absence of punctuation with
its at once liberating and compacting effect, the enjambement that pulls
us on, the feeling, as the eye catches an anticipatory glimpse of the unified
mass of language to come, of being drawn into a vast complex of signs and
signification – these are factors that, without diminishing our liminal sense of
expressive elegance and mental lucidness, prepare us for the long and quasi-
classical unfolding of the signifiers and signifieds to come. The second line,
self-reflexively meditating on the poem's own emerging process, is one of liberation (unrhymed, metrically shifting verse) and relative constraint (length of
sonnet, free but roughly constant syllabic count: 19-16-19-18-17-21-15, etc.).
It evokes the poem's natural, instinctual flow; compulsive, seemingly in affinity rather with the Reverdyan principle of (broadly aesthetic and not simply
metaphorical) *justesse* than with Breton's tipping of the scales in favour of the
'convulsive' and the phantasmagorical. Titus-Carmel's work, whether plastic or
poetic, always remains both aesthetically and ethically alert. As such, its lyricism constantly clips its own wings. Its melancholia, its capacity for plainly
affirming its 'presence to the world' is oddly fragilised by a sense of the unfin-
ishableness of saying and doing, which, in consequence, are condemned to
iteration, renewal, seriality, and the (dis)accomplishment of creative fatigue.
Titus-Carmel's cutting into the sheer givenness of artistic gesture, the collag-
ing, and at times veiling over and quasi-burial of its fragments – this, as well

as the dogged and exhausting (though deeply aesthetically and ontologically exploratory) nature of his very often long-term and serial creations, testifies to such tensions at the heart of his *poiein* (act of making). The third line of what we may think of as the sonnet's overture, its opening up of itself to what it is becoming, kickstarts the long single sentence that the poem slowly and intricately unravels, and which we may have thought to have stalled – using that wonderful conjunction *et*, which Michel Deguy has shown to be central to Claudel's verse, and of course poetic rhythm in general, with its additive, cumulative, pulsing and (com)pulsional measure and flow. Once more, the present participles breed suspension of time, action, completion: the *souffle*, the poetic *enthousiasmos*, are much ampler; consciousness is large, broad in its embrace, just gathering pace, in fact, as it seeks its spontaneously disciplined deployment in the particular space of this poem.

The third line pushes us to determine to what degree 'ces fleurs de première brassée' may be deemed purely descriptive or more essentialised, pure metaphors: is the poet alluding to the artist's contemporaneous flowers and other proliferating vegetal forms of, for example, *Feuillées* or *Jungles*, or is he constituting his poems-now ('ces') as Baudelairean creations conjured up from what will soon be understood to be the relative *mal* of existence (and even all doing therein) as a paltry even if exquisite *consolatio*? Certainly these flowers are not those of Victor Hugo's 'Demain, dès l'aube' or Marceline Desbordes-Valmore's 'Roses de Saadi', picked from the gardens of the earth to be offered to the other. But, if no direct representation is at stake, neither is figuration stable: in effect, all language is figure, as Deguy has argued, and, as figure, it is a gift – for it may remain an open offering – an *être-comme* (a being-like or being-as), as Deguy has termed it. Seen in this perspective, moreover, all saying becomes a saying-to-the-side, by-the-side, of the object of desire: a kind of unsaying, which explains why Titus-Carmel may regard, not unlike Bernard Noël or Jacques Dupin, poetic or plastic space as 'unspace', *non-lieu*. This, in turn, urges the artist–poet to repeat his gesture in the (soon to be avowed) vain hope of miraculously transmuting the art-being equation. In effect, lines 3–7 and beyond are written under an admittedly confessional sign ('avouant'); although if the poem inevitably remains the locus of a depiction of self's body (auto-bio-graphy), no simply determinable narrative emerges: all is anti-anecdotal, snatched away from sociological and even psychological context and explication, its precise articulacy oddly shrouded in that residual 'obscurity' and *pudeur* René Char and Pierre Reverdy respectively espouse. Certainly there are elements of affective intensification: the exclamation at the poem's core ('ah quand cesserons-nous'), the accumulation of fruitless and undesirable ontological strategies ('prétendre que. . .', 'que. . .', 'que. . .'), the final delyricised switch to the ampersands (&) from the repeated conjunction *et*, and, of course, the many enjambements that enable this poetic *souffle* breathlessly to reach that almost cathartic point of aesthetico-mathematical fulfilment which the finished (yet, in a sense, unfinished, as there is no definitive punctuational closure) mosaic implies – as with any sonnet. The use of the first-person plural *nous*, in conjunction with the *je*, may somewhat undermine any purely confessional, subjective tendency, but equally it tends to raise such private enunciation to the status of a vast and shareable philosopheme. In that sense the use of the *nous* becomes subtly persuasive, sophistical even in flashes ('c'est à ce prix seul que s'ouvre en nous le jardin'), yet we are largely inclined to see the *nous* as a synonym of the *je*, a metaphor perhaps for the infinite complexity of the self that, in effect, the poem mirrors.

To listen to Gérard Titus-Carmel declaim a poem by La Fontaine is to understand that the author of *Seul tenant* is a poet of mathematical, rhythmic, syntactic self-discipline. 'Or battant. . .' is, however, far from offering the only formal, modal blueprint embraceable: *Seul tenant* alone provides perfect oblong prose sonnets (the *Paysage de chutes* sequence: e.g. pp. 70, 71); an italicised three-line poem, unrhymed, metrically unstable (p. 24); many free verse poems, now italicised, now roman, of medium length (9, 10, 11 lines); the parenthesised seven-line poems of the book's central *volet*; the *Recitativo obbligato* suite of italicised sonnets, slightly more compact metrically than 'Or battant. . .'; and so on. Certainly Guillevic's *quanta* are not to be found in Titus-Carmel's modal arsenal, any more than Francis Ponge's prose poems with their poetics of *objeu* and *objoie*, or even Jacques Réda's fine experimentation with rigorously constrained *versets*. Titus-Carmel's admiration for Coleridge or Edward Young, for the work of the great Japanese haiku poets, or that of Bonnefoy or Dupin, Vargaftig or Jaccottet, reveals a large, open sensibility attuned to a wide diversity of manner and form. It also reveals an understanding that, if the latter may be deemed to have highly relative value, what in global terms we may call *forme* yet constitutes a significant *fond* for Titus-Carmel. For him it is an act and place of meaning, gathering, caressing, providing a framework where pure dispersal and entropy might otherwise threaten: all physical incarnation, whether of limb or wing or verse or drawn shape, is of the realm of a form that is critically, though half-invisibly, near-blindingly, embedded in meaning – it is the challenge of the physical thrown down to thought, the meta-physical. The endless formal niceties of 'Or battant. . .' offer, by way of example – merely, though intensely, centrally: all microcosms of being and doing (*poiein*), are absolute/relative synonyms for the macrocosm – the opportunity to realise the pure symbiosis of *forme* and *fond*, of expressive vessel and the potential, real but ever deferred, ever expandable thought contained therein.

And what thought, what intangibleness, what 'meta-physicalness' 'Or battant. . .' contains, turn out to be very considerable. The liminal discourse of destruction of dawning promise (l. 1), of a doing, a poetico-ontological *faire*, that undoes, is in many ways at the heart of Gérard Titus-Carmel's entire work, felt to be an oeuvre of Blanchotian *désœuvrement*. His beautifully executed early art reveals a fascination with the forms and meanings of breakage, deterioration and alteration and, as here, soon shows its affinity with the larger logic of death in works such as *The Pocket Size Tlingit Coffin*, so finely accompanied by Derrida's *Cartouches*, taken up in *La Vérité en peinture*, or the extensive *Nielles* series, or the remarkable suite of close to 200 paintings, inspired by Grünewald's Isenheim altarpiece, with its powerful crucifixion. From the outset, then, destruction, the deconstruction of illusion, is argued, felt – logic is emotional, not available to truly definitive rationality; hence the very problem with which the poet–artist wrestles – to be justified by, in sympathy with, the inherent structure of life lived as a dyingness. The transitory nature of our doing (l. 4) confirms, too, at once ironically but naturally, that dying 'suits us', accords with our very being. Yves Bonnefoy has sought to reconcile such tensions of absence and presence, tragicality and what lies beyond, both in his own work and with respect to Titus-Carmel's art and poetry, and the gesture has very recently been reciprocated in Titus-Carmel's *Un lieu de ce monde* (2008).

The second major discourse 'Or battant. . .' develops is centred upon the process of enunciation, saying, *poiein*, in the light of what precedes it. To write, it is initially stated (l. 2), would seem to be to allow speech its instinctual, visceral, pulsional flow. But, as I have suggested above, all of Titus-Carmel's work, from the tantalising *Joaquin's Love Affair* (1971) or the hyperconsciously constructed *Suite italienne* (1976) to the intricate orders of *Demeurant* or *Ici rien n'est présent*, is predicated on self-imposed discipline, on an exploration of the many forms of doing, which, far from gratuitousness or ludicity, seizes upon such exploration in order to meditate its relation to the self's being, its/his 'presence to the world', as Titus-Carmel has recently indicated in an interview with Jacques Darras. To 'abandon' the surging language of the self may thus be seen as a freeing (l. 3) of pent-up expressive, creative energy into the channels of the poet–artist's instinct-ive, but by now long-meditated sense of aesthetico-ontological order, rightness and correspondence with his deepest preoccupations. Unstintingly, and without a banal 'measuring' (l. 4) of *poiein*'s deployment – for, again, as Reverdy argued to Breton, poetico-artistic *justesse* involves not rational prescription, but spon-taneously, instantaneously judged mental activity – the inscription of the self's complex traversal of time and space now (l. 5) is at once discussed and enacted via the very discourse in the poem's unfolding. This said, the nowness of crea-tion, as of all doing and being, is equally the time of the poet's entire livedness: to discourse upon and write this poem now is, for Gérard Titus-Carmel, to enter the vast realm of memory, and with it, the question of both desired and undesired forgetting. Much of his work is deeply concerned with such matters, both psychologically (the death of the father, of the poet's young wife) and formally (the practice and logic of the original model, palimpsest-like covering and uncovering, seriality, self-exhausting creation, etc.). To speak here (l. 6) of an ever recurring sense of pain is thus to continue to turn the poem – as Titus-Carmel has turned his artwork – into a complex self-reflexive act of fused sharp, if discreet, or even fading memorialisation and impossible though half-sought

oblivion. Bloodiedness, crucifixion, burial, loss and excavation can thus prolif-
erate as obsessive *blasons*, and iterative modal and formal processes echo and
'practise' the discourse of consciousness.

At the very heart of the sonnet (ll. 7–9), these preoccupations plunge Titus-
Carmel into the central discourse of 'Or battant. . .': the question of end and
unendingness. The self criticises and emotionally deconstructs its own 'claim'
(l. 7) that attainment, arrival and accomplishment are feasible; that, via the
self's poetic and plastic doing, a 'garden' of beingness, perhaps secure, repose-
ful, edenic and original even, may open up within consciousness (l. 9). Such
felt self-delusion, however, seems unlikely to disappear; the question posed
('ah quand cesserons-nous. . .') seems quite rhetorical, and the entire production of the poem flies in the face of any notion that the self's creative struggle
with its own perception of the paradoxes and aporias of purpose, meaning and
outcome is likely to flag. Moreover, what then: suicide? Titus-Carmel's studies
of the life and work of Hart Crane (*L'Élancement*, 1998) or Gustave Roud (*Une
solitude dans les saisons*, 2005) or his *101 questions posées au pérégrin* (2001),
bear witness to his way of delicately mulling over the knotted imbrications
of desire. He is concerned with persistent traversal (of being and art), ideality,
and a Beckettian 'immobilité' (l. 10), a sense of unendingness without fruition,
absolute access or accomplishment. The metaphor of the seemingly all-powerful
shark (ll. 10–12) with its voracious appetite gives great energy to this affective
self-conceptualising discourse that thrusts undeterred ever 'faithful' utopian
vision and idealising purpose up against forces, seemingly external, but no
doubt implicitly internal, psychologico-philosophical, that wear away the very
medium of being and doing (l. 11). This poetics of erosion of feasibility and
resultant futility – and a 'bitterness' (l. 12) that ironically mimics the medium
offered to the poet–shark's movements, now condemned to haunt abyssal places
rather than loci of illumination – naturally finds itself in harmony with the sonnet's liminal discourse on death.

Mortality – of self, of other, of all that enters 'presence' or seems to lie beyond
on the obsessing horizon of dream, of the imaginable – weighs down such
dreaming, flattens and overshadows such buoyancy (l. 13). Is death's smiling-
ness (l. 14) a sign of its trickery, its seeming capacity to have the last laugh? Is it
the sign of an embraceable and ironically comforting finality which art cannot
provide, a smiling in sympathy with some deeply anchored death wish (l. 1:
'mourir nous sied') leading to the only apparent contradiction of the destruction
of dawn's promise (l. 1)? Powerfully and iteratively cadenced as the sonnet's last
line is, no definitive response to such questions can be said to emerge: death's
shadowiness may offer no 'redemption' ('in the mirror' of the self's consciousness and poetico-plastic *poiein*?), its enigmatic smile may persist, but, in even
the ever renewed consciousness of death's shadowing of self, it is life itself that
continues and, with life, art's Sisyphian round of desire and disillusionment; a
dogged self-inscription in the endless passing instants and yet its melancholia of

an unachievable end at the heart of this passingness. 'Or battant. . .' thus stages and debates – it is action and discourse, inextricably – deferral, ontological *différance*, that ourobouros-like circular chase after Z that leads back to A. Its logic of (its own) creation interlocks seamlessly with a *poétique du peu*, a (self-)negatory logic broadly reminiscent of a Michaux or a Frénaud and forming a compacted tensional unit which we may, perhaps presumptuously, hold to be rather more elegiac than tragical. Desire, in effect, remains powerful, transcendent in its tireless pursuit of something – it will be the poem, the painting, even the appreciation of the work, and all it may imply ontologically, of a Munch or an Ernst or a Bonnefoy and, of course, a wry sense of the self's own improbable grittiness – something, rather than nothing. And this mere something – here, our simultaneously self-lacerating and self-constituting sonnet – is, at least, the lingering trace of that fleeting, so easily deflated, ironised 'victory' that, in his *Notes d'atelier* (1993), Gérard Titus-Carmel calls 'Beauty'. 'Let us dare', he adds, 'for once, to call it thus' (*Notes d'atelier*, p. 146). Beauty: a fragile, but real, realisable experience, once deemed synonymous with Truth and the Good.

Note

1 Gérard Titus Carmel, *Seul tenant* (Seyssel: Champ Vallon, 2006), p. 70.

Further reading

Bishop, Michael, *The Endless Theory of Days: The Art and Poetry of Gérard Titus-Carmel* (Amsterdam: Rodopi, 2007).

Jean-Michel Maulpoix, 'Le bleu ne fait pas de bruit'

LAURE HELMS

Le bleu ne fait pas de bruit.

C'est une couleur timide, sans arrière-pensée, présage ni projet, qui ne se jette pas brusquement sur le regard comme le jaune ou le rouge, mais qui l'attire à soi, l'apprivoise peu à peu, le laisse venir sans le presser, de sorte qu'en elle il s'enfonce et se noie sans se rendre compte de rien.

Le bleu est une couleur propice à la disparition.
Une couleur où mourir, une couleur qui délivre, la couleur même de l'âme après qu'elle s'est déshabillée du corps, après qu'a giclé tout le sang et que se sont vidées les viscères, les poches de toutes sortes, déménageant une fois pour toutes le mobilier de nos pensées.

Indéfiniment, le bleu s'évade.
Ce n'est pas, à vrai dire, une couleur. Plutôt une tonalité, un climat, une résonance spéciale de l'air. Un empilement de clarté, une teinte qui naît du vide ajouté au vide, aussi changeante et transparente dans la tête de l'homme que dans les cieux.

L'air que nous respirons, l'apparence de vide sur laquelle remuent nos figures, l'espace que nous traversons n'est rien d'autre que ce bleu terrestre, invisible tant il est proche et fait corps avec nous, habillant nos gestes et nos voix. Présent jusque dans la chambre, tous volets tirés et toutes lampes éteintes, insensible vêtement de notre vie.

From *Une histoire de bleu*

Une histoire de bleu is the best-known and most widely read book by the poet, critic and academic, Jean-Michel Maulpoix, who was born in Montbéliard in 1952. First published in 1992 by Mercure de France and reprinted many times between its famous blue covers, it appeared in paperback with Gallimard in the autumn of 2006. It has been translated into many languages and the author today views the work as having almost cult-like status: 'Et ce bleu, ce vieux bleu fétiche qui en voit de toutes les couleurs',[1] he wrote in the final chapter, as if foreseeing the book's good fortune.

No doubt the book's success lies primarily in the colour it evokes: blue, firstly presented by Maulpoix as being just what it is – a stereotype, cliché, or platitude, the exact colour of what we might call the lyrical feeling. Jumbled up in Maulpoix's 'couleur-valise'/'case of colours', we find lovers' dreams (the 'little blue flower' aspect) as much as sad nostalgia (the blues), belief (blue is the colour of the Virgin Mary) and ideas of infinity and the faraway (the blue of the sky and the sea). The poet plays on all these levels; moreover, he explores them one by one, since these are precisely what give rise to the work's nine parts.

Each of the nine parts is composed of nine short texts: the work's architectural rigour constitutes one of its keys. Certainly, far from letting himself get carried away to some dreamy, ill-defined azure, the author meticulously frames his subject in a series of small pictures which echo each other in pairs: the texts are positioned opposite each other and have the same dimensions, as if to suggest the idea of a face-to-face between the subject and more distant things. In addition, each opens with a title phrase which is detached from the rest of the text and establishes the theme to be developed. In this way the musical nature of the composition as a whole is reinforced: 'Nous connaissons par ouï-dire l'existence de l'amour', 'Les femmes aux yeux noirs ont le regard bleu', etc.

At the centre of the book is a lengthy nine-page poem entitled 'Le Grand pavois'. Strikingly polychromatic, the poem breaks with the determinedly monochromatic nature of the rest of the volume. In embarking on the semblance of an ode to the ocean, its style parodies the intense outbursts of panegyric elsewhere. It also seems to provide the pivot on which the whole work turns, in that the four sections preceding it ('Le Regard bleu', 'Journaux du soir', 'Une incertaine église' and 'Le Marchand de couleurs') are consistently concerned with a lyrical analysis of blue itself, whereas the four later sections ('Adresse au nageur', 'Carnet d'un éphémère', 'Diverses manières de mourir' and 'Dernières nouvelles de l'amour') successively address specific subject-pronouns: 'tu', 'je', 'ils', and lastly, 'elle'.

The text we have chosen to discuss here opens the section entitled 'Le Marchand de couleurs', without doubt the poem in which the attempt to define the colour blue is most obvious: Maulpoix endeavours to determine the essence of the mysterious 'colour' – which for him is not a colour at all – without having recourse to any associated theme (love, belief, etc.). More specifically, this particular text brings together the essential elements of Maulpoix's critical and lyrical effort and is therefore one which articulates the author's intentions most clearly.

The work is composed of four regular paragraphs reminiscent of stanzas and it makes the fullest use of the space available without carrying over to another

268

page. One might almost think that this is prose passing itself off as poetry and all the more so because even without a title, which would have clearly conferred on it the status of a prose poem, the text opens – as do all the others in the collection – with a title phrase: here 'Le bleu ne fait pas de bruit'. The practice will remind readers of Maulpoix's critical work, particularly of his analyses[2] of Paul Valéry's celebrated statement: 'Le lyrisme est le développement d'une exclamation'. Certainly, this text's achievement rests partly in its lyrical, critical and melodic development of the opening theme. We note that this practice, which is used throughout the book, is in this case systematised within the text itself. Two of the four paragraphs (the second and third) open with what might be called a 'theme phrase', whereby 'blue' finds itself in the position of subject: 'Le bleu est une couleur propice à la disparition'; 'Indéfiniment, le bleu s'évade'. Thus the text proceeds as a coherent series of overlapping slippages, gradually working its way into the heart of the colour blue.

From the outset, blue is characterised by its quiet discretion. In contrast to fiery colours such as yellow and red, blue does not suddenly make itself known or push for attention, but opens our gaze to a space of infinite regression, although it also might represent the opportunity for a total and tranquil fusion. This is the theme of the first paragraph, in which blue finds itself personified to the point of being endowed with its own soul. Here Maulpoix uses hypallage and metonymy to bestow on the colour its own capacities of human perception and interpretation. Now blue acquires the subtle gift of seduction and, like a true narcotic, it numbs our vigilance and swamps all rational doubt in the flood of its transparency.

Under the effect of this strange spell, slippage occurs between the first and second paragraphs and we find that the idea of discretion has slid into that of disappearance. The colour that welcomed and absorbed has now taken on a sepulchral hue. And yet this imaginary blue of death, which could even be the hideous tint of a corpse, here turns out to be preserved in its unreality, similar to the ideal colour and emblematic of the soul's deliverance. The central concern of this paragraph is indeed nothing other than the illusory separation of body and soul, to which the composition of the paragraph itself lends consistency, at the same time adding, no doubt, a certain expressionist violence. Indeed, in opposition to the blue-tinged deliverance of the soul, there now comes a violent blood-letting and a visceral purgation: a frightful corporal materiality, brutally ended by death. We receive a passing reminder of the vanity of intellectual construction, which is compared here to a kind of 'furniture', which has to be removed from the premises.

A further slide of logic opens the third paragraph and leads from the image of removal to that of escape. The tactic, reminiscent of Rimbaud's *en-allée*, allows the author to pass to a new level: the colour which was simultaneously shy ('timide') and vertiginous (paragraph 1) and then ideal, unreal and sepulchral (paragraph 2), is now seen to reject its own identity as a colour, to efface itself chromatically and dissolve in space, becoming nothing more than the hue of the void itself – that, or simply an optical illusion. Readers realise that the text's whole motive was precisely to guide them towards this mysterious vanishing point: the blue that 'ne fait pas de bruit' is merely the 'résonance spéciale de l'air'. But at the exact moment that the azure-space-become-empty-space fully opens out, readers find themselves just as easily led back to the narrow dimensions of the human 'head'. We realise that the distances in question here are in fact those particular 'lointains intérieurs'– as Henri Michaux so finely describes them.

This idea is more fully developed in the text's final paragraph, which brings back what is most distant towards what is most near, whilst also giving authority to the idea of a 'bleu terrestre', and which finally pursues its grasp or understanding of the azure skies to the very inside of a room with closed shutters. In contrast to certain Romantic and Symbolist tendencies to escape to the underworld or a more beautiful otherworld, Maulpoix is here undertaking an enterprise of *repatriation*. Moreover, he offers blue a grounding, and makes of it a kind of skin: 'insensible vêtement de notre vie'. Far from being a tool for escape, any more than a place of lamentation for lost ideals, here poetic discourse is delivering a lesson in focus and a way of acceptance: it aims to teach us to live precisely *here*, where we find ourselves – not by turning away from the ideal, but by acknowledging that it causes anxiety and by recognising its presence – far-flung yet near – in the world of the senses.

The significance of *Une histoire de bleu*, as this particular page attests, lies partly with its effort of revaluation, which invites us to call an end to the dramatic opposition between the real and unreal, the near and far. In this respect, the poetic prose found in this volume could perhaps be compared with those optical instruments which not only enable us to focus on one or other aspect of human life, or to study mankind by revealing our own hidden traits, but also to confront the most private and the most unknown, the 'inner depths', and the 'celestial heights'. It is towards a similar *rapprochement* between the Azure and 'l'en bas' that one of the final texts in *Chutes de pluie fine* invites us – a text entitled, fittingly, 'Le Ciel d'en bas':

> Penchez-vous et tendez l'oreille. Au bord du puits, la pierre est chaude, d'un rose de brique usée par la corde, le seau de fer et le soleil. Au fond, des chants, des cris, des cloches, tant de paroles depuis toujours tenues secrètes. Des voix pareilles à celles des morts, et qui vous parlent des lointains lorsque vous approchez l'oreille, comme on entend la mer au creux d'un coquillage.
>
> Penchez-vous davantage. Au fond de ce puits est une bouche, un œil, votre visage, vos poumons peut-être. Entendez-vous ce souffle ? On est venu souvent pleurer ici. C'est tempête sur un lac de larmes ! Les pièces d'or ou les mots que vous y jetterez ne remonteront pas. Même la prière descend profond. Puisque là-dessous est l'Azur, maçonné d'un anneau parfait. Ce vent d'en bas a le vertige, qui aspire à soi tout le bleu du ciel

et toute la pensée. Aucun dieu caché n'y respire, mais l'absence, le rien extrême par quoi toutes choses existent et se défont.

Penchez-vous. Sur la margelle du puits la pierre chaude est muette. Elle désire tant votre chaleur et votre voix. C'est un baiser de vie, ce poids de chair. Ainsi la nuit du corps et la nuit de l'âme échangent-elles dans l'amour leurs appuis.

– Un puits disais-je encore, où jeter vos vêtements. Un puits de nudité. Un nu de pierre et d'eau, ainsi que les statues des dieux près des fontaines. Mais creusé profond : un corps vide. . . Il tremble de froid sous la neige. Et répète : « Il est temps, il est grand temps de prendre corps ! »

Entendez-vous le bruit des pioches, des pelles, et du gravier qui crisse ? La terre se soulève et s'entrouvre, offrant son ventre à qui le veut – et même s'il n'en veut pas. Il est temps, il est tard.

– J'appelle azur le ciel d'en bas, le ciel du fond du puits. Dans l'encre, son reflet m'est rendu visible, presque proche, accueillant au visage soudain reconnu nimbé de clarté.

Sur le papier, j'appelle azur ce puits d'eau sombre, tel que le ciel bleu lui-même, très loin, très haut, insiste pour s'y pencher.

Translated by Jane Yeoman

Notes

1 *Une histoire de bleu* (Paris: Mercure de France, 1992), p. 47; reprinted in *L'Instinct de ciel* (Paris: Gallimard, 2006), p. 128.
2 Jean-Michel Maulpoix, *Du lyrisme* (Paris: José Corti, 2000), p. 221.

Further reading

Maulpoix, Jean-Michel, *A Matter of Blue*, trans. Dawn Cornelio (Rochester, NY: BOA Editions, 2005).
The Inkwell's Monologue, trans. Dawn Cornelio (Halifax, NS: VVV Editions, 2005).
Pour un lyrisme critique (Paris: José Corti, 2009).
www.maulpoix.net, the official Jean-Michel Maulpoix website (in French, Spanish, English).

31 Amina Saïd, 'Trois continents dérivent'

ROSEMARY LLOYD

trois continents dérivent
dans mes veines

l'un m'a fait don du jour
sans me guérir de la mort

j'ai hérité de l'autre le chant   5
le clair rivage de l'île

l'aptitude à toujours chercher
mon orient

le soi et l'au-delà de soi
beaucoup d'amour d'incertitudes   10

quatre murs de vent
le soleil pour toiture

un lot d'angoisses

l'espace paisible
défini du tombeau   15

désignant le parfait horizon
le troisième m'a condamnée
à l'erreur à l'errance

à la conscience aiguë
d'une déchirure du temps   20

je déchiffrerai un jour leur message
inscrit en lettres noires
sur feuille de soie pliée en huit

il indiquera que la manière
dont j'ai construit ma vie   25
est l'exact contraire
de ce qui aurait dû être

pourtant je la taille à mon usage
(une ombre reproduit mes gestes)

dès le soleil levant   30
j'accomplis mon chemin de ronde
                    (une ombre me suit
                          ou me devance)

dans un livre jamais refermé
je transcris de mémoire   35
ma passion de la nuit
                    (une ombre pèse
                          sur mes rêves
             de tout son poids de rêve)

l'autre versant des choses   40
sécrète ses sortilèges

From *Gisements de lumière*

A poet driven by the desire to capture the beauty of both the world and the word, Amina Saïd immediately pulls her reader into a universe of light, into poems that shimmer with layers of physical and spiritual light evoked by the apparently paradoxical title of her 1998 collection, *Gisements de lumière*.[1] The clash between, on the one hand, the hard materiality of *gisements*, suggesting seams of coal, and, on the other, the idea of light, the conflict between the blackness and subterranean nature of the first and the aerial whiteness of the second nicely prepares us both for the central conflicts of the collection, and for their resolution, as the printed word is made to contain the vast layers of time and space the poet recreates through her use of language and rhythm.

Born in the harsh desert light of Tunis in 1953, to a Tunisian father and a French mother, Saïd now lives in Paris, that city of a very different kind of light, a northern light diffracted through moisture. She began publishing poetry with *Paysage, nuit friable* in 1980 and has since written over a dozen volumes of verse, as well as two collections of short stories. Having studied English and anglophone literature at the Sorbonne, she is also the translator of the well-known Filipino writer Francisco Sionil José, whose works she translates from English into French. There can be little doubt that her work as a translator concentrates her attention on language in ways that in turn fertilise her task as a poet.

Gisements de lumière is very much focused on poetry and its ability to seize, refract and transform our experience of the world, together with the ease with which that experience still eludes our grasp. A poem, Saïd proclaims in the collection's opening piece, is a ritual of light, a thread tied to the tree of life. 'Nos mots', she adds, 'sont fragiles et pourtant ils vivent' (*Gisements*, pp. 13–16). That

273

life, moreover, is not just instantaneous, like photography, but has duration, like cinema:

> dans une syllabe
> la lumière s'attarde
>
> je marche avec la vie
> pour compagne
>
> vers le ciel ininterrompu
> de mon enfance. (*Gisements*, p. 53)

But poetry is not just a means of understanding, projecting light on, the past: it also allows the poet to explore 'la frontière / entre mémoire et oubli' (*Gisements*, p. 115), transforming an anthology of poems into a 'herbier du temps' between whose pages memories, albeit dried and pressed, are preserved, for an attentive reader who might then in turn become a richer and more creative repository of memory, one capable of recreating and transforming 'l'histoire de notre solitude' (*Gisements*, p. 118).

That kind of active response from the reader is also what is invited, indeed demanded, by the opening words of 'trois continents dérivent'. But just as that frontier between memory and oblivion is one in which each can enrich the other, what is forgotten giving shape and density to memory, so misreadings can be fertile, especially those provoked by the poet herself. Too rapid a reading here will produce the more conventional sense that the poet's blood stems from three continents, with that image's invitation to explore the contemporary predicament of those whose lives have led them to live in multiple places, to think in multiple languages, to experience multiple cultural frameworks. What, in this reading, might the three continents be? Africa and Europe, obviously, because of the poet's parentage, but the third? The continent of the French language, of poetry, of imagination? In a sense the poem simultaneously invites and draws on this misdirected start to its own dark continent, both by its exploration of three continents and by the way in which our reading is inflected by the two quotations that lead us into the poem. The first of these, from fellow poet Claude Paradis, draws our attention to the question of physical and linguistic exile: 'Je suis d'un autre chant / comme d'une autre terre'. The second, from Armel Guerne, born in Switzerland of French parents, but choosing to live in France, suggests the universal longing for an elsewhere that can blind us to the beauty of what we have: 'Et grandit cet ailleurs au détriment d'ici.'

Nevertheless, a closer reading reveals that the poet is not claiming derivation from three continents but rather asserting that they 'dérivent dans mes veines', wander or drift through her blood. (Etymologically, *dériver* refers to boats breaking free of their moorings on the bank (*rive*) of a river and wandering with the currents, as Rimbaud's drunken boat does.) Our reading, moreover, should be guided by the epigraph to the collection as a whole, which comes from yet another poet exile, the Romanian-born Lorand Gaspar's *Journal de Patmos*: 'Il se trouve toujours quelqu'un qui veille aux rives divisées de la parole'.[2] The poet, one might argue, watches over the meanders and fissures of language, especially the poet who is multilingual, as in the case of Saïd. Both drawing on and deflecting the overtly autobiographical, the opening lines thus suggest that the poet, like her anthology-herbarium, carries these continents, these containers of memory and language, within her, forming them rather than simply being formed by them. An oblique commentary on this can be found in the recipe poem that begins with the words 'prendre une poignée de mots', where Saïd insists that the mixture that makes up a poem must be kneaded incessantly 'comme argile souple', like the clay of continents (*Gisements*, p. 94).

The first continent is succinctly evoked as the one that gave life without removing the need to die. Death, after all, is what gives both urgency and power to the poet's search to transform experience into language. It is worth noting, however, that Saïd uses the hackneyed term *donner du jour* to convey the idea of giving life, but like all fine poets she is able to transform cliché by means of the context in which she places it. Here *jour*, through the presence of the layers of light that run through her collection, is restored to all its power, its sense of illumination.

Saïd, however, is clearly more eager to give weight to the second continent. Where the first, one feels almost by an accident of fate, gave her life and death, this second continent is what has shaped her as an individual and a thinker. It is associated with songs and brightness, as well as, more intellectually and perhaps more paradoxically, the tendency to orient herself, to seek out the East even when in the West, to look for the light of the rising sun rather than of the sunset. Cartesian clarity, so deeply set into the contemporary concept of what it means to be French, is here gracefully but nevertheless ironically nudged into a different form, a different direction. Like Freud's *unheimlich* being in fact that which is most intensely *heimlich*, the mystic East, from which Saïd herself comes, is also that which allows Westerners to find their bearings. No wonder she also offers thanks to this continent for giving her 'le soi et l'au-delà de soi': the sense of self but also that which is more than self.

The fluid, unpunctuated lines of Saïd's verse also enable the kind of plural readings for which the play on 'orient' has prepared us. Among the gifts from this second continent we find 'beaucoup d'amour d'incertitudes'. Is this to be read as two separate gifts, both love and uncertainty, or does this point to yet another turn away from Cartesian logic and certainty: the positive love of the indefinite, of doubt, of imprecision? The poet's habit of breaking the line at the end of sense groupings, together with her generally taut constructions, preferring logical linkings to mere lists, suggest the latter, but it is part of the wandering nature of this poem not to allow us to be certain.

While these gifts from the second continent are primarily abstractions, what follows is both more concrete and more closely linked to those gifts associated with the first continent – those of life and death. The central word here is *lot* meaning not only prize (what you might win in a lottery), but also fate, a share, and a plot of land. In this case, the plot of land is defined by the tomb, that peaceful spot with its four walls of wind and with the sun for a roof. However peaceful it may be, however, it is also a place of *angoisses*, literally somewhere so narrow as to induce feelings of suffocation, and more broadly a place whose very existence arouses anxiety. This becomes the perfect horizon for the poem, which draws its intensity and much of its meaning from the poet's mortal condition.

The third continent, unlike the first, which suggests a unidirectional movement from birth to death, or the second, with its emphasis on the skill of orientation and on the existence of a guiding, if limiting, horizon, is introduced as the one associated with error and wandering, both geographically and chronologically, for, the poet adds, it has made her aware of a rift in time. Is this the rift we all experience between our own fluid sense of time and that which the clock measures? Or a rift between the time of the first continent, that of the orderly progression of life, and that of the second with its songs and anguish remoulding time to its own needs? Or again, a rift between Western and Eastern historical chronologies or even between two concepts of time itself? The poet allows these questions to surface, but sets them gently aside with the statement, which is also an affirmation that she shares our perplexity, that one day she will decipher their message, written, as if in a costly limited edition of the octavo book we hold in our hands, in black letters on silken pages folded into eight. If this line reminds us of Mallarmé's quietly resigned affirmation that even when seeking to depict the brilliance of the stars the poet is condemned to limit himself to black on white, the black of ink and the white of paper, there is another echo embedded in this statement: that of the earlier reference to the 'soi et l'au-delà du soi'. The expression 'feuille de soie' thus acts as an aural if not visual invitation to hear this poem as being written on the self.

This is where the poem shifts direction, as if, hidden behind its apparently free form, there were a traditional sonnet turning on the axle of the change between quatrains and tercets. The four lines that indicate this shift also offer hints of a traditional form, quickly suppressed but nonetheless powerful. The rhyming of the first and third lines (*manière/contraire*) draws attention both to the lack of aural rhyme and to the presence of a conceptual rhyme between the second and fourth lines, where *vie* and *être* have no phonetic parallels but do offer parallels of meaning. Equally reminiscent of traditional diction is the central phonetic block created by *construit* and *contraire*. A construction – of a life or of a poem – always, inevitably, holds within it not just the possibility but the desirability of its opposite. The wandering continents might be organised differently, or might simply line up differently, following alternate paths of continental drift as the psychological tectonic plates transform themselves, revealing unpredicted rifts provoking unforeseen realignments.

However much this possibility may be an inescapable if unpalatable truth,

Saïd calmly reasserts her own autonomy over her own life. 'Pourtant je la taille à mon usage', she declares, an affirmation in which the use of the present tense indicates not just a determination to assert her own rights, but also the continuous nature of her action. Even if we know that what we are doing is against some pre-ordained law, we continue because this is how we choose to live our lives, she seems to be maintaining in this understated but unbending claim. It is, however, followed by a parenthesis which suggests something less clear-cut: 'une ombre reproduit mes gestes'. Is this the shadow that in the world of light, on which she places so much emphasis, affirms that a person or an object is really present? Or the shade that she will become after death? The poem leaves both possibilities open, wrapping the words in parentheses as if simultaneously to draw attention to them and to set them apart from the world depicted so far.

Shaping a life, rather than allowing the continents within to direct it, involves keeping watch. Daybreak, Saïd tells us, finds her completing her nightly rounds, watching over both past and future as the shadow, following or leading her, reveals. This image projects a different light back on to the earlier reference to orienting oneself, allowing it now to carry together with its other meanings that of looking to the sunrise. The experiences of that nightly round then find expression in a book, drawing on memory to capture passion, in the word's multiple senses of love, suffering and enthusiasm. We should note that the word used here for the action of writing is not the simple *écrire* but *transcrire*, which, while it might also contain the sound *cri* that she claims drives her writing – 'j'écris . . . parce qu'il y a le mot cri dans écrire' (*Gisements*, p. 13) – suggests that the passion itself has given her the words and all she needs to do is passively transcribe them. Here, moreover, the shadow no longer merely replicates the gestures of writing but instead places all its weight on her dreams. Itself a dream, one might think this shadow as impalpable as dreams, but it is also possible to imagine it acting as the keystone that holds the dreams in place, or the weight laid on a flower that is being pressed in a herbarium to make it lie perfectly flat. Here, too, Saïd plays with, while not quite reverting to, traditional techniques to intensify the meaning of her words, using monosyllables as the final word of each of the stanza's last three lines to create a kind of pattern that, like a rhyme, bonds the idea of dream and weight more strongly together: ('une ombre pèse / sur mes rêves / de tout son poids de rêve').

The poem ends with an appropriately enigmatic couplet that playfully locks together a deliberately prosaic opening line with an ostentatiously poetic closing line:

> L'autre versant des choses
> Sécrète ses sortilèges.

The deliberate banality of *choses*, heightened by the word's position at the end of the line, offers a sharp and thereby provocative contrast with the complex phonetic patterning and poetic lexicon of the final line. Yet again, Saïd has taken a cliché (one of the many variants on 'the hidden face of the moon') and transformed it by setting it in the context of the continents drifting within her. Since poetry has long been closely allied with magic, the Latin word *carmen*, for instance, suggesting both song and magic charm, it is not surprising to find this poem ending on the powerful word *sortilèges*. Nor, given Saïd's emphasis on the suggestive power of the everyday, is it surprising to find those charms associated with objects: in the poems that follow this one in her collection, it is objects such as lamps and the rough bark of palm that play an essential role.

What is particularly satisfying in this apparently understated conclusion, with its final word including a mildly encrypted demand to read (the Latin imperative *lege*), is its openness, its invitation to reread the poem while thinking of that secret other side. But it is also, of course, an invitation to read the poems immediately following it in the light of what it has had to say. Her poems are at once defiantly independent and subtly linked to one another: layers of light that reflect on each other in unexpected ways. In inviting us to ponder on the continents that wander within her, she is also inviting us to see them drifting through the whole of *Gisements de lumière*, and to seek equivalents in our own existence.

Notes

1 Amina Saïd, *Gisements de lumière* (Paris: Éditions de la Différence, 1998), pp. 71–2.
2 In Lorand Gaspar, *Égée, suivi de Judée* (Paris: Gallimard, 1980), p. 99.

Further reading

Moatamri, Ines, 'La Quête du lieu dans l'œuvre d'Amina Saïd', *Littérature et nation: revue d'histoire des représentations littéraires et artistiques*, 30 (2005), pp. 77–90.
  'Poétique de la relation: Amina Saïd et Édouard Glissant', http://trans.univ-paris3. fr/, 2007 (accessed September 2009).

Pierre Alferi, 'Une défense de la poésie'

MICHAEL SHERINGHAM

Une défense de la poésie

Cela se passe
Ici
Entre la sensation aiguë et le sentiment latent
Entrant tu
As troublé le vieux jeu de l'âme
Et du paysage
Alors j'ai bien besoin de toi pour avancer.

Quel bonheur te voir surmarcher
Mon territoire, échanger quelques mots
Insignifiants de passe avec les nains
Du jardin. Les figures humaines s'étaient tues
Dans la partie construite du domaine   5
À la frontière à peine un vieillard retenait-
Il l'attention en tranchant la queue d'une banane
Affublée d'un code-barre avec un couteau suisse.
Oui, dès la première sensation
La face visible annonce la couleur   10
Le code du jour : la nature
De son lien avec la cachée. Cela se passe
Ici, non pas dans le « non-dit »
Mais entre les vues du moment
Du quartier tout à fait fidèles   15
Et ce qu'elles couvrent qu'il faut dire.
Un vérin hydraulique soutient la galerie
Je m'y appuie, j'éprouve sa résistance
À chaque ligne. Chaque ligne mesure
La distance entre le décor   20
Constat que l'on dresse et son ombre
Inventaire que l'on couche par écrit –
Entre la sensation aiguë et le sentiment latent, entre

Entre. Or cette proportion capricieuse qui règle
Mon débit maladif, le rythme, le débite   25
Avait gelé dans les lieux familiers. Tout un pan
Gagné par le désert et ses nuits froides
Et son vent-fou-que-nul-n'écoute-impunément.
Le même manège : regards d'habitués qui s'évitent
Préfèrent se rendre la monnaie des paroles de profil   30
Murs et chaussée lustrés par la rêverie
Pour la rêverie, sketches mille fois répétés
Devant une assemblée de chaises. Entrant tu
As troublé le vieux jeu de l'âme
Et du paysage. L'air que tu déplaces en marchant   35
A regonflé les figures de cartes d'ici.
– Cela nous fait un peu beaucoup d'images
Non ? De quoi parlait le téléfilm hier soir ?
Même pas compris si c'était un docudrama
Ou quoi. – Oui, tout se mêle ce matin   40
Plutôt se juxtapose, une vue clap une autre
Dosages inégaux de soleil, passants, voitures, ciment
Que rien ne lie sinon l'analogie dont la raison
Fuit dans la vue suivante. – Au moins j'espère
Qu'en les cousant tu cernes un peu mieux   45
Ce qu'elles couvrent dans ta pauvre petite tête.
– En deux mots j'appelle ça le sentimental
Alors j'ai bien besoin de toi pour avancer
D'une comparaison à l'autre ironiquement
Naïvement dans cette lumière indirecte   50
Cette « réalité » qui se cite elle-même
Et se distance. Car derrière elle, loin derrière
Le réalisme et l'imagination piétinent
Dans un mortel docudrama. – C'est tout ?
– C'est tout, j'ai trop parlé, c'est de ta faute.   55
Maintenant changeons de terrasse
Cherchons du silence mais dehors.

From *Sentimentale journée*

The title of Alferi's poem, from his 1997 collection *Sentimentale journée*,[1] links it with innumerable poems about poetry, such as Verlaine's 'Art poétique', but alludes most directly to Shelley's 1821 treatise, *A Defence of Poetry*, which claimed that poetry 'purges from our inward sight the film of familiarity which obscures from us the wonder of our being'.[2] In fact, most poems in *Sentimentale journée* can be said to be 'about' poetry since, as in 'Une défense de la poésie', Alferi repeatedly confronts the reader with hyperactive linguistic performances that include, among many other things, commentary on their own status and progress. With everything moving so fast it is often hard to see what is going on: items stand out momentarily before being swept away in a helter-skelter of words and images. As Alferi has observed, the 'flux' of poetic language necessarily engenders a certain 'flou'. His back-cover text for *Sentimentale journée* invokes the improvisatory arts of conversation and soccer: in these poems 'on voit en gros de quoi ils parlent . . . mais pas très bien ce qu'ils veulent dire'; meaning is kicked around like a football: 'ils repoussent le sens d'une image à l'autre, qu'ils défont, d'une phrase à l'autre, qu'ils coupent, un peu comme on frappe dans un ballon'.[3] The word 'image' here also points to cinema, an art form constantly invoked by Alferi. Like talk, football, and film, poetry is a 'chemin de la / Coupe':[4] cutting in, cutting across, and cutting up find their equivalents in the segmentation of utterance and vision accomplished by poetic lineation, especially when heightened by the frequent enjambement that is central to Alferi's poetics.

Each poem in *Sentimentale journée* has an epigraph made up of fragments of the text to follow. These 'edited highlights' constitute a sort of 'trailer'-poem, a speeded-up version that singles out certain topics whilst allowing the same words to function differently. Here, we zoom in to the enjambement of lines 12–13, pared down to a stark assertion of 'hereness': 'Cela se passe / Ici', and we then jump to a truncated version of line 23, which locates 'Ici' as an intermediate realm ('Entre . . .'). We then speed along to the double enjambement of ll. 33–5 which refer to the upsetting of a traditional balance between inner and outer worlds, and finally land at line 48 which points to the role of interlocution and exchange. Filtering out most of its details and loops, the 'trailer' highlights the main poem's ongoing concern with its own mechanisms, with whatever 'se passe / Ici'. Yet this concern with poetry itself is far from exclusive. On the contrary, Alferi's poetic practice, like that of others of his generation (Anne Portugal, Olivier Cadiot, Nathalie Quintane) associates poetic language directly with the processes of everyday existence. In many respects, including a passion for cinema and multimedia inventiveness, Alferi harks back to the avant-garde movements of earlier twentieth-century Modernism where linguistic and visual experimentation sought to be directly experiential and to break down the barriers between expression and reality, thus capturing the processes of perception. To be sure, the Modernist belief in art's capacity to transform life would be alien to Alferi's sceptical postmodern temper. But by contrast with the emphasis on a heroic struggle between language and being, or the disjunction between word and world, which has often marked modern poetry from Char and Ponge to Bonnefoy and Dupin, Alferi's work – taking cues in this regard from Deguy and Roubaud – questions demarcations between self and language, and between language and world. In so doing, it promotes the capacity for poetic, or more broadly literary, language to sponsor perceptual processes that are generally discouraged by routine and convention.

From start to finish, 'Une défense de la poésie' puts language on display. If we encounter a motley array of familiar things, including garden gnomes, bananas, Swiss army knives, hydraulic jacks, and TV movies; and familiar types of utterance, including first-person narration, *style indirect libre*, dialogue, and rumination, the poem has a pervasive air of suspended reality. Alferi's aesthetic, as articulated in his treatise, *Chercher une phrase*, affirms a belief in the creative and heuristic power of defamiliarisation. This does not operate through unusual combinations of words, or clusters of images, but through sentences. For Alferi, literariness occurs at the level of the sentence because sentences demarcate syntactic structures, while syntax establishes rhythm, the balances, ratios and vectors that produce meaning: 'le sens d'une phrase est l'effet global de son rythme'.[5] Literature, and poetry in particular, where the sentence is character-istically a group of lines making up a sequence, offers the possibility of new sentences. If anything is primal for Alferi it is 'l'élan de la profération' (*CP*, p. 27),[6] a propensity for utterance that does not channel desire or crave meaning but articulates life itself as an embodied process. In each of us this 'élan' can remain on fixed pathways, giving us the same old types of experience. Poetry, however, can reroute it, offering us, temporarily at least, through the dual process of writing and reading, new encounters with reality. One way it can do this is by fostering a verbal flow where rhythm is not the regular return of the same but a constant, open-ended mixing and matching, operating at every level of signification, where familiar things are made both recognisable and strange: 'la phrase met en rythme les choses. Elle est une expérience' (*CP*, p. 35). This kind of 'mise en rythme', favouring the dislocating agency of enjambement, can produce a convergence of the referential and the hallucinatory (Alferi's terms are 'référence' and 'apparition'). Through the curving paths of syntax, 'la phrase fait scintiller la référence: elle crée ainsi un flottement dans les choses' (*CP*, p. 38); but this disorientation is followed by recognition: 'la phrase s'achève en les [les choses] laissant se poser de nouveau, s'offrir comme pour la première fois' (*CP*, p. 40). The poem constantly gives the illusion that it is describing a pre-existing state of affairs, whilst in reality 'la phrase invente une expérience', constructing in its wake an 'antérieur absolu' (*CP*, p. 14). Everything in the poem – including its way of making our ordinary world visible to us in new ways – is the outcome of this sentence-making activity, of its 'élan': nothing was there, but retrospec-tively a world is created.

Conversational in tone, and making frequent reference to the language and technology of filmmaking, most of the poems in *Sentimentale journée* feature quick-changing scenarios where a protagonist, who often adopts a succession of (dis)guises, undergoes a series of strange experiences that can often seem to mirror the poetic activity that generates them. 'Une défense de la poésie' is one of the poems that makes this most explicit. From the start, the speaker comments approvingly on a force, addressed as 'tu', that affects what the world looks like, and in the course of the poem he (like Alferi, the protagonist is male) will seek to pin down the modus operandi of this 'tu', locating it outside or *between* various types of representation – 'entre' is a key word throughout. Put very crudely, this identifies the 'tu' as poetry itself; and in the course of the poem it becomes evident that the speaker's disquisition concerns his own activity, which makes him the poet, or rather a subject in the throes of what poetry does. In the last segment (from l. 37), another voice enters the poem (heralded by the dash indicating speech), and challenges the primary speaker to express himself more clearly. The ensuing cut-and-thrust dialogue resembles a comedy sketch in which a creative artist is pestered by a sceptical down-to-earth friend.

The poem is in *vers libres*, with a capital letter at the head of each line, and a norm of eight to eleven syllables. Lineation frequently replaces punctuation, favouring parataxis and appositional constructions with few commas. This highlights the frequent enjambement (ll. 1, 2, 3, 6, 11, 12, 14, etc.), which in turn draws attention to the segmentation whereby sentences generally end in mid-line, creating a mixture of staccato jerkiness and fluidity. The poem falls naturally into three sequences (ll. 1–16, 17–36 and 37–57), marked at ll. 16 and 36 by two of the infrequent end-stopped lines. Other end-stopped lines (at ll. 8 and 28) provide a caesura in mid-sequence, without interrupting the rhetorical shape.

In the first sequence the speaker ascribes the euphoric experience of a change in his perception to a sort of 'trans-coding' that happens to his 'territoire' when it is 'surmarch[é]'. This neologism, with its comic echo of 'supermarché' (which surfaces later in the 'code-barre'), suggests walking in the air, floating just above the surface, and feeds into the various bits of scenario that follow, where artifice and a blurring of familiar categories predominate, and where everything seems to hover between reality and unreality. The matter-of-fact tone is belied by the constant incongruities, befitting the way these are generated by the discourse. The syntax parallels '*surmarcher* / Mon territoire' and '*échanger* quelques mots', while the enjambement at lines 2/3 separates the components of the phrase 'mots de passe' so that 'Insignifiants' becomes ambiguous. Making us strongly aware of the language, this 'stuttering' effect, where a word is followed by two predicates, or is repeated with a different sense, will recur repeatedly in the poem, often in connection with enjambement (e.g. ll. 10–11, 11–12, 14–15, 19, 23–4, 31–2). Familiar binaries (nature/culture, animate/inanimate, human/inhuman, reality/ artifice) are toyed with by the syntax. For example, the *rejet* 'Du jardin' (varied in 'du domaine' (l. 5)) is juxtaposed with the periphrastic 'partie construite', which, if it connotes civilisation, sounds more like a stage or film set, just as the 'figures humaines' seem more like 'figurants' than ordinary mortals. In this conjuncture (implicitly that of 'poetry') what grabs attention is situated 'À la frontière' (l. 6): *between* realms. The 'vieillard' (l. 6) would be unexceptional were it not for the way poetic language zooms in on the tiny barcode on his banana ('affublée', suggesting a theatrical prop, underlines the artifice), and for his rather theatrical way of slicing the fruit with his penknife.

Beginning with a discursive and approbatory 'Oui', the second half (ll. 9–16) of the first sequence has a similar structure (two sentences, winding syntax), and reflects meditatively on the 'experience' recounted in the first, picking up the question of attention and the visible, and the idea of codes. Through brilliantly performative language, lines 9–12 ruminate on the connections between the seen and the unseen, while lines 12–16, focusing on representation and the links between the said and the unsaid, affirm that '[ce] qu'il faut dire' is to be found between them rather than in either of the two. Line 9 links the unsettling of customary appearances with the field of sensory experience: 'la première sensation' and 'jour' suggest morning awakening and the beginning of the day's stream of perceptions (the 'journée' is a common motif in Alferi's writing). The idiomatic phrase 'annonce la couleur', meaning to lay one's cards on the table (card games recur further on), fits the day's new colours but cleverly suggests the plain 'literality' of 'la face visible'. Syntactical ambiguity first allows 'annonce la couleur' to stand alone, and then, via the kind of 'stuttering' I referred to, allows for an enjambement where 'Le code du jour' is a second object of 'annonce', reinforcing the neutral quality of the 'face visible' by construing 'la couleur' as a 'code'. This is further reinforced, but then questioned, via repetition of the same device: line 11 initially stands alone, reaffirming 'codedness' by associating the visible with the natural, but enjambement then makes a bridge, opening up a 'lien' between the 'face visible' and – the word is cunningly made invisible – '[la face] cachée' (l. 12).

In lines 12–16 the opposition between the merely visible and the possibly invisible is replayed in terms of banal 'vues' that are firstly momentary glimpses, 'vues du moment', but then, via more 'stuttering' at lines 14–15, more like picture postcards: ('[vues] Du quartier tout à fait fidèles'). But a bid is made to locate the real 'action' – 'Cela se passe' – neither in the codedly visible, nor in some symbolic 'non-dit' that would lie beneath the cover of visibility, but rather 'entre'. This is '[ce] qu'il faut dire'.

The middle segment of the poem (ll. 17–36) maintains the mix of linguistic play, fabulation and rumination that is characteristic of Alferi's poetry. Here, as elsewhere, it is as if the poetic voice were constantly trying to account for the strange contraption it constructs as it proceeds. The 'élan de la profération' manifests itself in linguistic performances, and syntax weaves together different discursive modes: meta-poetry and poetry are wired into the same circuitry. Lines 17–19 seem initially to re-specify the physical location as some sort of mine or cave where tunnelling ('galerie') is jacked up hydraulically. Hitherto only implicit, the pronoun 'Je' (l. 18) now briefly places the speaker in the diegesis: as wielder of the jack he feels the force needed to create the space in which he finds himself (the comma in line 18 emphasises 'j'éprouve' by lengthening the vowel sound). But the repetition of 'ligne' in line 19 dissolves the diegetic space and lays bare the metaphorical play where 'ligne', linked to 'mesure', can allude to the verbal structure of the poem. The connection with engineering is consistent with Alferi's view of poetry as a 'mécanique lyrique'.[7] Here, the poem engineers equivalence between its structure of lines and a hollowed-out, subterranean or adjacent space. This culminates in the enjambement and repetitive stuttering of lines 23–4, where the first 'entre' is a preposition designating interstitial spaces between the manifest and the latent, and the second 'entre' is an imperative inviting us to enter this space (a homophone, 'antre', is flickeringly perceptible here). Lines 20–4, where the word 'entre' occurs four times, echo the specifications regarding 'Ici' and '[ce] qu'il faut dire' in lines 12–16. The 'space' of poetry is connected with a resistance to and a distance from other constructions of experienced reality. It lies between the purely objective, dispassionate 'constat' of observation (l. 21), and any fastidious verbal 'Inventaire' (l. 22) that could register this (the paralleling of the verbs 'dresser' and 'coucher' is apt). But as line 23 asserts, poetic space is not to be confused with extreme sensations or buried (unconscious) feeling. As line 23 insists once again, with its 'entre' at either end, and a further 'Entre' as its *rejet*, the space of the poetic is between.

Alferi's poetry is insistently present-tense, as it manifests its own becoming, but it often generates flashbacks that help to situate the 'action', creating different time zones within a single poem. Here, lines 24–33, starting with 'Or', constitute an analeptic excursus that conjures up a sterile universe of non-communication connected with a time when the speaker's mode of utterance, his 'débit maladif', had lost its capacity to find the right 'proportion capricieuse' between the various factors (objectivity, emotion, etc.) that seek to regulate or monopolise it. In the first scenario, 'Les lieux familiers' (l. 26) become a kind of arctic wasteland (the portmanteau word in line 28 suggests the artifice of a theatrical or cinematic wind-machine, whose job is to add portentous symbolism). In the second (ll. 29–33) we have people habitually ('le même manège') avoiding verbal exchange (l. 29), a transaction given negative connotations via the expression 'se rendre la monnaie' (to reciprocate) which, in another instance of 'stuttering', linking it to both 'des paroles' and 'de profil', seems more of a snub than a greeting. Equally, the 'stuttering' in lines 31–2 associates reverie with an activity that is anaesthetising rather than enlivening, like addressing an audience of empty chairs (l. 33). In lines 33–6 the scenario of a sterile, dysfunctional, bogusly stricken world, is curtailed by the advent of 'tu' – of poetry or something like it – which effects a reanimation or re-enchantment by disrupting the 'old game' where 'l'âme' found its image in the 'paysage' – the pathetic fallacy, inherited from Romanticism. The poetry defended in Alferi's poem subverts a traditional symbolic order – one where self and world mirror each other in a specular relationship without any real outside ('dehors' will be the poem's last word). Line 35 links the animating force of poetry with walking (a recurrent motif in Alferi), a bodily activity that effects constant displacement. And the slipstream this creates is credited metaphorically with the capacity literally to inject breath ('regonfler') into figures as lifeless as playing cards, and to return us 'ici' (l. 36), to the here and now.

Amusingly, the chaotic piling-up of metaphors does not go unremarked. In the last sequence (ll. 37–57), a dialogue strikes up between the main speaker and a heckling friend who insists on clarification, colloquially bemoaning the poem's plethora of images, and then asking whether last night's made-for-TV film was a 'docudrama' (ll. 37–40). As the speaker strives to clarify what he has been saying, Alferi's poem closes its defence of poetry with a consideration of genre. In his opening rejoinder (ll. 40–4), he affirms that, 'ce matin' (as in the famous opening sequence of Apollinaire's 1913 poem, 'Zone', the new day stands for the present, the 'now' of perceptual experience), reality consists of a juxtaposition of items in 'uneven doses' – sunlight, passers-by, cars, cement. This 'material' could be edited together in such a way as to deliver an underlying 'non-dit', an unstated, allegorical meaning – 'ce qu'elles [the 'vues'] couvrent dans ta pauvre petite tête' (l. 46), as the friend puts it, revealing his appetite for conventional verisimilitude. But being run through the mill of generic conventions would destroy the content of experience, turning what was live perception into the inert elements of a 'mortel docudrama', dominated by the coded verisimilitude of conventional realism or a conventional 'imaginary' (l. 53). (The colloquial 'mortel' in line 54, meaning 'dead boring', cleverly enfolds the deathlier meaning.) By contrast, this stream of perceptions can be left in its raw unedited state, as 'rushes' (the 'clap' of a clapper board in line 41 invokes the discontinuity of film shooting). If so, the link between one percept and another will be analogical rather than symbolic: 'Dosages . . . Que rien ne lie sinon l'analogie', notes line 43, with a nice internal rhyme. Provisional and momentary, such linkages dissolve, as one 'vue' succeeds another. Pressed by his interlocutor, the speaker offers a definition of this analogical successiveness (his way of 'sewing' (l. 45) the images together). 'En deux mots', he avers sententiously, it is 'le sentimental'. The joke here is that any idea of conventional sentiment or sentimentality seems wide of the mark in this context. But the word 'sentimental' could be stretched to make 'deux mots', and 'le senti-mental' would suggest the intermingling of feeling and intellection, the physical and the mental, that characterises the kind of poetry this poem wants to defend. We are referred implicitly here to the title of the volume, *Sentimentale journée*, and to the end of another poem that clarifies the bilingual pun *journée/journey*, and the allusion to Laurence Sterne's eighteenth-century travel narrative, *A Sentimental Journey*.[8] The span of a *journée* can be seen as an unbroken journey of perception. But this is where poetry comes in, for it takes a particular form of utterance, always involving an addressee ('j'ai besoin de toi', l. 48), to invoke a mode in which 'reality' is not turned into something other than itself but apprehended or appropriated in its unfolding. It takes the ironies and naïveties of poetic analogy-making (l. 49), its 'lumière indirecte' (l. 50), to enact 'Cette « réalité » qui se cite elle-même' (l. 51).

In the poetry defended, or celebrated, here the entities we encounter are not representations of reality but, momentarily at least, before language's headlong progress drags our attention forwards – so that what was 'there' a micro-second ago recedes into distance – citations or samples of the real. In Alferi's hands the dual *journée/journey* is uniquely exhilarating, but the need to move on is pressing: 'Maintenant changeons de terrasse' (l. 56).

Notes

1 Pierre Alferi, *Sentimentale journée* (Paris: P.O.L, 1997), pp. 53–5.
2 P. B. Shelley, *Selected Poetry, Prose and Letters* (London: Nonesuch Press, 1951), p. 1052.
3 Alferi, *Sentimentale journée*, back cover.
4 *Ibid.*, p. 21.
5 Pierre Alferi, *Chercher une phrase* [1991], rev. edn (Paris: Christian Bourgois, 2007), p. 30. Hereafter, page references will be given in the text, following the abbreviation *CP*.
6 See the poem 'Allegria', in Alferi, *Sentimentale journée*, pp. 97–9.
7 See the issue of *Revue de littérature générale* co-edited by Pierre Alferi and Olivier Cadiot (Paris: P.O.L, 1995).
8 See Alferi, *Sentimentale journée*, p. 20. The title also alludes to the famous Doris Day song from the 1940s Big Band era: 'Sentimental Journey'.

Further reading

Alferi, Pierre, *Personal Pong*, trans. Kevin Nolan (Cambridge: Equipage, 1997).
    Natural Gaits, trans. Cole Swensen (Los Angeles: Sun and Moon Press, 2000).
    Oxo, trans. Cole Swensen (Providence, RI: Burning Deck Press, 2004).
Pesty, Éric, 'Pierre Alferi "pas un geste inutile / pas un qui ne soit libre"', *Critique, Les Intensifs. Poètes du XXIᵉ siècle*, 735–6 (août–septembre 2008), pp. 612–24.

Afterword: Reading twentieth-century French verse

CLIVE SCOTT

The twentieth century generated a crisis in the reading of verse, which verse analysts, and indeed readers, have been slow to confront. We might begin this brief enquiry by looking back from a mid-century vantage-point. With the arrival of the tape-recorder in the early 1950s, verse had the opportunity to escape from the page and the written, an opportunity foreseen by Apollinaire in his casting of his own *Calligrammes* (1916) as a typographical swansong, and in his promotion of cinema and the gramophone as the future vehicles of poetry's reproduction and transmission: 'Quant aux *Calligrammes*, ils sont une idéalisation de la poésie vers-libriste et une précision typographique à l'époque où la typographie termine brillamment sa carrière, à l'aurore des moyens nouveaux de reproduction que sont le cinéma et le phonographe'.[1]

From the outset, Apollinaire had imagined the further implications of phonographic recording: to be able to compose on to disc with all the ambient noises: '(Comme si le poète ne pouvait pas faire enregistrer directement un poème par le phonographe et faire enregistrer en même temps des rumeurs naturelles ou d'autres voix dans une foule ou parmi ses amis?)'.[2] What underlies the investigation that follows is the paradox that this new departure seemed to produce: the voice was called upon to discredit a verse – and to discredit a way of describing verse (metrical analysis) – which had ostensibly always had the voice in mind. But there, perhaps, is the rub: *the voice in mind*; the new poetry was bent on restoring the voice to the body.

We have assigned the arrival of the tape-recorder to the early 1950s. We might be more exact and identify as the pioneer of its use, from 1953, François Dufrêne, with his *Crirythmes*. Dufrêne's example was soon to be followed by, among others, Bernard Heidsieck, Henri Chopin and Ferdinand Kriwet; and then, in the early 1960s, by Pierre de Vree, and Pierre and Ilse Garnier. For these poets, the tape made possible a mining of vocal resources which up to that point had been beyond the reach of exploitation. The tape restored to the voice its multidimensionality, its true acoustic range:

> Mais ce qui aujourd'hui favorise son [la poésie phonétique] développement c'est l'apparition d'un instrument remarquable: le magnétophone; l'impossible d'hier devient le possible d'aujourd'hui: la connaissance exacte et approfondie de sa langue par le poète lui-même, l'étude directe aux différentes vitesses, aux différents tons, les montages, les superpositions, les perspectives soniques, donc la création

de paysages linguistiques, la possibilité pour le poète d'enregistrer son
émotion, enfin les multiples attraits soudain découverts d'une œuvre
poétique créée exclusivement pour l'oreille.[3]

Suddenly the voice seemed to rediscover itself, in its raw physicality, polarised
now, in a dialectical tension, between the sounds of its primitive origins and the
possibilities of its science-fictional futures.

In the same year that Garnier published his *Spatialisme et poésie concrète*
(1968), Denis Roche published his collection of poems *Éros énergumène*, prefaced
by 'Leçons sur la vacance poétique (*fragments*)' which explain his intention to
'dé-figurer la convention écrite'.[4] This intention partly expresses itself in the
desire to replace the language of standard rhythmic analysis with something
more appropriate to the new poetries. Metrical rhythm, Roche suspects, is no
more than a support mechanism, of purely practical and limited interest; rhythmic analysis should focus on the 'pulsional' dynamic of the verse:

> déroulement de l'écriture, rythme d'arrivée des enchaînements méta-
> phoriques et des ellipses, rythme de déroulement de la lecture, rythme
> des thèmes, de leur apparition et de leur destruction, rythme des
> structures du discours, de leur arrivée et de leur disparition, rythme
> de disposition, d'étalement, d'enserrement, d'écoulement des textes
> imprimés, rythme de succession des pages et de leur imbrication
> possible et de leur succession comme autant d'*empreintes* (au sens
> biologique).[5]

Correspondingly, scansion should cease to have as its business the evaluation
of verse measures, whether quantitative or syllabic, and should, rather, trace
the pulsions ('units of energy'/drives) propelling the verse, or what he calls the
'bousculade pulsionnelle'.[6]

But did the direction of poetry suddenly, at mid-century, change, and court
orality above all else? Or did the tape-recorder merely highlight the difference
between two conceptions of the auditory perception and vocal realisation of
poetry, one still firmly established on the page, the other floating free in the
space of performance? The latter is nearer the truth. But this sudden intensification of the voice's demands does compel a reassessment of current methods of
describing poetry's acoustic activity.

The development of the voice over the past century has occurred on two
principal fronts: (i) in the properties of the voice itself; and (ii) in the voice's
extension beyond its own known boundaries. The development of the properties of the voice itself partly relates to what our ears are now sensitive to. If, in
the late nineteenth century, the acoustic aspect of verse was associated with
the poet's *chant profond*, with the personalisation and psychologisation of text,
with verbal impressionism, in the twentieth century it has perhaps been treated
more as the eruption of the psycho-physiological, as in glossolalia, echolalia
or Tourette's syndrome – that is, as an incipient vocal pathology. And as this

has happened, so a cleavage has occurred between the expressive voice and the psycho-physiological voice, between the discursive and the enunciatory, between rhythm and timbre. It is this cleavage which is traced in the contrary pulls of the linear text and the tabular text, and which defines an ongoing conflict central to the poetry of the twentieth century. At the same time a collision has occurred between, on the one hand, acoustic patterns cultivated for their *rhetorical* value, embodied in alliteration and assonance, and in familiar intonational curves; and, on the other, voices and ears attuned to *psychophonetic* values, to articulatory modulations, to the wilful autonomies of phonemes and morphemes. Let us remember Apollinaire's call for a new body-functional acoustic language in 'La Victoire':[7]

> On veut de nouveaux sons de nouveaux sons de nouveaux sons
> On veut des consonnes sans voyelles
> Des consonnes qui pètent sourdement
> > Imitez le son de la toupie
> Laissez pétiller un son nasal et continu
> Faites claquer votre langue
> Servez-vous du bruit sourd de celui qui mange sans civilité
> Le raclement aspiré du crachement ferait aussi une belle consonne

Let us also remember that even a classicising poet like Valéry insisted on the bodily source of poetry in the voice.[8]

Apollinaire's poem begins to indicate what might be meant by our second concern: the extension of the voice beyond its own known boundaries. We might identify two trends: first the intrusion into the text of Futurist *bruitismo* – noises which might be recorded into the text, or which the voice might be asked to perform; second, different degrees of dehumanisation or devocalisation of the voice under pressure from a language without syntactic or rhythmic discursiveness, or without vocal origins (in what voice does one read dictionary entries, or posters, or shop signs?). In his instructions to the modern declaimer, entitled 'Dynamic and Synoptic Declamation' of 11 March 1916, Marinetti, aside from advising his subject to make use of a certain number of elementary instruments such as hammers, little wooden tables, automobile horns, etc. to produce simple or abstract onomatopoeias, also decrees that the Futurist declaimer must: 'Completely dehumanise his voice, systematically doing away with every modulation and nuance'; and 'Metallize, liquefy, vegetalize, petrify, and electrify his voice, grounding it in the vibrations of matter itself as expressed by words-in-freedom'.[9]

One of the elements which, in free verse, is likely to imply a 'traditional' lyric voice, is the single margin: it establishes the poem's linearity and acts as a consistent speaking position and guarantor of unchanging identity. In the opening lines of the fourteenth of Louis Calaferte's *Îles* (1967):[10]

Indécise cité des femmes   8 (3+3+2)
vos mains   2 (2)
beaux peignes effilés   6 (2+4)
vos mains de feuilles fortes ô mains fidèles et adroites
    14 (2+4+(e)+4+4)

the margin is where the voice originates; it is the zero point from which tone and intonation and tempo find their appropriate configurations. Where such conditions obtain, the likelihood is that reading will wish to confirm recognisability and will adopt well-tried scansional methods.[11] Not surprisingly, therefore, in scanning these lines, I have found my way back to *vers pairs* (lines with an even number of syllables) and I have done so by counting so-called e mutes in the traditional way, and by dispensing with the –es of 'fortes' on the assumption that it is a so-called 'epic caesura', or, put another way, that this fourth line is a combination of a hexasyllable and an octosyllable, and that this justifies my treating the –es of 'fortes' as if it were a line-terminal –es which traditional scansion does not count. This poem appears to have an octosyllabic infrastructure – lines 2–3 might be a 'vers démonté', a single octosyllable split in two. Given this firm and reliable foundation, I have no need to treat the blank space as anything other than something left by the line, a surplus, something unused because not needed. And the play of phonemes I interpret thematically: the repeated unvoiced /f/ is the feminine which permeates the hands, becoming voiced, or rather expressed, in the /v/ of '*vos* mains'; the /i/ of /si/ ('Indécise cité') and /fi/ ('effilés', 'fidèles') convey a certain exquisite intensity and refinement which does not exclude strength and capability ('fortes', 'adroites'). In other words, syllabification and accentuation are chosen as the principal vehicles of rhythm, and acoustic patterning is called upon to play a role of semantic enhancement or euphonic decoration.

Out of anxiety, perhaps, or out of not knowing how to read/listen otherwise, we operate here on the assumption that the old frameworks are in place and that free verse derives its expressive resourcefulness from a re-motivation and adaptation of *known* metrico-rhythmic materials, that the metrico-rhythmic interest of free verse derives from its intertextual relationship with a past, and that free verse is in some sense 'political' and thrives on a polemic built into its very structure – a polemic of trespass, appropriation and *détournement*. But if the line of eight syllables is not treated as an octosyllable, and the line of six syllables is not treated as a hexasyllable, but as syllabic sequences in which the reader is invited to discern 'all possible combinations and interrelationships of eight or six tonal values',[12] then the nature of accent and syllable shifts from the quantitative to the qualitative, from the homogeneous to the heterogeneous, to nuanced and very specific auditory sensations. And, as this happens, so correspondingly a concern with linguistic features (syllabic number, syntactic accentuation) gives way to a concern with paralinguistic features, features of vocal input (pausing, tone, speed, loudness, differing degrees of accentuation, expressive accentuation). We no longer attend, principally, to what measures add up to the syllabic aggregate of the line; instead, we listen to what they create as an unfolding dynamic; in other words, the rhythmic measures of a line are no longer treated as a sequence of juxtaposed, self-immobilising, recuperable units, but as a metamorphosis of evanescent spans of voice.

A second extract, a page (compressed) from André du Bouchet's first 'Fraîchir',[13] presents a very different verse-landscape, a tabular rather than linear text:

comme plié.

parole

qu'à nouveau le corps, quand il a hésité,

ouvre.

comme ciel.   trouée du ciel qu'alors je longe,

vivant.

ou sur ses jambes

flamme, à nouveau, qui vacille.   mais il faut

Here we should make three observations which relate to other poems with radical spatial dispositions. First, quite clearly we may think of the tabular page as a stage or a score as much as a text, that is to say, as a space in which the world 'takes place' through the voice. As on the stage, every entry onto the page is an entry-into-an-action, is an encounter with the pressures and pitfalls of a particular destiny. And space is everything that any words or sets of words might attract to themselves: opening, void, limbo, air, sky, nowhere, loss, breath, suspense. How, then, do I speak this landscape through which words/the voice pass, how express in the voice that the landscape is an emanation of the voice? The voice enters the page as an actor, but not as the voice of an actor speaking his lines; rather, as the actor of the existentiality of the voice. The page has a first person – 'qu'alors je longe'. Is this 'je' assumable as an identity? Or do I assume it as a shifter, which offers *me* a place, but where everyone else can be too, at the same time? Or do I rather read this first person as a *predicament* of the voice?

Second, the move from the linear to the tabular transforms a perspectival vocality (a single voice moving towards an horizon) to a planar vocality (a voice shifting between the vocal, the devocalised, different kinds of oral enunciation). We may say too that the tabular replaces perspectival time with planar time, that is to say, a time which is teleological, directional, homogeneous, made up of regular intervals, is replaced by a time whose very continuity is made up of its heterogeneity, elasticity, digressiveness. The linear page is the page we pass through; the tabular page is the page we spend time in.

And, third, we might say that the move from the linear to the tabular involves a cinematisation of discourse. Tabular verse sacrifices the articulation of discursive syntax to the splicing together of cuts, to editing by 'shot'. Suddenly a window opens on to the world, and anything can enter, can be montaged into the voice. Rhythm then lies not in syntagmatic continuities, but in the enchained discontinuities of shot, in what is put together with what. Mallarmé, in his preface to *Un coup de dés* (1897), already adopted this language of image-sequence, in which space itself is the instrument of the cut: 'Le papier intervient chaque fois qu'une image, d'elle-même, cesse ou rentre, acceptant la succession d'autres.'[14] This rhythm of adjustment, this preparedness to reorientate structural and emotional drives, is the essence of the reading of tabular verse. Cutting and collage are tireless processes of vocal adaptation.

Tabularity disengages text from its firm moorings on the page. What conventions of the page, of linearity, tell us there should not be six margins, or eight, or twenty-eight, that the line spacing should be even, that lines should begin with capital letters, that lines should move from left to right, or should be horizontal? In the extract from du Bouchet's work, there seem to be seven margins, but these margins do not represent a known grid of phrasal beginnings, measured out at equal intervals across the page, a scale of layerings. Instead, they propose themselves as misalignments, not as margins but as slippages of margin. From one point of view, tabular space is a space of dispositional anarchy. From another point of view, it is a space of the infinitely constructible.

What kind of reader, then, do these pages seek to project? The answer is 'an experimental reader', a reader ready to try out different ways of describing textual dynamics and acoustics in order to make best sense of the text and to make the reading of it maximally fruitful; a reader with, at their disposal, not only all the sensitivities to linguistic detail that the past century has made them heir to, through psychoanalysis, linguistics, cultural anthropology, but also all those kinds of listening/reading – Cubist, Expressionist, Futurist, Orphist, Surrealist and so forth – that the various styles of perceptual consciousness have made available to them since the century's beginning. We need to recover the qualitative and the heterogeneous in our experience of accent and syllable; we need to make the ear more responsive to latent performance features in verse – those paralinguistic features such as volume, tempo, pausing, timbre, tone; we need to multiply our modes of analysis; and we need to develop a scansional language able to cope with that multiplicity. Conventional metrico-rhythmic analysis has three potential drawbacks: (i) it operates as a prescription for reading; (ii) it makes the paralinguistic invisible and thereby implies that it is secondary, accidental; (iii) it produces a perception of the poem's acoustic structure which does not tally with phenomena responded to at a live performance. The scansion of modern verse should perhaps activate a larger number of voice-properties than traditional scansion has been wont to do; should ask us to think of voice, not as an instrument that plays language as already given, but as a complex psycho-physiological apparatus for which poetic language serves as a means of self-scrutiny. In this way, reading a poetic text would individuate the reader; and the text, conversely, through the agency of the reader, would engage in a constant process of self-exploration.

Notes

1 Letter to André Billy, 29 July 1918, quoted in Michel Butor (ed.), *Guillaume Apollinaire:* Calligrammes (Paris: Gallimard, 1966), p. 7.

2 Guillaume Apollinaire, *Œuvres en prose complètes*, vol. II, ed. Pierre Caizergues and Michel Décaudin (Paris: Gallimard, 1991), pp. 976–7.

3 Pierre Garnier, *Spatialisme et poésie concrète* (Paris: Gallimard, 1968), p. 41. For more on 'poésie sonore', see Henri Chopin, *Poésie sonore internationale* (Paris: Jean-Michel Place, 1979). For an overview of post-Second World War trends in experimental poetry, see David Seaman, *Concrete Poetry in France* (Ann Arbor, MI: UMI Research Press, 1981).

4 Denis Roche, *Éros énergumène suivi du Poème du 29 avril 62* (Paris: Seuil, 1968), p. 10.

5 *Ibid.*, p. 13.

6 *Ibid.*, p. 16.

7 Guillaume Apollinaire, 'La Victoire', in *Calligrammes* (Paris: Gallimard, 1966), p. 180; first published in *Nord–Sud*, 15 March 1917.

8 'Chaque fois que vous aurez affaire à un poème, c'est toujours sonnant dans une bouche humaine', Paul Valéry, *Réflexions sur l'art* (1935); quoted in Francis Scarfe, *The Art of Paul Valéry: A Study in Dramatic Monologue* (London: William Heinemann, 1954), p. 60.

9 R. W. Flint (ed.), *Marinetti: Selected Writings*, trans. R. W. Flint and Arthur A. Coppotelli (London: Secker and Warburg, 1972), p. 144.

10 Louis Calaferte, *Îles*, in *Rag-time suivi de Londoniennes et de Poèmes ébouillantés* (Paris: Gallimard, 1996), p. 88.

11 For accounts of the versification of regular verse, see, for example, Michèle Aquien, *La Versification appliquée aux textes* (Paris: Nathan, 1993); Benoît de Cornulier, *Art poëtique: notions et problèmes de métrique* (Lyon: PUL, 1995); Clive Scott, *The Poetics of French Verse: Studies in Reading* (Oxford: Clarendon Press, 1998); Jean-Michel Gouvard, *La Versification* (Paris: Presses Universitaires de France, 1999); Brigitte Buffard-Moret, *Précis de versification avec exercices corrigés* (Paris: Armand Colin, 2004).

12 This is an adaptation of Mallarmé's description of the 'liberated' alexandrine, a description which sounds peculiarly prescient of Schoenbergian ways of thinking: 'Les fidèles à l'alexandrin, notre hexamètre, desserrent intérieurement ce mécanisme rigide et puéril de sa mesure; l'oreille, affranchie d'un compteur factice, connaît une jouissance à discerner, seule, toutes les combinaisons possibles, entre eux, de douze timbres.' Stéphane Mallarmé, *Œuvres complètes*, vol. II, ed. Bertrand Marchal (Paris: Gallimard, 2003), p. 206.

13 In André du Bouchet, *Ici en deux* (Paris: Mercure de France, 1986), n.p.

14 Stéphane Mallarmé, *Œuvres complètes*, vol. I, ed. Bertrand Marchal (Paris: Gallimard, 1998), p. 391.

Biographies of the poets

Pierre Alferi (1963–)
Pierre Alferi is the author of several collections of poetry including *Les Allures naturelles* (1991), *Le Chemin familier du poisson combatif* (1992), *Kub Or* (1994), *Sentimentale Journée* (1997), *La Voie des airs* (2004), and of a treatise on poetic language, *Chercher une phrase* (1991). He has also written novels (*Fmn*, 1994, *Le Cinéma des familles*, 1999) and essays on cinema (*Des enfants et des monstres*, 2004). He co-founded the *Revue de littérature générale* with Olivier Cadiot in 1995. Alferi has translated English and American poetry into French as well as works by Giorgio Agamben, and has made a number of films (*Cinépoèmes et films parlants*, 2002), and sound pieces (*En Micronésie*). Working on the borders of the visual arts and music, as well as poetry, he has devised a number of exhibitions and performances with musician Rodolphe Burger and the sculptor Jacques Jullien (*Ça commence à Séoul*, 2007). He has been awarded the Grand prix de poésie de la Société des gens de Lettres.

Guillaume Apollinaire (1880–1918)
The years before the First World War saw an explosion in the arts in Europe and in Paris in particular, and Apollinaire was at the centre of it. He is a creative force in poetry, prose fiction, drama, and in the early developments of film. His art criticism is integral to the conceptual energy driving the avant-garde of the period. He was instrumental in the development of Cubism, and introduced Braque to Picasso; after the war he also introduced André Breton to Philippe Soupault, and was then instrumental in giving birth to Surrealism as well, having himself coined the word 'surréaliste'. In addition to Cubism, his writing before the war engages with Fauvism, Futurism, Orphism and Dadaism; he not only describes but illuminates and develops the creative values involved. His energy derives from his sense that his was a time of momentous change. Modernism in all its forms was beginning to live and breathe. Artists and thinkers in Paris faced the new technological world symbolised by the Eiffel Tower, automobiles, Blériot's flight across the Channel and the advent of radio. At the same time, the people of Europe faced a new cultural world typified by the statuettes and masks from Africa and the Oceanic islands that could now be seen everywhere in the curiosity shops of Montmartre. European history was there to be rewritten; and the arts were there to make that history part of the fabric of lived experience. Apollinaire's driving ambition was to make the new art not just modern, but self-renewing as

well; to have it shape life and not just respond to it. 'Lettre-Océan', first published in 1913, is both a statement and a realisation of that ambition – a moment of Modernist creative optimism which came under such pressure from the battlefields of the Great War. Passionately in love twice over in 1914, the year he enlisted, Apollinaire responded to the war with nationalist pride, with erotic energy, and ultimately with melancholy and grief. 'Lettre-Océan' stands at a crossroads. As we watch it clamour for the power to re-shape the past and re-form the present, we wonder now about its power to renew the future.

Louis Aragon (1897–1982)

Aragon was born and died in Paris. He was raised by his mother and maternal grandmother, believing them to be his sister and foster mother, respectively. Having been involved in Dadaism from 1919 to 1924, he became a founding member of Surrealism in 1924, with André Breton and Philippe Soupault. In the 1920s, Aragon became a fellow traveller of the French Communist Party (PCF) along with several other Surrealists. He would remain a member for the rest of his life, writing several political poems. In 1939 he married Russian-born author Elsa Triolet, the sister of Lilya Brik. Aragon and Triolet collaborated in the left-wing French media before and during the Second World War, going underground for most of the Nazi occupation. Aragon was mobilised in 1939, and awarded the *Croix de guerre* and the Military Medal for acts of bravery. He was one of several poets, along with Robert Desnos and Paul Éluard, to join the Resistance both through literary activities and as an actual organiser of Resistance acts. Along with Paul Éluard, Pierre Seghers and René Char, Aragon would maintain the memory of the Resistance in his post-war poems. In 1950 Aragon was elected to the central committee of the PCF, sponsored by Maurice Thorez. He became the director of *L'Humanité*'s literary supplement, *Les Lettres françaises*. In 1956, Aragon supported the Budapest insurrection, provoking the dissolution of the Comité national des écrivains. Despite his criticisms, Aragon remained an official member of the PCF's central committee until his death. During the last ten years of his life, he published at least two further novels: *Henri Matisse Roman* and *Les Adieux*, as well as helping publish the works of dissidents. After the death of his wife on 16 June 1970, Aragon came out as bisexual, appearing at gay pride parades. Louis Aragon died in Paris on 24 December 1982. Various of his poems have been sung by Hélène Martin, Léo Ferré, Jean Ferrat, Georges Brassens, etc. His prose works include *Le Paysan de Paris* (1926), *Les Cloches de Bâle* (1934) and *Les Beaux Quartiers* (1936, Prix Renaudot). His volumes of poetry include *Les Yeux d'Elsa* (1942), *La Diane française* (1945), *Le Roman inachevé* (1956), *Le Fou d'Elsa* (1963).

Marie-Claire Bancquart (1932–)

Marie-Claire Bancquart has published some twenty volumes of poetry since the short *Projets alternés* (1972), the most recent being *Avec la mort, quartier d'orange entre les dents* (2005). A prolific writer and one of France's foremost women poets, she is also a novelist (she has written six novels to date) and a professor of French literature. She is currently Professor Emeritus at the Sorbonne (Paris-IV). Her literary studies include numerous essays on French literature between 1880 and 1914 with a particular focus on the writings of a small number of favourite authors such as Anatole France, George Sand and Guy de Maupassant. In 2000, she edited *André Frénaud, la négation exigeante*, a collection of essays devoted to a fellow twentieth-century poet whose work echoes many features of Bancquart's own. She has also written studies of Surrealism and an overarching analysis of French literature in the twentieth century. In recent years she has published studies focusing on representations of Paris in post-war French literature and in Surrealism. She was awarded major national literary prizes for her poetry in 1984 and 1985 and has won numerous other awards. Each of her collections of poems stands in dialogic relation to the rest, echoing and developing key themes, and an important personal anthology of her poems, *Rituel d'emportement*, was published in 2002.

Yves Bonnefoy (1923–)

Yves Bonnefoy is a poet, a translator (notably of Shakespeare and Yeats), an essayist and an art historian with particular interest in the works of Giacometti and Miró. He is considered to be the greatest poet of his generation, rising to instant prominence with his first important collection, *Du mouvement et de l'immobilité de Douve* in 1953 whose particular thematic concerns with existence, nature, death and the role of poetry would continue to be elaborated over the next fifty years. He has travelled and taught widely in Europe and the United States, and has received many awards for his work, including the Hudson Review's Bennett Award (1988) and the Franz Kafka Prize (2007). He held the 'Chaire d'étude comparée de la fonction poétique' at the Collège de France from 1981 until 1993. His volumes of poetry include *Hier régnant désert* (1958), *L'Arrière-pays* (1972), *Dans le leurre du seuil* (1975), *Début et fin de la neige* (1991), *La Vie errante* (1993), *Les Planches courbes* (2001). His essays include *Peintures murales de la France gothique* (1954), *L'Improbable* (1959), *Rimbaud* (1961), *Alberto Giacometti, biographie d'une œuvre* (1991), *Dessin, couleur et lumière* (1995), *La Communauté des traducteurs* (2000), *L'Imaginaire métaphysique* (2006), *L'Alliance de la poésie et de la musique* (2007) and *Ce qui alarma Paul Celan* (2007).

André du Bouchet (1924–2001)

André du Bouchet, of French and Russian origin, was born in Paris, but in 1940 his family moved to the United States, where he lived for eight years. He studied there and taught at Amherst College. He is reported to have said that when he returned to France, the French language appeared strange to him; this sense of strangeness permeates his poetry and his writing on translation. As a reading of his poetry would suggest, he spoke very little about himself. He divided his time between Paris and the tiny commune of Truinas in the Drôme, where he is buried. Philippe Jaccottet's account of his funeral is published as *Truinas, le 21 avril 2001*, a title that pays homage to du Bouchet's own tribute to Hölderlin in the text 'Tübingen, le 22 mai 1986'. Since his death an increasing number of essays and collected volumes have been devoted to his work; as well as discussing his poetry, they focus on his engagement with the writing and art of others. His books of poetry include *Air* (1951), *Dans la chaleur vacante* (1959), *Sur le pas* (1959, with illustrations by Tal-Coat), *La Lumière de la lame, avec des eaux-fortes de Joan Miró* (1962), *Laisses* (1975), *Pourquoi si calmes* (1996), *L'Ajour* (1998) and *L'Emportement du muet* (2000).

André Breton (1896–1966)

André Breton was one of the founders of Surrealism (with Éluard, Desnos and Aragon), its leading theoretician (*Manifestes du surréalisme*, 1924 and 1929), and its often-contested leader. He was a poet (*Clair de terre*, 1923; *Le Revolver à cheveux blancs*, 1932), a prose writer (*Nadja*, 1928; *Les Vases communicants*, 1932; *L'Amour fou*, 1937), an editor (*La Révolution surréaliste*, 1924–9; *Le Surréalisme au service de la révolution*, 1931–3), and an exhibition curator (exhibitions in Paris and New York). His exploration of the unconscious and his experiments in automatic writing, dream transcription and free association drew on Freudian psychoanalysis; his concept of the surreal as the merging of dream and reality was grounded in the Hegelian dialectic; and his idea of revolution and liberation in both the individual and the collective spheres was informed by Marxist, and later by Trotskyist revolutionary thought. His aesthetics evolved from a celebration of the single hallucinatory image as the juxtaposition of disparate elements (influenced by Reverdy's poetics), to the idea of 'convulsive beauty' grounded in the dialectic process, and finally to the concept of analogical thought informed by alchemy.

Blaise Cendrars (1887–1961)

Born Frédéric-Louis ('Freddy') Sauser in La Chaux-de-Fonds, Switzerland, Blaise Cendrars's early life was one of family moves and disrupted education. In 1905, he was employed by a jeweller/watchmaker in St Petersburg, amidst the early manifestations of revolution. After returning to Switzerland in 1907, he pursued university studies in Berne, moved to Brussels in 1908 and then, in the following years, to London, Paris and back to St Petersburg, before embarking in 1911 for New York. Back in Paris in 1912, he published *Pâques à New York*, whose manuscript he had already sent to Apollinaire. With Apollinaire he frequented the studios of avant-garde artists (Picasso, Braque, Chagall, Léger, Robert and Sonia Delaunay). Sonia Delaunay provided the kaleidoscopic decoration for Cendrars's *Prose du Transsibérien*, the 'premier livre simultané' (1913), and his association with these artists significantly influenced his *Dix-neuf poèmes élastiques* (1919). In 1914, he married Féla Poznanska, and was soon serving in the Foreign Legion at the front, where, in September 1915, he lost his right arm. In 1924 he resumed his globe-trotting habits with his first visit to Brazil; but after 1924, when he published *Documentaires* (originally entitled *Kodak (Documentaire)* and a re-modelled version in verse of a text from Gustave Le Rouge's *Le Mystérieux Docteur Cornélius* (1912–13)), he abandoned poetry for prose as his chosen expressive medium (e.g. *L'Or*, 1925; *Moravagine*, 1926; *L'Homme foudroyé*, 1945; *Bourlinguer*, 1948). In 1949 he remarried. His second wife was the actress Raymone Duchâteau. He died in January 1961.

Aimé Césaire (1913–2008)

Aimé Césaire was born in the small town of Basse-Pointe, in the north-east of Martinique, under Mount Pelée, a volcano which erupted in 1903, destroying the fashionable capital Saint-Pierre and its thirty thousand inhabitants. The volcanic became a theme as well as a model for his poetry. The island of Martinique was colonised by France in the seventeenth century (the French colonisation of Africa only started in the second half of the nineteenth century). Its indigenous population was replaced largely by African slaves. Their descendants gained French citizenship after the final abolition of slavery in 1848. French was the language of education and all the cultural references were to the *métropole*. Most inhabitants are of 'mixed races' which, during Césaire's youth in effect meant that they perceived themselves as anything but 'black'. Césaire recounted that very early on he developed an aversion to the stiflingly 'bourgeois' atmosphere of his island. He won a scholarship to study in Paris, arrived there in 1931 and met Léopold Sédar Senghor, future poet and president of Senegal, who 'revealed' Africa to him, and introduced him to the milieu of black artists and intellectuals, in particular from the US and the Caribbean, which had flourished there since the 1920s. It seemed that a new consciousness was taking shape and Césaire gave it a name: *négritude*. He wrote *Cahier d'un retour au pays natal* during his studies at the prestigious École Normale Supérieure and published it in 1939. He then returned to Martinique, taught at the Lycée Schoelcher in Fort-de-France and co-edited the journal *Tropiques* during the war.

André Breton, the founder of Surrealism, met him in 1941 and hailed him as the greatest lyrical poet of the time. After the war Césaire started a political career as mayor of Fort-de-France and deputy for Martinique, initially as a Communist. His major political decision of the period was to campaign for the *départementalisation* of Martinique, which became a full part of France (for him the disastrous economic situation of the island made independence as yet impossible, and the main desire of the population was assimilation). In 1956 he decided to leave the Communist Party to protest against its Stalinism and its inability to deal with the colonial situation. Throughout he continued writing and publishing poetry, for instance *Soleil cou coupé* (1948), *Ferrements* (1960) and *Moi laminaire* (1980), and also produced an important dramatic oeuvre, in particular *Et les chiens se taisaient* (1958), *La Tragédie du roi Christophe* (1963) and *Une saison au Congo* (1966).

These works reflect on postcolonial situations – a subject he explored theoretically in many texts, among them his crucial *Discours sur le colonialisme* of 1953. Césaire retired from his elective positions in 1995 but remained an important public figure. In 2005 he published a book of interviews with Françoise Vergès, *Nègre je suis, nègre je resterai.* He died on 17 April 2008.

René Char (1907–1988)

Born at L'Isle-sur-la-Sorgue, René Char grew up in a Provençal landscape for which he conceived a lifelong attachment. In 1929 he joined the Surrealist movement in Paris, contributing to its creations and agitations alike until quietly withdrawing in 1934, shortly after publishing his Surrealist poetry as *Le Marteau sans maître.* Having survived a grave illness in 1936, he published *Placard pour un chemin des écoliers* in homage to the child victims of the Spanish Civil War. Progressively more politicised, though never joining any party, he fought in the Resistance after the collapse of France in 1940, leading a guerrilla group against the Occupation forces; he later helped assure the Allied advance through Provence. After the war, Char was able to publish again, producing the collection *Seuls demeurent* (1945) and the wartime notebook, *Feuillets d'Hypnos* (1946), both later subsumed within his most important compendium, *Fureur et mystère* (1948). His reputation now assured, he divided his time between Paris and Provence, cultivating intellectual friendships with Albert Camus and Yves Battistini, the philosopher Martin Heidegger and the painters Georges Braque and Nicolas de Staël. Volumes of poetry continued to appear: *Les Matinaux* (1950), *La Parole en archipel* (1962) and *Le Nu perdu* (1971). *Chants de la Balandrane* (1977) celebrated a region close to his native village, where he settled permanently in 1978. Major cardiac problems notwithstanding, Char kept writing until his death in 1988, at the age of eighty. *Éloge d'une soupçonnée* appeared in that same year.

Michel Deguy (1930–)

Michel Deguy is a poet and Professor Emeritus of philosophy and literature at the University of Paris VIII (Vincennes at Saint-Denis). Deguy is past president of the Collège International de Philosophie (1990–2), the Maison des Écrivains, and the Centre International de Poésie (Marseille). He is founding editor of the journal *Po&sie* and an editorial board member of both *Critique* and *Les Temps modernes.* After the Fénéon, Max Jacob, and Mallarmé prizes for various works, Deguy received the Grand Prix National de Poésie in 1989, the Encyclopedia Universalis prize and the 2004 Grand Prix de poésie de l'Académie française. Among Michel Deguy's latest books are *La Raison poétique* (2000) and *L'Impair* (2001). He has translated Heidegger and Paul Celan, and co-edited *21 poètes américains* (1980), *René Girard et le problème du mal* (1982), *L'Hexaméron* (1990) and *Au sujet de Shoah* (1990). His collections of poetry include *Fragments du cadastre* (1960); *Poèmes de la presqu'île* (1962); *Figurations* (1969); *Poèmes*

1960–1970 (1973); *Donnant donnant* (1981); *Gisants* (1985); *Poèmes II 1970–1980* (1986); *Poèmes III, 1980–1995* (1998).

Jacques Dupin (1927–)

Jacques Dupin was born on 4 March 1927 in Privas, Ardèche, and has lived in Paris since 1944. He studied law, history and political science. He formed friendships with René Char from 1947, with André du Bouchet from 1950, and from 1954 with Yves Bonnefoy, Philippe Jaccottet, Alberto Giacometti, and many other artists and writers. He married Christine Rousset in 1951. He was editor at the Galerie Maeght from 1955 to 1981. With du Bouchet, Bonnefoy, Louis René des Forêts, Paul Celan and Michel Leiris, he founded the journal *L'Éphémère* in 1966. In 1975 he purchased an old *mas* (farmstead) in the Roussillon, near Céret. His books of poetry include: *Gravir* (1963); *L'Embrasure* (1971); *Dehors* (1975); *De nul lieu et du Japon* (1981); *Le Désœuvrement* (1982); *Une apparence de soupirail* (1982); *De singes et de mouches* (1983); *Écart* (2000); *Coudrier* (2006). His essays on art are *L'Espace autrement dit* (1982); *Joan Miró* (1961, new edition in 1993); *Textes pour une approche sur Alberto Giacometti* (1962, new edition in 1991); *Matière du souffle* (on Antoni Tàpies) (1994).

Paul Éluard (1895–1952)

Born in Saint-Denis on 14 December 1895, Eugène-Émile-Paul Grindel had an uneventful childhood until health problems interfered with his adolescent life. In 1912, a year before his first collection of poetry, *Premiers Poèmes*, was published, he abandoned his studies and entered a sanitorium near Davos, Switzerland. Here he met a young Russian patient, Helena Dimitrievna Diakonova (Gala), who was to become his first wife five years later. Éluard's life among the Dadaists and the Surrealists began in 1919. During the next five years he met and collaborated with Louis Aragon, André Breton, Philippe Soupault, Tristan Tzara, Max Ernst and other writers and artists living in Paris. In 1926 he joined the Communist Party and published his first important work of poetry, *Capitale de la douleur*. Other collections followed: *Défense de savoir* in 1928 and *L'Amour la poésie* in 1929, the year he met Maria Benz, known as Nusch, whom he married in 1934. During the 1930s Éluard published several works of poetry, some in collaboration with writers such as Breton (*L'Immaculée Conception* in 1930) and many with illustrations by well-known artists of the time: Pablo Picasso, Salvador Dalí, Man Ray, Valentine Hugo, Hans Bellmer and Max Ernst. At the start of the Second World War he was mobilised and given the rank of lieutenant. After the fall of Paris in 1940 and the Occupation he reactivated his membership of the Communist Party (now officially outlawed by the Germans) and began a clandestine life. Under various pseudonyms, he wrote articles and poems and ventured secretly into areas where the Resistance was active. Thousands of copies of his lyrically patriotic poem, 'Liberté', were dropped over France by the Royal Air Force in 1942 to keep morale high among the populace.

The joy of liberation was short for Éluard. On 28 November 1946, while recuperating in Switzerland, he received a telephone call with the devastating news that Nusch had died suddenly. For the next few years, he travelled widely: England, Poland, Macedonia, Hungary and Mexico where, at an international peace congress in 1949, he met Dominique Lemor; they were married in 1951. On 18 November the following year, Éluard died of a heart attack and four days later was laid to rest in Père-Lachaise cemetery.

Claude Esteban (1935–2006)

Normalien, agrégé, docteur ès lettres, Claude Esteban combined a career in university teaching with that of poet, editor, translator and critic of art and literature. Any one of the following – *Argile*, the splendid review of poetry, essays and graphics that he edited in the 1970s; his penetrating art criticism; his translations from Spanish into French of such major poets as Paz, Lorca, Guillén and Borges; his exploration, in *Le Partage des mots* (1990), of the dilemmas posed by his French–Spanish bilingualism – would have earned him an important place in twentieth-century French letters. But it is above all for his poetry, at once elegant and tender, for collections like *Terres, travaux du cœur* (1979), *Le Nom et la demeure* (1985), *Élégie de la mort violente* (1989) and *Morceaux de ciel, presque rien* (2001), that Claude Esteban will continue to be read and admired.

Édouard Glissant (1928–)

Édouard Glissant was born in 1928 in Martinique, in the Morne Bezaudin which he left as a baby in his mother's arms, in her drift across the island towards the coastal Cohée du Lamentin – a *mythe d'enfance* and a source of poetic apprehension of the world. After the collections of poems *Un champ d'îles* (1952) and *La Terre inquiète* (1954), he was awarded the prestigious Prix Renaudot for his first novel, *La Lézarde*, in 1958, and simultaneously published *Soleil de la conscience*, the first of now five volumes of a *Poétique*, and *Le Sel noir* (1959). His Parisian years (1945–65) also saw the heyday of his political engagement in the Front antillo-guyanais pour l'indépendance, with travel restrictions confining him to metropolitan France (1959–65). Back in Martinique (1965–80), his activities as teacher and co-founder of the Institut Martiniquais d'Études enabled him to combine his perception of social realities with his inspiration as an essayist (*Le Discours antillais*), novelist (*La Case du commandeur*), and poet. From 1980 until 1988 he was back in Paris as the chief editor of the *UNESCO Courier*. Since 1988 he has been a visiting professor at several American universities; his residence at Louisiana State University produced the *Entretiens de Baton Rouge* with Alexandre Leupin (2008). Alongside several collections, amongst the more recent *Pays rêvé, pays réel* (1985), *Les Grands Chaos* (1993) and *Une nouvelle région du monde* (2006), he has started an *Esthétique*. He is the leading force behind the creation of the Institut du Tout-Monde, a cultural institution and society for the advancement of *Tout-monde* philosophies (at tout-monde.com).

302

Bernard Heidsieck (1928–)

Heidsieck is one of the pioneers of 'Poésie sonore', alongside François Dufrêne, Henri Chopin, and Brion Gysin (Paris, 1955). Exploiting his bodily presence as well as his voice, Heidsieck projects the text towards his audience, who are also his spectators, thus establishing a poetry 'which stands upright', resolutely embodying the whole of language, and the whole of man's and woman's being within that language. Between 1955 and 1961 he wrote sixteen *Poèmes-partitions* (*Scored Poems*) to be read by the unaccompanied voice of the poet. *Poème-partition* V evoked the insecure everyday life of an ordinary man in an urban environment and this was to become one of the recurrent themes of the whole of his future work. Between 1961 and 1980 there followed nine *Poèmes-partitions*, thirteen *Biopsies*, twenty-nine *Passe-partout*, recorded on tape and intended to be broadcast and acted out, as well as read aloud. The most persistent themes are the Cold War and the consumer society: in *Poème-partition B2B3* of 1962 he inaugurates the superimposition of live voices on stage over pre-recorded 'voices over'; in *Le Carrefour de la Chaussée d'Antin* of 1972 his own voice mingles with other voices and with the surrounding city hubbub. *Canal Street*, consisting of thirty-five 'Lectures' (1976), marks his first sustained poetic cycle, revolving around the leitmotif of 'communication', which is another major theme of his work. From 1978 to 1986 he wrote *Derviche/Le Robert* (26 'Lettres'), based on the first ten words starting with A, then B, down to Z, in the 'Robert' dictionary, whose meanings the author admitted escaped him. Between 1988 and 1995 came *Respirations et brèves rencontres*, sixty 'faux monologues' addressed to sixty absent authors, whose only response is an interlocking chain of recorded breathing. Heidsieck's published work includes: *Respirations et brèves rencontres* with three CDs in 2000; *Canal Street* with two CDs in 2002; *La Poinçonneuse* with CD in 2003; *Derviche/Le Robert* with three CDs, published by Al Dante in 2004; and *Partition V* with CD, published by Le Bleu du Ciel in 2002.

Nguyên Hoàng Bao Viêt (1934–)

Nguyên Hoàng Bao Viêt was born on 6 June 1934 in the Mekong Delta, South Vietnam. He is a poet, journalist and writer, and studied anthropology and sociology at the University of Saigon. He was imprisoned in a concentration camp (April 1975) because of his political views, and was one of the 'boat-people' who found temporary shelter in the refugee camp in Djakarta, Indonesia (April 1979). Since December 1979, he and his family have been living in Geneva, Switzerland. He has published four volumes of poems and prose poems: *Hy Vong* [*L'Espérance*] (1961, Prix national de littérature (Poésie) 1960–61), *Nhung Dong Nuoc Trong* [*Les Ondes pures*] (1962), *Quê Huong Nhu Môt Thanh Tich* [*Terre natale comme une relique*] (1969), and *Dâu Tich Phuong Hoàng* [*L'Empreinte du Phénix*] (2008). His poems and short stories have been published in various literary journals since 1950 and translated into more than twelve languages. He is an active member of the Centre des Écrivains vietnamiens en exil (CEVEX), PEN Club

Vietnamien in Europe and the Centre Suisse Romand du PEN International. He founded, and is a member of, the Ligue Vietnamienne des Droits de l'Homme in Switzerland (LVDHS). He was an editor-in-chief of the *Revue des Droits de l'Homme* (Vietnam, Cambodia and Laos), for the French edition in Switzerland.

Philippe Jaccottet (1925–)

Born in Switzerland, Philippe Jaccottet is one of the most prominent figures of the immediate post-war generation of French-speaking poets. He has lived in France since 1953, working as a translator and freelance writer. As well as poetry, he has published prose writings, notebooks and critical essays. He is particularly well known as a translator from German (Musil, Rilke, Mann, Hölderlin) but has also translated Homer, Plato, Ungaretti, Montale, Gongora and Mandelstam. He has won many distinguished prizes for his work both in France and elsewhere. His books include *L'Effraie et autres poésies* (1953), *La Promenade sous les arbres* (1957), *L'Ignorant* (1958), *Airs* (1967), *À travers un verger* (1975), *À la lumière d'hiver* (1977) and *Cristal et fumée* (1993).

Jean-Michel Maulpoix (1952–)

Jean-Michel Maulpoix was born on 11 November 1952 in Montbéliard. He is the author of twenty books of poetry, including *Une histoire de bleu* (1992), *L'Écrivain imaginaire* (1994), *Chutes de pluie fine* (2002), *Pas sur la neige* (2004), and *Boulevard des Capucines* (2006), all published by Mercure de France. He is Professor of French at the University of Paris X Nanterre and specialises in modern and contemporary French poetry. His essays include *La Poésie malgré tout* (1995), *La Poésie comme l'amour* (1998), *Du lyrisme* (2000) and *Adieux au poème* (2005), as well as studies on Henri Michaux, Jacques Réda and René Char. He is also currently editor-in-chief of *Le Nouveau Recueil*, a leading journal of literature and criticism.

Henri Michaux (1899–1984)

Born in a francophone family in Belgium, Michaux died in Paris. Between 1923, when he first started to publish, and 1984, Michaux never stopped writing, and published a prolific, original and influential body of works in several media – texts, drawings, paintings and one film. Michaux's best-known texts are, in chronological order: *Un barbare en Asie* (1933), *La Nuit remue* (1935), *Plume précédé de lointain intérieur* (1938), *Ailleurs* (1948), *Épreuves, exorcismes* (1945), *La Vie dans les plis* (1949), *Face aux verrous* (1954), *Misérable Miracle* (1956), *Paix dans les brisements* (1959), and *L'Infini turbulent* (1967). Gallimard has published an excellent critical edition of Michaux's complete works in three volumes (Pléiade, 1998, 2001 and 2004).

Bernard Noël (1930–)

Bernard Noël was born at Sainte-Geneviève-sur-Argence (Aveyron), on the high plateau of the Aubrac in the southern Massif Central. After a formative engagement in 1953–4 with the politico-gnostic phenomenology of Raymond Abellio and his Cercle d'études métaphysiques, Noël came to critical attention in 1958 with his first major collection of poetry, *Extraits du corps* (the second, *La Face de silence*, appeared only in 1967). His first novel, *Le Château de Cène*, came out in 1969 under the pseudonym Urbain d'Orlhac; its re-publication under his own name in 1971 led to one of France's last literary obscenity trials. The rich vein of work that has followed includes poetry, novels (*Les Premiers mots* (1973), *La Langue d'Anna* (1998), *La Maladie du sens* (2001) among others), essays (*Le Lieu des signes* (1977/2006), *L'Espace du poème* (1998)) and books on artists as diverse as David, Olivier Debré, Fred Deux, Géricault, Matisse, Magritte, Moreau, Opalka, Vieira da Silva, Zao Wou-Ki and *Les Peintres du désir* (1992). Many prefaces and poems on contemporary art are collected in *Onze romans d'œil* (1987), *Romans d'un regard* (2003) and *Les Yeux dans la couleur* (2004). Bernard Noël received the Prix France-Inter for *Journal du regard* (1988) and was awarded the Grand Prix National de Poésie in 1992 and the Prix Max Jacob in 2005. His principal poetic works are contained in two volumes in the Poésie/Gallimard series, *La Chute des temps* (1993) and *Extraits du corps* (2006).

Marie Noël (1883–1967)

Marie Noël was the pseudonym of Marie Rouget. Born in Auxerre, she lived most of her life in her beloved native Burgundy, well away from the literary ferment of the capital. Initially encouraged in her poetic vocation by a cleric, the abbé Munier, she came to be recognised as one of the foremost Catholic poets of her time. Writers as ideologically and stylistically diverse as Montherlant, Duhamel, Aragon and Valéry admired her. From her late thirties onwards, she brought out collections of verse, mainly with the publishing house Stock: *Les Chansons et les heures* (1920); *Le Rosaire des joies* (1930); *Chants de la merci* (1930); *Chants et psaumes d'automne* (1947). Her collected poetry was issued in one volume in 1957. She also wrote two collections of short stories, *Contes* (1942) and *La Rose rouge* (1961), some based on local folktales, and a play, *Le Jugement de Don Juan* (1955). Her autobiographical *Notes intimes* (1959) shows a struggle between hope for a God of love and the experiences that she sometimes felt belied that hope. Her writing takes as starting points the natural beauty of her region; God; her wish for a human love that, she said, passed in front of her door without bothering to stop; and the emotions that took her by surprise ('les soubresauts') during the apparently well-ordered life she led amid a provincial *petite bourgeoisie*.

Saint-John Perse (1887–1975)

Saint-John Perse is the enigmatic pseudonym of Alexis Saint-Léger Léger, a French diplomat who, following a posting to China became (briefly) General Secretary of the Ministry of Foreign Affairs, before being dismissed by the Vichy government in 1940, when he fled to America. He eventually divided his highly successful life as a writer between the south of France and Washington DC, winning the Nobel Prize for Literature in 1960. Born in Guadeloupe in 1887 to a lawyer father and a mother descended from the plantation-owning elite, he moved with his family in 1899 to Pau in southern France, attending university in Bordeaux. Although he had many friendships with literary figures such as Francis Jammes, Jacques Rivière, Valéry Larbaud, Léon-Paul Fargue and Paul Claudel (also a distinguished diplomat), he remained rather a lonely figure. Like that of Claudel, his work gradually adopted an oracular style marked by a rhythm of much broader sweep than that of the alexandrine. His poetics tended to become ever more recondite in diction and impregnated with his peripatetic interest in the natural world. His poetic oeuvre falls into four periods: if *Éloges* (1911) celebrates the lost Caribbean paradise, *Anabase* (1924) (translated by T. S. Eliot), and *La Gloire des rois* (especially 'Amitié du Prince') belong to the Asian period and in particular to the poet's attraction to the Gobi Desert. The American period produced the poems of *Exil* (1942), as well as *Vents* (1946) and *Amers* (1957). The work of his later period includes the epics *Chronique* (1960) and *Oiseaux* (1962).

Francis Ponge (1899–1988)

Francis Ponge, even though he aspired to be a scientist rather than a poet, is one of the most iconic, if fiercely idiosyncratic and independent, poetic figures of post-Surrealist France. Despite the friendship of the influential director of the *Nouvelle Revue Française* Jean Paulhan, and the relatively early interest such esteemed philosophers as Sartre and Camus took in his oeuvre, official recognition did not come about until the 1960s when Sollers, and later Derrida, celebrated him as a spiritual father of textualism and post-structuralism. First and still mostly known as the poet of everyday objects (see, in particular, *Le Parti pris des choses* published in 1942 but composed of much earlier texts), crafting brief, self-enclosed prose poems conceived as verbal equivalents of the referential world, Ponge's practice increasingly gravitated toward open-ended 'dossiers', finding inspiration in the example set by his painter friends. Through the inclusion of all the various stages and configurations of the writing process, such 'work in progress' exemplified the convoluted, often laborious, genesis of the poetic text as well as its intrinsic incompletion (see *La Rage de l'expression* (1952), *Le Savon* (1967), *La Fabrique du pré* (1971), *Comment une figue de paroles et pourquoi* (1977)). Retaining a similar concern for metapoetic considerations and definitional formulae, and maintaining an unabashedly anti-lyrical stance, the later texts thus accentuated the perpetually meandering, self-reflexive movement of poetic writing and continued to introduce novel notions or genres (the combined *objeu* and *objoie*, in particular, designate the 'jouissance' resulting from the self-functioning, self-perpetuating nature of an 'orbiting' text). Both his *Pour un Malherbe* (1965) and the Pléiade edition of his complete works (1999 and 2002) show him to be a unique reconciler of classicism and avant-gardism.

Jacques Réda (1929–)

Jacques Réda is one of France's leading contemporary poets, the author of over twenty volumes of verse and prose poetry since the influential early collections *Amen* (1968), *Récitatif* (1970) and *La Tourne* (1975). The publication of *Les Ruines de Paris* in 1977 launched Réda's reputation as a *poète-flâneur* in the Baudelairean tradition. Réda's alertness to the startling beauty of the everyday, his concern for the generative potential of the particular, translate into language that oscillates between moments of metonymic quickening and the richer, slower work of figurative expansion. Combining lyric generosity with piercing precision in his writing, Réda's poetry is shaped by a remarkable suppleness of tone and rhythm that complements – and impels – a flexibility of perspective as a particular memory or anecdote (often inscribed in material detail) suddenly takes wing, bringing a fluttering intimation of poetry's metaphysical or cosmological reach. An accomplished visual artist and a not infrequent illustrator of his own works, Réda's poetry reveals a painter's eye for the expression of colour and line. His writing crosses boundaries of genre: he merges poetry with the writing of narrative (*récits*, *chroniques*); he is the author of fictional autobiography inspired by his native Lorraine, and has produced a clutch of detective and spy novels; he is a prolific and distinguished jazz critic (his negotiations between jazz rhythm and improvised prosody have been highly influential for contemporary poetics). The work of the neglected Swiss poet Charles-Albert Cingria and the poetry of Jean Follain provided formative influences, but Réda's expansive humanism draws on Dante, Shakespeare, Racine, Wordsworth, Valéry and Robert Frost. A former editor of the literary journal *Nouvelle Revue Française* (1987–95), Réda has played a signal role in encouraging new literary talent, and he continues as a reader for the major French publisher Gallimard.

Pierre Reverdy (1889–1960)

Pierre Reverdy was born in the Mediterranean coastal town of Narbonne, not far from the Catalan border. His father and grandfather were monumental masons and sculptors of ecclesiastical statuary, and Reverdy, who adored his ebullient father, never lost his passion for the plastic arts. His happy childhood, much of which was spent running wild in the hot rocky landscapes around Carcassonne, remained an idyll, or a reality, that he sought in vain to recover. In 1910 he travelled to Paris, and thence by coach to Montmartre, where he soon counted among his friends the cutting edge of the avant-garde in poetry and painting – Apollinaire, Max Jacob, Picasso, Gris, Laurens, Modigliani – and other denizens of the Bateau-Lavoir. Despite the ambient effervescence, Reverdy held down a job as a printer's proofreader (where he first met Adrienne Monnier), and worked hard in solitary lodgings in the rue Cortot. Discharged from the army in 1914, during the war years he published his first collections *Poèmes en prose* (1915), *La Lucarne ovale* (1916), his first novel in verse *Le Voleur de talan* (1917) and his breakthrough collection *Les Ardoises du toit* (1918). From 1917 to 1918 he also founded and ran the highly influential avant-garde magazine *Nord-Sud*. The contents page of the first issue included poems by Apollinaire, Max Jacob and Reverdy himself, followed by Reverdy's seminal essay on the new movement in painting 'Sur le cubisme'. Succeeding issues contained many of his most penetrating and densely argued essays on poetics and aesthetics including 'Essai d'esthétique littéraire', 'L'Émotion' and 'L'Image': these and later essays on aesthetics are collected in the complete edition of Reverdy (Flammarion). To the surprise of many, Reverdy announced his conversion to Catholicism in 1921, and followed it up by removing to the secluded monastery town of Solesmes, and settling at the foot of its famous abbey. 'Libre penseur, je choisis librement Dieu' was one gnomic aphorism he offered by way of explanation in *Le Livre de mon bord* (1948) – a kind of spiritual apologia. Reclusive years of intense introspection followed, during which he rewrote several of his poems. In 1948 he published the first of his 'livres d'artistes', *Le Chant des morts*, in collaboration with Picasso. Later works include *Au soleil du plafond*, with lithographs by Juan Gris (1955), and *La Liberté des mers* with his long-time friend and ally Georges Braque, which appeared in 1960, the year of Reverdy's death.

Jacques Roubaud (1932–)

Jacques Roubaud's various published works since 1967 include *La Belle Hortense* (a novel, the first in a series, 1985), ∈ (the mathematical symbol for 'is an element of', poetry, 1967), *Trente et un au cube* (poetry, 1973), *La Vieillesse d'Alexandre* (essay on the iconic French poetic line, 1978), *Quelque chose noir* (1986), and *La Forme d'une ville change plus vite, hélas, que le cœur des humains* (poetry, 1999). *Le Grand Incendie de Londres: récit avec incises et bifurcations (La Destruction)* (1989) was the first of currently five or six 'branches' of *le Projet*, what is referred to as Roubaud's 'increasingly autobiographical' project. He has long been a member of the OULIPO (Ouvroir de Littérature Potentielle) group of mathematicians and writers, founded by Queneau and Le Lionnais as a kind of counterpart/contrast to Surrealism and the mathematical group Bourbaki; Roubaud gives his own description in his piece 'Écrit sous la contrainte' (in *Poésie, etcetera: ménage* (1995), pp. 197–219). His favoured disciplines of mathematics, critical argumentation and medieval and modern poetry mark him out as a serious intellectual with a love of rigorously formal games pursued to their finish; these are carried out with a gently sidelong glance, wit and punning anglophile humour as well as a broadly humane outlook. He has published many collaborative books.

Amina Saïd (1953–)

Amina Saïd was born in Tunis and moved to Paris in 1978 to study at the Sorbonne. She now lives in Paris, where she is an active promoter of poetry, giving recitals of her poems and working with young writers in literary workshops. To date she has published eight works of poetry and two volumes of re-created Tunisian folktales. In 1989 she was awarded the Jean Malrieu Prize for *Feu d'oiseaux* and, in 1994, the Charles Vildrac Prize for *L'Une et l'autre nuit*. In addition to her creative writing, she is also a translator, in particular of the novels and short stories of the Filipino writer Francisco Sionil José whose work she translates from English into French.

Her books of poetry include: *Paysage, nuit friable* (1980), *Métamorphose de l'île et de la vague* (1985), *Sables funambules* (1988), *Feu d'oiseaux* (1989) (Prix Jean Malrieu), *Nul autre lieu* (1992), *L'Une et l'autre nuit* (1993) (Prix Charles Vildrac), *Marcher sur la terre,* (1994), *Gisements de lumière* (1998), *De décembre à la mer* (2001), *La Douleur des seuils* (2002) and *Au présent du monde* (2006). She has published folktales – *Le Secret* (1994), *Demi-coq et compagnie* (1997) – and a CD, *L'Horizon est toujours étranger* (2003). Her translations include Ahmed Ben Dhiab, *Chants tatoués* (1987).

Victor Segalen (1878–1919)

Victor Segalen was born in Brest. He trained as a naval doctor in Bordeaux, and spent his first posting (1903–4) in French Polynesia, where his experiences led him to write a novel, *Les Immémoriaux* (1907). He returned to France for several years, when he collaborated with Debussy on a pair of ultimately abandoned operas and began to learn Chinese. In 1909 he left for China, where he would spend much of the remainder of his life. An initial expedition with Gilbert de Voisins resulted in *Briques et tuiles*, a text from which a number of his subsequent works – including *Stèles* (1912) – emerged. He fulfilled several professional roles, including professor of medicine and personal physician to the son of the first president of the Republic of China. A major topographical and archaeological expedition from north-east to south-west China was led by Segalen in 1914, but this was interrupted by the outbreak of war in Europe. Segalen requested a posting to the Front, but having fallen ill spent much of the remainder of the war in Brest, where he completed his poetry collection *Peintures* (1916). He returned to China in 1917 to recruit indigenous workers for wartime service in France. Segalen was a polymath, with interests in fields as diverse as medicine, music, the visual arts, archaeology and cartography. His literary production ranged across a variety of genres, including poetry, novels, theatre, libretti and essays. At the time of his premature death in Huelgoat in 1919, the majority of his oeuvre – keys texts such as *René Leys* and the *Essai sur l'exotisme* – remained unpublished, and these only became available when interest in Segalen increased from the 1950s onwards.

Léopold Sédar Senghor (1906–2001)

Léopold Sédar Senghor was born at Joal in Senegal on 9 October 1906. Following primary schooling at a Roman Catholic mission, and at secondary level in the capital Dakar, he attended the Lycée Louis-le-Grand in Paris, followed by a degree at the Sorbonne. In 1935, he was successful in the fiercely competitive *agrégation* in French grammar, opening the way to a teaching post at the Lycée

Descartes in Tours. While there, he pursued studies in Paris in African languages and linguistics. Called up in 1939 for war service, he was taken prisoner in 1940 and invalided out in 1942, allowing him to join the Resistance. From 1944 to 1960 he occupied the chair of Black African Civilisation and Languages at the École nationale de la France outre-mer. The year 1945 saw the publication of his first collection of poetry, *Chants d'ombre*, and the start of his political career as deputy for Senegal, becoming Secretary of State in 1955 and then ministerial adviser in 1959. When Senegal obtained independence in 1960, he was elected president, a post from which he resigned twenty years later, having been demo-cratically re-elected four times. Poetry collections accumulated: *Hosties noires* (1948), *Éthiopiques* (1956), *Nocturnes* (1961), *Lettres d'hivernage* (1972) and *Élégies majeures* (1979). He continued his cultural activities intensively, spoke and published many essays, and was awarded numerous major prizes for his work. In 1983 he was the first black writer to be elected to the Académie française. He died on 20 December 2001.

Gérard Titus-Carmel (1942–)
Born in Paris, Gérard Titus-Carmel studied art at the École Boulle from 1958 to 1962. The death of his father (1949) and of his young wife (1967) was to influ-ence all his work. There were early meetings with André Breton, Elsa Triolet and Louis Aragon, Matta and Ernst. In 1969 he abandoned painting for nearly twenty years, concentrating on drawing and engraving. In 1970, he wrote *Joaquin's Love Affair*, and created *7 Constructions possibles* and *25 Variations sur l'idée de rupture*. He met Joan Robinson in Japan and they married in 1971. From that time to the present, he has maintained a remarkably intense level of crea-tivity, offering great plastic works such as *The Pocket Size Tlingit Coffin* (1975), *Caparaçons* (1981), *Forêts* (1986), *Quartiers d'hiver* (1999), *Feuillées* (2000–3) and *L'Herbier du seul* (2006). He has written widely and influentially on the global aesthetics and ontology of art and poetry, devoting studies to specific artists and poets such as Ernst, Bonnard, Chardin, Schwitters, Crane, Goya, Munch, Bonnefoy, Roud, Michaux and Bram van Velde; and since 1987 he has produced a powerful poetic oeuvre of some twenty volumes from *La Tombée* (1987) and *Le Motif du fleuve* (1990) to *Travaux de fouille et d'oubli* (2000), *Ici rien n'est présent* (2003), *Jungle (non-lieu)* (2005) and *Seul tenant* (2006). In addition, he has col-laborated with many of France's great contemporary writers by illustrating their work (Apollinaire, Dupin, Aragon, Jaccottet, Bénézet, Quignard, Bonnefoy, Faye, Frémon, Vargaftig and many others).

Paul Valéry (1871–1945)
Paul Valéry was born at Sète near Montpellier. As a young man he was attracted to the circle of Stéphane Mallarmé in Paris and published a number of Symbolist poems under Mallarmé's influence, but in 1892, visiting his mother's family in Genoa, he underwent a severe moral and intellectual crisis and decided to

abandon poetry. He did, however, continue to write prose, such as the essay *Introduction à la méthode de Léonard de Vinci* (1895) and the dramatic monologue *La Soirée avec monsieur Teste* (1896), two profound explorations of self-analysis and creativity. It was only in 1912, at the instigation of his lifelong friend André Gide, that he agreed to rewrite the poems of his youth, which he finally published in 1920 as *Album de vers anciens*. In the process of rewriting, he composed a new, 500-line poem *La Jeune Parque*, which, when published separately in 1917, was acclaimed as an innovative masterpiece for its musical rendering of the variations in consciousness in a single night. These two volumes freed Valéry's creative drive and led to the publication in 1922 of *Charmes*, one of the most famous volumes of French verse of the twentieth century. His own voice is heard most clearly in 'Le Cimetière marin', an elegiac meditation on the meaning of life and death, set in a graveyard by the sea.

Valéry's personal and professional life was largely uneventful. In 1900 he married Jeannie Gobillard, the niece of the painter Berthe Morisot. They had a son and a daughter. Valéry worked for much of his adult life as an administrator in the Havas newspaper agency. He was elected a member of the Académie française in 1925 and Professor of Poetics at the Collège de France in 1937. After the publication of *Charmes* he continued to give lectures and write essays on literature, art, architecture, music, science, philosophy, psychology and society (many collected in five volumes of *Variétés*, published between 1936 and 1944). Indeed, for some critics, Valéry's greatest achievement is the collection of his private notebooks entitled *Cahiers*, in which he wrote his thoughts on these topics every morning for most of his adult life. On his death he was buried in the cliff-top cemetery overlooking the Mediterranean that inspired 'Le Cimetière marin'.

Glossary

accidental in music, a mark which indicates raising or lowering a note by half a tone.

adnominatio a warning or censure.

agentive of an affix or suffix signifying the agent (subject) of a verb or noun.

alexandrine twelve-syllable line of verse. When it is regular, a line is divided by a caesura into equal halves (called hemistiches).

allegory a narrative or work of art intended to be understood symbolically.

alliteration the recurrence of the same initial sound in words in close succession.

allocution an exhortation or formal address.

alveolar sound produced with the tongue against the roots of the teeth ('l', 'd', 'n').

amphibology an ambiguous or equivocal statement.

anacoluthon an abrupt change within a sentence from one syntactic structure to another.

anadiplosis repetition of the last word of one line or clause to begin the next.

anagram a word or phrase formed with the letters of another in a different order.

analeptic restoring to consciousness, or a restorative medicine.

anamorphosis (anamorphotically) a distorted figure which appears regular when viewed or mirrored from a certain angle.

anaphora the rhetorical device of starting successive lines or phrases with the same word.

anastrophe inversion of normal word order for the sake of emphasis.

antiphrasis use of words in a sense opposite to the literal one, usually for the sake of irony.

antithesis a figure of speech in which words or phrases are balanced in contrast.

apocryphal of doubtful authority.

apophasis (apophatic) effectively saying something by claiming to deny having mentioned it.

apostrophe address to an absent person or thing or to an idea, often preceded by a declamatory 'O'.

apotropaic intending to avert or avoid evil.

approximant a speech sound, such as a glide or liquid, produced by narrowing but not blocking the vocal tract.

arbitrary in Saussurean linguistics the notion that there is no innate link between objects in the real world and the words conventionally used to denote them.

aspect verbal form expressing the inception, duration or completion of an action.

assonance the repetition of sounds, which, including vowels but not usually consonants, falls short of rhyme.

automatic writing a type of writing while in a state of self-induced trance, inspired by dream or the unconscious, practised by the Surrealists.

blazon a depiction in heraldic terms, or a celebratory text listing a series of personal features.

caesura a break, especially a sense pause, usually near the middle of a verse.

canon composition where the melody is repeated by one part following another in imitation.

cheville redundant word or expression used in verse less for meaning than to maintain rhythm or metre.

chiasmus parallel repetition in reverse order either of sounds or words.

contre-rejet the isolation, at the end of one line, of a short element that is bound syntactically to the next line.

couplet pair of lines of verse, usually rhyming.

Dada an anarchistic movement of poets and writers developed between 1916 and 1923 by Max Ernst and Tristan Tzara attempting to overthrow literary and artistic values from within by their chaotic anti-artistic practice.

deixis (deictic) reference by means of an expression whose interpretation is relative to the (usually) extra-linguistic context of the utterance, such as: who is speaking; the time or place of speaking.

dental a sound produced by applying the tongue to the teeth or the gums ('d', 'n', 't').

dialectic a form of logical debate or disputation which seeks to resolve the conflict between two opposing theories rather than prove or disprove either, typically using a thesis–antithesis–synthesis structure.

diegesis a factual narrative, history; a recital or account.

ekphrasis the figurative representation in literature of real or imaginary works of art.

elegy (elegiac) a song of mourning, a funeral lament.

ellipsis a figure of syntax by which words are left out and merely implied.

elocutionary the art of public speaking in which gesture, vocal production and delivery are emphasised.

end-stopped having a pause at the end of each line, rather than letting the phrase or the sense run on.

enjambement (or **enjambment** in English): the spilling over of grammar and sense from the end of one metrical line into the next.

enunciator the speaker or writer of a distinct statement or utterance.

envoi the author's final words, closing a poem and 'sending' it to the reader.

epanadiplosis repetition at the end of a phrase or line of a word used at beginning.

epanalepsis repetition at the end of a line, phrase or clause of the word or words that occurred at the beginning of the same line, phrase or clause.

epic elevated style as of a long poem narrating heroic events.

epigraph a citation or motto at the start of a book or section.

epiphany a sudden revelation or insight.

epiphora repetition of a word or phrase at the end of several successive clauses.

euphonia a pleasant-sounding sequence of words, often produced by modulating the original sounds.

fable (fabular) a folktale, obviously fictitious or mythical, but intended to instruct and amuse.

free verse *see vers libre*.

fricative a consonant, such as f or s in English, d and t in French produced by the forcing of breath through a constricted passage.

glossolalia the speaking of wholly or partly unintelligible phrases seemingly part of an unknown language.

haiku a type of Japanese poetry with only three lines, of five, seven and five syllables.

hemistich a half-line of verse.

hermeneutic concerned with interpretation.

heuristic of an argument whereby readers or listeners are guided and encouraged to discover meaning by themselves.

hexameter a line of six metrical feet.

hexasyllable a line of poetry using six syllables.

homophone (homophonic) a word pronounced like another which differs in spelling and meaning.

hypallage the reversal of the syntactic relation of two words; an interchange of two elements in a phrase or sentence from their expected relation.

hyperbaton an inversion of normal word order.

hyperbole extravagant statement, obviously exaggerated.

hypotyposis vivid description of a scene, event or situation.

ideogram, ideograph a graphic symbol that stands not for a word or a sound but for the thing or concept itself; in Apollinaire, a graphic arrangement of words which depicts something additional to or other than what is denoted by the individual words themselves.

idiolect a particular variant of a language, shared by a small professional or social group, like a dialect, but more restricted.

image a figure of speech, especially a simile or a metaphor, representing one thing by another.

imperative a verbal mood expressing a command.

incipit the beginning or opening words of a text.

intertextuality the process whereby a text takes on its full meaning only by reference to other texts which are embedded, cited or alluded to within it.

isochronic (isochronal, isochronous) of equal time, performed at the same time, at equal intervals.

isotopy 'a redundant set of semantic categories which make possible the uniform reading of a narrative' (Greimas). A sequence of expressions joined by a common 'semantic denominator'; identifies one of the themes of a text.

labial consonants articulated either with both lips (bilabial articulation) or with the lower lip and the upper teeth (labiodental articulation). (p, b, m, f, v, w).

langue in Saussurean linguistics, the ensemble of a whole natural language.

lateral consonant produced by air passing over one or both sides of the tongue (l).

lexeme a single word or basic unit of vocabulary.

lexis vocabulary; the entire stock of words in a language.

literariness for Roman Jakobson, those stylistic features of a text which alert us to its literary nature as opposed to language used for everyday purposes.

lyric relating to a category of poetry that expresses subjective thoughts and feelings, often in songlike style or form. Contemporary poets tend to focus on a more enigmatic 'lyrical subject' (Jean-Michel Maulpoix).

mantissa an addition of trivial importance to a discourse.

metaphor the figure in which one thing stands for another due to resemblance, similarity or association.

metatextual something implied by the text but not actually written.

metonymy the figure in which one thing stands for another due to contiguity. Reference to something or someone by naming one of its attributes.

metre the organised rhythm of accented or unaccented syllables.

metrics the study of the rules and patterns of metre.

mimesis the attempt to imitate reality as directly and literally as possible in language.

mise en abyme the effect of mirroring by embedding a similar model within another: a play within a play, etc.

montage the cutting and editing (originally of film, but now often of text, rather as in 'cut and paste') of fragments of narrative or dialogue into a new, usually irregular, order.

morpheme the smallest meaningful grammatical element of a language, say a prefix or a suffix.

mute 'e' the 'e' at the end of a French word which is unstressed in everyday speech, but which may be spoken or read and included in the syllable count of a line of verse.

nasal a sound uttered through the nose (in French, 'en', 'in', 'on').

octosyllable a line of verse containing eight syllables.

onomatopoeia imitation of the sound associated with a thing or an action.

optative verbal mood that is expressive of wish or desire; sentence that is expressive of wish or hope.

orphism term coined about 1912–13 by Apollinaire to describe the abstract and colourful paintings

315

of Robert and Sonia Delaunay. The term was derived from Greek mythology (the poet and musician Orpheus). Aiming to appeal to the senses, this style of painting employed overlapping planes of contrasting colours.

OULIPO 'Ouvroir de Littérature Potentielle', a literary movement writing poetry inspired by random verbal connections (say every 'nth' word in a text or a dictionary).

oxymoron an expressive phrase or epithet formed by placing two contradictory terms adjacent to one another.

paralepsis, paralipsis stating and drawing attention to something in the very act of pretending to pass over it.

parataxis (paratactic) a string of phrases which lack connecting words or subordination.

paronomasia, paronomasis the use of a play on words which sound alike but differ in meaning.

performative in J. L. Austin, a use of language whereby the very utterance of the words performs the act mentioned (as in 'I thee wed', or 'I name this ship').

periphrasis (periphrastic) using more words than are necessary to explain or describe; circumlocution.

phoneme the smallest contrastive unit in the sound system of a language.

plosive of, relating to, or being a speech sound produced by complete closure of the oral passage and subsequent release accompanied by a burst of air, as in the sound 'p' 'b'.

poème-partition a 'sound poem' which uses instrumental sounds following a musical 'score' as well as words spoken by the poet.

poetic persona the first-person speaker of a poem or implied by the poem – not necessarily explicitly identified, not necessarily the biographical author.

poetics the theoretical study of poetry; or the stylistic system of a poet.

polyptoton repeating a word, but in different cases or inflexions in the same sentence.

preterition a rhetorical figure of speech wherein the speaker or writer briefly mentions something while claiming to omit it.

prose poetry poetry which is written out as if it were prose, but where the reader detects phrasing, and traces of rhythm, assonance and alliteration which reveal a poetic intent (*see* **vers libre**).

prosopopoeia a figure of speech in which an imaginary or absent person is represented as speaking or acting; the personification of something which is inanimate or abstract.

quatrain a stanza of four lines of verse.

referent *see* **sign, signifier, signified**.

refrain a line or phrase or verse recurring at the end of each stanza of a poem.

rejet the isolation, at the beginning of one line, of a word that is syntactically bound to the previous line.

rhizomatic, rhizomatous seeming to flower from the root, i.e. of a text, throwing up meanings whose connections are invisible on the surface (Deleuze).

rhyme the pairing of homophonous words in verse. 'Rime léonine': a very rich rhyme containing at least two syllables; 'rime riche': containing more than two elements in the tonic syllable; 'rime suffisante': rhyme of tonic vowel + following consonant(s); 'rime pauvre': a weak rhyme, containing only one identical element; 'rimes croisées': rhyme scheme alternating, or crossing rhymes (abab); 'rimes embrassées': embracing one pair of rhymes within another (abba); 'rime plate': rhyme scheme following the pattern aabbcc.

rhythm regular recurrence and pattern of tonic stress or of long and short sounds.

ritornello a short instrumental passage, like a prelude, interlude or refrain, in a vocal work.

rondeau a form of poem of thirteen lines characterised by closely knit rhymes, with the opening words repeated as a refrain after the eighth and thirteenth lines.

scansion the metrical patterns of verse and their analysis.

scholion, scholium (in Francis Ponge) marginal explanatory annotation, as in the margin of a manuscript or a classical text, providing explanation and comment.

semantic relating to the meaning of words.

seme an elementary unit of meaning.

semiotic dealing with a text as a system of linguistic oppositions, rather than given meanings.

sens meaning.

sibilant having, containing, or producing the sound of or a sound resembling that of the 's'.

sign, signifier, signified in Saussure's linguistic system, communication is operated by the 'sign' (a linguistic item or event). The sign comprises the 'signifier' (normally a written or spoken word), the 'signifed' (what it evokes in the mind of the reader or listener), and the 'referent' (what it refers to in the real world).

simultaneity, *simultanéisme* (simultaneous) a poetic movement (led by Apollinaire) which was inspired by the simultaneous multiple perspectives of Futurist and Cubist painting.

sonnet a poem of fourteen lines, often divided into stanzas of four, four, three and three lines, but different stanzaic groupings, or one undivided stanza, are also frequent.

stanza sometimes loosely called a 'verse' in English. A separate group of lines of verse within a poem.

Surrealism a movement of poetry calling on the unconscious and the world of dreams for its inspiration, rather than the real word (Aragon, Breton, Desnos, Éluard).

Symbolism a nineteenth-century French poetic movement, typified by Mallarmé, where poetry was intended to evoke indirectly through symbolic and suggestive language, rather than describe or relate.

synaesthesia the exchange of different modes of sensorial experiences; the expression of one sense in terms of another, say the sight of 'blue' as the feeling of 'cold'.

synecdoche a trope substituting a part for the whole.

syntax the grammatical organisation of phrases, particularly their word order.

techne the technical craft and features of poetic writing, as opposed to its inspiration and messages.

theophany a manifestation or appearance of God or a god to man.

toponym a place name.

topos a traditional or conventional literary or rhetorical theme or topic.

transferred epithet figure of speech where qualities of people or things are transposed, as in 'sol indolent' where it would normally be the feet rather than the ground which were numb.

trope word or expression used in a figurative, non-literal sense (metaphor, irony, etc.). Displacement of the reference of words.

valency (agentive) the power or capacity of a verb to combine with or displace dependent elements within a sentence.

vernacular the everyday conversational use of language, as opposed to more formal registers used in writing.

vers in French is either (a) poetry/ verse as opposed to prose, or (b) a single line of poetry. Never a 'verse' in the English sense of a stanza grouping a set of lines together.

***vers libre*,** **free verse** verse that has neither regular rhyme nor regular meter, but is written in separate lines, as poetry. Free verse often uses cadences rather than uniform metrical feet, and assonance and alliteration rather than formal rhyme schemes (*see* **prose poetry**).

vers pairs*/*impairs even or uneven lines. Typical 'pair' lengths would be six or twelve syllables; typical 'impair' would shift between five and seven, or eleven and thirteen.

verset a long, loose line of verse (or a short complete 'verse', in the English sense), with fluid rhyme and rhythm. Originally from the Bible, as in, say, the Psalms. The 'verset' calls for oral declamation.

versification the study of, or the system of, the techniques used by a poet.

zeugma a general term describing when one part of speech (most often the main verb, but sometimes a noun) uses the same structure to govern two elements of a sentence which normally convey contradictory meanings.

318

Select bibliography

Items selected below are supplementary to Further reading sections

I Anthologies and other works of reference

Aquien, Michèle, *Dictionnaire de poétique* (Paris: Livre de Poche, 1993).

Auster, Paul (ed.), *The Random House Book of Twentieth-Century French Poetry* (New York: Random House, 1982).

Beausoleil, Claude (ed.), *La Poésie suisse romande* (Vevey: Les Éditions de L'Aire, 1993).

Boulanger, Pascal (ed.), *Une action poétique de 1950 à aujourd'hui* (Paris: Flammarion, 1998).

Breunig, LeRoy C., *The Cubist Poets in Paris: An Anthology* (Lincoln: University of Nebraska Press, 1995).

Broome, Peter and Chesters, Graham (eds.), *An Anthology of Modern French Poetry (1850–1950)* (Cambridge: Cambridge University Press, 1976).

  The Appreciation of Modern French Poetry (Cambridge: Cambridge University Press, 1976).

Caws, Mary Ann (ed.), *Surrealist Love Poems* (London: Tate Publishing, 2001).

  Surrealist Painters and Poets (Cambridge, MA: MIT Press, 2001).

  The Yale Anthology of Twentieth-Century French Poetry (New Haven, CT: Yale University Press, 2004).

Chénieux-Gendron, Jacqueline (ed.), *Il y aura une fois: une anthologie du surréalisme* (Paris: Gallimard, 2002).

Chevrier, Jacques (ed.), *Anthologie africaine*, vol. II: *Poésie* (Montréal: Hurtubise HMH, 2006).

Dannemark, Francis, *Ici on parle flamand & français* (Bordeaux: Le Castor Astral, 2005).

Décaudin, Michel, *Les Poètes fantaisistes* (Paris: Seghers, 1983).

  (ed.), *Anthologie de la poésie française du XXème siècle*, vol. I (Paris: Gallimard, 2000).

Deguy, Michel, Davreu, Robert and Kaddour, Hédi (eds.), *Des poètes français contemporains* (Paris: ADPF, 2001).

Deluy, Henri (ed.), *Poésie en France 1983–1988, une anthologie critique* (Paris: Flammarion, 1989).

Dent, Alan (ed.), *When the Metro is Free: An Anthology of Contemporary French Counter-Cultural Poetry* (Middlesbrough: Smokestack, 2007).

Dia, Hamidou (ed.), *Poètes d'Afrique et des Antilles* (Paris: La Table Ronde, 2002).

Eagleton, Terry, *How to Read a Poem* (Oxford: Blackwell Publishing, 2007).

Frontier, Alain, *La Poésie* (Paris: Belin, 1992).

Gavronski, Serge, *Towards a New Poetics: Contemporary Writing in France* (Berkeley: University of California Press, 1994).

(ed.), *Six Contemporary French Women Poets: Theory, Practice, and Pleasures* (Carbondale, IL: Southern Illinois University Press, 1997).

Giraudon, Liliane (ed.), *29 femmes en poésie* (Paris: Stock, 1997).

Gouvard, Jean-Michel, *La Versification* (Paris: Presses Universitaires de France, 1999).

Grégoire, Bruno, *Poésies aujourd'hui* (Paris: Seghers, 1990).

Jean, Georges, *Nouveau trésor de la poésie pour enfants* (Paris: Le Cherche-Midi, 2003).

Herbert, W. N. and Hollis, Mathew (eds.), *Strong Words: Modern Poets on Modern Poetry* (Newcastle upon Tyne: Bloodaxe, 2000).

Hocquard, Emmanuel and Raquel (eds.), *Orange Export Ltd. 1969–1986* (Paris: Flammarion, 1986).

Hollier, Denis (ed.), *A New History of French Literature* (Cambridge, MA: Harvard University Press, 1989).

Jarrety, Michel (ed.), *Dictionnaire de poésie de Baudelaire à nos jours* (Paris: Presses Universitaires de France, 2001).

Jones, Edward Allen, *Voices of Negritude* (Valley Forge, PA: Judson Press, 1971).

Kelley, David and Khalfa, Jean (eds.), *The New French Poetry* (Newcastle upon Tyne: Bloodaxe Books, 1996).

Kesteloot, Lylian (ed.), *Anthologie négro-africaine* (Vanves: Edicef, 2006).

Lambersy, Werner, *Poésie francophone de Belgique* (Paris: Le Cherche-Midi, 2002).

Linkhorn, Renée and Cockran, Judy (eds.), *Belgian Women Poets: An Anthology* (New York: Peter Lang, 2000).

Mailhot, Jean and Nepveu, Pierre (eds.), *La Poésie québécoise des origines à nos jours. Anthologie* (Montréal: Les Presses de l'Université du Québec, 1980).

Martin, Graham Dunstan, *Anthology of Contemporary French Poetry* (Edinburgh: Edinburgh University Press, 1972).

Maulpoix, Jean-Michel (ed.), *Poète toi-même, une anthologie de poésie contemporaine* (Bordeaux: Le Castor Astral, 2000).

Para, Jean-Baptiste (ed.), *Anthologie de la poésie française du XXème siècle*, vol. II (Paris: Gallimard, 2000).

Prendergast, Christopher (ed.), *Nineteenth-Century French Poetry: Introductions to Close Reading* (Cambridge: Cambridge University Press, 1990).

Queneau, Raymond, *Cent mille milliards de poèmes* (Paris: Gallimard, 1961).

Rees, William (ed.), *The Penguin Book of French Poetry: 1820–1950* (London: Penguin Books, 1992).

Reuzeau, Jean-Yves (ed.), *French Poets of Today* (Toronto: Guernica Editions, 1999).

Romer, Stephen (ed.), *Twentieth-Century French Poems* (London: Faber and Faber, 2002).

Rothenberg, Jerome and Joris, Pierre (eds.), *Poems for the Millennium* (Berkeley: University of California Press, 1995).

Roubaud, Jacques (ed.), *128 poèmes composés en langue française* (Paris: Gallimard, 1995).

Seghers, Pierre (ed.), *La Résistance et ses poètes* (Paris: Seghers, 2006).

Sorrell, Martin, *Modern French Poetry* (London: Forest Books, 1992).

(ed.), *Elles* (Exeter: Exeter University Press, 1995).

Taylor, Simon Watson and Lucie-Smith, Edward (eds.), *Modern French Poetry Today: A Bilingual Anthology* (New York: Shocken, 1971).

Terr, Patricia and Gavronski, Serge (eds.), *Modern French Poetry: A Bilingual Anthology* (New York: Columbia University Press, 1975).

Velter, André, *Orphée Studio: Poésie d'aujourd'hui à voix haute* (Paris: Gallimard, 1999).

Wolosky, Shira, *The Art of Poetry: How to Read a Poem* (Oxford: Oxford University Press, 2008).

II   Critical works (historical, general and individual studies)

Abraham, Nicholas, *Rhythms*, trans. Benjamin Thigpen and Nicholas T. Rand (Stanford, CA: Stanford University Press, 1995).

Acquisto, Joseph, *French Symbolist Poetry and the Idea of Music* (Aldershot: Ashgate, 2006).

Adamson, Walter L., *Embattled Avant-Gardes: Modernism's Resistance to Commodity Culture in Europe* (Berkeley: University of California Press, 2007).

Adorno, Theodor W., *Notes sur la littérature*, trans. Sibyle Muller (Paris: Flammarion, 1984).

Agamben, Giorgio, *Idée de la prose*, trans. Gérard Macé (Paris: Christian Bourgois, 1998).

  The End of the Poem, trans. Daniel Heller-Roazen (Stanford, CA: Stanford University Press, 1999).

Allaire, Suzanne, *La Parole de poésie: Lorand Gaspar, Jean Grosjean, Eugène Guillevic, Philippe Jaccottet* (Rennes: Presses Universitaires de Rennes, 2005).

Aquien, Michèle, *L'Autre versant du langage* (Paris: José Corti, 1997).

Armand, Louis (ed.), *Contemporary Poetics* (Evanston, IL: Northwestern University Press, 2007).

Balakian, Anna Elizabeth, *Surrealism: The Road to the Absolute* (London: Unwin Books, 1972).

Bancquart, Marie-Claire, *Poésie de langue française 1945–1960* (Paris: Presses Universitaires de France, 1995).

  La Poésie en France du surréalisme à nos jours (Paris: Ellipses, 1996).

Barthes, Roland, *Le Degré zéro de l'écriture* (Paris: Seuil, 1953).

Bei, Huang, *Segalen et Claudel: dialogue à travers la peinture extrême-orientale* (Rennes: Presses Universitaires de Rennes, 2007).

Benjamin, Walter, *Selected Writings*, vol. II, ed. Michael W. Jennings, Howard Eiland and Gary Smith (Cambridge, MA: Belknap Press of Harvard University Press, 1999).

Berranger, Marie-Paule, *Les Genres mineurs dans la poésie moderne* (Paris: Presses Universitaires de France, 2004).

Bishop, Michael, *The Language of Poetry: Crisis and Solution* (Amsterdam: Rodopi, 1980).

  Contemporary French Women Poets (Amsterdam: Rodopi, 1995).

Bishop, Michael and Elson, Christopher (eds.), *Contemporary French Poetics* (Amsterdam: Rodopi, 2002).

Blanchot, Maurice, *L'Entretien infini* (Paris: Gallimard, 1969).

321

Bobillot, Jean-Pierre, *Trois essais sur la poésie littérale* (Paris: Léo Scheer, 2001).

(ed.), *De la poésie scientifique & autres écrits: René Ghil* (Grenoble: Ellug, 2008).

Bombarde, Odile (ed.), *Poésie et rhétorique* (Paris: Lachenal & Ritter, 1997).

Bonnefoy, Yves, *The Act and the Place of Poetry*, trans. John T. Naughton (Chicago: University of Chicago Press, 1989).

Entretiens sur la poésie (Paris: Mercure de France, 1990).

Alberto Giacometti: biographie d'une œuvre (Paris: Flammarion, 1991).

Breton à l'avant de soi (Tours: Farrago, 2001).

Sous l'horizon du langage (Paris: Mercure de France, 2002).

Bonnejean, Bernard, *Clio et ses poètes: les poètes catholiques dans leur histoire 1870–1914* (Paris: Éditions du Cerf, 2007).

Braud, Michel and Hugotte, Valérie (eds.), *L'Irressemblance: poésie et autobiographie, Modernités 24* (Bordeaux: Presses Universitaires de Bordeaux, 2006).

Briolet, Daniel, *Lire la poésie française du XXe siècle* (Paris: Dunod, 1995).

Brophy, Michael and Gallagher, Mary (eds.), *Sens et présence du sujet poétique: la poésie de la France et du monde francophone depuis 1980* (Amsterdam: Rodopi, 2006).

Burch, Robert and Verdicchio, Massimo (eds.), *Between Philosophy and Poetry* (New York: Continuum, 2002).

Cantaloube-Ferrieu, Lucienne, *Chanson et poésie des années 30 aux années 60: Trenet, Brassens, Ferré ou les enfants naturels du surréalisme* (Paris: Nizet, 1981).

Castin, Nicolas, *Sens et sensible en poésie moderne et contemporaine* (Paris: Presses Universitaires de France, 1998).

Castin, Nicolas and Simon, Anne (eds.), *Merleau-Ponty et le littéraire* (Paris: Presses de l'École normale supérieure, 1998).

Caws, Mary Ann, *The Inner Theatre of Recent French Poetry* (Princeton, NJ: Princeton University Press, 1972).

Chol, Isabelle (ed.), *Poétique de la discontinuité* (Clermont-Ferrand: Presses Universitaires Blaise Pascal, 2004).

Chrétien, Jean-Louis, *La Joie spacieuse* (Paris: Éditions de Minuit, 2007).

Clancier, Georges-Emmanuel, *La Poésie et ses environs* (Paris: Gallimard, 1973).

Cohen, Jean, *Structure du langage poétique* (Paris: Flammarion, 1966).

Collot, Michel, *L'Horizon fabuleux*, 2 vols. (Paris: José Corti, 1988).

La Poésie moderne et la structure d'horizon (Paris: Presses Universitaires de France, 1989).

La Matière-émotion (Paris: Presses Universitaires de France, 1997).

Paysage et poésie du romantisme à nos jours (Paris: José Corti, 2005).

Collot, Michel and Rodriguez, Antonio (eds.), *Paysage et poésies francophones* (Paris: Presses Sorbonne Nouvelle, 2005).

Collot, Michel and Mathieu, Jean-Jacques (eds.), *Espace et poésie: rencontres sur la poésie moderne* (Paris: Presses de l'École normale supérieure, 1987).

Confluences poétiques (2 mars 2007).

Cook, Jon (ed.), *Poetry in Theory, An Anthology 1900–2000* (Oxford: Blackwell, 2004).

Critique, Les Intensifs. Poètes du XXIe siècle, 735–6 (août–septembre 2008).

Darras, Jacques, *Arpentage de la poésie contemporaine* (Amiens: Éditions In'hui, Trois cailloux, 1987).

Dastur, Françoise, *À la naissance des choses* (Fougères: Encre marine, 2005).

Deguy, Michel, *La Poésie n'est pas seule* (Paris: Seuil, 1987).

 L'Impair (Tours: Farrago, 2000).

 La Raison poétique (Paris: Galilée, 2000).

Delaveau, Philippe, *La Poésie française au tournant des années 80* (Paris: José Corti, 1988).

Doumet, Christian and Halpern, Anne-Elisabeth (eds.), *Ce que le poème dit du poème* (Saint-Denis: Presses Universitaires de Vincennes, 2005).

Ducros, Franc, *Le Poétique, le réel* (Paris: Klincksieck, 1987).

Eigeldinger, Marc, *Poésie et métamorphoses* (Neuchâtel: la Baconnière, 1973).

Esteban, Claude, *Critique de la raison poétique* (Paris: Flammarion, 1987).

 Ce qui retourne au silence (Tours: Farrago, 2004).

Europe, L'Ardeur du poème, 875 (mars 2002).

Fletcher, Angus, *A New Theory for American Poetry* (Cambridge, MA: Harvard University Press, 2004).

Frey, Jans-Jost, *Studies in Poetic Discourse: Mallarmé, Baudelaire, Rimbaud, Hölderlin*, trans. William Whobrey (Stanford, CA: Stanford University Press, 1996).

Friedrich, Hugo, *Structure de la poésie moderne*, trans. Michel-François Demet (Paris: Librairie générale française, 1999).

Fumaroli, Marc, Bonnefoy, Yves, Weinrich, Harald and Zink, Michel (eds.), *L'Identité littéraire de l'Europe* (Paris: Presses Universitaires de France, 2000).

Gadamer, Hans-Georg, *Truth and Method*, trans. Joel Weinsheimer and Donald G. Marshall (London: Sheed and Ward, 1975).

 La Philosophie herméneutique, trans. Jean Grondin (Paris: Presses Universitaires de France, 2001).

Gallagher, Mary, *Soundings in French Caribbean Writing since 1950: The Shock of Space and Time* (Oxford: Oxford University Press, 2002).

Garnier, Pierre, *Spatialisme et poésie concrète* (Paris: Gallimard, 1968).

Gikandi, Simon, *Writing in Limbo, Modernism and Caribbean Literature* (Ithaca, NY: Cornell University Press, 1992).

Gleize, Jean-Marie, *Poésie et figuration* (Paris: Seuil, 1983).

 À noir (Paris: Seuil, 1992).

 Le Principe de nudité intégrale (Paris: Seuil, 1995).

Glissant, Édouard, *Soleil de la conscience, Poétique I* (Paris: Gallimard, 1956).

 L'Intention poétique, Poétique II (Paris: Seuil, 1969).

 Poétique de la relation, Poétique III (Paris: Gallimard, 1990).

 Une nouvelle région du monde, Esthétique I (Paris: Gallimard, 2006).

 Philosophie de la relation. Poésie en étendue (Paris: Gallimard, 2009).

Greimas, Algirdas Julien, *Essais de sémiotique poétique* (Paris: Larousse, 1972).

Guermès, Sophie, *La Poésie moderne* (Paris: L'Harmattan, 1999).

Guillaume, Daniel (ed.), *Poétiques et poésies contemporaines* (Cognac: Le temps qu'il fait, 2002).

Hamburger, Käte, *Logic of Literature*, trans. Marilynn J. Rose (Bloomington: Indiana University Press, 1973).

Hamburger, Michael, *The Truth of Poetry* (London: Anvil Press, 1982).

Jaccottet, Philippe, *L'Entretien des muses* (Paris: Gallimard, 1968).

La Semaison, carnets 1954–1979 (Paris: Gallimard, 1984).

Une transaction secrète (Paris: Gallimard, 1987).

Jackson, John E., *Mémoire et création poétique* (Paris: Mercure de France, 1992).

À la source obscure des rêves (Paris: Mercure de France, 1993).

La Poésie et son autre (Paris: José Corti, 1998).

Jenny, Laurent, *La Parole singulière* (Paris: Belin, 1990).

La Fin de l'intériorité (Paris: Presses Universitaires de France, 2002).

Kaufmann, Vincent, *Poétique des groupes littéraires (avant-gardes 1920–1970)* (Paris: Presses Universitaires de France, 1997).

Kelly, Michael G., *Strands of Utopia. Spaces of Poetic Work in Twentieth-Century France* (Oxford: Legenda, 2008).

Khalfa, Jean (ed.), *The Dialogue between Painting and Poetry: Livres d'Artistes 1874–1999* (Cambridge: Black Apollo, 2001).

King, Russel and McGuirk, Bernard (eds.), *Reconceptions: Reading Modern French Poetry* (Nottingham: University of Nottingham Press, 1996).

La Charité, Virginia A., *Twentieth-Century French Avant-garde, 1907–1990* (Lexington, KY: French Forum, 1992).

Lacoue-Labarthe, Philippe, *Poetry as Experience,* trans. Andrea Tarnowski (Stanford, CA: Stanford University Press, 1999).

Lallier, François (ed.), *Avec Yves Bonnefoy. De la poésie* (Saint-Denis: Presses Universitaires de Vincennes, 2001).

Lapprand, Marc, *Poétique de l'Oulipo* (Amsterdam: Rodopi, 1998).

Leuwers, Daniel, *Introduction à la poésie moderne et contemporaine* (Paris: Bordas, 1990).

(ed.), *De francophonie et de France, le poème, aujourd'hui* (Tours: Presses Universitaires François-Rabelais, 2005).

Littérature, De la poésie aujourd'hui, 110 (1998).

Little, Roger, *The Shaping of Modern French Poetry: Reflections on Unrhymed Poetic Form, 1890–1990* (Manchester: Carcanet, 1995).

Louette, Jean-François, *Sans protocole: Apollinaire, Max Jacob, Henri Michaux* (Paris: Belin, 2003).

Maldiney, Henri, *L'Art, l'éclair de l'être* (Chambéry: Éditions Comp'Act, 2003).

Mandelstam, Osip, *The Complete Critical Prose and Letters,* trans. Jane Gary Harris and Constance Link (Ann Arbor, MI: Ardis, 1979).

Maulpoix, Jean-Michel (ed.), *Poétique du texte offert* (Fonteney: ENS Éditions, 1996).

La Poésie comme l'amour (Paris: Mercure de France, 1998).

Du lyrisme (Paris: José Corti, 2000).

Le Poète perplexe (Paris: José Corti, 2002).

Adieux au poème (Paris: José Corti, 2005).

Merleau-Ponty, Maurice, *La Prose du monde* (Paris: Gallimard 1969).

Meschonnic, Henri, *Le Signe et le poème* (Paris: Gallimard, 1975).

Mole, Gary D., *Beyond the Limit-Experience: French Poetry of the Deportation, 1940–1945* (New York: Peter Lang, 2002).

Montale, Eugenio, *La Poésie n'existe pas,* trans. Patrice Dyerval Angelini (Paris: Gallimard, 1994).

Montefiore, Jan, *Feminism and Poetry* (London: Pandora, 2004).

Mossop, Deryk Joseph, *Pure Poetry: Studies in French Poetic Theory and Practice, 1745 to 1945* (Oxford: Clarendon Press, 1971).

Mounin, Georges, *Sept poètes et le langage* (Paris: Gallimard, 1992).

Nancy, Jean-Luc, *Résistance de la poésie* (Bordeaux: William Blake and Co., 2004).

New, Elisa, *The Line's Eyes: Poetic Experience, American Sight* (Cambridge, MA: Harvard University Press, 1998).

Noël, Bernard (ed.), *Qu'est-ce que la poésie?* (Paris: Jean-Michel Place, 1995).

Nolan, Carrie, *Poetry at Stake: Lyric Aesthetics and the Challenge of Technology* (Princeton, NJ: Princeton University Press, 1999).

Onimus, Jean, *La Connaissance poétique* (Paris: Desclée de Brouwer, 1966).

Perloff, Marjorie, *21st-Century Modernism: The 'New' Poetics* (Oxford: Blackwell, 2002).

    The Futurist Moment (Chicago: University of Chicago Press, 2003).

Petterson, James, *Postwar Figures of* L'Éphémère: *Yves Bonnefoy, Louis-René des Forêts, Jacques Dupin, André du Bouchet* (Lewisburg, PA: Bucknell University Press, 2000).

Peyré, Yves, *Peinture et poésie: le dialogue par livre 1874–1999* (Paris: Gallimard, 2001).

Pinson, Jean-Claude, *Habiter en poète: Essai sur la poésie contemporaine* (Seyssel: Champ Vallon, 1995).

    Sentimentale et naïve (Seyssel: Champ Vallon, 2002).

Pinson, Jean-Claude and Thibaud, Pierre (eds.), *Poésie et philosophie* (Tours: Farrago, 2000).

Pleynet, Marcelin, *Poésie et révolution: la révolution du style* (Nantes: Éditions Pleins Feux, 2000).

Pollard, Charles, *New World Modernisms* (Charlottesville: University of Virginia Press, 2004).

Pondrom, Cyrena N., *The Road from Paris: French Influence on English Poetry, 1900–1920* (Cambridge: Cambridge University Press, 1974).

Prétexte, La poésie contemporaine en question, carnet 9 (juin 1998).

Prigent, Christian, *Ceux qui merdrent* (Paris: P.O.L, 1991).

Rabaté, Dominique, de Sermet, Joëlle and Vadé, Yves (eds.), *Figures du sujet lyrique* (Paris: Presses Universitaires de France, 1996).

    Le Sujet lyrique en question, Modernités 8 (Bordeaux: Presses Universitaires de Bordeaux, 1996).

Rancière, Jacques, *Les Noms de l'histoire* (Paris: Seuil, 1992).

    Malaise dans l'esthétique (Paris: Galilée, 2004).

Raymond, Marcel, *De Baudelaire au surréalisme* (Paris: José Corti, 1992).

Renard, Jean-Claude, *Notes sur la poésie* (Paris: Seuil, 1970).

Richards, I. A., *The Philosophy of Rhetoric* (Oxford: Oxford University Press, 1948).

Ricœur, Paul, *Lectures*, vol. II (Paris: Seuil, 1999).

Riffaterre, Michael, *Semiotics of Poetry* (Bloomington: Indiana University Press, 1978).

Ritm, Horizons de la poésie moderne, 15 (1997).

Roubaud, Jacques, *L'Invention du fils de Leoprepes: poésie et mémoire* (Saulxures: Circé, 1993).

La Vieillesse d'Alexandre (Paris: Ivrea, 2000).

Rowlands, Esther, *Redefining Resistance: The Poetic Wartime Discourses of Francis Ponge, Benjamin Péret, Henri Michaux and Antonin Artaud* (Amsterdam: Rodopi, 2004).

Scott, Clive, *Reading the Rhythm: The Poetics of French Free Verse, 1910–1930* (Oxford: Clarendon Press, 1993).

The Poetics of French Verse: Studies in Reading (Oxford: Clarendon Press, 1998).

Shaw, Mary Lewis, *The Cambridge Introduction to French Poetry* (Cambridge: Cambridge University Press, 2003).

Stamelman, Richard, *Lost beyond Telling: Representations of Death and Absence in Modern French Poetry* (Ithaca, NY: Cornell University Press, 1990).

Steinmetz, Jean-Luc, *La Poésie et ses raisons* (Paris: José Corti, 1990).

Les Temps sont venus (Nantes: Cécile Defaut, 2005).

Stewart, Susan, *Poetry and the Fate of the Senses* (Chicago: University of Chicago Press, 2002).

Sud, 'Questions de poésie', 118/19 (1997).

Thélot, Jérôme, *La Poésie précaire* (Paris: Presses Universitaires de France, 1997).

Thomas, Jean-Jacques, *La Langue, la poésie* (Lille: Presses Universitaires de Lille, 1989).

Thomas, Jean-Jacques and Winspur, Steven (eds.), *Poeticized Language: The Foundations of Contemporary French Poetry* (University Park: Pennsylvania State University, 1999).

Vadé, Yves, *Le Poème en prose et ses territoires* (Paris: Belin, 1996).

Walcott, Derek, *What the Twilight Says* (London: Faber and Faber, 1998).

Zambrano, Maria, *Philosophie et poétique*, trans. Jacques Ancet (Paris: José Corti, 2003).

Poetry reviews

Action poétique (1950–), founded by Henri Deluy.

L'Éphémère (1967–1972), founded by Yves Bonnefoy, André du Bouchet, Louis-René des Forêts and Gaëtan Picon.

Europe (1923–), founded by Romain Rolland.

Nioques (1989–), founded by Jean-Marie Gleize.

Le Nouveau Recueil (1995–), directed by Jean-Michel Maulpoix.

La Nouvelle Revue Française (1909–), founded by Jacques Rivière.

Po&sie (1977–), founded by Michel Deguy.

Poésie 2008, founded by Pierre Seghers.

TXT (1969–89), founded by Christian Prigent and Jean-Luc Steinmetz.

Websites: poetry and journals (all accessed September 2009)

Recordings and texts

www.alalettre.com. Good section on French poets.

www.gallica.bnf.fr. Very thorough archival site with thousands of full texts online.

www.poesie.net. *Le Club des poètes*. Very entertaining website on French poetry.

www.poesie.webnet.fr. Very good selection of poets.

www.ubu.com/sound. A very comprehensive survey of twentieth-century and
    twenty-first-century sound artists.
www.writing.upenn.edu/pennsound. Wonderful series of poetry recordings.

Other select websites

www.culturesfrance.com. Well-informed website on French poets and writers.
www.english.cam.ac.uk/vclass. Good glossary of literary terms.
www.etudes-litteraires.com. Excellent website with helpful pedagogical tools.
www.fabula.org. The best French website for information on French literature.
www.lehman.cuny.edu/ile.en.ile. Excellent website for francophone poetry.
www.lmda.net. *Le Matricule des anges*. Very good journal on contemporary writing.
www.maulpoix.net. Arguably the best website on French and world poetry.
www.remue.net. Very good website on French poetry and culture.

Index